For Tony Bravo

1-15-23

# *Bachelor* Father

### The first single man to legally
### adopt a child in America

*Bill W. Jones*

a memoir **Bill W. Jones**

I dedicate this book to my son, Aaron Hunter Jones.

# Contents

## Part Two – Aaron

Contents

## Part Three – After Aaron

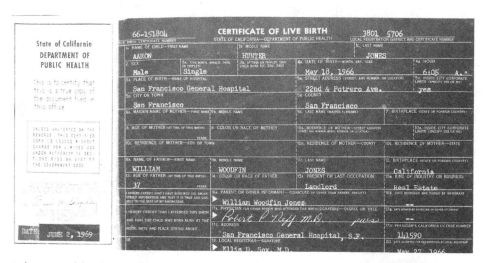

A historical birth certificate – only one parent listed, and it's the father!

Not flesh of my flesh,
Nor bone of my bone,
But still miraculously
My own.
Never forget for a single minute,
You didn't grow under my heart
But in it.

—Fleur Conkling Heyliger

I want the world to know you don't have to be chaste or perfect to love and care for your child. You don't have to be married or even a couple. You can be straight or gay, a man or a woman, or something in between. Any race, any religion, any time, or any place. Rich or homeless. Athlete or handicapped.

Belonging, devotion, and caring intensely are the common denominators. To hold your child and feel the bond, that sacred bond, is worth living for. And in my case, fighting for.

Bill W. Jones

# Introduction

This is my story about the document I signed as a single man in 1969 that became a worldwide news item – a historical milestone that has forced our American lawmakers in every state to battle over making it a law (or forbidding it) in their constitutions for the past 52 years. More than half the states still deny this human right, by law, to their citizens. One more reason to take a memoir writing class at the age of eighty-six.

By signing up for an OLLI workshop at San Rafael's Dominican University of California, I hit the jackpot: OLLI's most inspiring writing teacher, Diane Frank. I was thrilled for the first time in my life to turn in "homework."

This is not an apology, but rather an explanation of what you are about to read here. The book is in two parts. The first part is from my birth to the age of thirty-nine before Aaron, my son, came bursting into my life, mostly memories I wrote for Diane's class.

The second part was written for a support group of writers hoping to publish a book. Its raw honesty may make you want to avoid me, but it tells of my incredible dream that came true, turning my life into a perfect storm, flooding it with a love that has kept me alive these ninety-four years. Some of the chapters were so gut-wrenching for me that Diane or my friend Elinor Gale had to take over reading them to our group because I choked up and couldn't stop the tears. The second part of this book is about what I went through as a closeted gay man who, by chance, became the first single man in America to be allowed to adopt a child through a government adoption agency…that child being Aaron Hunter Jones, my son.

So, the good news for you is this: You have just bought two books for the price of one. If you don't want all the sordid details of my early years in Part One – Before Aaron, you can skip to Part Two – Aaron, the story of the homosexual who lied, begged, cheated, prayed, and fought an invisible monster to become the first single man to legally adopt a child through the Department of Social Services Adoption Services of a city and county in America.

Bill W. Jones
Father's Day – 2020

# Part One

## Before Aaron

## Chapter 1
# Diaper Memories

**W**hat kind of a (choose *your* preferred word) queer, pervert, faggot, homo, fairy, pansy, queen ... would *want* to adopt a kid? Why would *this* particular homosexual want to, and how in *hell* did it ever happen?

In 1969, these would be normal questions. Gays and lesbians were deviates, hiding their secret passions, not ready in that hostile world to be guardians of children, right? So, I was never asked these questions to my face, but I saw the questioning behind the eyes of strangers and even my family and friends. I couldn't answer them then anyway. I think the way to find the answer to these questions is to start at the beginning – July 12th, 1928, when my mother, Pearl, labored for hours in great pain, as she reminded me so many times, to finally give birth to little Billy.

My father, Bill Jones Sr., spent most of the eight hours my mother was snarling and cursing the nurses at the Marysville hospital, across the street in a bar. He was getting drunk with his newest best friend, whom he had met just hours before, and whose wife was also in the maternity ward with my pissed-off mother.

As the hours and drinks went by, my dad and his new best friend grew to be such intimate comrades they decided to exchange middle names for their firstborn. I ended up William Woodfin Jones and unfortunately, somewhere there's an old, annoyed woman, trying to explain how she ended up with the middle name of Henry.

Mother once told me, "Bill and I waited four years to have you so we would have enough money. And we wanted to be sure. You know. Absolutely sure."

I thought, *Sure of the money or sure they wanted a kid?*

"And wouldn't you know? Two years later, he's packed and running." She barely pauses, "with *Maude*!"

*     *     *     *     *

I have three distinct memories of before I was two years old and abandoned. I know it was before I was two because my mother, Pearl, and my father, Bill, separated when I was about to celebrate my second birthday. My first memory is of my father sitting on the toilet, his pants and shorts draped over his shoes. The bathroom, filled with his cigarette smoke in the afternoon sun, seemed as large as an airplane hangar to me. I toddled toward him, but fell on the yellow-tiled floor in terror as he bellowed at me, "Get out of here, Billy! Get the hell out of here! Damn kid!" I remember crawling out as fast as I could and hearing the bathroom door bang shut so hard that the floor beneath me shook.

My second memory is of my mother, kneeling down to be with me at a wire fence that ran around our backyard, pointing at a green car driving out of the Live Oak Garage across the street where my father worked as a mechanic and saying, "See, Billy. See that woman driving Daddy's car? See that woman?" She could hardly ask the question, her voice was so intense and raspy. "That woman is taking Daddy away from us. That woman is going to hell, and so is your Daddy! They can both go to hell!"

Instead of a party for me with two candles on a chocolate cake, I was farmed out to our neighbors, the Umshieds, to live with them when my distraught mother whined that she couldn't work as a telephone operator and take care of me at the same time. She worked at the switchboard because my father, who took a job as a guard at Folsom Prison, claimed there wasn't enough money left over in his meager paycheck to send any to us.

The Christian Umshieds were not the kind of people to give a party of any sort, especially for a kid who had never been baptized, but they obliged my mother and took me in, as good Christian families were required to do in 1930.

The separation and eventual divorce left my mother a mass of seething, boiling emotions, filling every crevice of her thin body. She once told me that for months after my father left her for Maude she couldn't sleep lying down. She could only pass out after a few drinks sitting up in a chair. It led her later in life to be a very nasty drunk, but in the meantime, I was left in a house that was not a home with a family of religious nuts who told me quite often that my *divorced* mother and father were going to fry in hell in a fire that was seven times as hot as their wood-burning stove.

When they closed my bedroom door at night after hearing me recite, *Now I lay me down to sleep, I pray the Lord my soul to keep. If I should die before I wake, I pray the Lord my soul to take,* the sudden darkness of the room would silently start to expand into a pitch-black infinity. The dark that came with the click of a closing door quickly turned into a blackness that I floated helplessly away in, frightened out of my wits that the Lord was taking my soul. I crawled down beneath the sheets to the bottom of the bed so the Umpshieds wouldn't hear me crying.

They belonged to a church in Live Oak, California, that had a huge white plaster tub filled with murky water next to the pulpit. The baptism tub sat directly beneath a plaster statue of a very naked Jesus painted in flesh tones, who watched us down below singing and praising him on the hard, wooden pews. They called themselves Dunkards. I spent many Sundays gazing up at that naked Jesus, trying to imagine what was under that carefully draped towel around his middle.

Going to hell meant nothing to me then. It might as well be the next town up the highway from Live Oak. It wasn't until one Sunday morning in the Dunkards' church, with that naked Jesus looking down on me and the minister dunking Mrs. Umshied in the white plaster tub, that it occurred to me that my mother wanted with all her heart for my father to be fried to a crisp in hell, a hell that was seven times as hot as the Umshieds' wood stove.

*   *   *   *   *

My third memory is of a nightmare that first came during one of my drifting-through-black-space nights when I slipped into another kind of darkness. I had what I now know was a nightmare, but at the time it was so real my mouth and throat went dry, preventing me from screaming. Not just any old nightmare, but a scene that I would relive again and again – throughout my childhood – through my twenties, thirties, sixties, and yes, eighties. A nightmare I have told and interpreted for at least three therapists. It won't go away and it's as clear as a bell to me what it means.

*I am in the back seat of our green car with the wooden spoke wheels. I can smell the dusty upholstery and feel the mousey brown velour beneath my bare legs. The two front suicide doors open and my mother and father are standing outside the car with their hands on the door handles on either side of the car. They both start to get in and are almost in their seats when there's an explosion of feathers and wings, flapping wildly between them. A bird so big that it could be another human is squawking so loudly that I can hardly hear my parents screaming. It is mammoth, billowing dark gray with a brilliant orange beak, baring long white teeth. The black wings are flapping furiously, banging against my father on one side of the car and against my mother on the other side. I hear the car doors slam shut and the front seat is empty. No Mama. No Daddy. No wild bird. I am alone.*

"So, what do you think the dream means?" Each shrink asks me. And it is so obvious to me that I wonder why I have to reply. But it gives me smug comfort to analyze it each time.

I lean back, assured. "The frightful, out-of-control gigantic bird is the divorce. It separates my mother from my father, and leaves me alone, bewildered, and terrified in a vehicle that will drive on without them. I am alone moving through the rest of my life in a car with no driver on a highway that is full of ruts and bumps and the car drives me to an unknown destination. Isn't that everyone's nightmare?"

## Chapter 2
# A Snake in Our Mouths

I have acrophobia so badly that my toes curl down under my soles when I'm climbing a ladder or even standing at the top of a staircase. I was determined to cure myself of it and thought I had when I jumped out of a small plane to skydive and to celebrate my 79th birthday – and my 80th, 81st, 82nd, 83rd, and finally, the last time on my 84th. But just yesterday, my toes started to tingle and twitch when I used the kitchen stepladder to get the sugar from a high shelf. I guess I'll have to live with it.

My other panic-striking fear is of snakes. Not just poisonous ones, but *any* snake. A garter snake at my feet in a garden can make me nauseous. I stopped my subscription to *National Geographic* because its pages were full of hideous multicolored snakes draped in the black branches of jungle trees.

After years of therapy, I came to the conclusion that the revulsion I feel toward reptiles started one day when my mother told her story to me and anyone else who would listen about the time she fainted when she saw me with a snake in my mouth. She has told the story so often, and with such dramatic flair, she makes Norma Desmond look like Minnie Mouse. Now I even think of it as part of my own memory. Her memory has become *my* memory! Until I heard her tell it, I had absolutely no recollection of that terrible day, but I can tell it to you in exquisite detail.

It happened one day in the fall of 1929 when I was 18 months old and just starting to walk on my own, with a little help from my dad's old mutt and retriever, Bozo. He stoically strolled with me and allowed me to hang on to one of his long, droopy ears to balance myself. We were inseparable, in and out of rooms, up and down stairs, under tables, and over piles of dirty laundry. Wherever he roamed, I was by his side. Mother had to separate us at his mealtime or I would be on the floor chewing on one of his bones.

My grandfather, Lou Dunning, had built a primitive summer cabin on the edge of a rushing creek in the Butte Mountains near Paradise, California, so his family could escape the blistering summer heat of Live Oak and Gridley in the Central Valley. It had two rooms, a small bedroom for Grandma and Grandpa, and a larger room that was used for storing most of our food, cooking on the iron stove, and for the rest of the family to bed down on rickety used army cots at night if they didn't want to sleep out on the deck. Food that had to be kept cool was stored in gunny sacks and left in the icy water of the creek that rushed past the deck of the cabin. The "family room" had a drop-leaf table with a kerosene lamp hanging over it, big enough for the adults to play cards on it or work together on a jigsaw puzzle. All of our meals were at a long table made out of redwood planks with benches for seats out on the massive deck, teetering on the edge of the creek, under the shady pine trees, and so close to the rushing water that you had to raise your voice to be heard over its constant babbling and splashing. I cherish that sound. It lulled me to sleep and woke me in the early morning, mornings filled with promise, not to mention the smell of coffee and fried bacon, and the fun of being with my family. It's a memory I resort to when life turns nasty on me. It brings me joy.

Mother says that she and my dad were playing cards with Aunt Ruth and Uncle Elzie out on the deck after lunch. They had lost a couple of games and were intent on winning back their nickels. Bozo and I walked slowly around the table two or three times, but my parents were squinting at the cards in their hands and not paying any attention to the dog and the toddler.

Bozo's black, wet nose was exactly the same height as my nose when we were standing together. Mother didn't like the dog licking my face, and she really didn't like me kissing his nose, but the dog had become a perfect companion for me – my guardian, and my babysitter. So as long as I was with Bozo, my mother thought I was safe. None of the adults realized Bozo had become bored just circling the table, and decided to explore the thick bushes that surrounded the house and deck.

Mother said they all leaped to their feet when they heard Bozo's fierce rapid-fire barking, which changed to a howling. Over the years, Mother perfected

Bozo's howl when she told her story but never felt she could do the barking justice, so she would just do the howl. The howling stopped abruptly, and she said that sent a chill through her body, thinking that both of us were drowning in the creek. Everyone panicked when we were nowhere to be seen.

"Billy! Billy! Billy!"

My mother and my aunt yelled as loud as they could, staggering toward the steps that led down to the dirt driveway.

My father and uncle joined in, "Bozo! Bozo! Here, Boy! Bozo! Come here, Boy!"

"Billy!"

"Bozo!"

"Billy!"

"Bozo!"

"Billy!"

Bozo was the first to peer out from under the deck, and he almost backed down under it when he saw how crazy the adults were acting. My aunt was the first to scream. She realized that the bloody rope Bozo had in his mouth was not a rope at all, but a snake, a snake still managing in the throes of death to undulate its blood-covered body to escape from Bozo's long teeth. The snake's head was hanging just inches from the dog's jaw, limp, blood trickling from its open mouth. Dad and Uncle Elzie were shouting, "Oh, my Gawd!" and "Damn!"

That shock was nothing compared to what they saw next. Bozo came farther out from under the deck, and I came out with him, clinging to his ear and happy to show everyone how well I could walk, as long as I had hold of my best friend's ear. And I was also proud to show that whatever Bozo could do, I could do, too.

My mother fainted and was caught by my uncle just before she rolled toward the edge of the deck and off into the creek. Bozo had one end of the snake in his mouth, and I had the other end of the snake, the end with the rattles on it, in mine.

## Chapter 3
# The Monkey's Tale

It blows my mind to think that when I was just five years old in 1933, my mother did something with me that would have shamed her in a courtroom if she did it today. She took my hand at the station in Marysville, led me to a seat in a Pullman car, and told me to sit there while she looked for the conductor to tell him that I was traveling to San Francisco. I heard her ask him to show me the walkway to the ferryboat when the train came to the end of the line in Oakland. Which he did! He lifted me off the steps of the Pullman and sent me trotting along with the other passengers to board the ferryboat.

Even if we could afford to buy a newspaper, no articles ever appeared about child abuse or pedophilia. It was something parents weren't worried about during the Depression. There was enough to worry about – having enough money to get food on the table, worrying if kids would come home before dark, late for supper, and the soup getting cold. Traveling alone on a train for 60 miles and then on a ferryboat across the San Francisco Bay should be easy for a five-year-old. What could go wrong?

It was an adventure for me, especially when the conductor gave me a box of Cracker Jacks with a whistle in it. Even though I couldn't get it to make a sound, I was thrilled to find it with the caramel popcorn. But even more than the train ride, the boat ride, and the whistle, the thing that excited me most was that my Aunt Ruth and Uncle Elzie would be waiting for me when the ferryboat docked at the big building with the tall tower and gigantic clock. I pulled myself up on the handrail that ran around the deck just enough so I could peer over it. There they were, waiting at the bottom of the gangplank. Aunt Ruth, wearing her fox fur draped over her shoulders, and Uncle Elzie stood beside her, smoking his pipe.

I ran down the gangplank and leaped into their waiting arms. Aunt Ruth was warm and soft, and Uncle Elzie smelled of Bay Rum aftershave. He was a car salesman and drove an apple-green Plymouth sedan that he'd parked right outside the Ferry Building. I sat on Aunt Ruth's lap, and as we drove, she pointed out the Christmas decorations in all the shop windows on Market Street. Uncle Elzie parked in front of Woolworths, where the cable cars spun around on a turntable before heading back up the steep Powell Street to the expensive hotels on Nob Hill.

We crossed Market, dodging autos and streetcars, to go into the Emporium, the largest department store in Northern California. I was fascinated by the glass tubes that vacuumed money in capsules from the sales desks to a mysterious vault hidden away in the basement. We took an elevator up to the rooftop, and to my amazement, I saw a bright and happy merry-go-round with wonderful, clanging music coming from it.

I gazed at the Ferris wheel and booths where you could throw wooden donuts at pegs. To make it even more wonderful, Santa Claus sat on a golden throne and invited children to sit on his lap, while a photographer took their picture. I was too afraid of him to sit on his lap but not afraid of riding on the back of a colorful merry-go-round horse that went up and down, as long as my uncle held me.

I loved walking up the two flights of stairs to their apartment on Filbert Street. The minute Uncle Elzie unlocked the big beveled glass door to the lobby, I smelled the carpet, rich with ancient dust mixed with the musty smell of family dinners cooked long before I was born.

They had lived in the same apartment from the day they'd married 12 years before. It smelled like a *home*, not like the hotel rooms my mother and I moved in and out of. The walls were papered with pale, faded red roses. The walnut furniture squatted on the red and blue oriental carpet with straight and curved roads woven into the design, perfect highways for me to play on with my toy car.

A small lighted Christmas tree sat on top of the Philco radio cabinet, center stage in front of the bay windows. Their bedroom was separated from the living room by glass-paned doors that slid magically into the walls on each side of the arch that extended across the living room, making it seem larger.

But the room I loved most was the kitchen where I could sit on a high stepstool to watch Aunt Ruth cook our meals. Two kitchen cabinets with glass doors faced the small eating area. In one of the cabinets sat a never-used porcelain teapot and cups, and in the other was Uncle Elzie's collection of pipes and tobacco jars. The cookie jar on the counter close to my stool was always filled to the top with fresh-baked cookies, and there was never a warning that I would ruin my appetite for supper.

I loved my aunt and uncle and often told them that I wished they could have been my mother and father. Uncle Elzie taught me to swim at the Sutro Baths and took me to movies. Aunt Ruth hugged and kissed me and was always interested in my life away from them in the months that separated our weekends and holidays together. My dad was a bartender in Oakland and lived in a small studio over the bar, so when I came to visit him, it was better for us that I stayed with my aunt and uncle. I couldn't have been happier.

I slept on a day couch that took up most of their entry hall, but that night, which was Christmas Eve, I couldn't sleep, thinking that Santa Claus would have to go right by my bed if he came in the front door on his way to the Christmas tree. I remembered him being terribly big with a huge white beard that scared me. I started to whimper, and then to cry, finally slipping out of bed and going into my uncle and aunt's bedroom. For some reason, they found my fear of Santa amusing, and I was allowed to crawl into their bed to sleep between them, safe from intruders.

"Billy, Honey. Wake up, Sweetie. Guess what? Santa's been here. He left a present for you. It's sitting on top of the radio under the tree."

I couldn't believe my eyes. A little brown monkey sat waiting for me. He wore a red silk suit with green piping around the jacket's edge. Perched on his head was a red cap with a gold tassel on its tip, sticking straight up in the air. His pants were short, and his long legs and tail stuck out from them.

I found out a few years later that Santa Claus hadn't actually left my monkey, Toby, for me. It was my Aunt Ruth. She had sewn it by hand from a pattern her mother had used to make a monkey for her when she was four. The cloth that covered the stuffing was material from a man's pinstriped suit. She had clipped the furry hair that hung below his cap from her fox stole, and his eyes were brown buttons from a high button shoe worn by her grandmother in the 1800s.

Toby became my life's companion who comforted me, snuggling with me when I hid away from my grandparents in cardboard boxes. Later, much later, Toby was wet with tears after I had cried myself to sleep over a lost love. He waited for me to come home drunk when I was in college. My son cuddled him every night in his crib. My dog, Lily, chewed his legs off. He is now resting on a shelf in my bedroom next to Snoopy and Teddy, my son's dearest companions. Who could throw a faded, ripped apart monkey like that out with the trash? Not me!

## Chapter 4
# Two to Eight Is a Little Blurry

When I was about five, my mother and her older sister, Myrtle, took over a rundown concession in a fruit and vegetable packing plant in Brentwood, California. No. Not the slick Brentwood in Southern California where O.J. murdered his wife.

*Our* Brentwood, near Stockton in Central California, was the end of the road for the "Okies" and "Arkies," driven out of the Dust Bowl to find work during the Great Depression. Any kind of work. The whole family, Pa, Ma, and all the kids worked 10 to 14 hours a day in the fields, orchards, and packing plant for 15 cents an hour and were glad to get it.

My mother and Aunt Myrtle ran the company store where the workers bought their food and work clothes. Most of the workers set up housekeeping in a row of tiny shacks that had been quickly erected during World War I. Some, like my mother, lived in tent cabins, impossible to tolerate under the burning, midday summer sun and drafty at night. My mother didn't want to spend the rest of her life in one of the flimsy shacks, so she was pleased with herself for "camping out" until something better would come along.

Somehow, my mother and Myrtle managed to latch onto a lot of turkey chicks, and during that summer of 1934, they were called the *Turkey Queens of Diablo Valley* in the *Brentwood News*. Knowing my Aunt Myrtle, who knew how to use her tall frame and movie star good looks to get whatever she wanted from horny farmers, I don't see her getting all those turkeys with hard-earned cash. I hated her. But because Myrtle was such a wheeler-dealer, my mother thought she could finally afford to raise me by herself. So, I left the Umshieds' home and the church with the naked Jesus and moved into a one-room tent cabin at the packing plant with my mother.

I have several memories of my short time there that might give you a clue to what kind of a man I eventually grew up to be … and why I wanted a child of my own … a family of my own. For the first time in my life, I felt secure, having my mother with me every day, eating when she ate, sleeping in the same room (tent) at night.

The only time in my entire life I can remember feeling intense love for her was one evening when she was getting dressed to go out dancing with her boyfriend, Jerry. She smelled so good. Her hair was curly and soft, and she was smiling. She was wearing a billowy ivory silk blouse and a floor-length black velvet skirt. I touched the velvet and my head started to swirl. She was so beautiful and happy that I started to cry.

Several times in my life I've become teary-eyed simply because someone I loved looked so unbelievably beautiful. And I always flash back to that evening, seeing my mother for the first time as warm, loving, and desirable.

But I have raw terrible memories about that time, too. One morning I struggled with another little boy over a toy airplane. I don't know if it was his or mine, but the push and pull ended when I bashed his head with the airplane and blood cascaded down over his face. Myrtle said she was going to call the police and have them take me to jail, which scared the shit out of me. I spent the rest of the day hiding under my mother's bed.

Apparently, Myrtle was the disciplinarian for my mother. I crossed the highway several times with the boy I'd hit and we placed rocks on the railroad tracks that ran parallel to the highway. It was great fun to see them fly into the air as gravel and dust, crushed under iron wheels, but when my mother and Myrtle found out, Myrtle warned me that I was "really gonna get it" if I did it again, which I did.

Dismissing her threats, the very next day my playmate and I crossed the two-lane highway and were ready with our rocks on the iron rails, waiting for the next train to come along. All I remember was Aunt Myrtle taking me by my shirt collar and dragging me across the road and through the store to the back where there was a huge walk-in refrigerator. The farmers paid to use it to hang their slaughtered and skinned pigs and cows. And hunters left their venison, raw and bloody, hanging from huge iron hooks next to them. Myrtle yanked the thick door open, pushed me inside, snapped off the lights, and slammed the door shut.

It was freezing cold. Dark as black ink. Smelled of death, blood, meat. You can imagine how a five-year-old felt being punished by a hated relative for a terrifying time that seemed to never end. She was right about one thing, though. I never crossed the highway and played on the tracks again. The other thing you can be sure of. I never shed a tear when she died decades later.

The last bit of trouble I got into then made my mother throw up her hands in shock and despair … and to usher me out of her life again. A stringy little blonde girl also lived at the packing shed. She said she wanted to play a game with me that the grownups played. I think she was about 10 or 11, much taller than me, but I doubt if she weighed much more than me. The lack of food made her growing body cling to her bones. It must have been in the morning when everyone was at work because we were absolutely alone. No adults in sight.

She took me into one of the community bathrooms and told me to take off my clothes, which I did. She slipped out of her dress and dropped her panties. We were in the shower room that smelled of mildew and old wet soap. She lay down on a wooden bench and told me to lie down on top of her. Which I did. It was sorta fun except that she smelled like piss, or maybe she hadn't wiped her butt clean enough.

Later that afternoon in our tent, my mother put me on her bed and told me it was naptime. She had been up since dawn and was tired, so she lay down beside me and closed her eyes. I turned to her and said, "Mama, let's play the grownup game."

"What game is that, Billy?"

"The fuck game, Mama."

The next thing I knew, I was taken to Grandma Nettie's house that she shared with her second husband, Wallace. It was on the other side of Brentwood, but far enough away from the packing shed that I never set foot there again. Mother would visit me occasionally, but she spent most of her time with me talking and drinking with my grandmother and Wallace.

I would get bored and retreat to my cardboard box under the porch with Toby, where I could close the flaps and be in a world of my own. My monkey was better company than any grownup I knew, and besides that, I knew my monkey loved me, no matter how bad a boy I turned out to be.

## Chapter 5
# Komiko, Machiko, and Binky

A couple of years before Pearl Harbor, when I was nine years old, two of my best friends, Komiko and Machiko, who also went to the Excelsior Grammar School, gave me a white Wire Hair Terrier puppy for my birthday. Binky filled my lonely days. Soft smelling, baby clean, and clinging to me like Peter Pan's shadow, we played and rolled around on the floor, his soft fur, cold nose, and wet tongue always an inch away. I couldn't wait to come running home to him after school. Binky slept with me under the sheets, not on top of the bed. Binky ate his dinner with me. Binky ran beside me when I was on my bike. I was in love.

A moment in Binky's and my life haunts me to this day. Like an ugly tattoo, it is cursed but will never fade away until I finally do. I was walking on the side of the road that led to our school, about half a mile from our motel cabins. Binky at my side. It was a sunny Saturday morning, and I was on my way to play with Komiko and Machiko, who lived on their daddy's farm across the road from our three-room schoolhouse.

Komiko was in the third grade with me. Mrs. Johnson, a big-boned Swedish woman, who hugged each and every one of us as we arrived in the morning, was our teacher. We shared her motherly teaching and our room with the first and second grades. Machiko was a year older and was in Mr. Johnson's room, upstairs, with the fourth and fifth grades.

The girls and I spent a lot of time on our bicycles on sunny days in the summer, riding on the dirt roads that ran through the walnut orchards and alongside the irrigation canals. We went to each other's birthday parties, and on rainy days, their mother would lay out coloring books on the kitchen table and serve us cups of tea half-filled with milk. Binky was always given a bone to chew on as he sat under the table.

Very few cars drove on Highway 4 during the Depression, so it was startling to see a shiny new Chrysler looming toward us. Its waterfall grill of vertical chrome bars was blinding. The blue-green paint was brilliant and shiny, not like the dusty cars and trucks the ranchers drove around Brentwood and Byron.

Binky started barking excitedly as it neared, and then for some god-forsaken reason, leaped out in front of it! I heard a terrible thud and I watched, in sheer panic, the body of my beloved tumble through the air and land hard in the dry ditch beside the road. His body was convulsing and blood oozed out of his mouth. I ran to him and clutched his body to my own, crying so hard that I didn't hear the squeal of the brakes or of the footsteps coming toward me. A man's hand reached down, put a dollar bill in my shirt pocket, and I heard him say, "I'm sorry, kid. I'm so sorry." Then he drove away.

Binky stopped breathing. That moment haunts me to this day. Sometimes I wake up in the middle of the night, because I have stopped breathing, and my thoughts go back to his warm soft body in my arms, so still, so very still.

Three years later, in the early spring of 1942, Komiko and Machiko didn't show up for school. It didn't occur to me that anything but very, very bad colds could keep them away from school, but after a week of our teachers calling out their names for the morning roll call and not hearing them answer, "Present," I began to wonder if I should take some of their school books and homework assignments to them.

Since their farm was just across the road, I rode my bike over to their front gate. It was locked. I had never seen a lock on it before, and now a new padlock was on the outside. I peered through the wooden slats and saw their daddy's pickup parked by the side of the house.

That meant that they were home, so I yelled out their names, "Komiko! Machiko! Come unlock the gate! It's me – Billy!"

No one came to the screen door on the front porch, but I could see a paper nailed to the front door. I climbed over the gate and ran up the steps to the screen door, but it had a lock on it, too, and I couldn't read the legal paper attached to the front door through the dirty screen.

I went around to the kitchen door, and to my amazement, it also had a lock on it. The blinds were pulled on every window, but I managed to peer through a few of them. The rooms were still furnished just as I had last seen them. Even the girls' bedroom looked exactly like it did a few months before when I went to Komiko's twelfth birthday party. So, they hadn't moved to another farm, I thought.

They couldn't have been on a vacation. The school was still in session. Why didn't they tell Mr. Johnson they wouldn't be at school? Why were there locks on all the doors and the front gate? No one ever locked their doors unless they were leaving on a long, long trip. Especially on any of the ranches or farmhouses.

I told Mr. Johnson about the locks the next morning, and during recess, he walked over to their house to see for himself. He looked worried when he came running back into the schoolyard and whispered something to Mrs. Johnson. Then I saw her take out her hanky and wipe her eyes.

I still feel pangs of guilt because when the girls wrote to me and told me how much they missed Excelsior School, Mr. and Mrs. Johnson, and especially how they missed me, I never answered their sweet letters. In my undeveloped mind full of bullshit slogans and stereotypes, in my juvenile, blinding patriotic fervor, they were now the enemy. They were JAPS!

If only I could see them now, I would plead with them to forget how stupid, cruel, and thoughtless I had been. I would beg for their forgiveness – the quieting forgiveness I cannot give myself no matter how many times I have prayed for it. I can never turn the hands of the clock back to be with Binky and my Japanese friends again. They are gone. Gone, but not out of my life, not out of my memories.

## Chapter 6

# Mother
## Pearl Helen Dunning Jones Crist Kelso

She would appear occasionally, sometimes leaning out of a car window to talk to me, sometimes waking me in the middle of the night to bring me a new pair of shoes. Since she and my father divorced, my meals and my bed were in the home of our neighbors, the Umshieds, who took me in when my mother obviously wasn't capable of caring for me. Her long hours as a telephone operator and the extreme grieving she felt as a deserted and betrayed wife overwhelmed her.

I can't remember a single time she ever picked me up to sit on her lap, read me a book, or kissed me goodnight, warning me not to let the bedbugs bite. She did try to have me live with her several times, but it never seemed to work out. My father didn't have any interest in raising me either. So, I drifted from one relative's home to another from the time I was two until she remarried when I was eight.

I stayed with her for a short time in the only hotel in Brentwood during the Depression. She was without a job, so she would stroll through the nearby cafes and steal the sugar, soda crackers, and cream that were a part of every table setting, along with salt, pepper, mustard, ketchup, and toothpicks. We each ate a bowl of crackers, sugar, and cream on her good days.

Some nights she took me out to the bars with her where free drinks came steadily her way, and even a hard-boiled egg for me once in a while. I was six and in the first grade, usually alone at night in a dark hotel room except for the nights she took me with her. I dreaded those nights more than the lonely ones I spent in our room.

I was frightened and repulsed by the men in their shabby clothes and sweaty felt hats, their hot liquor breath flowing over us, claiming their barstool next to my mother for the price of a drink for her. I think she used me as a shield, avoiding their unwashed bodies by telling them her "little man" needed his mama to put him to bed, and the hotel wouldn't allow "visitors" to help her do that, especially after midnight.

One night after the bar closed, we were walking back to the hotel on an unlit street. My mother stopped abruptly and slurred, "I gotta piss!" She pulled me in with her behind a pump at a closed gas station, and pulling her dress up and her panties down, squatted.

The thought of my mother "going to the bathroom" right in front of me was appalling, but what completely grossed me out was when she asked me to help her fasten her silk stockings to an undergarment I had never seen before. I still have visions of her white thighs above the dark silk stockings, and it disturbs me.

Buddy (4), Corky (6), and Billy (8)

Two years later, my Aunt Myrtle, whom I had dreaded since she locked me in a walk-in freezer full of hanging carcasses, took me in for a long weekend. While she was driving me back to my mother's rooms behind the restaurant where she cooked, Aunt Myrtle informed me that my mother had married the bartender, Louie, and from then on I should call him "Daddy."

I hated his guts. We didn't speak to each other unless it was absolutely necessary. The only really good thing that came from that marriage was the soul-satisfying gift he brought to it. In a matter of days, I was sharing a motel cabin in the back of the bar restaurant my mother and her husband ran, with a stepsister, Corky, two years younger than me, and a stepbrother, Buddy, two years younger than her. My lonely days were over!

There were four old motel cabins behind the Borden Junction bar-restaurant. We three shared one with a double bed. My mother and Louie had the only cabin with a bathroom. The Japanese janitor-and-dishwasher couple, who spoke no English, stayed in another, and the hired bartender and his wife, the cook, occupied the last cabin. We peed outside and used the gas station's restroom for anything else.

Two bedrooms and a complete bathroom were attached to the bar, but they were for the use of the customers. We used that bathroom for baths once a week, and my mother, God rest her soul, used it to give us enemas any time she felt like it. It's incredible, but she must have gotten some kind of creepy kick doing it. If she suspected one of us was constipated, she got us, one after the other, to lie naked on the bathroom floor in a fetal position. Then she forced warm soapy water up our butts even when we screamed with pain. Long after we screamed with pain.

I realize I'm painting a detestable picture of my mother, and to be fair, she did clothe and feed us well. She enjoyed decorating her aluminum Christmas tree every year in all red or all blue lights. It stood in the bar, and that's where we would open our presents on Christmas morning. On her birthday, we would drive into San Francisco, 60 miles west of Brentwood, to see the Ice Follies at Winterland Ballroom and to have dinner in one of the swanky restaurants in the International Settlement block on Pacific Avenue.

Corky, Buddy, and I stayed up as late as we wanted because there was no one to tell us it was bedtime. We giggled and told scary stories to each other as we lay in the darkness of our cabin, lit only by the headlights of the cars speeding by on Highway 4 outside our window.

My joy in having a brother and sister was sporadic at best. When my mother and Louie would have one of their loud and public name-calling quarrels, her revenge would be to pack Corky and Buddy's suitcase and order them to catch the next Greyhound bus to Stockton, back to live with their alcoholic mother. All my tears and pleading wouldn't change her mind. Only Louie's abject apologies could do that. It tore me to pieces to watch Corky and Buddy disappear into the whale-sized Greyhound bus and see it grow smaller and smaller as it carried them away from me.

As lesser revenge against Louie, instead of ordering Corky and Buddy to move back to Stockton, she would take me in our Willys sedan to see a movie in Brentwood, leaving Corky and Buddy with tears running down their cheeks, bewildered, wondering what they had done to be punished again.

When I was eleven, I was completely surprised one afternoon to learn from the cook and the bartender that my mother was in the Stockton hospital and that I had a baby brother! I ran back to Excelsior, my three-room school a mile away, to tell my teacher, breathlessly, how excited I was about having a brother, a real brother, who would never be sent away. Mother had wished for a girl, whom she was going to name Geraldine, and she was so disappointed the baby was a boy it took her three days to finally name him Jerald.

Mother and Lou were popular with their customers, drinking most of them under the table and laughing at their crude jokes. Their whole social life revolved around their work and drinking, leaving the raising of Jerald mostly up to me. I loved it. I loved keeping him clean and feeding him. I loved carrying him in the basket on my bike, peddling down the lanes through the orchards and farms. I loved holding him and reading to him. He was mine!

From 1958 to 1960, I was living in Greenwich Village as a professional model and actor in commercials, happy to be 3,000 miles away from the drunken arguments of my mother and Louie. One morning, the phone rang and I picked it up immediately, hoping it was a booking from my agent.

"Billy, it's me." Mother blew her nose and I could hear her sniffling. "Louie died last night."

I couldn't think of anything to say, except, "Oh, dear me. What did he die of?"

"Drinking two quarts a day accordin' to the doctors."

"Two quarts!"

"Yeah, isn't that the livin' end? Fat around his heart gave him a heart attack."

"Gee, Mom, I'm sorry."

"I bet!"

I pursed my lips and let that one fly by. "Well, you might be interested to know he quit drinkin' six months ago and went to them damn AA meetings. He practically begged me to go with him, but why should I? I'm not a drunk."

"Depends on the time of day."

"What's that?" she said as if she didn't hear me.

"Nothing, Mom. I just asked what day's the funeral."

"What do you care? I know damn well you won't fly home to go to it … to support your mother in her hour of need."

Mother could be funny and affectionate, to a degree, but it usually took a couple of highballs to get her there. Long after I had moved to Sausalito after graduating from College of the Pacific, I wrote her a letter and addressed it with all her last names. She had been married three times and her maiden name was Dunning, so the envelope read to: "Pearl Helen Dunning Jones Crist Kelso, The Wild Idol Inn, Byron, California." She called me two days later.

"Hi, Billy, I got your letter this morning."

"I wasn't sure you'd get it. With all those names and all."

"Oh, I got a kick out of it, and so did Nick down at the post office. In fact, I took it down to the bar and tacked it up on the board. Those dumb farmers have been laughin' their heads off cuz of it and buying me highballs all day."

\*     \*     \*     \*     \*

My brother, Jerry, and Bill Randles, his lover of 19 years, died of AIDS, but not before Jerry saw to it that Mother was safely ensconced in a retirement home near him in Hayward. She lived to ninety and died after a long illness in a convalescent facility in Mill Valley. I'd put her there after Jerry died so I could visit her often. I took albums of family photos for her to look at with me, but they bored her and she was too feeble to respond to them – even if she was able to recognize us.

She complained bitterly about her condition every time I visited her. It was frustrating for me because we had discussed taking our own lives many times in the past if life was no longer worth the trouble. But she kept on living, and I wasn't about to put a pillow over her face to help her.

One day, she motioned for me to come as close to her as possible so she could speak to me. Her eyes were red and brimming over with tears. "Billy, why does God hate me so much?"

"Mama, God doesn't hate you. Why do you say that?"

"Cause if he loved me, he'd take me, wouldn't he?"

"He will in time, Mama. It's just not time yet."

"I want to die. I want to die!" She was weeping now. "I want to go to heaven! I wanna be with Myrtle and Ethel and Dad and … I wanna die!"

I leaned in and whispered in her ear, "Mama, *you* have the power. You could take care of that, you know."

"How am I supposed to do anything? I can't even wipe my own butt!"

"Just tell the nurse to stop feeding you through this tube, Mama. That's all you havta do. They have to do what you tell them."

She glared at me for a long time. I knew she was thinking it over. Then she said in a low and steady voice, "Billy."

"Yes, Mama?"

"Go home."

\* \* \* \* \*

The phone rang early one morning, and it was the day nurse at the hospice. "Mr. Jones, I am very sorry to tell you this, but your beloved mother passed away at two a.m. this morning. We thought it best not to call you at that hour, so we waited until a reasonable time."

"Thank you. I'll be over there as soon as I can. She wanted to be buried in our hometown cemetery, so I'll make all the arrangements to have her picked up."

All I could think of is my mother calling out, "Two a.m., everybody. Last call! Get your asses home!"

She had bought burial plots for Louie and herself in 1959, and prepaid for all of her funeral expenses, including the most expensive casket available at the Brentwood Mortuary. But when I sat down with the mortician to finalize the funeral plans, it turned out the price of the casket she ordered was now 10 times more expensive, and I did *not* want to pay the difference! We negotiated for a *much* less expensive casket, and, to my amazement, the mortician told me that in her prepaid plan, she had *not* made allowances for a tombstone!

"But," he quickly added, "by buying the least expensive casket, you have enough for a marble marker that would be larger than the one she bought for Louie, and of course, they would be standing side by side. What would you like carved on her tombstone, Mr. Jones?"

It may have been a little vengeful of me, but I hope she'll look down and appreciate my sense of humor at what I had engraved. I wouldn't have done it if I thought she wouldn't get a kick out of it. I've visited their graves several times in the past 10 years, spending some of that time pulling the weeds away so the engraving on her stone can be read. I hope it makes her smile.

**R.I.P.**
**Pearl Helen Dunning Jones Crist Kelso**
**1906–1996**

## Chapter 7
# My Mama Done Told Me

Verla went to the Byron Grammar School in Byron, and I went to the Excelsior Middle School – about three miles apart. Because she lived in town, her school had a room for each class. Out where I lived, Excelsior had three rooms for all eight grades. The one thing the two schools shared was our 8th-grade graduation at the Byron Odd Fellows Hall in June of 1942. It was a hot, windowless wooden box, the size of a church, between the post office and Stanley's hardware store.

Verla had curly reddish-brown hair, a halo caressing her freckled face, and bright blue eyes. She was wearing an all-red outfit, a red skirt with a white blouse under a red jacket. She wore white socks and white shoes. I had never seen a more beautiful human being. Even in the movies. We received our diplomas and said "Hi" to each other. My cheeks blushed as red as her dress. I thought about her that whole summer, nearly floating on the warm night air as I listened to Frank Sinatra singing "In the Blue of Evening" and "All or Nothing at All." I was in *LOVE*.

When school started in September, I was the happiest of freshmen for several reasons. Verla rode the same yellow school bus as I did into Brentwood, a seven-mile stretch through hay fields, apricot and walnut orchards, and past the cemetery. I got to sit next to her, my heart pounding every minute of the ride. And then, since we both lived so far from the dance floor in the auditorium of Liberty High, and since neither one of us was old enough to drive, our parents took turns driving us into Brentwood about once a month for the school dances. To my relief, I didn't have to ask her for a date and take a chance on her rejecting me. Since we arrived together and left together, it was easy to be eventually known as a couple.

I loved it when Verla's older sister would chauffeur us to the dance or a game and then pick us up. She was always laughing and playing the radio as loud as she could. When my stepfather, Louie, had to drive us, we sat in complete silence, opening all the windows in the back seat to blow out his breath, heavy with whiskey and cigarettes. I felt so much shame and embarrassment, but Verla never mentioned it. She just squeezed my hand.

I had been driving our family car, a blue Willys, since I was eleven, mostly at night when my mother and Louie were too drunk to care who was driving. They would take us, my stepsister, Corky, and my stepbrother, Buddy, to the movies in Stockton, have dinner at On Lock Sam's, and then stop at every bar between Stockton and Borden Junction to have a "nightcap." We kids were left in the car to fight over who would get to stretch out and sleep on the back seat, and which two would have to share the bench seat in front. We usually took turns between "nightcaps."

Eventually, Louie would begrudgingly let me use our car to drive Verla on our dates, but he glowered at me every time he handed over his keys. By the time we were juniors, we had our first real kiss and were the school cheerleaders. She wore my oversized class ring, and we spent all the nights after games and dances, sometimes until nearly dawn embracing and kissing – long, slow, and very dry kisses.

Sometimes we would lie in a haystack and sometimes we would face each other on a Byron schoolyard swing and swing back and forth as high as we could – almost reaching the stars, our bodies close and warm together. Once we stood only a few feet away from the railroad track with our arms around each other, hugging as tight as we could, and kissing as long as it took the train to go roaring by, causing us to breathe heavily and feel the thunderous vibration in our bellies.

Looking back, I am amused *and* disappointed. Yes, we hugged and kissed and lay in each other's arms for hours, but it never occurred to either one of us to let our hands slip cautiously down below our necks to touch any one of those secret, forbidden places. In those war years, the movies were about virgins who *never ever* slept with a man until after the final credits played over their church wedding.

As far as I know, that was the way it was during my high school days. I suppose some of my classmates went "all the way," but if they did, it was in absolute secrecy, shame, and fear of losing the love and respect of their parents and friends. It simply could not happen in Brentwood. The "fast" kids were the ones that drank coffee.

So, you can imagine my surprise and chagrin one afternoon when I opened the kitchen screen door and found my mother, the drama queen, sitting at the table dabbing her eyes. She looked up at me and I didn't know if it was a startling look or a glare, but I knew she was about to give me holy hell.

"I was doin' the laundry today." She let out a huge sigh. "Billy, your father should be talking to you instead of me. Damn him. Never was around when he shoulda been. I looked at your underwear. I saw your underpants." Her eyes welled up with tears. "Verla is a *good* girl."

"Yes, Mama. Verla is a very good girl."

"Then you mustn't do anything bad to her."

"I don't, Mama."

"Billy, there's *blood* on your underwear. And hay. And the stuff that comes out of a man."

"Mama, Verla, and I were just playing in the hay after the dance. Nothing else. And I haven't told you cuz I'm embarrassed about it, but I have hemorrhoids. Sometimes they bleed. A lot."

"Well, Billy, I guess it's up to me, and I better tell you about the house in Tracy. I sure don't want you to do something bad with Verla. She's a *good* girl."

"I know. I know."

"There's a house in Tracy. Stanley was talkin' about it in the bar the other night. I can get the address for you." She blew her nose. "Louie told me to tell you that if you tell the woman that it's your first time, she'll be really good to you and be very understanding. He says they have hearts of gold. And it costs $5."

"I won't be going there, Mama, but thank you. Thank you, and don't worry about Verla. I would never do anything to hurt her."

But I did hurt her in the fall of '45 – hurt her deeply, a pain she felt for the rest of her life. I fucked with her heart, and it never healed.

## Chapter 8
# Verla (in 2004)

In 1946 there were 55 in my graduating class from Liberty Union High School in Brentwood, California. Fewer than 10 are still walking on this earth. The others have moved on to the Marble Orchard. Most of the living are still entrenched in that two-block-long town and live within 20 miles of it. About 10 of us have lunch at Sweeny's once a month. Brentwood is about 60 miles from San Rafael where I live, so I don't make that boring trip as often as the others.

Verla has become reclusive and doesn't show up as often as I do, so it's always a special occasion when we're there at the same time. I try to sit next to her, but she turns her attention to anyone else but me at the table, and we part with a "Goodbye," which makes our conversation all of two words, "Hi" and "Goodbye."

I can't remember who phoned me to tell me that Verla's husband, Tom, had died, and I should come to the burial and memorial service for him at the Brentwood Cemetery, but I was grateful even if the invitation hadn't come from Verla.

She was so special in my life, and there was a chance to show her that I cared enough to make the 120-mile round trip and also to show her that I honored her marriage to Tom. I was eager to see her children and grandchildren, and I couldn't stop thinking her grown sons and daughter could have been mine. Turning into the cemetery I wondered if she still remembered those moonlit nights after school dances when we fogged up the car windows parked among the tombstones.

Verla still had that bouncy, youthful movement in her body, and I could see her smooth, happy face under the wrinkles. Her hair was now gray, but as curly as when I first saw her in that red dress reaching for her grammar school diploma. Her slim athletic body was now full and voluptuous, and her eyes and mouth worked as one to make a smile. How I loved that smile!

I have been to dozens of memorials, mostly in the eighties when my friends were dropping like swatted flies around me, dying of AIDS, but this one was one to remember!

I parked behind a row of pickups and dusty SUVs and walked on the gravel road to the long white awning that had been pitched on a brick walkway. To one side of it was a freshly dug grave, but so small that you could have stepped into it if it hadn't been under a canopy. The awning was shading a long narrow table overloaded with food at each end. The centerpiece was a box of wine, cabernet, I think, surrounded by a variety of flowers in assorted vases and candles that flickered in the autumn air. Golf clubs encircled the flowers. VERY odd!

I was pleased to see how good-looking her children were as they each spoke endearing words about their father, who apparently was an avid golfer and traveled with Verla to every golf course on the West Coast in their motor home. Oh, yes, they each told us how very much he loved his boxed cabernet wine ... a lot!

Finally, it was time for the burial, and I had to choke down a laugh. Verla had never lost her sense of humor, and I could hardly believe what I was seeing. They were burying the table centerpiece! Verla walked over to the box, bent down, patted it for a few seconds, made a slight nod to the cemetery worker, who lowered the wine box holding Tom's ashes into the dark brown hole.

It took a long time before I could work my way down the line of friends and family who were hugging her and wiping away their tears. By the time I got to her, most of the mourners were well into their second helping of the tuna fish casserole. She wasn't hungry, so we decided to sit in the shade on the white plastic chairs under the awning.

I took her hand for a moment, and it was as if we were in the loge seats at the Delta Theater again, as we had been so many times, holding hands watching the *March of Time* or some Betty Grable musical. A feeling of comfort and warmth swept over me. It was the same feeling I'd felt when she touched me all those decades ago. Then she let go. The conversation was a little stilted and predictable. She got up and greeted some of the other guests, turning her back to me.

I hung around longer than I should have, and when the cemetery worker started to shovel dirt into the tiny hole, I knew definitely it was time to go. Verla left her son after kissing him on the cheek and came over to me. "Bill, I am so glad you drove here today. It's a long way. Thank you."

I gave her an awkward hug and asked, "Are you driving? Can I walk you to your car?"

She said, "Just a minute." and walked back to her son to kiss him again. Then she went over to the table and picked up the golf clubs. We strolled down the gravel roadway, saying few words. Verla had arrived early to set things up and had parked her car under a huge oak tree to keep it shaded and cool. All we could hear was the crunching of the gravel as we walked. At least it drowned out the constant hum from Highway 4.

When we got to her car, I opened the door for her and started to say some meaningless thing, but she looked directly at me and for the first time all afternoon, I saw a tear welling up in her blue eyes.

"Bill, I have wanted to tell you something for about 50 years."

"What, Verla?"

A tear rolled down her cheek. "You will never know how much you hurt me, Bill. How many times I cried over you!"

"Oh, Verla! I'm so ..."

She sat down and closed the door, staring straight ahead for a few moments to compose herself. She started the engine, and I thought she was going to drive away, but she rolled down her window and looked at me. I knew she wanted to say something more, so I leaned down to hear her over the motor. She was barely speaking above a whisper.

"On my wedding night ... on my wedding night to Tom ... I was thinking about *you*. All I could think about ... I was thinking of *you*." With that, she rolled her window up, drove away, and left me standing alone among the marble tombstones with a hollowness in my chest as big as an open grave.

\*   \*   \*   \*   \*

December 10, 2004

Dear Verla,

The most profound thing I've ever done in my life all started one night on the swings at the Byron school when you told me that you wanted to run an orphanage. Your dream was the seed in my mind that grew to be my obsession to adopt a child. So, really, you were the one who inspired me to do something that would make my whole life meaningful. I owe so much to you, Verla.

I also owe you something else. I owe you an explanation about what happened to me during the summer between our junior and senior years. It was something so bizarre, so terrible, that I couldn't talk about it to anyone. Especially you. I thought God was going to send me to hell and that I would burn there forever because I fell in love, miserably in love with, of all people, another man. He was a counselor at the Methodist Youth Fellowship camp at Lake Tahoe. He was 27 and had just returned from the war. It wasn't mutual. There was no sex and no talk of love. I was just swept away. He was on my mind night and day, and there was no way I could tell you or even explain it to myself. I was living in a hell that I didn't choose. It was simply there and I had to live through it alone and in secret.

If we had married, as I thought we would, it would have happened to me sooner or later and I would have ended up a drunk or a bastard husband who would come home and kick the dog. I'm glad that I didn't put you through that. It was bad enough as it was. I knew you were in pain, and I felt that pain, but there was no way I could think of to help you. Believe me, I was torn up inside and had no one to turn to.

If it comes as any consolation, I have never loved any other woman as I loved you. Besides my son, I have never felt as loved as I was by you. I hope we can, at last, become friends and that I get to see you once in a while. You are special to me, Verla. Very special.

Love, Bill

## Chapter 9
# Cora Lee Murray aka TWAT

My monthly salary as a fourth-grade teacher in Novato in 1953 was less than $250, and I had to be very creative about my budget. A trick I picked up in a gay bar put me on to ushering at the Opera House. It cost me about 25 cents in gas and a 25-cent toll each way over the Golden Gate Bridge. Eating out, even a 35-cent hamburger was not an option, but I loved the ballet, and even though I had to stand for the entire performance, I was in a cost-free heaven. Free musicals like *Call Me Madam* with Ethel Merman and *Peter Pan* with Mary Martin! I even was thankful to stand for the five-hour-long performance of Wagner's "Parsifal."

One night at the ballet, I was teamed up with a young woman about my age to usher on the first tier. We took turns handing out programs and leading fashionably dressed patrons to their seats. She wore black-rimmed, thick-lensed bifocal glasses that magnified her brown eyes so much you could see every emotion and thought she had. Her hair was dark brown like mine, and it was thick, running down over her shoulders. Her clothes were voluminous, dark, and made of heavy woven material that disguised her young body, but didn't hide the slight hump in her back.

I watched her lead people to their seats, then make a grand, sweeping gesture for them to sit and enjoy the show. She didn't just walk back up the stairs to where we were stationed. She leaped up the steps two at a time, landed at the top in the fifth position, and twirled around, making her long black skirt bellow out. She looked so ridiculous and clumsy that I had to stifle a giggle.

Then I took a look at her feet and gasped. She was wearing ballet slippers that once had been pink but now were stained and dirty.

The curtain went up and she strained forward to watch every graceful turn, every extended arm or leg, moving her own body slightly in unison with the dancers. During a pause between ballets, we seated late-comers. After the curtain rose again, we were free to go behind the railing and stand for the rest of the night. Cora Lee tugged on my sleeve.

"Bill, come with me. Hurry, so we can beat the others!"

I assumed she wanted to go back down to the main floor to watch in "Standing Room," which would be a little closer to the stage, but instead she ran ahead of me and darted up the side marble steps that led to the second tier.

"Don't ever tell anybody, but we can sit on the aisle steps up here and nobody's the wiser. Sometimes you can even find an empty seat!"

I began to like this girl. She was a little daffy, and not a great beauty, but she amused me and I liked her spunk and resourcefulness. Maybe it was because I was gay and felt a kindred spirit with females, but all through high school and college, my best friends were girls. Emotionally, I had more in common with them than I did with my straight male classmates. I never wanted to *be* a girl, but I found them sensitive, loyal as friends, and eager to explore all facets of life. My "girl friends" all had a wonderful sense of humor. They could be sarcastic or coy, but they made me laugh, and I found I would put up with all kinds of bad behavior as long as they could crack me up.

Cora Lee chatted during the next intermission, revealing the basics of her life. She worked as a temp secretary but didn't really want a regular nine to five. That would interfere with her guitar lessons and her chance to usher at the matinees. Most of all, she wanted to take ballet lessons. Free ones if possible. She was forced to leave home when her family discovered she had had an abortion. She *loved* San Francisco, bragging that she had learned how to protect herself from ever getting knocked up again, and I distinctly felt she was hinting at something, when she asked me, "Bill, what you doin' after the performance?"

"I'm going to a bar and have a beer. I've got a damn quarter in my pocket that's burning a hole in it. Then I'm driving back to Sausalito."

She put me on a spot, asking, "Can I go with you? I'd just like to talk to you some more. Which bar?"

"It's called Keeno's, and the beers are 25 cents, and that's all I have in my pocket."

"Oh, I'm not asking you to buy me a drink, Bill. I have a juicer at home, carrot juice mostly. No. I just thought you might like some company."

"Cora Lee, I, eh, well, you see, eh, I don't think you'd feel comfortable hanging out with me in the bar I'm going to … Keeno's."

"Why not?"

"Well, ah, well, it's a gay bar. Keeno's is a gay bar down on Golden Gate Avenue, 'cross from the Golden Gate Theater."

"That's *wonderful*, Bill. I *love* gay bars!"

I couldn't believe my ears. This was the first girl I had ever known who even knew what a gay bar was. "You've been to a gay bar, Cora Lee?"

"Up in Portland. Lots of times."

We ended up at Keeno's, a bar with no name on the outside, just the street number over the door, and we shared the beer, passing it back and forth, taking tiny sips to make it last as long as possible. Keeno catered to the casts that toured shows at the Golden Gate and once a month he redecorated his bar with themes. That night was "Roman Baths" and all the bare-chested bartenders wore towels around their waists, over their pants, with "Jack's Baths" stenciled on them.

One month, Keeno painted all the Peanuts characters on the wall. Snoopy, Charlie Brown, Lucy. The next month's theme was Paris, and he erected an Eiffel Tower in the middle of the floor that reached the ceiling, sprinkled with live yellow daisies. He called the looping garland of daisies encircling the bar his "Daisy Chain."

Cora Lee and I did become good friends. She asked me to come to dinner one time, boasting that for the first time we would have a steak dinner. The steaks were a little tough and chewy, but Cora Lee smothered them with a thick layer of hot mustard and it wasn't until we were eating dessert that she told me where she bought the steaks.

"Promise not to hit me, Bill. I get them all the time at a shop on Maiden Lane off Union Square."

"Maiden Lane? There's no butcher shop there."

She offered me another cookie. "Bill it's just across from that Frank Lloyd Wright building. Robison's."

"Robison's pet store?"

"Yeah, it's filet of filly. Horsemeat. Not too bad, eh? And cheap!"

When it was my turn to do dinner, I told her we would be having steak, too, but steak I would be getting in a meat market. When I put the dinner dish in front of her, she let out a wail.

"Weenies! Weenies and sauerkraut! I thought you said we were goin' to have steaks!"

"It is. Tube steak."

We were honest with each other, pulling no punches, laughing mostly at our own faults. But there was one thing I couldn't bring myself to tell her. Even though she took ballet lessons every time she could afford it and practiced until her feet were swollen and even bloody at times, in my opinion, she walked across the room like a pregnant elephant and there was no way in hell she could ever get a job as a professional dancer. That's what I thought until the night she phoned me, panting into the phone.

"Bill, I'm soooo. I'm soooo happy! Can't believe it! I can't believe it!"

"Can't believe what?"

"I got a job dancing! I'm going professional! They pay me. Me! Pay me money to dance! I'm so excited, I think I'm going to pee my pants!"

Now she had my attention. "What company, Cora Lee? Where? Here in the city?"

"Yeah, right here on McAllister Street."

"On McAllister?"

"Yeah, at the President Follies on McAllister."

"Honey, that's a burlesque theater!"

"I know. I know, but they're going to pay me to dance in the chorus, and they said if I don't quit right away, they might let me do a solo."

"You do a strip? You mean with your tits hanging out and everything?"

"Sure, as long as they let me dance while I'm stripping. Why not?"

"Jesus Christ, Cora Lee. I dunno. I dunno. You as a stripper. Wow!"

"Bill, I'm so excited! I rehearse tomorrow afternoon and I get to go on tomorrow night! Isn't that great?"

"What time's the show?"

"Three times a night. Seven, nine, and eleven. I'll have time for my guitar and ballet lessons. Isn't this perfect?"

By nine o'clock the next night, I had seven of my friends chomping at the bit and deliriously happy to be going to a burlesque theater for the first time in our lives. We gladly paid 75 cents a ticket. In the darkened theater only a dozen or so men slouched in their seats, sitting far apart. The first five rows were empty, and we happily sat in the center of the front row, all the better to see Cora Lee make her debut as a professional dancer.

A bored and tired-looking drummer, pianist, and horn player shuffled down into the orchestra pit right in front of us. After dragging on a cigarette or two, they lurched into "A Pretty Girl Is Like a Melody." The curtain jerked open and a follow spot lit the left side of the stage. Out came a line of women, none of them smiling, all of them grossly made up and wearing identical blonde wigs. One by one, they shook off a shiny black cape and kicked it into the orchestra pit, some falling on the drummer. They were wearing yellow high-heeled shoes, a sequin-covered red bikini, with red and yellow tassels that covered their nipples and hung down from their breasts, flopping against their stomachs, some with glistening stretch marks.

Cora Lee was the last in the line to appear, and even though her face was painted with make-up so thick it looked like a plaster cast, and she was wearing a bouffant blonde wig, we had no doubt it was our Cora Lee. The horned-rimmed glasses gave her away.

She kicked her outer garment off the stage into the pit, but not like any of the other women. After the kick, she extended her leg with her foot pointing to the back of the theater and held it there as long as she could, and was left behind by the rest of the chorus who had moved on to the right side of the stage, sashaying their hips to the beat of the drum, and tugging at their bikinis to bare a little more skin.

Cora Lee hurried to catch up to the chorus line, but suddenly stopped when she saw us looking up at her. She broke out into a big smile and we applauded wildly as if she had just completed a handstand on the back of a bucking bronco. She came over to the edge of the stage and smiled again.

"Hi, guys!"

We all yelled back, "Hi, Cora Lee!"

By that time, the rest of the chorus started to giggle at what was obviously eight gay friends in the front row with their pants zipped up, who came to support the new girl. After that, the entire show was played to us. Cora Lee told us later, when we met at Keeno's for a nightcap, that the girls *loved* having us there. Most of them were like Cora Lee. Department store clerks, single mothers, students … just doing it for the money and despising the men who sat in the dark, peering at them with their hands pumping their crotches.

The women bumped and ground for us as they never had for the straight men sitting in the dark. It was fun for them that night because to them, the show was a joke, and they loved the fact that we were in on it.

I had never seen Cora Lee anywhere near naked. It was a revelation to me. Aside from having a slightly rounded back, her body was limber. Her skin was clear and firm. I even complimented her about her big breasts that made the tassels swing back and forth.

"Oh, Bill, I hate to tell you this, but my tits are so flat that one of the girls put eye shadow under each one to make them *look* bigger."

"Size isn't everything, Cora Lee. You're a performer. A little girl who's a BIG performer with really big tits as far as I'm concerned."

She eventually was allowed to do a solo striptease, introduced by the comedian MC as Miss Va Va Voom, and became a draw as the stripper that strips out of a tutu, dances on the toe, and as the only stripper that refused to shave off her pubes, which enticed one drunk in the audience to yell out, "Hey, Va Voom, show us your hairy twat!"

We gave each other nicknames, never shared with any of our friends. I affectionately called her TWAT, and she addressed me as VICE VERSA. Good friends.

## Chapter 10
# Bee Vee

In 1955, I was denied tenure after teaching for three years in the Novato School District because Mr. Lavaroni, my principal, *suspected* I was gay. *Gay* – meaning pervert, evil, sinful, child molester, criminal.

His reasoning: I lived in the art colony of Sausalito with another single man. And I thought my love was a secret!

The year 1954 was the Year of the Blessed Virgin. When I saw an ad in the *Chronicle* that baby skunks were available for loving families at a pet store in Sacramento, I grabbed my lover's arm and we were out the door. On the way back to Sausalito, Jim drove and I held our tiny, soft, furry baby skunk in the palm of my hand. "What shall we call her? She could be a nun. All black and white."

Jim chuckled, "The Blessed Virgin!"

"I can't tell my fourth-grade class their mascot is a virgin. I'd be fired for saying a word like that in front of them."

Jim pulled into our driveway. "Then just call her Bee Vee ... Blessed Virgin."

"Yeah. If anyone asks, I'll say it stands for Black and Vite!"

And so, Bee Vee came into our lives. You couldn't sit down anywhere, even on the toilet, that she didn't want to climb onto your lap. She was affectionate and needy. She waited outside the bedroom door until we were done with our lovemaking. The minute we opened it, she crawled up the side of the bed and wiggled her way down between us under the sheets to our bare feet, where she slept for the rest of the night. At breakfast, she would rear up on her

Jim Young and Bee Vee when she was a baby

front feet and slap the floor until she got her strip of bacon. She emptied her bowl of kibble right after I filled it.

What she really liked were the nights I put a harness and leash over her shoulders and we went out into the garden's darkness, where she devoured nasty little bugs and insects, her gourmet meal. She dutifully used a cat's litter box and groomed herself constantly when she wasn't dozing. I have never had such a clean pet and one so eager to be loved. She was adored by everyone who met her, and she drew Jim and me closer as a couple, a couple defined as a family by a pet skunk!

We almost caused a couple of serious fender benders when tourists driving by craned their necks to see us walking down Bridgeway with Bee Vee on her leash, going to Willie's Marin Fruit store or to the No Name Bar. The squeal of their brakes never seemed to jar Bee Vee. She just kept waddling with her nose to the sidewalk, looking for bugs.

I took Bee Vee to school with me every day where she slept most of the time on the bottom shelf of a cupboard. The first one to finish his or her lesson got to hold her. Even the slowest tried to beat the rest of the class for this wonderful reward.

Bee Vee was the reason my class excelled in almost everything. Her snuggly ways inspired even Michael French, the class clown and major terrorist, to do his best so he could hold her on his lap to pet her.

Jim and I spent the night of our second anniversary in a panic, flashlights in hand, walking every street in our neighborhood calling for Bee Vee. One of our dinner guests, even after warnings that every door had to be closed tight as a drum, forgot or dismissed the importance of our warning. Sometime during our laugh-filled night, Bee Vee went out alone into the darkness to dine on bugs.

Her loss affected every one of us, our friends, and the kids in my fifth grade. Eventually, the bitterness and sadness became a wedge between Jim and me. Over a silly argument – the reason escapes me – we called it quits. What a fool I was to let him walk out!

I don't know what I missed more. Our lovable skunk or the chance to live the rest of my life with Jim. When you're young, you are young and foolish. I regret losing Jim to this day, and the loss of a defenseless pet can hurt as much as a death of a friend or lover. Pain is pain.

It was a deep and tragic loss but almost a miraculous happy ending, when I was driving home two months later and saw a skunk hurry across the road and dash into an open garage. I slammed on the brakes, whipped back the emergency brake, jumped out, and ran into the dark garage. The skunk raised its tail and slapped the dirt floor with its front paws as a warning not to come closer.

"Bee Vee? Bee Vee? Come to Daddy, Honey. Come to Daddy." I slowly approached the animal, and it slapped the floor again as its tail shot up and flared out.

"Bee Vee, come to Daddy." I got down on my hands and knees and crawled forward as slowly as I could while still whispering, "Bee Vee. Bee Vee. Bee Vee."

The fanned-out tail floated down and the mass of black and white fur sank to the floor, her head resting between her front paws. My hands were trembling as I reached under her belly and lifted her up to my face.

It *was* Bee Vee and the next day at the vet's I was told she had distemper and was dying. I stayed home from school for the next few days, petting her as she lay in my lap or slept with me under the covers. She died on my lap. When I finally phoned him that evening, Jim drove from his new apartment in the city back to Sausalito. We buried her in the garden she loved so much … in the dark of night.

**Chapter 11**

# Miss Va Va Voom and I Fly to the Big Apple

The "Toast of Paris who taught Gypsy Rose Lee everything she knew, the Femme Fatale who was Banned in Boston, the star of the Monte Cristo Ballet, the hot and sexy Miss Va Va Voom, flown here this very night for your pleasure from 42nd Street in New York City …" actually stayed as a featured stripper at the President Follies for about six months. Whenever I had a new hot affair, she would sneak us in through the stage door. Then we would take a couple of seats in the front row and cheer her on. My dates were all impressed that I knew a female stripper in person, and sex was always hot and heavy that night when I took him back to my apartment.

We did fly to New York together in the fall of 1958. It was the first time either one of us had ever been on a plane, and not knowing the airline provided meals and drinks, Cora Lee had fried a chicken and I made a salad to eat on the eight-hour flight. The hostess on the plane glared at us and at the mess of greasy chicken bones and wet lettuce leaves we left on the seats and the floor.

My plan was to teach school in New York for a year, then teach at an army base somewhere in Europe. I had no plans to return to Sausalito or San Francisco. Cora Lee was invited to stay with a couple of gay lovers who lived in Brooklyn that she had met in a dance class in San Francisco. The invitation was for a long weekend, just long enough to see several ballets and hopefully, *West Side Story*.

We flew TWA and joked that if you just added one more T, it would spell the endearing nickname I gave her, and it could be her airline. When we landed at the airport, she took a bus to Brooklyn, but I splurged and took a helicopter to fly into the city at dusk. The buildings rose through the smoky brown smog like a crowded mass of rusty I beams, and lights in thousands of windows flickered as if sunlight was shining through moving branches of a poplar tree. The setting sun shot arrows of gold light that reflected on the windows that weren't lit from within.

I was excited almost to the point of near orgasm and kept humming "Autumn in New York" over and over. The flight was something I have remembered, visually, emotionally, and cherished all my life. It was like the overture to a new musical. It was the wrapped Christmas present under the tree with your name on it. It was the smell of popcorn when you rush through the lobby to see a movie. My life was now full of possibilities! Dreams could come true! Something great and powerful and thrilling was about to happen.

The reality was that I had to lug two suitcases on a hot night in Manhattan through streets that smelled of urine and pizza. The YMCA where I had reserved a room seemed to be miles from where we landed, and since I knew nothing about the subway system and was too cheap to hail a taxi, it took hours before my head finally hit the pillow.

## Chapter 12

# I Take a Bite Out of
# the Big Apple

I had brought a letter of recommendation and a composite of modeling photos from the Ann Brebner Agency in San Francisco for the Rice-McCue Agency in New York. Joel Rice and Burke McCue were very cordial and accepted me as one of their exclusive models right away. They handed me a file of names and addresses of photographers, ad agencies, art directors, and casting agents that I would have to approach and show my composite to. That meant to get started I would have to walk up every avenue and down every street in the city. It meant sitting in waiting rooms of bustling advertising agencies, sometimes leaving my composite with a receptionist, or climbing rickety stairs to a loft studio of a photographer. I did it eight hours a day, five or six days a week, all the time trying to look fresh and cool in my sweaty shirts with the "ring around the collar."

It was not what I planned. My intention was to continue as I had in San Francisco, teaching full-time and modeling part-time. After a year or so in New York City, I intended to teach in Europe, probably at an army base so I could travel and see London, Paris, and Venice. After I'd lived in Europe a few years, I might return to San Francisco or Sausalito, but being a teacher was my ticket to that dream.

To my complete surprise, my full-time job became selling myself as a model, and even more surprising, because I was a fresh face and a perfect size 38 regular, I started getting bookings right away. My plans had been changed. I was no longer a teacher. I was a piece of meat, an object to be molded and lit, to make an appealing pitch, marketing products. I was ordered around and admired at the same time. A phony, delusional, attention-getting thing, bought and sold.

Did I hate it? Hell no. Being a model in New York was a step down from being an actor, but many steps up from any businessman you see on the streets. The businessman walking toward you may be more handsome than you, have a better body, dress better, or even be sexier, but when he sees you with the large, black leather modeling portfolio, he's impressed. He gives you a second look. You are something special in the evolution of men ... in New York City.

It didn't take me long to realize that modeling took little or no talent. I was blessed with average good looks, and the photographers and their crews embellished on that, making me look more "whatever" than I really was. I eventually felt less attractive than I actually was, and the thought that my life was superficial and that I wasn't achieving anything substantial began to bother me. A little over two years after I'd arrived, I was ready to go home and start over where my family and friends were waiting for me.

I have never regretted the two years I lived in the Big Apple. How can you regret seeing the original cast in *West Side Story* and Ethel Merman in *Gypsy* three or four times? I learned to sneak into Broadway shows during intermission and grab an empty seat. Since almost every theater had standing room, I would worm my way through the standees and lean against the half-wall behind the last row. I don't regret seeing only the second half of most of the shows on Broadway, and I don't regret paying for the musicals that have become like family to me, bringing me comfort.

My stint in New York City was crammed full of excitement, and things happened, people happened. I had sex. Lots of sex, but more importantly, I had love affairs. I met friends who became lifelong friends, and I made a dangerous and foolish trip to another country when I heard a rumor they were allowing adoption of orphans to single people. I don't regret a thing.

Just a few days after Thanksgiving, which I'd celebrated alone in a Chinese restaurant floodlit by fluorescent bulbs hanging from the ceiling, Rice-McCue booked me for a print ad as a golfer caught in a sand trap but wearing very chic Levi's khakis.

"Burke, I guess I won't be able to take the booking. I've never played golf. Gee, I'm so sorry."

"If we book you as a golfer, you play golf. If they want a Marlboro cowboy, you get on a horse and ride it. If they want an Olympic swimmer, you swim. Fake it. Fake it, but don't let 'em know you're faking it. I've been fakin' it for years!"

I didn't have to fake it as it turned out. The shot called for me to show rage and frustration as I missed the ball time after time and hit the sand with my club, but at least I was wearing smart-looking Levi's khakis with perfect creases. It was a sunny November day, but the chill breeze pierced my bare arms like darts of icicles. The thermometer read 20 degrees, and the cameraman and the crew stood nearby, wrapped in their parkas and wearing fur-lined leather gloves.

The photographer saw that I was shaking and had goosebumps on my arms.

"Okay, Bill, just a couple more and you can head home for a hot shower. Just a couple."

The crew quickly circled me, smoothing out the sand as if it had never been touched, then balanced the golf ball on the tee in front of me.

My muscles cried out to be used to keep from freezing, so I swung the club as hard as I could. It made a cracking sound as it slammed the ball into the air. I turned to the account executive and sheepishly apologized for hitting the ball.

He shrugged it off. "Accidents happen."

The crew was setting up another ball for me to swing at and miss when a caddie in a golf cart drove up. He leaped out and ran directly over to me.

"Congratulations! My god that was the first time since I've been here, and that's goin' on six years!"

The photographer, who was worried about losing the light and didn't want any distractions, wailed, "What the hell are ya talkin' bout?"

The caddie was pumping my hand and excitedly yelled out, "From the goddamn sand trap! The sand trap! A hole in one! Wow!"

For a few days after that, I was referred to as the "Hole-in-One Model" at the agency. That is, I was called that until they changed it to the "Ten-a-Day Model."

Burke phoned me to go on a "go-see" at a large advertising agency on Sixth Avenue for a Lucky Strike commercial that would run nationwide and pay thousands of dollars. He told me the ad executive liked my composite. I was just what they were looking for – an average-looking guy, probably from Kansas or Ohio, who was healthy-looking and enjoyed a good smoke.

"But, Burke, I don't think I should go on that one, cuz I've never smoked. In fact, I hate the smell of cigarettes, and, well, I think smoking is bad for you."

"Bill, this is what every model and actor in this berg wants – a national commercial. Get over it. 'Member what I said? If they want somethin', give it to 'em. Now cut the crap and get up there."

The ad agency took up several floors of a skyscraper. I waited in the reception area along with a half dozen or so other male models from other modeling agencies. We all were wearing our medium gray suits and nervously sat with our portfolios on our laps. All of the others were chain-smoking. The competition for this booking was fierce. I looked at their extremely handsome faces and felt depressed. Any one of them would be chosen over me. Bill Jones from Brentwood, California? No way.

My name was called, and I hesitantly walked through a double doorway into a vast conference room with a floor-to-ceiling glass wall that demanded you be overwhelmed by the view of downtown Manhattan, the Empire State Building towering in the center. In the middle of the room seated at a long glass conference table were 10 men in dark suits, a woman in a gray suit with a man's necktie, and the photographer, in a leather jacket, who sat expressionlessly.

My portfolio was passed around the table and each person took their time to study each photograph. When it reached the last person, they all stared at me for a moment, then the account executive asked me to walk around the room. I could feel the nervous beads of sweat on my forehead as their eyes followed me.

"Bill Jones, is it? Rice-McCue?" The ad executive asked, not expecting me to respond. "You're new in town, right? I like that. Fresh face."

The woman added, "Not pretty like the others. Looks Middle America to me, and that's what's called for."

The photographer asked me to turn so he could look at my profile, then told me to smile. "Easy to light. I'm in."

The client from Lucky Strike asked, "You smoke Luckies, Bill?"

Burke's voice came out of my throat. "Oh, yeah. I've been smoking Luckies for years! Love 'em!"

The woman clapped her hands. "As far as I'm concerned, you've got the job, Bill. Great smile. Sincere. Not fake, and I like it."

One of the men in a black pinstripe approached me and said, "Bill, this is going to be the easiest money you've ever made. All you gotta do is take a deep, really deep drag, and when you exhale, give us that smile we all like. How much would you say you smoke a day?"

Burke's voice, not mine, casually said, "Oh, five or 10 a day, I guess."

The man looked at me in disbelief. "Packs?"

I knew I should have corrected him by saying cigarettes instead of packs, but Burke's voice boomed out, "Sure! As long as they're Luckies!"

I was handed a cigarette by the photographer and then lit it with a shaking hand.

He was in charge now. "Okay, Bill, now a deep inhale looking up at heaven as if it were the best thing you've ever put in your mouth. Exhale. Then a big smile. Contented."

I took a deep, deep drag on the cigarette, the acid smoke filling my lungs, and then as if I had swallowed fire itself, I began to cough so violently that two of the men rushed to my side, and keeping me upright, led me out of the room as fast as they could.

When I got back to the Rice-McCue waiting room, I was a mess. My eyes were bloodshot and the icy winds had blown my hair into a clown's wig, but I didn't care. My extreme embarrassment and humiliation were all I could think about. Luckily, sitting next to me, was a man, about my degree of good looks, average, not pretty, who leaned into me with empathy in his eyes, and calmed me down.

"Hi. My name's Wyatt. Wyatt Cooper, and you look like you need a friend, Buddy."

Wyatt offered to teach me how to smoke so I wouldn't cough myself to death, and he told me how to hold a cigarette in a masculine way, how to light one and look butch at the same time. It was all precious knowledge if you wanted to succeed as a male model. I asked him if I could buy him a drink.

Our backgrounds seemed very similar. We both had been brought up in rural farming communities but felt isolated and "different," desperate to leave as soon as we were old enough to move out. We were disappointed our families didn't seem to love us, at least, not as much as we wanted, and we were terrified about their reaction if they knew we were homosexual.

We both longed for a loving family of our own, and even after we admitted to each other that we were gay, we wondered if our lives had to be as single men. Would we never have the one thing we wanted most, to be a father and raise a child differently from the way we were raised, with more love, and more meaningful time spent with our kids? We both wanted to be parents, but it didn't look like that would ever happen.

The more I saw of Wyatt, and the more time we spent in bed together, the more I had dreams of a cottage in the country, picket fence, station wagon filled with our kids, and in my wildest dream that I knew was impossible, wedding rings on our fingers.

That dream came to an abrupt end a few weeks after we had spent our first night together when he told me in a rather matter-of-fact tone that I would have to share him. He was also sleeping with Chita Rivera, one of the female stars in *West Side Story*. I slept with him that night and said goodbye to him for the last time the next morning.

Christmas was coming, and I didn't want to spend it alone, knowing Wyatt was with someone else. It was going to be bad enough staying in Manhattan, freeze-your-balls-off Manhattan, away from family or friends.

As Christmas came closer and the models I had met at the agency left for the holidays, I felt more isolated and lonely than I had ever felt in my life. The loneliness grew exponentially each time I thought of Wyatt, and I began to seriously regret leaving him. My apartment was a white solitary confinement cell in the prison of my solitude, but I had nowhere to escape to. No one to wrap presents for, to cook for, to decorate a tree with.

I woke up two days before Christmas and said aloud, "This is bullshit! I'm drowning in self-pity! Get off your ass and do something! Something for someone. You're not the only lonely asshole in the city who's feeling sorry for yourself!"

I grabbed the phone book and looked under hospitals. I talked to the head nurses in the children's wards of several hospitals, offering to spend Christmas reading to hospitalized children and giving them art lessons. They all rejected my "kind" offer, most of them telling me that they used only volunteers who would be consistent on a weekly schedule.

I put the phone down on Christmas Eve morning after a few more calls, almost in tears, the rejections echoing in my head. I had already bought large tablets of newsprint, colored construction paper, crayons, and colored chalk. I was ready. Ready, but discouraged. By then, I had phoned a dozen hospitals in Manhattan and been turned down one after another. Finally, I found one in Brooklyn that cautiously said they would be willing to give it a try. I dressed in a hurry and ran to the nearest book store, feeling like Scrooge the morning after his nightmare of the three ghosts, happy and ready to buy books to read to the kids in the hospital.

I spent Christmas Eve and Christmas Day in the children's ward of the hospital in Brooklyn and went back every day the next week, including New Year's Eve, to read to the children and do art projects with them. To see them forget they were confined in an institution and break out in big smiles as they showed off their artwork, made me smile inside and out – a lot. More than a few times I even forgot to remember Wyatt.

*    *    *    *    *

I was cast quite often as "the young father," mostly in insurance or furniture ads, but also as the "mature" daddy at the family table, driving the family car, or at a playground pushing my kid on a swing. On the cover of *Parents* magazine, I was in bed with my "wife" and baby, all smiling, of course. I enjoyed those bookings more than the fashion ones. I signed a contract to be Howard Clothes' exclusive model for a year after they saw the full page of me in *Esquire* that introduced the flared trouser bottom from England. With the children in the "family" ads, I could let loose and distract them so we all looked more relaxed and intimate. I missed those wonderful days in my classroom with the kids hovering around my desk.

The legwork I'd done all over Manhattan to introduce myself to photographers and ad agencies paid off in 1959. The Howard Clothes contract was steady work, and the "young father" bookings were icing on the cake. I could afford jazz and tap dance lessons with Chee Davis and acting lessons from Dan Daley's sister, Ann, but it was in those classes I learned my limits. As far as acting, I just didn't have the fire in my belly. In a scene we did in Ann Daley's class from *Separate Tables*, I stood stunned as a younger woman who had an emotional scene with me said her lines with real tears streaming down her face. She had a fire in her belly that I couldn't even fake.

## Chapter 13
# Free Kids in Cuba

As usual, I was attending the business of being a New York model, which was – sitting by the phone, hoping it would ring. Bookings were all that I seemed to be living for. It rang.

"Hi, Bill, guess who this is?"

I am impatient with guessing games like that, but I responded as politely as I could. After all, it might be Mr. Right.

"George?"

"No."

"Tom?"

"No."

"Dick?"

"No."

"Harry?"

The caller sounded sorry he had ever started this guessing game and said, rather curtly, "It's me, Bill. Wyatt."

"Wyatt? Wyatt Cooper?"

"I know. It's been a long time, Bill, but I think of you now and then, and specially today."

"How's that, Wyatt?"

Wyatt Cooper

"I saw an item in the *Times* about orphans in Cuba, and I thought of you immediately. You know. The revolution. Castro and all that. Anyway, it says there are hundreds of orphans they can't find homes for in Cuba and they're open to letting them find homes here in the U.S. of A.!"

"But I'm not married, Wyatt. What's the use?"

"Bill, they're desperate. The country's a mess. All blown up. Poor kids livin' on the streets. It might be worth a try. And by the way, there's also a full-page ad in the *Times,* trying to get Americans to come back and spend money. They need money so bad that Castro is offering everything – hotels, food, transportation, everything – half price! Even the airfare to get down there, Bill."

It was wonderful hearing Wyatt's voice again, but as much as I wanted to ask him to fly down to Cuba with me and bring back a child for *us*, I knew that would never work. I could share a child with him, but not with his other lovers.

I cleared a week with Howard Clothes and Rice-McCue, bought a round-trip flight to Cuba that would be reimbursed by half the price on arrival, and packed a small bag with tennis shorts, bathing suits, seersucker shirts, and suntan lotion.

I found that the orphanage I wanted to visit was housed in Batista's former summer home, isolated on the beach near the resort town of Veradero. It was a two-hour bus ride from Havana, with a resort hotel on the beach nearby. The magnificent resort sat like a queen on her throne, ruling over the surf and sand. It could accommodate several hundred guests, but since Castro's victory, it stood nearly empty.

I was the 25th and the last guest to sign in that day. The dining pavilion was mammoth, circular, with a full-size Broadway stage at one end. A long line of waiters and busboys stood against the outer curved walls, waiting to serve the few diners at the tables. The dinner entertainment was Las Vegas showy, with long-legged showgirls in outlandish headdresses and male dancers in tight pants that showed off their round, tight buns, as they snapped their fingers and stamped their feet to sensual flamenco.

The 25 of us huddled together in the center of the room, eating our beef Wellington and fretting over the economy of Cuba with its empty hotel rooms and a waitstaff that would be jobless as soon as we left. Castro had chased Batista and all his mobsters who ran the casinos out of Cuba, fleeing like rats from a sinking ship into the wasteland of Florida.

Our solution? The moon was full, the Caribbean breeze warm, so all 25 of us walked, ran, and danced down to the beach after dinner, took off our clothes, and went skinny-dipping.

## Chapter 14

# Chased by a Witch on a Broomstick

The desk clerk at the resort, who spoke perfect English with just the slightest Cuban accent, told me there were two ways to get to Batista's summer home, which was only a couple of miles away. One was by a gated, private road that led through a thick grove of palm trees, and the other was to follow the beach until I came to the first and only structure on it.

"Last year, both approaches were heavily guarded. You would have been shot before you got 10 steps down the road or on the beach. They shot first, and said, 'stop!' after. You know what I mean?"

I nodded, but he could see I was worried, so he reassured me.

"The guards? They're long gone. The ones who were defending the house when the mobs came, ran away or were killed if they put up a fight. That was last year. Not to worry. The nuns are there now. Running an orphanage for Castro. Castro's orphans. Here's a lunch housekeeping packed for you. See you later, and good luck to you. You're gonna need it. Will you be staying another night?"

I shrugged my shoulders and answered, "That depends."

The morning sun had already started to heat up the white sandy beach, and I was glad I'd decided not to go barefoot. The wide highway of sand stretched before me, shaded on my left by a wall of palm trees and to my right, succumbing to the thrusts of clear turquoise waves that rolled in one after another. One after another.

It was midafternoon when I got my first glimpse of the mansion and its for-saken formal garden that lay between the arches, ceramic-tiled steps, terracot-ta-tiled roofs … and the unrelenting, pounding ocean surf. I walked cautiously around the empty swimming pool enclosed by a barbed-wire fence, toward a row of tall arches at the top of the steps. I could hear children laughing and scream-ing, as children do when they are playing, but their voices echoed.

I assumed they were playing inside, keeping away from the heat of the day and the little wild beasts that might scare them or even bite them.

The house was so immense and imposing that I assumed I was approach-ing the front entrance. Later, I found out I was at the back of the mansion where the great hall on the lower floor and the master bedrooms and baths on the second floor could take advantage of the ocean view, with its manicured garden and swimming pool. Most of the glass panels in the French doors lead-ing to a loggia from the great room were broken. As I moved closer, I real-ized the pockmarks on the tiled arches were bullet holes. I stood mesmerized, absorbing its past beauty, imagining the violent attacks that had damaged it, and fretting about how I could get inside. I saw no door to knock on or bell to ring.

I climbed the few broad steps and stood in the loggia facing the bullet-riddled French doors, but I couldn't see beyond them because of heavy, torn drapes that hung behind the doors.

I eventually yelled out, "Hello. Hello! *Yo estoy Americano por las ninas y los ninos.*" It was too late, but I wished with all my heart that I had paid the desk clerk to come with me. I needed a translator badly.

The dusty green drapes parted slightly, and two wrinkled faces with wor-ried looks stared out at me. I spread my arms out and turned slowly around to let them know I was unarmed. Then I gave them a thin smile to show I was friendly. They returned thin smiles and drew the drapes back so I could walk in. The cavernous room was so dimly lit, it took me a few minutes to adjust. I squinted to see who had motioned for me to come inside. Their black habits seemed to blend in with the darkness around them, but the two nuns radiated kindness. Their old, tired faces bore sweet smiles, and their bony hands were graceful as they beckoned me to follow them.

They led me silently through a maze of rooms and anterooms, down hall-ways bustling with children playing hide-and-seek, through a butler's pantry with empty shelves and a dining room filled with children chasing each other and yelling. I thought of the old woman who lived in a shoe and had so many children, she didn't know what to do. This looked like one family. Brown eyes. Dark hair. Coffee and cream skin. All of them are beautiful. Although they seemed happy playing with each other, I saw sadness, a sadness that comes from terrible experiences, in those lovely brown eyes.

The two small-framed nuns led me up a secondary staircase, then through a series of rooms that were once walk-in closets and dressing rooms. We continued through a spa-like bathroom whose mirrored walls were smashed. The tiled tub had been chopped away by angry revolutionaries with hatchets and hammers.

Eventually, they opened a floor-to-ceiling door and I was politely ushered into what I thought might have been Batista's own master bedroom. Instead of a bed, an arrangement of crates and wooden barrels was used as a desk. Behind the "desk" sat the mother superior, a nun taller than my escorts, and younger, too, but with a face so worn with worry and fear that she looked like their mother. Their real mother.

She was very gracious and offered me a lukewarm glass of tea, apologizing for what I assumed was the lack of ice. She knew a few words of English and for a while listened politely as I tried in my faltering Spanish to tell her that I had been a teacher and how much I loved the kids in my class. How my brother Jerry had a boy and a girl, and that I loved them, too, as my own. I tried to tell her about my Christmas with the children in the hospital, explaining as best I could why I had made the long trip there, hoping to adopt one of their wards, and take a child home with me.

She looked at me quizzically, and in her faltering English started to ask me personal questions. As she began to realize I wasn't married, that I was a single man who wanted to take one of her wards away from this orphanage, away from Cuba to a foreign country, she began to show signs of irritation.

She grew agitated, crossing herself, and speaking to my two sweet nuns in a voice that grew louder and louder. Then they began crossing themselves, looking at me with contempt and ferocious anger. One of them started to scream at me. Then the other nun screamed at me, too. I had no idea what they were calling me, but, no doubt about it, it was the Spanish word for a pedophile.

Without *knowing* what they were calling me, I *understood* what they were screeching about. Pedophilia! I got up from my chair and slowly walked backward, sort of bowing to them as I headed for the door. One of the nuns grabbed a broom and came toward me, snarling and shrieking at me. I reached the door and started to run for my life, not knowing which way was out. I came to a balcony hallway that led to the grand staircase cascading down in a wide curve into the entry hall and the front entrance. The two nuns were running after me, one of them still swinging the broom in the air as I rushed out the front door and ran as fast as I could down the driveway toward the private road that would take me back to the hotel in Veradero. I packed my overnight bag and caught the next bus back to Havana.

When I arrived in Havana, I registered at the same hotel I had stayed in before. Lying in bed that night, I mulled over every detail of my visit with the nuns, and at first, felt a shuddering depth of shame and embarrassment, but then I began to visualize it as a scene from a movie and came to the conclusion there was nothing to be ashamed of. After all, it would be a comedy, not a tragedy, a simple case of miscommunication. I couldn't help laughing out loud and could hardly wait to tell Wyatt how the little old nun chased me out of Batista's mansion, poking her broom at me. I hoped he would see the humor in it, not the embarrassment and fear I was trying to forget.

My return flight to New York wasn't for a few days, so I spent the first day back in Havana desperately looking for a gay bar. I didn't dare take a chance to ask a cab driver to take me to one. I certainly didn't want to get chased out of a cab by a driver swinging a broomstick at me. I had had enough of "miscommunication."

In a way, I did finally communicate with some hot Cubans. As I was passing a bar that night, I heard a great jukebox blasting out Bobby Darin singing "Mack the Knife." I went in, grabbed a barstool, and felt right at home. The music was all American pop hits, and it was fun watching the couples dance. It was a straight pickup bar for prostitutes, and I eventually felt comfortable enough to tell each one that sidled up next to me and asked me *if I was looking for a little fun*, "Me gusto harmanes, no gusto hermanas."

They giggled at first when I told them I liked men, not women, but when they found out I could jitterbug *and* rumba, the Cuba libres came sliding down the bar to me. I trotted back to the same bar every night until I flew back home.

On the plane back to "The Big Apple," I kept thinking about that bar and the fun I had dancing with the girls who hung out there. One of the whores, a woman who called herself Lela, became my "date" each night. She was a dead ringer for Elizabeth Taylor, including the come-hither look in her violet eyes. She asked me to dance, and from then on, she was the only one I danced with. Johns would coax her with $20 bills to leave with them, but she turned all of them down and put more nickels in the box so we could keep dancing. Those couple of nights dancing with Elizabeth *Lela* Taylor made the trip to Cuba unforgettable and worth all the creepiness.

That trip to Cuba was another failure in my attempt to adopt a child, but I was young, only thirty, and sooner or later, even if I had to marry some woman, I was determined to be a father. I felt it in my bones.

## Chapter 15

# More Bites Out of the Big Apple

As soon as the propellers stopped chopping the thick air at Idlewild, I made a beeline for the exit. When I'd boarded the plane in Cuba, the air had been warm and smelled of seaweed and coffee. The stewardess unlatched the plane's door and a gust of muggy soot blew over me. No doubt about it. I was back in New York City.

What the hell! New York was where it was at, and I was glad to be back – watching the second act of all the Broadway shows, dance classes with Chee Davis, cruising the East Side bars, chain-smoking, bookings, cruising the subways, mingling up close with celebrities and pretending they weren't there to give them "space."

I was able to afford to fly my mother and brother, Jerry, to visit me for a week, but got carried away and bought tickets for us to see *West Side Story* the night they arrived. What a mistake! I had forgotten how tiring traveling can be, and during Carol Lawrence's singing "I Feel Pretty," my mother let out a loud snore. She slept through *Flower Drum Song, The Music Man, Gypsy,* and *The Fantasticks,* but I take the blame. Jerry was only eighteen and loved every minute of it, but my poor mother in her late fifties was exhausted after a full day of sightseeing and a four-course dinner (with drinks) at a different restaurant every night. Then it was off to some music, and for her, a nice snooze.

After we took Mother back to my apartment to go to bed, I'd take my brother out bar hopping, which was a real treat for him because he couldn't buy a drink in California until he was twenty-one. I took him to the Upstairs at the Downstairs to hear Mabel Mercer and Bobby Short and to the Bon Soir, a basement dive in the Village, where we howled at Lenny Bruce and Phyllis Diller. One night I cautiously took him with me to the Red Lion to meet Burke McCue to listen to the current talent winner, and Jerry never realized we were in a gay bar.

One night stands out above all the others. Mother told me she'd had enough of Broadway and would rather stay in my apartment to watch some of her favorite TV shows, which let me off the hook because that night I had tickets to a new play that was in previews, and I didn't think she would like it.

It was Tennessee Williams's *Sweet Bird of Youth*, and my heartthrob, Paul Newman, was the star. I didn't give a damn what the reviews would say. I knew from the minute I read in the *Times* that he was going to be in it, that I had to see it! Because it was a preview and also playing on a Monday night when most of the Broadway shows were dark, I was able to get two fantastic seats in the fourth row, center, and I was breathing hard with excitement.

I made sure Jerry and I got there early because I had heard that actors from other Broadway shows took advantage of "dark Mondays" to see new plays and musicals they would miss otherwise. I was hoping to impress my brother if we were lucky enough to see one of these actors, and sure enough, we did.

We were drinking Cokes in the lobby before the curtain went up. I looked around and was disappointed I didn't see anyone I recognized. I knew Jerry would be king of the roost if he could go back to school and brag about seeing a real live celebrity, but it didn't look like that was in the cards. At least it wasn't until one of the men standing in a group near us turned around.

"Jerry, see that guy who just turned around over there by the bar?"

"Which guy, Bill?"

"The good-lookin' one facing us."

"Yeah."

"Remember the first night you were here and Mother snored in the middle of a song? *West Side Story*. Remember?"

"Yeah."

"Well that guy lookin' this way is … I'm sure it's … Larry Kert … Tony."

"Oh, yeah!"

We stood there mesmerized, staring at the young man who was killed just before the final curtain. It had brought tears to our eyes, and now we were looking at that very man, just a few yards away, whose tragic death made us cry.

Then Larry Kert announced to everyone in the lobby, "No matter how much they stare at me, I'm NOT going to get any prettier!"

The men in his group smirked and glanced at Jerry and me. I felt my face flush with embarrassment as I took Jerry's arm and quickly guided him to our seats. Then I leaned over to hide my angry, red face in the playbill. I could tell by his silence that Jerry was shocked and embarrassed, too.

It never occurred to me was that there was even a greater shock and embarrassment in store for us within the next few minutes. My head was bent over the playbill, and I was still mulling over the terrible experience that had hurt us so much, so I wasn't aware right away of the excitement and murmurings of the audience that seemed to grow more intense.

Jerry nudged me and asked, "What's goin' on, Bill? Why are some people standin' up? What's happenin'?"

I looked around, first at the people in front of us, then to the sides. They all seemed to be looking at us! I stood up and turned around. Jerry stood up, too. We looked at the audience in the back of us and then I looked up at the loge and balcony. They all seemed to be looking right at Jerry and me! Some were pointing at us. The chattering got louder.

I looked helplessly at Jerry, and said, "I don't get it. What that asshole Larry Kert said about us couldn't be this big a deal! I don't know why in hell everybody is looking at us and pointing"

I decided to ignore the whole damn bunch of them and take my seat. It was then that I glanced down and saw who was sitting directly behind us. I spun around and sank into my seat.

"Bill, nobody was lookin' at us, were they?"

"No, Jerry."

"So, they were lookin' at that pretty blonde lady and the guy with her?"

"Shh! Yeah."

"Who do ya think they are, Bill?"

"Jerry, I'm telling you, don't look around, and don't look at them at intermission, okay?"

"Who?"

"Shh. Marilyn Monroe and Arthur Miller."

"Really? Really? So, who's Arthur Miller?"

## Chapter 16
# Home Is Where the ...

I flew to New York in the fall of '58, and by the time Central Park slipped on her new gown of gold, red, and yellow autumn colors in '60, this guy was ready to go home to Sausalito, my cozy nook by the Golden Gate. I know I was becoming the biggest bore at any gay cocktail party in New York.

The jasmines and geraniums bloom and smell so good all winter long ... You never see the sunset or stars at night *here*. You should *see* the sunset behind the Golden Gate Bridge! You should *see* the moonlight over the Ferry Building ... Ocean Beach is just across town ... The redwoods are only 20 minutes away ... *real* artists live on houseboats in Sausalito ... not like the ones in Greenwich Village, which isn't a village at all! BORING!

I hadn't soured on the Big Apple, but more and more, I was hungry for my home on the bay and my adopted family, John, Muffer, Enid, and even for my "blood" family. Especially my brother Jerry. One by one, my New York friends made casual suggestions about different scenic routes I could take if I ever decided to drive back to San Francisco. It was tossed off as a joke, but since they had already told me to shut up about the gardens that bloomed all year, I began to take notes on how I could get home. One of the problems was that my wardrobe had put on weight – and size – and I would need steamer trunks to hold it all. The other problem was that I *loved* my little one-cylinder, door-in-front, bubble-car Issetta and wanted to keep it to show it off when I got home, but there was no way I could drive it home – 3,000 miles across deserts and two mountain ranges.

The Christmas parties ran continuously through New Year's Eve. Rice-McCue threw a big one in a photographer's studio on the West Side with most of their models strutting around in gowns and tuxedos. My Fire Island friends held one in an empty warehouse, carpeted in white sand, where we all had to wear shorts or bathing suits and we drank vodka through straws stuck in watermelons. Burke McCue threw a bash in the Red Lion that went on for several days, and a few of my friends had goodbye dinners in my honor. I loved living in New York, but I didn't know how much I'd miss it until I was leaving.

Even though New York City was a joy and ablaze in Christmas glory right after Thanksgiving, the one downer I felt was choosing between Nixon and Kennedy for president that November. Nixon had made his nastiness known when he ran for governor of California a few years before, and I thought he was an asshole. As movie-star attractive as Senator Kennedy was, I thought I might have to hold my nose and pull the handle for Nixon because John F. Kennedy was a Catholic, and I was fearful that that church would end up running the country. Women would be forced to bear children they didn't want or couldn't afford. We would have to buy fish on Fridays – no beef. Homosexuals would be beaten and incarcerated – if not tortured by the inquisition! Movies and books would be censored again. Certain works of art couldn't be shown in museums!

I mistrusted the Catholic Church more than I despised Nixon, but Kennedy promised he wouldn't put his church before his duty as president, and finally I believed him enough to vote for him. Of course, his athletic handsomeness played no part in my decision.

A week before Christmas, I did a real dumb-ass thing. I had bought presents for both my families in California (adopted in Sausalito – blood in Brentwood) and took great pains in packaging them separately to be sent in the mail. I made several trips down the four flights of stairs from my minuscule apartment, to stack them neatly in my Issetta, leaving barely enough room for me to squeeze into the driver's seat.

Just as I started the one-cylinder motor, I realized I'd left my wallet in my apartment. I took the keys with me but forgot to lock the door to the Issetta. When I came back to the car, I found it empty, and a dead weight fell from my throat to the pit of my stomach. The little door that swung out in front of the car with the steering wheel attached to it seemed to sneer at me. The little red bench seat and the wide shelf behind it were empty, starkly lit by the streetlamp above. I stared at the empty space, unable to accept that someone had done something I would never do myself. It didn't make sense. As usual, I was living in a delusion.

The next day I mailed gift certificates from Brooks Brothers to my friends and "family" in Sausalito, and Sears Roebuck gift certificates to my "blood" family That got me off the hook, but I was left with a bitter taste that was hard to spit out.

I found an ad in the *Times* asking for a driver to deliver a station wagon to Northern California, all fuel paid for by the owner on delivery, with the understanding the driver would *not* be allowed to tow a trailer of any size. I signed up for it immediately, then rented a trailer I could drive my Issetta on to. I filled the station wagon with belongings and stuffed most of my clothes into the Issetta. Then I encased the little car with more bric-a-brac, covered the whole thing with a bedsheet, tied it down, and took off for California the day after Kennedy's inauguration.

## Chapter 17
# The Accidental Fuck

It was a dark and stormy night in Sausalito. I was just finishing my Swanson's TV fried chicken dinner and starting to watch *Route 66*. A beam of light from the headlights of a car that had pulled up on the dirt road outside my houseboat shot through the window, flooding the room. I recognized the putt-putt-puttering of the dying motor. It was a Ford Model A, and I knew it had to be Cora Lee. Before I could get up, she was bounding up the gangplank and banging on the door.

She was yelling at the top of her voice, "Bill, Bill, open up! I'm soaking wet out here! Open up! It's *me*, dammit! Open up!"

I threw the aluminum tray into the sink and rushed to unlock the door. As soon as I had turned the key, she pushed the door open and swooshed in, hair hanging limp, her glasses fogged over with rain. Her gypsy blouse, two skirts, sailor's peacoat, Spanish shawl, and tennis shoes were dark and wet. She held something wrapped in a towel, and for a brief moment, I thought she might have had a baby! She crossed the room immediately, leaving a trail of water on the floor, and went directly to the electric heater whose bright orange coils glowed, radiating waves of heat. Before she took her coat off, she lowered the bundle to the floor and unwrapped a sad-looking black and white cat.

"That's Roginsky, Bill. He's hungry." She got down on her knees to pet Roginsky. "Aren't you, Sweetie?" Then without even looking up at me, she asked, "Got any milk?"

Cora Lee was allergic to cats and couldn't live without at least two, three, or four of them. She had to inject herself with anti-allergy serum once or twice a week, the needle marks on her forearms and buttocks disguised with body makeup left over from her Va Va Voom days.

I poured milk over the remains of my chicken bones, still in the tray, and gave them to Roginsky while Cora Lee got out of her wet clothes and took a hot shower. Seeing her naked was not exactly new to me, but I turned away, feeling modest and uncomfortable in such a small, intimate setting. It was *not* the President Follies Theatre, after all.

We hung her clothes over the backs of chairs, a hanging light fixture, and doorknobs to dry out, and I gave her a pair of clean Jockey shorts, a shirt, and a sweater to wear until her clothes were dry. We sat in the glow of the heater for hours, drinking wine and filling each other in on some of the things, good and bad, that had happened to each of us while I had been in New York for the past two years and she was in Mill Valley.

She'd received an inheritance and had bought a house in Sausalito but decided it was too urban for her. She sold it and bought a more isolated one in Mill Valley.

She knew how much I wanted to be a father, to have a child I could care for, and to make a family of my own. After she was rudely "expelled" from the Follies, we'd had several serious conversations about the possibilities of *us* siring a baby. She liked the idea that I had been a teacher who loved teaching and the kids I taught. We'd agreed that if she would bear a child for me, I would have to pay her enough to live on, including guitar and ballet lessons, for the nine months she was pregnant. It meant I would have to take on several part-time jobs to afford it, but I was eager to try.

Obviously, there was one big elephant in the room. I was a virgin – at least as far as women were concerned. I had tried. God knows I had tried. One lovely and decent girl, Emily, whom I dated in college, explored my body and let me explore hers. We would spend hours "necking," as Verla and I had, but unlike Verla, Emily put my hand on her breast as we were driving somewhere on a date, and Emily would press up next to me naked on a sofa or a bed, as we French kissed skin to skin. But she drew the line at touching each other's genitals. I never had an orgasm, even though I had a hard-on that became painful after an hour or two without any release.

It didn't bother me too long because after I left Emily lying on her rumpled bed, I drove my Model A convertible a short distance from the Pacific campus to the apartment of my literature professor and knocked on his door. He opened it for me no matter what time it was any night, and I drove back to my room with a smile on my face after I left him lying on his rumpled bed.

The two other times I'd tried were with whores, but because of their painted faces and lacquered hair, the smell of other sweaty men on them, and their disinterested, business-like attitude, I failed to respond. I couldn't get an erection. I was repulsed. So, in a strange way, I was a virgin.

Cora Lee was intrigued when I suggested, if it came down to me fucking her to introduce one of my sperm to one of her eggs, we could have another gay man with us to get me hot and ready for the grand-entrance moment. Hopefully, I would be primed and ready to cum instantly, doing my duty, as it were. That determined, we went on to discuss more pressing things. She and I agreed that from the time she gave birth to the time I could enroll the infant in childcare, it would have to be taken care of, and since I was still working, who would do that?

"My mother's not working in the bar anymore, TWAT. Her days are free and she's bored! I bet she'd love to do it. You know, take care of my baby."

I drove us to Byron, where my mother lived with Lou, my stepfather, in a house behind their bar, the Wild Idol Inn. I introduced Cora Lee to my mother, and at first, it looked like it was going to be a pleasant afternoon, drinking cold beers on her front porch. Unfortunately, after the initial chatter about the weather and the increasing cost of beauty parlors, Mother thought she would entertain us with rumors about infidelities of the married men in Byron who drank at the Wild Idol. When she finished those stories, she gabbed on about the funerals of her friends who used to be neighbors, but I could see she was saving the best for the last.

"Has your brother told you about the girl he's *madly* in love with, Billy?"

"Yeah, he phoned me and told me how pretty she is, and how smart, how polite and everything. Esther, isn't it?"

She took a couple of gulps of beer from the can. "Esther Maria *Garcia*. A spic!"

"Jerry told me her grandparents were from Honduras, Mom. They came here 60 years ago. You shouldn't call her a spic."

"Oh, shouldn't I? Well, I don't want to have to learn no Spanish to speak to no daughter-in-law!"

"Daughter-in-law? What's this about? He didn't say anything about marriage."

"You just wait and see, Billy; she'll see to it to get knocked up. That'll do it. I know her kind."

When we got into my car, waved *goodbye*, and were driving away, Cora Lee smoothed her skirt, looked out the window and said just two words that almost broke my heart.

"No *way!*"

\*     \*     \*     \*     \*

That was in 1957. Three years had passed and both of us had matured. As we reminisced that night with the rain beating down on the roof of my tiny houseboat, we laughed at our naivety and simple-minded solutions to life's problems and promises. Our lives still had problems and promises, but now they felt real, and we hoped we could face them as adults, not as children in grown-up bodies. By morning, we would be pressed to see if that were true because during that night something unexpected happened.

Cora Lee had been driving back in the rainstorm after seeing *Swan Lake* for the eleventh time at the Opera House, and she was going through Sausalito when her Model A sputtered a few times. She realized her gas tank was nearly empty. Luckily, it happened just as she was about to drive past my little houseboat.

It was past midnight when we ran out of memories to talk about. Her clothes were still damp, and the one gas station in Sausalito wouldn't be open until the next morning, so she had to spend the night.

We had slept in the same bed several times during the nine years we'd been friends and, of course, nothing sexual had ever happened between us. We could cuddle, usually with one or two cats pressed between us, and it was comfy and cozy. That night we had to share my much smaller single bed, and since I usually slept naked and didn't use pajamas, there were none for us to wear. She was, by that time, back in her panties and bra, and I was wearing my boxer shorts and a tee shirt. So, we crawled in together. We were sleeping spoon fashion, Cora Lee's back warming my chest and stomach, and

Roginsky, purring loudly, cuddled in her arms. The rain pitter-pattered against the window, and within seconds I was sound asleep, full of red wine and happy thoughts.

A clap of thunder woke me, and I was embarrassed to find my cock fully erect and poking out from the fly in my boxers. Cora Lee felt it pressing against her buttocks, and without muttering a sound, she pulled her panties down and wiggled back, guiding my family jewel into her jewel box! I came almost immediately, then, shocked at what I had just done, turned over away from her, not saying a word.

She was very sweet the next morning. Fully aware that I had fucked her without intending to, and that I had no desire to ever let it happen again, she shyly suggested that it would be all right with her if I ever wanted to try it again – while I was awake. It was a generous offer from one loving friend to another that I never took advantage of.

## Chapter 18

# Gate Five of Sausalito's Shipyard

Johohn Kennedy's murder threw everyone I knew into deep despair. During that nasty November, my lover, Jack Claydon (Clay) and I lived on the top floor of a houseboat that had been the Spreckels's boathouse when the Spreckels "Sugar" family had lived in a brown-shingled waterfront mansion on the south end of Sausalito at the turn of the century. The mansion had burned down, leaving only the empty boathouse sitting on the edge of the estate overlooking the bay waters. The estate's valuable acres of waterfront were to be covered with condominiums in the sixties.

The charming old boathouse had been lifted off its pilings and attached to a large wooden barge, then towed over to the north end of town, where a small rag-tag community of barges, old houseboats, tug boats, and ferry boats huddled together sheltering a ragtag bunch of "outsiders." Artists, musicians, writers, bohemians of every ilk, including homosexuals, were drawn to its rough frontiersman charm. Clay and I lived in the caretaker's apartment over the yacht's garage. Later, two more apartments were built in that empty space below us.

Squatting like a beached whale, the old side-paddle ferryboat, *Charles Van Damme*, was our neighbor and the destination point for hungry Marinites at three in the morning after the bars closed at two. Juanita's Galley, the funky restaurant on the ferryboat, was open 24 hours a day. Juanita was a woman larger than life in more ways than one, but her mammoth plates of delicious

I adopt friends as a loving family, L to R below me – Cousin Howard,
Grandmother Witchcraft, Muffer, Dad

food and her loud screeching insults thrown at customers made the wait to be
served – sometimes over an hour – worth it.

The "road" into our floating home community and Juanita's Galley on the
*Charles Van Damme* was nothing more than dredged silt from the Richardson
Bay's shoreline. It was a leftover of World War II when the north end of
Sausalito changed from rickety fishing piers to a crunching, banging, 24-hour-
a-day shipyard, turning out liberty ships at the rate of one a week.

Gate Five Road, the last of five "gates" into the shipyard, was ungraded,
bumpy, muddy, and sometimes disappeared under a high tide. Our so-called
utilities, gas, water, and electricity were about as reliable as the Gate Five
"road." They had a habit of disappearing too, especially if we were all home at
the same time, cooking a holiday dinner.

The sewer system was simple. A pipe from our toilet ran down one flight
and then abruptly made a right turn to run under the waters of the bay for
about 30 feet. End of sewer system story.

It was during one of those godawful nights that Clay and I were having my "family," John, Muffer, and Enid, over for dinner that our gas stove wouldn't turn on. Clay was in a panic.

We searched but couldn't find the hot-plate burner we had used once before. Enid suggested we use a can of Sterno and heat beans over it, which brought a round of groans from the rest of us.

Our deck and front door faced south, and a very large window next to the doorframe reflected the moon on the vibrating waters of the bay and the lights of San Francisco. The Bay Bridge blinked at us from afar. A man, silhouetted against this bright view, crossed our deck and knocked on our door. He was taller than me and wore a worried look on his face. I opened the door.

"Hi, I'm your neighbor, er, ah, three houseboats down. Did your gas go out? Ours did, and the chicken we put in the oven is colder than a witch's teat, oozing blood as a matter of fact."

"Yeah, ours too, dammit. I mean our gas. You know. Not a chicken. Clay was about to put in a roast. This seems to happen all the time, you know."

He smiled and rolled his eyes. "I know. I know. Polish luck!"

"Who's *us*?" I asked, hoping to find out if he was single or married, gay or straight.

"Oh, us? My roommates, Zahn and Don."

"Zahn and Don? Are you putting me on? So, your name's Ron, right?"

"Ron? No, my name's …"

Clay interrupted him and introduced us one by one. "I'm Clay. This is my … eh … my roommate, Bill, and this handsome man is my … eh, Bill's dad, John, and his mother, Elizabeth. We call her *Muffer* – Enid Foster, the artist. You've probably seen her on Bridgeway with her pet duck on a leash. Everybody knows Enid and Emily … now you do."

The man smiled a really big toothy smile. He reminded me of Dick Van Dyke or Danny Kaye, sorta goofy but rather handsome at the same time. "Oh, yeah. I almost bumped into the car in front of me on Bridgeway cuz I was gawkin'. I mean, *looking* … at her and … the duck."

Enid quickly chimed in, "Emily Duckinson. That's her name. *Miss* Emily Duckinson, and I'm Grandmother Witchcraft … Pleased."

"That's terrific! I love it! Wait 'til I tell Zahn and Don!" He paused for a just a second and then proposed, "Hey, how about me bringing my roommates back here to meet you, and I'll go over to Juanita's and pick up hamburgers for all of us?"

I looked at Clay for approval, probably too late after I had blurted out, "That's a great idea, and we can pay you for ours when you come back."

Clay hesitated a moment too long and then added, "I baked a cheesecake this afternoon, and there's plenty for all of us … but … and … can you bring a bottle of wine?"

Enid pulled herself up until she was ramrod straight. Looking over her framed glasses at the stranger as if he were a lowly page or jester, she disdainfully said, *"Ham*burgers? My good, good man, *ham*burger for me?" Pause. "Medium rare, please. Not too much, but *some* blood."

He walked out the door and then sort of loped across the deck to the stairway. We heard him take the stairs two at a time. In less than a minute, we heard the clumping of feet on the stairs and then saw the stranger and his two roommates standing on the deck looking in awe at the view of San Francisco. The rising moon created a shimmering pathway of silver, leading to the most beautiful city in the world. They came in for a quick introduction, and then the three of them turned to go back down the stairs and pick their way through the mud puddles of Gate Five to Juanita's.

I ran out on the deck and yelled down at the stranger, "Hey, what's *your* name? I didn't hear you if you said it!"

He looked back up at me and began to chuckle. "It's Bill. Just like yours! Bill! But I tell you what … so not to confuse everybody, you can call me Polly. That's what my friends call me sometimes. Polly Pasek, that's me! Oh, hell, just call me Pasek."

## Chapter 19
# Santa's Revenge

Icouldn't have been happier that November morning.

Jack was clipping hair in his barbershop downtown when it happened. I was having a cup of coffee at the bait shop next to the entrance of Gate Five, but to my annoyance, Old Mack turned up the sound on his black-and-white TV to an ear-splitting volume. "We interrupt this broadcast to bring you this special report. The news we have from Dallas, Texas, is that the president of the United States, John F. Kennedy, has been shot. It is unknown at this point in time ..."

The news stunned me and all the fishermen there. Our hands and bodies froze. There were grunts and groans. We all stared, horrified, at the black-and-white messenger on the shelf behind the counter. Old Mack was talking to himself, "Mother of Christ! Dear Mary, mother of Jesus!"

I grabbed Lily's leash and ran back to our houseboat and up the outside stairs, pulling her behind me, threw the door open, and rushed for the phone.

"Clay, Clay, do you have the radio on? Oh, my god! Oh, my god! Hang on. I think I'm going to need a tissue."

His voice sounded strained, tense. "I've already dirtied two handkerchiefs. Bill. I've canceled everybody, and I'm locking up to come home."

When he came up the stairs, I saw his face, his wonderful face, stained with tears. We sat together on the couch, Lily sleeping at our feet, and watched the television late into the night with our neighbors, Pasek, Donald, and Zahn. We had no dinner that night, but we threw an empty wine jug over the railing into the bay before Clay and I finally turned off the set and went to bed, hugging each other for hours before we could get to sleep.

I phoned my agent, Ann Brebner, the next morning. "Ann, they'll call off the Santa gig Sunday, won't they? After what's happened?"

"Bill, the contract you signed is airtight. If they call it off, they'll owe you for a whole month's work. They had full-page ads this morning in all the newspapers that the helicopter will be landing at 11:30 Sunday morning. I don't know what to tell you. After what happened yesterday, I think it would be in good taste to cancel the whole damn thing, but it's their money and their decision. I'll get back to you as soon as I hear from them. Have a nice Thanksgiving, Bill."

"I'll try, Ann. I'll try. You try, too."

On Friday, the day after Thanksgiving, I phoned her again, this time pleading with her to get me out of doing the job.

"Bill, you do not squirm out of a signed contract if you want to continue in this profession. I've talked to them and they are determined to go through with it. Please remember that this agency's name is in bold print on the paper we signed. I have a reputation in this town to uphold, Bill, so grit your teeth. Just do it and it'll be over in less than four weeks. We're all counting on you."

By Saturday, I was a drained, emotional wreck, floating among all the other emotional wrecks in a sea of tears.

*　　*　　*　　*　　*

"Yes, this is Bill Jones."

The voice on the other end sounded overly polite, like a head waiter with attitude. "This is the general manager at Penney's and I want to go over the details for tomorrow with you. First of all, we will …"

"You know, I don't think anyone will show up for this thing. Everybody's home, crying their eyes out. Is there *any* chance you will change your mind and call it off? Besides, it looks like it's gonna rain tomorrow."

"Mr. Jones … may I call you Bill?"

"Of course."

"Bill, we did this at the Penny's in El Cerrito last year, and it was an awesome, awesome event to start the Christmas season."

"Of buying," I sneered.

"Yes, of buying. Our economy is based on it, you know." He was beginning to sound a little edgy, then decided to cool it in his very polite business manner. "Please be at the Sausalito heliport no later than 10:30 a.m. The display staff will meet you there with the Santa Claus suit and beard and stuff. Have your wife drive you …"

"I'm not married."

"A friend then. Bring a small suitcase for your clothes. She can …"

"My friend's a guy."

"*He* can deliver the case to you at the store. Bill, I know you don't want to do this, but we have thousands of dollars invested in it, and do you really think President Kennedy would want to take this joy away from the children who are looking forward to Santa coming out of the clouds to land right in Penney's parking lot?"

"No, he loved children. Caroline. Little John." I started to choke up again.

Sunday was overcast and chilly. Clay drove me to the Sausalito Seaport and waited with me in the men's restroom while I undressed and put my clothes in the suitcase. Then he drove off to meet us later at Penney's parking lot.

Two men from Penney's window display helped me get into the red velvet pants and coat outlined in white rabbit fur. "We sewed these thick foam pads onto the thighs so your legs will look huge, and this pillow, with a strap to tie it on, goes here to make your belly look jolly and fat. I stood while they finished dressing me and hung a big white beard on my rouged face that hung from my ears. They plopped a white wig and a red velvet cap on to my head.

"Hey, it's time to get in the copter."

"Good grief!" I wailed, "This beard smells like it's been soaking in whiskey and wet cigar butts!"

"Yeah, they had to fire the Santa last year for coming in plastered half the time."

I gagged, "And he smoked cigars! A lot!"

"Yeah, you shoulda seen the little kids fanning away the smells when they sat on his lap. Funny as all getout."

I was so restricted by the foam in my pants and the pillow that I had to be hoisted up into the helicopter. The pilot leaned over and yelled over the pounding of the rotors, "Last year in Santa Rosa, the Santa got out when we landed and raised his hands over his head when he was givin'em the old Ho! Ho! Ho! … and the blades took off three of his fingers!"

He watched me wince.

"So, whatever you do, wait 'til you get out from under the blades!"

I nodded *yes* so hard my beard slipped down to my chin. The day was gray. Like the mood of the entire nation. We rose slowly as if we were in a freight elevator, then tipped our nose toward Corte Madera, and flew like a seagull in a straight line for just a couple of minutes until we hovered over the parking lot at the mall. I couldn't believe what I saw there. I had been expecting a few families, probably right-wingers who hated the Kennedys anyway and wouldn't mind having an excuse to smile and laugh at a time like this, but I was wrong, wrong, wrong.

A gigantic wreath of human bodies waited below us. A circle of thousands, thousands of families, holding a wide red and green ribbon that formed a wheel as big as a football field, guiding us to land in its center. As we descended, I could see the delighted faces of children, cheeks red from the icy winds, and their parents behind them, solemn with eyes still reddened from crying over Kennedy's bloody assassination.

The wheels touched the pavement, and a minute later, the pilot gave me a little shove toward the door. I grabbed the black sack of lollipops and eased my blimp-like body down until my black boots touched the ground.

I waddled out toward the crowd, not looking at them because my eyes were focused on the blades above me. When I was sure I was safe from being sliced like so much baloney, I dropped the sack of lollipops, lifted my arms as high as I possibly could, deepened my voice to an octave below a frog's croak, and let out the happiest "Ho! Ho! Ho!" I could muster.

I picked up the sack and looked straight ahead at the crowd, puzzled by what I saw. Children weren't laughing anymore. They were shell-shocked, it seemed. Eyes wide. Mouths open slightly. But the adults behind them, some bent over holding their stomachs and sides, were all laughing so hard that they were gasping for breath. I tried to walk toward them, but I couldn't move my feet!

I saw Clay and the two display men running toward me as fast as they could. I looked down at my feet, but couldn't see beyond the red hill of the red velvet belly, but I felt a chilly breeze around my legs, blowing up under my boxer shorts.

"Bill, Bill, your pants fell down and are hanging over your boots!" Clay cackled.

One of the display men yelled, "Damn foam! Too thick and heavy. Musta pulled 'em down when you raised your arms!"

The three of them pulled my pants up and cinched the belt so tight it hurt. Then I made my way around the circle of families, the little ones thanking me, wide-eyed, for the suckers, and the adults, almost every one of them, thanking me for the first laugh they had had in four days.

"Kennedy would have *loved it* and laughed at your skinny chicken legs propping up Santa's fat belly." At least that's what Pasek told me, with tears of laughter running down his cheeks, as he reached out over the head of a little girl for a lollipop.

Penney's general manager was not amused.

## Chapter 20
# Lillie Langtry

Our mutt, Lillie, aka Lily, was almost left an orphan one terrible night when Clay and I rolled over and crashed my maroon '62 Corvair Spyder convertible on the Sausalito Boulevard exit off 101 on the Waldo Grade, the car landing upside down.

We had been invited to a very posh dinner party given by two very rich queens we hardly knew, to celebrate the finalized construction of their home on Strawberry Point. It was a two-storied stucco house that was contemporary, but you had the feeling of tradition and wealth when the hand-carved wooden gates opened to their driveway. The house was painted a rich orange-red, with all the wooden trim and windows left natural. The tall entry hall and staircase were as large as our one-bedroom houseboat, and a huge floral arrangement stood in the center of the entry, spotlit from above. I was impressed, but Clay stiffened with obvious envy and resentment.

We were handed gin martinis and led into the vast living room, dimly lit, with spotlights lighting enormous Jackson Pollock and Rothko paintings that hung on three walls. The fourth wall was floor-to-ceiling glass doors and beyond them was a carefully landscaped patio overlooking Richardson Bay and Belvedere.

The conversation never veered far from the description of the trials of the design and construction of their home. One of the most difficult problems was the choice of color for the stucco exterior. They finally settled on the peach/burnt orange they found in a Degas painting and had it mixed in the stucco, not just painted on afterward. I was so relieved to hear they no longer were struggling with such decisions.

I never understood why rich people always ate dinner so late, and it was nearly nine o'clock before one of our hosts rang a small silver bell to announce grub was finally going to be served. In the hours since we arrived, many more gin martinis were consumed, and Clay's nastiness became more and more evident. He took the carefully stacked, oversized architecture and garden books on the glass coffee table and slid them every which way. He plucked an orchid from the entry bouquet and wore it out of his breast pocket, but the worst thing he did to humiliate me and cause embarrassment around the dining room table was yet to come.

Ten of us, all gay men in suits and ties, sat at the steel and glass table. Our hosts sat at the ends with four of us on each side. I sat across from Clay and watched him, through the glass tabletop, drape his napkin over his knees. It was distracting to look at each man at the table, and also see their napkins and knees below it. All eyebrows raised when Clay slowly moved his left hand over to the thigh of the man sitting next to him and started the approach to his crotch like a spider stealthy advancing to the fly caught in her web.

Since there was only silence and no objection from the half-drunk guy sitting next to him, we all continued eating and watched Clay grope his prey through the main course. But before dessert and coffee were served, I stood up and asked our hosts to please excuse me.

"I'm having a monumental migraine headache and need to get home and into bed immediately."

One of the offended hosts not only agreed that we should leave but ran to open the front door so we could get out as soon as possible.

I was livid and too drunk to drive. Too much in a hurry to put the convertible's top up on the car. Too humiliated to even cuss Clay out, and driving much too fast to take the curve on to the Sausalito Boulevard exit. One minute we were speeding up the Waldo Grade, the warm air blowing our hair and the motor roaring so loud that we couldn't hear the radio. The next moment, actually minutes later, I was lying on my back staring up at the stars. I could smell gasoline and I could hear the sputtering radio. I looked and saw the front wheels still turning as they pointed up to the sky.

My head throbbed and a little blood flowed down from under my hair on to my shirt collar and coat. I moved my legs and arms, but they ached, so I lay down again, trying to figure out what had just happened. Cars were whizzing by on 101 and in spite of their steady hum, I heard something that shocked me into a reality that I didn't want to face. Clay was groaning in pain.

I was in front of the car, its headlights blinding me. The car had flipped over and was upside down with its windshield crushed. Clay was lying close to the side of the car. His groans were growing into screams of pain as I crawled over to him. His left arm was under the car door, pinning him down across his elbow. I tugged at him, but he just screamed louder. I tried to rock the car back and forth so he could get out, but I couldn't budge it, so I ran back up to the freeway and waved my arms madly at every car that went by, but no one stopped. I ran back to Clay, who was now crying with pain. "Get me out of here! I've got gas all over me!"

I ran, limping, back up to the freeway. This time, I didn't just wave my arms standing on the shoulder of the road. I stood right in the middle of a lane until finally a car slowed down and stopped. Two men got out and we went back to Clay and the wreck.

Panicked, I yelled, "See if you two can lift the car up enough so I can pull him out!" They tried several times, but the car didn't move an inch.

One of the men shook his head, and muttered, "We better go get help. A tow truck can lift it."

Clay was sobbing. "Please! Please!"

I grabbed at the two who were leaving. "For god's sake, don't leave yet! One more try! Please!" I hobbled around to the front of the car and reached under the fender closest to Clay. "I'll lift and you two pull him out!" Then something happened that is still hard to believe. With the headlight braced against my sore stomach, I wrapped my arms under the slick upside-down fenders, and with a strength I had never felt before or since, lifted the front of the car up a few inches. Just enough for the two men to slide Clay's arm out from under it.

The sun was just lighting the starless sky over the bay when I finally got home that morning after spending a sleepless night in the emergency waiting room. The doctors came through the swinging doors with horrible news for me. Clay would recover, but his right arm had been ground up at the elbow like so much hamburger, and he would live with it in a rigid right angle for the rest of his life.

I sat by his bed, holding his hand until one of the nurses gently ordered me out of the room so he could get complete rest. She also noticed my blood

Clay before the accident

stains and offered to clean my scratches and told me my clothes, which were ripped and covered with blood and dirt, should be thrown away as soon as I got home.

I phoned the only person I knew who might be up that early, my houseboat neighbor Pasek, and asked him to pick me up at the hospital. He came rushing into the lobby, still in his pajamas and bathrobe, a very worried look on his face.

"Holy shit, Bill! What the hell happened? You've got blood all over you! Jesus! What's the other guy look like?" He smiled at his feeble joke. "You've got to stop hanging out in those rough bars and pickin' fights." He saw I was not amused.

"Sorry, Bill, just trying to lighten things up. Come on, I'll take you home. Then I've got to go to work. Have you over for dinner tonight, okay?"

Lily was waiting for us at the front door and ran around barking excitedly until she smelled the blood on my clothes. Then it was hard to keep her from sniffing it and whimpering. She ran to the door several times, expecting Clay to appear, but he never did. Never.

During the next few days, while Clay was in the hospital, I went into his shop to ready it for sale to another barber if we could find one to buy his business. It was obvious to both of us that he could never cut hair again. I started by picking up his personal belongings in the back room, a room that until then was more or less off limits to me.

A dozen or so of his very small framed abstracts were leaning against the wall. His paints, brushes, and more empty frames were stacked on his drawing table. On the table I had made for him from a flush door lying on two sawhorses, were a couple of books, a coffee cup half full, an overflowing ashtray, a stack of unpaid bills, and a diary.

I felt sneaky and ashamed, but I opened the diary to the last page. I'm sure my face flushed as I read, "I want to travel. I want to paint. I don't want this domestic life any longer. I want OUT."

That afternoon, I told Clay what I had found in his diary as he lay in his hospital bed. Without looking at me, he turned his head toward the window and admitted it was how he really felt. He didn't hate me or his life with me, but he didn't love it either. He wanted to move back in with the group of artists he had been living with on Union Street. They made him feel free, free to go and come as he pleased.

That night, I sat in the dark with Lily's head on my lap. I heard footsteps on the deck, and for a split second thought, Clay had come home to me. Pasek knocked on the door tentatively, then pushed it open without me saying, "Come in!" He carried a hot bowl of tomato soup and a chilled bottle of wine for me. He put his arm around me and we sat in the dark for a long time, not saying a word.

I was immobile ... haunted by the thought of Clay's smashed elbow. It took days for it to sink in that Clay was actually going to be out of my life forever. The feeling of abandonment and loss filled my days and my nights, but I managed to sell the business for him and close the doors forever to JACK, THE CLIPPER, his shop on Bridgeway in Sausalito.

Ray Williams, my real estate buddy, found me a dilapidated Victorian on San Francisco's Bernal Heights, sprawled over two lots with a direct view of the city, OZ, pastel gray during the day and a treasure chest of jewels sparkling at night. It cost $14,000, and another couple of grand to remodel it, living in plaster dust and sawdust during the next two years. I still had Lily and a black cat, Mammy Pleasant, named after a famous San Francisco entrepreneur and abolitionist, to comfort me – and a friend I would have for the rest of our lives – Bill Pasek. Polly Pasek to his friends. Pasek to me. Our friendship lasted for the rest of our lives, and it was Pasek who held my hand through the 18 months of tribulation it took to adopt my son, Aaron, and then officiated as my knight in shining armor helping me raise him. But that's another story. Another book of stories.

**Chapter 21**

# The DAR Host a Belated Birthday Party for "Poland's Only Beauty Queen"

### Sept. 17, 1967, RSVP

The year 1967, the Summer of Love in San Francisco with hazy air reeking of marijuana. Thousands of hippies defiantly flowed into San Francisco, costumed in their tie-dyed tee-shirts with strings of beads hanging around their necks and flowers poked into their long, matted hair and beards. Mayor John F. Shelley and the entire Board of Supervisors specifically *uninvited* the inelegant, itinerant young misfits who clogged Haight Street, an *uninvite* that made headlines in the *San Francisco Chronicle*, but to no avail.

My unhip group of friends decided to crash the party and see what all the hoopla was about. We drove to Haight and Ashbury and squeezed into a parking space between a Volkswagen van and a small dilapidated school bus, both covered with psychedelic graffiti. As we opened the doors to get out of the car, our ears were nearly blown off. Jefferson Airplane's "White Rabbit" blasted from several cars' radios, including the bus and van, tuned in to the same station.

Michael and Bob had thoughtfully bought us all a string of beads, and Pasek dangled yellow daisies over our ears so we could blend in with the young crowd, mostly glassy-eyed and "tripping." We tried to be in tune with the times, all sporting sideburns. Gary and Bob even had full mustaches. We thought of ourselves as being very "hip," but when a couple of giggling girls blocked us, pointing at us, laughing, we stood speechless.

One of the girls, tall and thin, pointed at Pasek and me, screaming with laughter, "Cashmere sweaters and khaki pants! Who you kiddin', Daddy?"

The "Group" L to R: Bill Pasek, Bill Jones, Gary Fusfeld, Bob Lanci, Michael Vincent

The short one joined in, "Man, I haven't seen penny loafers since high school!"

We stood in disbelief, looking at each other until Michael blurted out, "I need a drink!" We piled back into the Lincoln and took off for the Buena Vista. The Irish coffees were better than drugs, and we didn't have to cloak what we were doing, hiding behind some dumpster down an alley either.

We tried being "hip," but when we clapped to the beat of Jimi Hendrix, the Who, or Janis Joplin, it was obvious that we were out of it. The only new music we liked was Jefferson Airplane *when* the Mamas and the Papas sang.

Pasek was the first to admit how square we were. "I just don't get it ... dancing without touching? Might as well dance alone! Give me the Polish polka!"

I agreed. "In high school I could twirl a girl, toss her around, slide her under me or up in the air, and never miss a beat, but I feel like an epileptic robot with all my nuts and bolts dropping off when I try to dance to this crazy rock music."

Gary quipped, "Let me know the next time your nuts drop off. That I gotta see!"

The Summer of Love left us cold, but Pasek's birthday was coming up and it was my turn to host for our potluck dinner and charades. Pasek said he was looking forward to blowing out 39 candles and getting a pile of absolutely filthy birthday cards, but he didn't want a big birthday party. Just our Group.

The Group, as we called ourselves, included Bill Pasek – Polly Pasek to his friends – head designer for a special events company based in South San Francisco; handsome with a comb-over.

Michael Vincent – British born and one of San Francisco's top interior designers whose work often appeared in Architectural Digest; pale with naturally blond hair.

Bob Lanci – Michael Vincent's lover, an exuberant Italian waiter at Enrico's; blustery with a handlebar mustache and a large mop of black hair.

Gary Fusfeld – head of display for Saks Fifth Avenue in Palo Alto; mustachioed with dark brown curly hair and long sideburns.

And me, Bill Jones – ex-school teacher, ex-bartender, model for Macy's ads, an extra in movies shot in San Francisco, and not too handy a handyman, but making a living at restoring houses.

In 1966, the prelude to the Summer of Love, we five watched The Group at the Royal Theater on Polk Street. After the movie, over drinks at the White Swallow, we joked about who was most like the women in it. The movie was shocking, dealing with pre-marital sex, contraceptives, abortion, spousal abuse, marital infidelity, and most shocking of all, lesbianism! Edgar Bergen's gorgeous daughter, Candice Bergen in her first film, played a lesbian, a rich, beautiful dyke! Occasionally, when a gay character *was* allowed in a film, he/she was comic relief, *never* attractive, and usually ended up either in jail or an insane asylum ... or dead.

Like the female characters in the movie, we were truly an odd bunch. You'd never suspect we were gay. Michael and Gary wore the latest fashion in men's wear, but none of us were "nelly" or "swishy." None of us felt a need to be accepted as a member of the "gay community." We got campy only at times in the privacy of our homes. We never assumed the leather or cowboy mindsets, and we didn't go to gay bars to stand with our legs apart, warm beer bottle in hand, elbows out at our sides doing a *male* impersonator act as a come-on for those who were less "butch."

We were just ordinary guy-friends who, like millions of other ordinary guy-friends, felt a warm, intimate bond, glued together with a common sense of right and wrong, a sarcastic and lethal sense of humor, and a common interest in hot sex. Homosexual sex. Sex on the QT, sex that was forbidden, ridiculed, preached against, costly, and dangerous. Sex that could put us in jail. But most of all, a constant desire to experience sex with a man whom we loved and who loved us. Thus, we were always looking for a possible long-lasting love affair in every trick we picked up.

We had two other things in common. 1. We were ambitious, focused on our careers, and 2. None of us had ever considered getting in to drag or appearing as a female. Ever. Until I came up with a bizarre idea of a surprise birthday dinner party for Polly Pasek.

The thought of wearing an outlandish, show biz, sequined gown and plastering my face with heavy smears of lipstick and eye shadow repulsed me. I felt the over-the-top drags were an affront to women, making them look grotesque and less desirable.

It's true I felt women were less desirable sexually, but I liked women in my life and never saw them as grotesque. Sometimes, however, I did see *attitudes* in certain women *and* men that deserved to be ridiculed. When I spelled out my thoughts about drag to Michael, Bob, and Gary, they agreed enthusiastically and with a giggle or two, we began planning for Pasek's birthday party.

On the morning of the party, I was nailing in the last row of shingles to the front of my house on Bernal Heights. As I tried to balance myself on the top of a 30-foot extension ladder, my baby blue Princess phone rang. I bounced down as fast as I could without spilling the nails or the bundle of shingles.

"Hi, Bill, it's Ann at Brebner's. There's a photo shoot for Macy's that just came in out of the blue, and they want you down there within an hour, and, Bill, Chaconni says to clean your fingernails this time."

The photo studio was on the top floor of Macy's, and after we finished the shoot, I always got off the escalator on the third floor. Even though I felt pressured to finish work at home for the big night, I took my usual few minutes to check out the children's department. As I walked up and down the aisles touching the soft baby blankets and bending over to smell the newness of a tiny sweater or bonnet, I felt a trickle of sadness, knowing I would never have a reason to buy them.

I rushed home to hang red, white, and blue bunting around large photos of President Hoover and Barry Goldwater and tacked up signs on the dining room walls reading, "Kill a Commie for Christ" and "In your heart, you know he's right. Faaar Right!" I taped a blown-up cartoon of a small cabin cruiser with two men on board to the wall at the top of the stairs. On the stern where the name of the boat is usually painted was a three-line message.

## The Boat That / Dare Not Speak / Its Name

My round dining room table that I'd made from an industrial wire spool was set for eight with a centerpiece of large American flags stuck in a pot of geraniums. In a corner of the dining room, a card table with a small Polish flag stuck in an overripe cantaloupe as its centerpiece was Pasek's place to sit with a banner over his table that read, "Separate, but Equal!"

For this very special occasion, I sheepishly asked my Aunt Ruth if she would bake her secret recipe, double-chocolate fudge cake. She had never met Pasek, but she baked it for me. I could hardly wait to hear the compliments and praise coming from my friends. Aunt Ruth's chocolate cake was unbelievably delicious.

I knew the cake with 39 candles would be the hit of the evening, and as much as I wanted to show it off, I hid it in my dishwasher until the time when I'd light the candles and we'd sing happy birthday to Pasek. I took one more quick survey of the decorations, and finding everything in order, made a beeline for my bathroom to shower before the Group showed up with five of our "groupies" in tow.

The Groupies brave enough to go with my theme were Don Lane, a third-grade teacher who later changed his name to "Sky;" Al Husar, a high school teacher, who flew up from West Covina as often as possible to be with us; Judd

Wirz, the architect who shared Dennis and David's studio; and Ray Williams, my ex-lover who sold real estate and eventually drank himself to death.

After showering and shaving, I went into my bedroom. On the bed, laid out very carefully, was the outfit I spent hours finding in thrift shops. The low-heeled pumps were topped by black leather bows. The black cotton stockings came up to my knees, and the sensible black dress with a large white lace collar hid the fact that I forgot to fill in the empty bulges that had once cradled full breasts. The gray wig didn't quite cover my dark sideburns, but a small-flowered hat distracted the eye, and with a pair of granny glasses perched on my nose, I looked in the mirror and was pleased with what I saw.

With no makeup and a beady scowl, tight lips, and an occasional judgmental twitch, the image I stared at in the mirror, if you squinted, looked like one of the DAR (Daughters of the American Revolution) who was about to celebrate the first Polish beauty contest winner in history.

The doorbell rang as if someone were leaning against it. I poured a gin martini into a teacup for the first guest and opened the door. It was Gary, looking a little frightened. He rushed past me, carrying a small suitcase and a round hatbox.

"Jesus, Bill, hand me that cup. I really need a drink. You know, last month the police rounded up a bunch of drags and tossed 'em in the pokey!"

"But, Gary, they were at that cafeteria. Out in public. Doin' their thing right out there where everybody could see 'em."

"Nevertheless, I don't want my mug shot taken in a dress! I've heard of those bad, bad things the inmates do to each other in the pokey. Imagine. *Forced* to have sex!" He paused and took a gulp from his teacup. "Come to think of it ..."

Just then the doorbell rang again and I rushed to the door with a teacup of gin. Michael and Bob stood outside, a gust of wind blowing Michael's blond hair straight up off his head. Bob's hands were full, balancing a large salad bowl and birthday gifts for Pasek.

"Open the damn door, Wilhelmina! It's colder than a witch's teat out here!"

I pressed the buzzer to open the door and Michael struggled up the stairs carrying two suitcases, a wardrobe bag, and two hatboxes. Bob took the salad bowl into the kitchen and plunked their red, white, and blue birthday gifts down on my coffee table, a dining table that I had salvaged and adapted to use as a coffee table. I had made a pitcher of gin martinis and filled an old coffee pot with Manhattans. Michael dropped their suitcases and hatboxes on my bedroom floor, then poured two Manhattans into the china teacups until they overflowed.

"God knows I need this drink. I'm nervous as hell, and, ah, what time's the beauty queen due? Oh, my dear! I haven't told you how very lovely you look this evening, but where *did* you pick up that ugly hat?"

Gary came out of the bathroom with a flourish, twirling like Loretta Young. He had painted pursed kewpie doll lips over his own with bright red lipstick and wore a wig of red curls, anchored by a large flowered hat.

I thought to myself, *a little too floozy for a Daughter of the American Revolution.* Then a stern, judgmental, very proper, very class-conscious mood took over. I was not only a character in a play about the DAR, I wrote the play, designed the scenery, and was determined to have the cast wear the costumes I designed for them ... conservative, drab drag. The point was to eventually get Pasek dressed as distastefully as possible.

He knew every Polish joke written and loved to make fun of his Polish heritage, so that night he could be his own Polish joke. He was to be the star of the evening, and the rest of us were there to set him off, a contrast in style. At least that was what I planned.

Even though I planned the party to look staid and right-wing conservative, it took off in its own raucous direction. With each teacup of booze and each flourish of brassiere fillers like grapefruits, bean bags, and sponges, the howls grew louder and the quips grew "earthier." The party was out of my control when Ray Williams, who was standing drunken guard at the front door, screeched out, "Ladies! Ladies! Take your positions! Polly's comin' up the steps!"

We scrambled to find American flags to hold, then limped in our high heels to get in line to receive the Polish beauty queen. As Pasek came into the room, we overwhelmed him.

"Happy Birthday, Polly!"

"Surprise, Polly!"

"Take off your pants, Polly!"

It took him a few seconds to absorb the scene of elderly, gray-haired ladies in dark dresses, teetering on their high heels. We saluted him, raising our teacups, pinky fingers held high. He burst out laughing as he tried to identify the faces of his friends, powdered, rouged, lips painted red. We rushed to him, hugging his shaking body, and left lipstick marks all over his cheeks, nose, and forehead. Ray and Al unbuttoned his shirt and pants.

Ray goochy-gooed Paskek under his chin and teased, "Come on, Polly, we got your Polish drag! Come on. Drop your drawers. We're gonna dress you like the beauty queen you are."

Pasek, visibly shaken by the spectacle around his entrance, pleaded for a drink, which Bob had waiting for him. He handed Pasek a teacup of vodka. He took a long slurp of his drink, then belched as loudly as he could. Finding himself the center of attention, he played his part to an adoring audience of prim and proper "mature" ladies.

Gary gave him a garter belt and pink panties. Al, a brassiere. Don, a crinoline. Ray, a pair of torn silk stockings and garters. Bob and Michael, the largest woman's shoes they could find. Judd, the blonde wig and a white hat that looked like a pot of flowers, and I gave him a tacky black lace dress with feathers hanging from the hem.

As he donned each present, he delivered another Polish joke as a *Thank you.*

"What's long and hard that a Polish bride gets on her wedding night?"

One. Two.

"A new last name!"

As soon as we finished dressing Pasek, Don pulled out his Polaroid camera and took photos of all of us, especially Pasek, gleefully picking his nose. He looked like he had just been assaulted by the *new* Polish navy, whom he claimed had glass-bottom boats so they could see the *old* Polish navy.

The dinner was wonderful, each dish a recipe out of *Sunset* magazine, and the conversation at the Daughters of the American Revolution table was loud, funny, and filthy, interrupted often by the Polish Beauty Queen sitting at his table in the corner.

In my drunken state, I remembered to rescue the birthday cake from the dishwasher, then lit the candles, rushed it to the table singing/yelling the birthday song and watched my friends tear into it with their hands. Bits of clothing flew through the air. Gray wigs were tossed around like beach balls, and when I put the soundtrack of *Thoroughly Modern Millie* on the turntable, five of us climbed on to my cocktail table (Julie Andrew's elevator) and started to tap dance in a frenzy.

I called an end to the party around three in the morning, primarily because it had gotten out of control. Michael had gone into my bedroom looking for his lover, Bob, and found him dry humping Al Husar, spread-eagle on the floor at the foot of my bed. Michael found a wastebasket, filled it with water and ice cubes, and then dumped it on the rutting couple, leaving my bed soaking wet. Chocolate cake crumbs sprinkled the floor; dresses, silk stockings, high-heeled shoes, and unmentionables covered most of my furniture or were draped over lamps and house plants, struggling to survive under my brown thumb.

It was time to sing "The Party's Over" and push the guests out the door to face the dawn. Everyone but Pasek. He had passed out in my bathtub wearing nothing but his boxers, a torn tee-shirt, and Michael's fur piece to keep him warm. I threw a blanket over the birthday boy and headed for my sofa to finish the night. At least the sofa was dry.

## Chapter 22
# Genie in a Bottle

"How'd I end up in your bathtub, and what's this smelly roadkill around my neck?" Pasek sat up in the tub and threw Michael's fox stole on the bathroom floor. Holding his forehead with one hand and using the other to massage his back, he groaned, "I'm dying. Call an ambulance, *quick*. A circular saw put a part in my hair, and my back is killing me. *Killing* me, I say. Who the fuck made me sleep in your bathtub, anyway?"

"You climbed in there yourself, Mister Beauty Queen. You could at least show a little gratitude for the blanket I threw over your royal body. I had to sleep on the couch cuz Michael dumped a bucket of water on my bed."

"Why on earth did he do that?"

"He was aiming for Bob's ass."

"Bob's ass?"

"Breakfast? I got some ham and three or four eggs I can scramble."

Pasek staggered through the house, searching for and finding bits and pieces of the clothes he had arrived in, then slowly dressed, groaning each time he bent over to pick up something from the floor.

"I want a pot of coffee all for myself." He paused as if to give another Polish punch line. "And a bottle of aspirin." He paused again. "Or strychnine. Whichever is the handiest. What day is it?"

"Sunday. Why? You hav'ta go to church?"

"You kiddin'? No, just had a thought. Wanna make a couple of ham and egg sandwiches and drive down to San Gregorio Beach?"

"You mean the nude one?"

"Yeah, yeah, yeah. I need a birthday present, and *he* might be waiting for me on a beach towel right now. Zowie! My head's feeling better already!"

We drove down the Pacific Coast Highway a few miles past Pacifica, where we pulled over and parked alongside a dozen or so other cars on a flat spot overlooking the gray ocean below.

A bleached, handwritten sign, "San Gregorio Beach" was posted at the beginning of a path leading down to the roaring surf. The beach itself was discreetly hidden by a cliff. When we came around the final sand dune, I couldn't help but think of Dorothy opening the gray door of her gray world to the rush of beauty in the multi-colored Land of Oz. But the rush of beauty I saw wasn't colorful. It was gray. Beautifully pale gray. Unlike the morning sun that had warmed my house on Bernal Heights earlier, a misty fog bank hung over the beach and erased any shadows, blending the sand, rocks, the cliff, and the fog into a monotone Japanese watercolor.

That didn't discourage Pasek. He trudged ahead of me, almost jogging at times, toward an outcropping of rocks that defined the end of the beach.

"This is where the action is, Billy. The gays own this end of the beach and the straights go to the other end. And, if we're lucky, some of the straight guys wander down here. Just "curious," don't ya know?"

We spread out the blanket Pasek had slept on, ate our breakfast sandwiches, and washed them down with black coffee from a thermos, taking turns drinking from the one thermos cup. The air was still and warm, and the waves beat the wide, sandy beach with a slow, deliberate crash of white foam. We sat in that grayish world, staring out at the horizon, the smashing surf the only thing to interfere with our silent daydreams.

Without saying a word, we took off our shoes and rolled up the cuffs of our pants. We left the blanket and strolled down to the edge of the Pacific Ocean, then walked on the hardened wet sand, leaving footprints behind. Our tracks were washed away by the next sheet of seawater the surf pushed toward the cliff, in its persistent drive to eat away the shore and reign over the earth.

Pasek picked up a smooth tiny green and marveled, "Look! Jade!"

My thoughts raced back to the hot, sunny afternoons Wyatt Cooper and I had spent on the beach at Fire Island. We had gathered and made a collection of smooth white pebbles that we called our "buried treasure." The collection became mine when we split up.

I saw something lying half-buried in the wet sand ahead of us and ran to see what it was.

"Look, Pasek, a wine bottle, and it's rough on the outside. Must have been rolling back and forth in the sand for a hell of a long time."

"Stick a candle in it and impress your friends, Mr. Jones."

"Pasek, you think there's a genie inside?"

"Let me see." He grabbed the bottle away from me and rubbed it with the flourish of three sweeping strokes. "Hey, Mr. Genie in there. You gotta grant me my wish." He held the bottle up to his ear. "My wish? Same as always. A husband! Good lookin' one with a big dick and … a job." Then he blew into the neck of the bottle making a hooting sound and handed me the bottle. "Here, take it. Now you can wish for a husband, too."

"Pasek, let's go back to the blanket. I need to get my lighter."

"You gotta make a wish. The genie's in there just waitin' for you to tell him what you want most in the world. Go on!"

"Okay. Okay. Here goes. A kid of my own, Mr. Genie, and I don't care if it's a boy or a girl. That's what I've *always* wished for."

Pasek glanced at me as if I had said something he didn't want to hear. Then he turned around and headed back toward our blanket. I blew into the neck of the bottle and tried to make the hooting noise Pasek had made, but the sound didn't come out, just a few grains of sand that stuck to my lips. I followed him to the blanket and sat next to him.

"Bill, next time you make a wish, wish for something you might actually get. Like me. Wish for a husband. You might never get one, but at least there's a possibility."

"I know. I know. You're right of course, but I can't stop thinking about it, you know."

"Do I have to remind you you're a gay man? We're at the gay end of the beach, for Christ's sake. If you want kids, you gotta go to the other end of the beach. That's where the breeders are."

It may have been his hangover, but Pasek was sounding annoyed with me. It was so unlike him. I should have just let the subject drop, but I felt cornered and whether it was the right time or not, I wanted to confide in him. Besides my brother Jerry, Pasek was my most cherished friend. I wanted to share the secret that for years had brought me nothing but disappointment and frustration.

Before I said a word, he broke the ice.

"Are you thinking of marrying a woman, Bill?"

"Nothing that drastic."

"Kidnapping a baby?"

"And spend the rest of my life in jail? Give up going to the movies with you? No. No. Don't think so."

"So, what's this all about? You and a kid?"

"I know it sounds like I'm a little off my rocker, but ever since Jerry was born, I've wanted to be a daddy. Really. It started with him cuz I took care of him while my mom and Louie worked their tails off in their bar ... and drank after work."

"And you taught school for a while, didn't you? Maybe you should go back to teaching, Bill. There're your kids. Lots of 'em."

"Not the same, Pasek. Not the same. I want one of my own. If I tell you 'bout the crazy things I've done to get one, promise not to tell anyone? Not Gary or Michael or Bob or *anyone*?"

"Shoot."

It was such a relief to spill my guts out to him! I told him about Michael French, the "bad boy" in the fourth grade, my first year of teaching in Novato ... a misfit at nine, and I wished I could have taken him away from his dad, a major in the army who browbeat Michael when he wasn't ignoring him, making him frightened and helpless. Hurt, knowing he wasn't wanted or loved. I knew I was the father Michael should have had.

I told him about my mind-boggling trip to Cuba in 1959 and how the nuns had chased me out of the orphanage with brooms and mops, thinking I was a pedophile. He knew Cora Lee was a friend, but it was shocking to him that she agreed to bear me a child – that is, until she met my mother. Then he was relieved to hear that a lawyer advised me against signing in at the hospital as the father when my pregnant tenant asked me to take her child. But the escapade that amused him most was my going to a Sexual Freedom League nudist party in Berkeley to see if I could learn to fuck a woman ... to screw a woman just so I could have a child of my own.

"You never cease to amaze me, Bill. You know ... miracles *do* happen. I believe genies exist in jars ... and wine bottles. Who knows? Modern science. You may be the first man on earth to give birth to a little brat."

The fog lifted and grew thinner. Suddenly the beach was bright with sunlight, and nude male bodies appeared from behind sand dunes and rocks, strolling up and down in front of us. Pasek stood up and took off all his clothes, but I was too shy, and stripped down only to my Jockey briefs. Besides, Pasek was built like a Polish stallion, and next to him I was just a ten-cent-a-ride pony.

## Chapter 23

# Mr. Genie Responds

I talked to two people every day. Either I would call them or Pasek and my brother Jerry would call me, so I wasn't surprised to hear the phone ring the morning after Pasek and I spent the day cruising San Gregorio Beach.

"Hi, Polly, did your moneymaker get sunburned yesterday? Mine sure did even through my underwear ..."

"It's Jerry, Bill. I need your advice real bad."

"Mother?"

"No, she's going to lend me the money to rebuild the kitchen just the way Glenda wants. Four thousand at 12% interest. Geez, I'll be paying her back forever. No, it's not Mom, but something happened to me on the Greyhound coming home from Mom's that has me upset. Ya know, I love my kids, and Glenda, of course, but I've been takin' scary chances, doin' it in johns and parks. I can't seem to help myself. If they find out, it'll kill 'em, Bill. I know it will. Just kill 'em!"

"Jerry, know what ya mean. Really. I get those same insane urges, and I shouldn't be giving you this advice, but, Jerry, a lot of married men go to the baths. At least, it's a little safer there cuz I hear the bathhouse owners pay off the cops, and they've stopped raiding 'em. If you get caught with your pants down behind some bush in the park, it'll be your job, and for sure, your marriage. You'd lose Allison and Mark."

"I gotta tell you what happened on the bus. This guy sits down next to me. We chat for a while. Weather, football scores, jobs, schools. You know."

"Okay."

"Then his knee starts pressing up against mine."

"And …?"

"I pressed back."

"Go on."

"He got off at the stop before mine and he hands me his phone number when he shook my hand. He bakes crackers in a factory in Oakland. What'll I do now? I can't stop thinking about him, Bill. When I kiss the kids goodbye in the morning. At school. At the blackboard. At night when I havta crawl into bed with Glenda. Drivin' me crazy. He smelled so good! And damn good-lookin'."

"Jerry, I'll give ya the dime to phone him. It sounds like it's gonna be love-at-first-fuck to me. This might be what you were really in search of when you went into those creepy places to get your rocks off."

The phone rang again right after Jerry hung up, and I was sure it was Pasek.

"Hi. Is this the Polish beauty contest winner with the sunburned moneymaker?"

"No, Dear, this is the genie you discarded on the beach yesterday. Guess what? Remember what I wished for? Well, I might get it. The guy I took behind those rocks gave me his phone number when we got through, and …"

"So, the genie's granting your wish … for a husband?"

"Next best thing … a married man!"

"Well, Dear Heart, there's no genie for me. Even *he* can't grant me some little tyke calling me Daddy."

"You're a hopeless dreamer, Bill, but if the genie can give me a husband, even someone else's, he can leave a bundle of joy at your front door … right there with the morning paper."

We decided to have Chinese takeout and watch *Ironside* that night at Pasek's place. I opened the *Chronicle* and read Peanuts first, as usual, then studied the entertainment section before going back to the front page that relentlessly detailed the brutal war we were losing in Vietnam.

I flipped through news pages to get to the editorial page as fast as I could, mostly to read the Letters to the Editor in the Opinion section. Later, as I was dumping the paper into my trash, a small item caught my eye.

The headline read, 850 KIDS IN SAN FRANCISCO NEED HOMES, and the article was written by Mary Tobin, a *Chronicle* reporter concerned mostly with human interest stories that I enjoyed reading.

She contrasted the adoption placements of the Department of Social Services in San Francisco with the Los Angeles County Department of Adoptions placements for the fiscal years of 1965–66. San Francisco – 225; Los Angeles – 2,427. San Francisco was able to place 225 kids that year, but over 850 were still waiting in foster homes for families who would embrace them and call them their own. Female white babies, up to six months old, were the first to be adopted. Then the white male babies, followed by mixed-blood babies, followed by black babies, followed by children older than six months, and lastly, handicapped and children over the age of two years up to eighteen.

Tobin announced a new brochure sponsored by the Carriage Trade, a non-profit organization of adoptive parents showing how easy it was now to adopt a child in San Francisco. I tore out the article and left it on my desk for about a week. Then, with a lot of courage, bolstered by a few swigs of Gallo's Hearty Burgundy, I wrote to Mary Tobin. I told her I would like to have the brochure sent to me, but that it probably would be a waste of postage since I was a single man, not a couple.

To my amazement, a few days later I received a letter and the brochure from Mary Tobin. Her note shook me to the core.

*July 27, 1967*
*Dear Mr. Jones:*
*Thank you for your letter. I would like to suggest that you call Miss Dorothy Murphy at the Department of Social Services in San Francisco.*
*Miss Murphy can be reached at 558-5381. She is eager to talk with anyone who is interested in offering their home as an adoptive single parent.*
Sincerely,
Mary Tobin

My jaw dropped. I reread her note a dozen times; then I read the brochure. It was titled, *Should You Adopt?* It began by asking the reader to be realistic, the choice of adopting being the most important decision a *married couple* will make. Then it followed with "Some Practical Questions."

Do you *both* want to adopt a child?

Have you *both* considered the needs of the child?

Are you *both* willing and able to meet these needs?

"The biggest question in the mind and heart of *couples* considering adoption is ... what kind of a baby will *we* get? The answer being: whatever kind of child the *couple* would choose for its own." The back page was about the adoption agency itself. Its purpose was "to place children in adoptive homes – not in ideal 'picture-book' homes with 'perfect *parents*.' But in happy homes with *parents* who would love and provide for an adopted child as *they* would for one born to *them*."

The agency offered safeguards: "(1) The child had been truly surrendered and legally freed for adoption **before** placement. (2) The agency has made careful studies of the child and his/her background. (3) The identity of the *couple* is protected. (4) A *couple* had a choice about the child *they* wanted and had the assurance the child would be selected especially for *them*. (5) The *couple* would have the service of a trained adoption worker during the initial months of adjustment **after** placement."

All well and good for *couples, married couples*, but obviously not written with a single person in mind! I sat at my desk, debating whether or not to call Miss Dorothy Murphy for an appointment. I wondered if Mary Tobin was pulling my leg, hoping to get another human-interest story in the *Chron* about this dumb-ass guy who actually went to the adoption agency, believing they would let one of their wards live in a home without a father *and* mother. Would I be considered a nutcase by Dorothy Murphy? Would she laugh at me? What was I getting into?

I wanted to call Jerry or Pasek to ask for advice, but a trickle of dread slid down my throat. Would they shake their heads over my foolishness, or would they laugh at me and talk me out of seeing Dorothy Murphy? Would they tell my friends and make me the butt of their jokes for months to come?

Oh, hell! It was Friday afternoon. The social workers had left for the weekend, and that would settle my quandary. At least I'd made an attempt, I could tell myself, hoping to put it all aside.

Everyone in the agency had left for the weekend except for one person, and wouldn't you know, it was Dorothy Murphy's secretary! I stumbled around, trying to avoid what I had phoned for, but she was determined to make an appointment for me. I was to see Dorothy Murphy Monday morning at 10:30 in the agency at 1680 Mission Street.

My heart began to rev up, and I spent the weekend obsessing about what might happen Monday morning. It was all the control I could muster not to phone Pasek or Jerry, but this was a secret I had to keep to myself for my own good. Trouble was, I had never kept a secret from Pasek. I had tried to keep my homosexuality a secret from Jerry, but that was understandable because he was straight, or so I'd thought. This secret, though, was like being unfaithful and dishonest. I felt as if I were cheating on a lover.

As I lay in my dark bedroom, I felt a smile widening my lips. Despite my suspicions that nothing would come of Mary Tobin's note and my fear of the appointment I'd made, when I closed my eyes, out of a bottle half-buried in wet sand, a pillar of smoke appeared, solidifying into a gigantic genie. He rose up above me into the overcast clouds, and I heard his voice boom out so loudly it shook the beach, the rocks, and the cliff.

"Make up your fuckin' mind, Bill Jones. Do you want a kid of your own? Some little brat that'll call you Daddy? This is the last wish you'll get from me!"

I couldn't speak I was so excited, so I gave him both thumbs-up. He broke out into a toothy grin and bellowed, "Okay, Buster, you asked for it!"

Then he dissolved back into a whiff of smoke, rapidly disappearing down the neck of the bottle. I lay there, smiling and thinking about genies and wishes. I'd been called a hopeless dreamer many times, but that night I wished with all my heart that this dream could come true, and I drifted off to sleep, smiling.

# Part Two

Aaron

## Chapter 24
# Nine Months of Pregnant Interviews

The adoption agency of the San Francisco Social Services was housed at 1680 Mission Street, a bland, utilitarian building that also held the Department of Public Works, where you stood in long lines to pay for permits to build or remodel. Since I never applied for permits to remodel the houses I bought and sold, it was the first time I had ever been inside this cold, barren building. Building inspectors were frightening enough to me, but as I searched for Dorothy Murphy's office, all I could think of was – *what am I doing here?*

I was dressed to the nines in my best cocktail party clothes, but it was only a little past ten in the morning. What was I thinking? Too late to run home and take off the suit and tie. Too late to look casual, as if I could take the adoption or not – as if I weren't trying so hard to impress her. By the time I reached the reception desk, I was so nervous that my palms were sweating and instead of breathing normally, I was gulping deeper and deeper inhalations.

The woman at the desk outside of Dorothy Murphy's office kept filing papers and answering the phone as I sat in the wooden chair, checking my fingernails and picking Lily's hairs off my suit. The clock's minute hand went past the 10:30 appointment time, and I watched it slowly tick away another seven minutes.

A buzzer sounded. The woman picked up a handset, listened, and then beckoning to me, said, "Miss Murphy will see you now."

As I opened the door, I watched Dorothy Murphy get up from her desk and walk toward me, hand outstretched to shake mine in a warm, firm grasp. She was shorter than me but gave the impression of being taller. Her wool skirt, blouse, and cardigan sweater draped comfortably over her motherly body. She wore glasses with no frames that enabled her to let her blue Irish eyes announce who she was … confident, friendly, inquisitive, compassionate, but unable to hide a tinge of personal sadness. She didn't wear makeup, only light rose lipstick that covered her fleshy lips, and her salt and pepper hair was gathered at the back of her head in a large bun.

"Mr. Jones, I was delighted when Mary Tobin told me you were interested in our adoption options. She sent your note to me, and I'm curious. Had you heard we were considering letting single women and men adopt? We've never announced it … uh … It's never been done successfully, you know."

"Well, I …"

"Last year a gentleman in Los Angeles tried it – to cope with an eleven-year-old boy – a boy who, unfortunately, had many emotional problems, but it was a failure. Very sad. The boy was returned to the foster care system. Los Angeles hasn't attempted to try it again, but *this* agency is eager to find homes for our foster home kids. There are hundreds, Mr. Jones, hundreds of children in this city in dire need of a loving, permanent home. Now tell me about yourself, Mr. Jones. How old are you?"

"Thirty-eight. Twelfth of July. Thirty-eight."

She broke out into a big grin. "We've decided our single adoptive parents should be between thirty-five and forty-five. Old enough to accept the serious responsibilities of raising a child and young enough to cope with the natural problems that are sure to arise, and also young enough to enjoy the physical and emotional needs of a child."

Her words floated through my mind, but I was having a secret conversation with myself that drowned out most of what she was telling me.

*Look at her! Direct. Honest. Irish. Like a mother. Treating me as an equal. How'd she felt if she knew I sucked cock the other night? She's vulnerable, and I'm deceiving her just like I've lied to everyone else. Mama, Dad, Uncle Elzie, Aunt Ruth. The whole damn school in Novato. The kids I loved in my classes. My agents and all the photographers I worked for. Lies. Lies. Lies. I fooled them all. Made 'em believe I was straight and not only straight but a playboy … love 'em and leave 'em … Me? Gay? Not on your life!*

"Mr. Jones, I can see you feel a little uncomfortable. Don't worry. This interview is just for you to ask me any questions you might have about adoptions, and for me to understand why you are interested in adopting."

*I can't lie to her. It isn't fair. If she gives me a kid and then finds out I'm a cocksucker, she might lose her job ... the respect of the people who work here. Fuck! I don't want to hurt this woman. Pick up your purse and head for the door!*

"My fiancée, Cora Lee, didn't want us to have a child once we got married, and I did, so we broke up over it. I even traveled to Cuba in 1959 because I heard they were allowing single people to adopt the war orphans. Unfortunately, I was misinformed, Miss Murphy."

*Cora Lee, my fiancée? Stop lying! You know you have no right to be here, so give her good reasons not to let you adopt. Reasonable reasons, Jerk-Off.*

Dorothy leaned in toward me, and it was as if she wanted to confide in me. "Life's an unsure road, isn't it? Sometimes fine and mature people fall in love but for some reason beyond their control are unable to marry. It doesn't mean they wouldn't make wonderful parents for a child who longs for love and a home."

I was quick to agree. "Yes. That's true. My mother was a single parent after my parents divorced when I was two, and I know she did a good job."

*Liar, liar, pants on fire!*

"Another thing we are looking for is a person who has family in the area. Extended families are important to children. You know, grandparents, aunts, uncles, cousins."

"My dad and his wife live in Oakland, and I have an aunt and uncle who live here in the city. My mother lives in Byron, and my half-brother lives in Hayward." I quickly added, "With his wife and two children, a boy and a girl. He's a teacher like I was. We're very close."

*Mostly true. Close to Jerry at least.*

"Are you financially secure, Mr. Jones? Employed?"

*Here's my chance to get out of it, and I don't have to lie to her either!*

"Not employed. No. I make money by buying up run-down homes ... fixer-uppers, and then I remodel them and sell 'em. It takes a couple of years sometimes because I run out of money. I hate to admit it, but I'm broke most of the time. I do odd jobs, you know, painting, handyman stuff, and I work as an extra in movies, and I model for Macy's ads occasionally. Not two cents to my name most of the time." Then I went for the closer with a sad look on my face. "Too broke to send a kid to college."

*There! That should nail it!*

"Mr. Jones, we aren't looking for the 'perfect' person who has achieved all their goals, a house, a car, a steady job. We're looking for warmth and understanding in loving homes for our children. You know, poor people can give all that to a child, a child hungry for love and security. Poor people find ways to support their children's dreams. Desperately poor families find a way to send their children to college. I see it all the time."

*She's winning every argument. I do want a kid of my own, but what I want doesn't matter. I shouldn't be here. She's making a mistake if she thinks I'm straight. I'm a fuckin' liar ... a fuckin' gay man who lies about it all the time. My life is a goddamn lie!*

"Come to think of it, the work I do on the houses would be really dangerous for a kid. You know, electric saws, nails on the floor, buckets of paint."

"So, you spend almost the whole day at home, don't you? That would be wonderful for a child ... to have their parent right there to attend to their needs. As far as your house being a minefield for a toddler, all you have to do is put him or her in a playpen. We placed a little girl with a charming couple in the middle of remodeling their home, just as you are doing, and it worked out just fine. Playpens do the job. Toys, a place to nap. Playpens."

*I've got to get down to the nitty-gritty. I've got to stop this before it's too late. Sex! That'll end it!*

"You know, Miss Murphy, I am a normal man and I do have a social life. I like to go out barhopping with friends, have dinner with them, go to movies. I'm in the prime of my life, and frankly, I like to go out on dates. Sometimes stay the night. I hope this doesn't put you off."

"Of course not. That's healthy. As for you going out in the evening, get a babysitter."

*My god, she's good. I'm tempted to tell her I'm gay. There's something so sincere and intelligent about her. I think she'd understand, but would she still consider me as a perspective adoptive parent? No. No way in hell.*

"Let me tell you how this could proceed. You would be treated exactly like the married couples that apply here. The applicants, and in your case, the applicant, if we agree to go ahead, will need letters of recommendation from four couples with children who will vouch for you. We require a letter from you stating your reason for wanting to adopt. Also, a list of relatives in the area. If we agree to start on this journey, a social worker will be assigned to you, and the interviews can take months. Up to nine months." Smiling, she quipped, "Think of it as a pregnancy." She then looked me straight in the eyes and finished our conversation. "Do you feel in your heart, Bill Jones, that you would like to proceed?"

*In my heart, of course, but, but, but …*

"Yes. Yes, I most certainly would like to proceed, Dorothy. May I call you Dorothy?"

Two days later a letter from the City and County of San Francisco, Department of Social Services jumped out at me from my mailbox. I took it inside, poured gin over some ice, eased myself into a chair at the kitchen table, and with trembling hands, opened the envelope, not knowing if it would be the start of a new life for me or the stamp of disapproval I felt I deserved.

The first paper I opened from the envelope made me utter to myself, "What the fuck! Are they pulling my leg?"

## **INFORMATION FOR ADOPTIVE APPLICANTS**

*During the application process, the following documents will be needed. We suggest that you secure them now, in order to save time.*

*Either photostat or certified copies of the following documents are acceptable. Since these documents remain part of the permanent adoptive file, you probably will not want to send the originals.*

(1.) *Present marriage certificate*

(2.) *All previous marriage certificates*

(3.) *Verification of termination of all previous marriages i.e., divorce, death, or annulment.*

(4.) *Snapshot of husband, wife, children – either together or separate pictures (one set)*

(5.) *If you are foreign born, proof of legal entry or naturalization is required.*

If Dorothy Murphy sent this thick envelope, she must have been in a hell of a hurry, but more likely, the woman at the reception desk stuffed the envelope and put in the usual papers, not realizing it was to be mailed to a single man. The first time it was ever done.

But it was the short, to-the-point letter from Dorothy Murphy that made me gulp the drink I held in my shaky hand. It was actually happening.

*August 25, 1967*

*Mr. William Jones*
*217 Montcalm Street*
*San Francisco, California*

*Dear Mr. Jones:*
*I am enclosing the application forms, fact and information sheets*
*and brochures.*
*If you have any questions, please feel free to call me.*

> *Sincerely yours,*
> *DEPARTMENT OF SOCIAL SERVICES*
> *(Miss) Dorothy A. Murphy*
> *Senior Social Service Supervisor*
> *Adoptions*

My first thought was that I wanted to share this letter with Jerry and Pasek so urgently that it made me dizzy, but that must have been the gin because I quickly came to my senses. I knew I shouldn't expose myself to them or any-one else for being crazy, hoping I could be a father this way. It was bound to go down the tubes, and I could confess what I was up to after it blew up in my face. Later, much later, we could all have a good laugh about it.

## Chapter 25

# Mary Davidson Helps
# Me Conceive a Child

Before it came in the mail, I assumed I could fill out all the information required in the application that Dorothy Murphy would send me. But one of the major requirements was that I get solid recommendations from four families with children, saying I would make a responsible and loving parent. I knew my agent, Ann Brebner, would write one for me, but who knew me better than my own brother, Jerry? Jerry, with a wife and two kids? So, in spite of my hesitations and fear of being ridiculed, I called him to break the news. His response came in one word,

"Terrific!"

He and Glenda promised me that they wouldn't tell any other members of the family, especially Mother – or any of their friends. They understood the importance of keeping this single adoption policy under lock and key. If my adoption failed, it might have a disastrous effect on all future adoptions. It was imperative not to let the world know about it until our adoption was finalized.

Once I had confided in Jerry, I realized there was only one other person in the world that I had to tell or lose his friendship if I didn't.

\*　　\*　　\*　　\*　　\*

"Billy, for the first time in this Polack's life ... I ... I'm speechless." He gulped his gin martini down in one dramatic gulp. "Speechless! Bartender, n'other round here, please." He stared intently into my eyes. "This is incredible, Billy, incredible! Do you have any idea what you're doing?"

"Pasek, you *do* realize why you can't tell anyone, *any* of our friends about it, don't you?"

"Mr. Speechless, that's me. I can't even find the words for what I'm feeling right now." The bartender laid two new napkins down before he poured the martinis from the shaker. "My father here is paying for this round, Barkeep, cuz he owes me one – or two – or three."

"Pasek, I need you to tell me it's okay. Okay?"

"Billy, I've been listening to you wail about this kid thing for years, but I was sure it was just a passing … bullshit whim and you'd grow out of it. Had no idea you'd actually get this far. You know damn well I want whatever you want, what makes you happy, but I'm afraid about this. Aren't you?"

"Afraid? Scared shitless is more like it."

"Billy, you're scared cuz you might *actually* have a kid on your hands. I, on the other hand … I'm afraid this is either a goddamn spooky joke they're pulling on you, or if it's for real, it might blow up in your face, and put you outta commission for a helluva long time."

*　　*　　*　　*　　*

*City and County of San Francisco*
*Department of Social Services*
*585 Bush Street*
*San Francisco, California 94108*
*November 22, 1967*

*Mr. William Jones*
*217 Montcalm*
*San Francisco, California 94110*
*Dear Mr. Jones:*
*All of the documents necessary for your application to adopt are now on file. A worker will be calling you soon to make the appointment for the first of the home study interviews. Please feel free to call on me if you have any questions.*

*Sincerely yours,*
*Department of Social Services*
*(Miss) Dorothy A. Murphy*
*Senior Social Service Supervisor*
*Adoptions*

\*     \*     \*     \*     \*

"Hello. Mr. Jones?"

"Yes."

"Dorothy Murphy sent you a letter last week …"

"Yes?" I waited for the second shoe to drop when the voice on the other end of the line would laugh, and say, *Sorry! We know you're gay, and the deal's off.*

"I'm Mary. Mary Davidson, and I'll be your home social worker for the next few months. When would be a good time for me to drop in for your first interview? Would you like to get started this week?"

The voice sounded confident and business-like, very much in command, and yet I detected a softness, a woman who was compassionate and, well, motherly.

I glanced around to see how much I had to do before I let her see the kind of house she would be allowing one of her charges to live in. "How 'bout the day after tomorrow 'round ten?"

"It's on my calendar. Ten it is. Bye for now, Mr. Jones. I'm looking forward to meeting you."

I tried to picture her. Thirtyish. Thin. Blue eyes. Irish, I thought. Red-headed Irish. I knew she was Irish because I tricked with a guy once who was from Boston, taught architecture in one of the universities there, and this woman had a brogue just like his. Works with another Irish woman, Dorothy Murphy. How Irish can you get?

Luckily, I had just finished remodeling the house in Bernal Heights. The rooms still smelled of fresh paint, and the dark walnut floors glistened from the varnish and wax I had applied while on my hands and knees. I crammed the single garage with my old Dodge pickup loaded with all my tools, ladders, and paintbrushes. Once the garage door was closed and all my junk hidden, I borrowed $500 from Pasek to buy a used Lincoln convertible to sit in the driveway, which lent a little class to my newly shingled Victorian. Then it was just a matter of driving to the graveyards in Colma that night to snatch a few fresh flowers to put in vases around the house. I considered every way I could possibly impress the social worker, even cleaning the *inside* of cabinets in the kitchen and bathroom. First impressions are so important!

I rolled out of bed just as the sun was coming up on the morning of our first meeting. After showering and dressing in my best tweed jacket and flannel pants, I made a last-minute inspection, making sure every speck of plaster dust was wiped away. I baked cinnamon rolls and had coffee perking on the stove, a trick I had learned from Ray Williams, a realtor who always made sure these wonderful "homey" smells filled the rooms of houses he showed to clients.

The doorbell rang precisely at ten. I rushed to open it, pausing for just a second at the hallway mirror to check if my tie was neat and be sure my cowlick wasn't standing straight up.

When I first saw her in the doorway, I thought maybe the Irishwoman I had talked to on the phone couldn't make it, and they had substituted another worker to interview me, but the minute she said, "Good morning, Mr. Jones. So glad to meet you," I knew it was the same woman I had talked to, and I broke out into a ridiculously wide grin, almost laughing, laughing at myself.

I watched her climb the stairs. She wasn't overweight but had a comfortable motherly figure, and took the stairs in an easy stride. She was dressed in fall colors. Burnt orange blouse, muted green skirt, and tan suede shoes. Very "casual chic," I thought, at the same time, wondering how she could afford such nice clothes. In my limited experience, I had never seen a black woman look so elegant.

She was a complete package. Good taste in clothes, hardly discernible makeup, a warm smile, large brown eyes that looked straight into mine, and a lovely, soft Boston accent. She glanced around the living room, noting the Robert Harvey paintings on the walls, remembering seeing them in Gump's. Robert, a gay friend who was raising his son, had done a series of paintings based on faded tintypes he found in my family's photo album. I didn't tell her that Robert had exchanged the painting of my mother and dad, sitting on the bumper of their honeymoon Model T, for me remodeling and painting his son's bedroom. It tickled me that she thought I could afford to buy it. First impressions and all that.

I gave her a guided tour of the de-*gay*ed house, smug that I had put away my signed headshots of Judy Garland and Bette Davis and had put plain book covers on *The City and the Pillar* and *The Well of Loneliness*. I'd even hidden the *Life* cover of Bobby Kennedy's handsome face, framed and sitting on the nightstand next to my bed.

We sat together on the sofa, talking for an hour or two, drinking coffee and nibbling on the cinnamon rolls. We discussed my family, living and dead, how much I wanted to send my child through college, religious practices, disciplining children, physical exercise, allowances, household chores, recipes, favorite movies, and musicals we both loved, but she never asked me why I was almost forty and never married.

All during this intense, serious conversation, with her gently questioning me, she and I looked at each other, our eyes fixed, looking into each other's souls. I had just told her about my experience with the nuns in Cuba, when, to my surprise, she put down her coffee cup and turned her head slightly away from me, avoiding our eye-to-eye contact for the first time since we'd started our conversation. What she said next riveted my attention and set the course we would travel together for the next 18 months. It thrilled me, chilled me, and I remember every word.

"You know …," She took a deep breath. "I've been doing this … finding real homes for desperate children … over 20 years now. I'm blessed, I tell you." She paused, collected her thoughts, then gave herself permission to admit something buried deep, and about to be released for the first time to a client.

Still looking away from me, actually up toward the ceiling, she seemed to be talking to herself, pondering. "In 20 years, we've never had a homosexual apply to adopt, you know."

I could feel the blood drain down from my head.

"Dorothy and I have discussed it on occasion. Never really came up. We talked about it. I, for one, and I've told Dorothy this … I, for one, believe in my heart that a homosexual is just as capable of being a responsible and loving parent as any of the couples I've dealt with, you know?"

I busied myself with sweeping the crumbs off the coffee table, unable to compute what Mary Davidson was saying. Was she just thinking out loud? Did she care if I heard what she was thinking? Was she actually talking to me? Should I comment?

"Trouble is … if a homosexual should apply, you know, to adopt, I hope he or she never tells me that he … or … she … is, homosexual, because, you know … because I'd be obliged to go back to the placement committee and tell them. And then they'd be *obliged* to deny the adoption. So, you see, I hope that never happens. Too many lonely, beautiful children will never find a parent who will care for them … care about them. I know a divorced woman, a friend who's raising her two kids, and she's a lesbian, one of the best mothers

I have ever laid eyes on. So, I hope if a homosexual ever applies, he keeps it to himself. There are more important things to consider in finding homes for my children."

I tried not to look stunned when she turned to look me in the eye again. I reached for the coffee pot to refill her cup, but she stood up, looking at her wristwatch.

"Oh, my dear, I'm going to be late for my afternoon appointment, and it's in Colma. Have you ever been to Colma and walked through the graveyards there? History in stone. Very lovely, Bill." She hurried to the door, then turned back to me. "I can't tell you how much I've enjoyed this time with you. So much that time just got away from me. Thanks for allowing me to see your beautiful home, but I've really got to run. I'll phone you to make an appointment for next month. Did Dorothy tell you our interviews and home visits might go on for eight or nine months? It's a long time, but *you* have to be sure and *we* have to be sure. You wanna be a parent? Think of our get-togethers … interviews, as a nine-month pregnancy, Bill."

*     *     *     *     *

One morning, a short time into my "pregnancy," Ray Williams called me panting and whizzing into the phone.

"You won't believe it, Billy, you won't believe it! I can hardly believe it! Wow, what a beautiful fuckin' day!"

"Try me, Ray, I'll believe you. What's up?"

"You sittin' down?"

"Yes, fer god's sake, Ray!"

"Got TWO for ya. TWO!"

"You been drinking? You promised not to before five."

"The *lessor* of the two, Wiseguy, is that your house in Bernal Heights is now in escrow! And the other … best … is … get dressed and I'll meet you on the corner of Larkin and Greenwich in half an hour! Bye-bye, Smart Ass!"

Burning with curiosity, I speeded Old Rust to that corner, and there was Ray squatting in the entrance of a four-story stucco apartment house, searching through a pile of papers.

"I got things in motion, Bill. Twelve units with views of the Golden Gate! Up your alley. Gonna need a *ton* of work, and I can get you a second at 20%. With the cash from Bernal, it's yours from a desperate seller for just ... hang on to your hat ... it's not cheap ... $165,000."

I looked down at a splattered piece of stucco at my feet and sighed, "OK."

## Chapter 26

# Anyone Can Fuck!

Being a child of divorced parents has certain benefits, believe it or not. The most important is that you celebrate your birthday twice, eat two Thanksgiving and Christmas dinners, go on two family vacations, and have two graduation parties. Although I should have been happier about that, I wasn't. Those celebrations with my mother were the fun ones, mostly because they included her tipsy brothers and sisters, my aunts and uncles, with crazy cousins to tease and annoy to distraction.

The holiday dinners with my father and his second wife, Maude, were both boring and confrontational with my father complaining about the $50 a month my mother was forcing him to spend on my college education to make up for the alimony and child support he didn't pay for years, and the education, itself, being too liberal and un-American. We were, of course, on opposite sides of the war in Vietnam, and at one Easter dinner, I called my father on making a joke about a Jew, a nigger, and a wop who got thrown out of a bar for ordering "faggy" drinks.

I threatened to leave the table if he made another racist remark. He started listing all the ways he was disappointed in me, then added insult to injury by listing all the ways his and Maude's son, Russell, had achieved goals I hadn't. Russell was 10 years younger than I, and already had been promoted to be a head accountant in his firm and had married Sandi, prettier and better behaved than any of the girls I had brought around. Maude wisely stayed out of the grousing, and my Aunt Ruth and Uncle Elzie tried to calm things down with jokes I had heard them tell for years. My father had long given up laughing at them.

The first time I ever saw my father break out into a big grin was at our Christmas Eve dinner in 1967, the year I started the procedure to adopt. I had been looking forward to this night since that day in June when I sat in Dorothy Murphy's office and agreed to be interviewed by a social worker for nine months before I could adopt. I was absolutely sure that when I told Maude and my dad I would, at last, make them grandparents, they would grin from ear to ear and shower me with unconditional love and approval … at last.

All the way over the bridge to Oakland, with Christmas carols flowing nonstop from the car radio, I envisioned how sensational it was going to be to stand there raising a glass of champagne and tell my family, especially my father, the news about me being allowed to adopt. That would make him a grandfather and Maude a grandmother! I was so excited I could hardly force the turkey and dressing down. I thought I'd wait for dessert and then … and then … stand up, pour everyone a glass of champagne, get their attention, and then … whammy!

Finally, they would have something they couldn't disapprove of … like my being arrested at a civil rights rally or not having a good, steady job like my half-brother, Russ, or not giving a damn about football scores.

I had discreetly hidden a chilled bottle of champagne away in a paper bag under my chair at the table. Regretfully, I gave up going to Pasek's Christmas Eve party to come to Oakland and offer a toast to my addition to the Jones family. Most of our gay friends and all of my "Group" would be at Pasek's party. They'd be half-drunk, planting kisses under the mistletoe, and I hoped, missing me and wondering why I wasn't there. But this was more important to me. Standing there with my glass raised high, I would drink in all the love and admiration I had longed for, for so many years.

The pumpkin pie dessert dishes were in the kitchen sink, and I was about to push my chair back and reach down for the paper bag when Russell, at the other end of the table, plopped a bottle of champagne down on the lace tablecloth and said, "Mom, Dad, next year there'll be another chair at this table … a high chair! It'll be the best Christmas ever! You'll love this. Sandi's pregnant." My father's face lit up and he began to grin. It became a smile so wide you could even see his chipped front tooth.

I swallowed, congratulated Sandi and Russell, kissed Maude and Aunt Ruth on their cheeks, waved at Uncle Elzie and my father, said goodnight, and bolted for the door, paper sack in hand. By the time I got back to Pasek's apartment on Bay Street, most of the guys had left. The remains of red and green popped balloons were scattered all over the furniture and floor. Michael and Bob Lanci were stashing paper plates and plastic glasses in garbage bags, and Gary was washing serving bowls.

I took Pasek's hand and led him out to the deck. The night wasn't chilly. Actually, it felt comfortable, as it does before a rain. It was starless with a low ceiling of rose-colored clouds, reflecting the city's lights. I closed the door to the deck to be sure what I was about to say couldn't be heard by the others, and then I blurted out how Russell had beat me to it, as usual. Russell got what I so desperately wanted. I had lost again. It had been my one chance to win my father's approval, my one chance to look "normal" to him, but I was hardly able to tell Pasek everything I felt because I was choking up.

Pasek took me by my shoulders and shook me. Then embraced me.

"I'm so proud to be your friend, Bill. I know I promised to keep it secret, but I've been dying to tell *everybody* what you're doing … and I will, I will, as soon as you get a kid and the adoption is finalized. And you give me the okay."

He gave me another hug then pulled back to look at me.

"Bill, you'll be the greatest dad, and I'll be the greatest uncle!" he snorted, "Uncle Polly!"

We both grinned to think of Pasek being Uncle Polly, but then he looked at me in a serious, intense way that was so unlike Pasek.

"I don't think you realize how special it is, what you're doing. You're doing something no single man has ever done before. Jesus, Bill, think of it! Besides …"

Then he took a deep breath and smiled again with a haughty, knowing look.

"… *Anyone* can *fuck!*"

# Chapter 27
# *Bullit*

I named my building Wildflower Apartments and moved into a large, empty area off the lobby on the first floor that was rented illegally during World War II as an apartment, but now was a dusty, forlorn storage room. It had rough plumbing for two baths and a kitchen, which I found after I attacked the space with a broom, mop, fly spray, and fierce determination. I desperately needed money at that point, being up to my teats in debt, and the nursery was *not* ready for a kid. If the adoption agency ever found out how broke I was, the whole adoption might sink into the What-Might-Have-Been Ocean.

The Vietnam mess was an orgy of bloody rage that came spilling into my "living room" every night on the five o'clock news, and I defiantly wore the peace symbol button to give the finger to anyone who supported it. I even considered having it tattooed on me somewhere, but that somewhere had to be hidden if I still wanted to model and do extra work in the movies. Practicality won over my sense of outrage. So, I wore the button except to auditions and "go-sees." It made me feel like a traitor to my own values, but a guy's got to eat.

"Bill Jones from Ann Brebner Casting," the second AD (assistant director) announced to Peter Yates, the director on *Bullitt*. I felt a wave of excitement as I walked into his trailer office. I was cast as an extra by Ann and occasionally picked out of the extra lineup to do a special business by the first assistant director, but never before this had I been sent straight in to be interviewed by

2459 Larkin St., the Wildflower Apts.

a director. I had no idea why Ann had picked me out from all the other extras she booked to "go-see" Yates, but my heart was pounding since she told me it might mean a four-week contract at $400 a week!

Ann warned me in the quiet, British way she had of telling you which way is up, "Wear a suit and tie. Get your hair cut. And take off that damn button."

Peter Yates wasn't movie-star handsome, but he had a quiet flair about him that was attractive and at the same time domineering. His British accent, pale skin, and flowing blond-gray hair belied what was really there. A man's man, strong and insightful. I worried that he might sense I was gay. It would be the end of the interview and my chance at a role if he even suspected. I panicked.

"I see you're against the war."

*Oh, shit!* I had put the pin on out of habit and forgot that Ann had warned me not to wear it. This might be worse than his realizing I was gay. He might even kick my ass as he told me to leave, but instead, he just said, "So am I."

I spent the rest of the afternoon sheetrocking the nursery and day dreaming about being a movie star. I wiped the doughy spackle off my hands and slid down the ladder to grab the Princess phone before it stopped ringing.

"Bill, this is Ann. I have terrific news for you. You got the part. You'll be playing Robert Vaughn's political aide. I don't know if you have any lines, but you'll be driving his car and hanging around him in all his scenes. Go back to Yates's office. They have a contract for you to sign."

I closed my eyes to savor this moment.

"You'll be making more money than you've ever made before, so don't blow it. Act very straight. Stand by and be focused. Don't make them have to go off and look for you. I'm so happy for you, Bill, and here's the funny part. Yates chose you because you were wearing that peace button, but even though that peace button got you the job, PLEASE don't wear it on the set."

I took the fastest shower of my life, jumped into my suit and tie costume, and gunned the motor of my '49 Dodge pickup to speed back to the *Bullitt* home office, which was just one of a dozen or so film trailers parked in the empty parking lot of Candlestick Stadium.

"Hi, Bill. I'm Walter Hill, the second AD." He was casual and a little scruffy with a full head of fluffy hair. He had a young, sexy way about him but was intense about his position. "Here's your call sheet for next week. Let's see. Yeah. You're on for Tuesday at 7 a.m. Report to Wardrobe first thing, then to makeup and hair. DON'T get a haircut before you get here. We'll take care of that. Do you need a car to pick you up?"

Wouldn't I have just LOVED that? But I knew I would need Old Rust to drive over to Goodman's for supplies every night after the wrap, so I shook my head and backed out the door, clutching the contract in my sweaty hands, hoping they wouldn't change their minds.

\* \* \* \* \*

The very next day I opened the letter I had been waiting and praying for.

> *The San Francisco Social Services Adoption Agency is pleased to inform you that after considerable consideration, your application for adoption was approved, and as you know, we have taken great pains to find just the right child for you. I am also happy to report that the search has been fruitful. He is almost 2 years old with blue eyes and brown hair like yours. Please be at the Agency at 10 o'clock Monday morning to meet your new son.*
>
> *Very truly yours,*
> *(Mrs.) Mary Davidson - Child Welfare Supervisor*

\* \* \* \* \*

My head was swirling and I couldn't breathe. *"I CAN'T do both at the same time! Shooting time for a movie can go on for 12 hours or more sometimes. I can't bring a baby on the set!"*

I felt tears of frustration welling up. Everything I had ever dreamed of was being offered me all at once, and I had to choose which I wanted more. To be a father or to be cast in a movie. What a wrenching choice for me to make! I had to choose. I had to choose. *"I want to be in this movie! I need the money. I need to be a parent! I want a family of my own. Please, dear God, what shall I do? What shall I do?"*

What I should have done was simply calm down. I can be such a drama queen! All it took was a call to Mary explaining what was happening, that I was tearing my hair out trying to decide between being a daddy or a movie star, and she waved her magic wand. The only problem she saw was the one I had in my head.

"Bill, I'm suppressing a giggle right now. You can't possibly think it has to be one or another. Don't you trust us? Dorothy and I have spent more time working on your case than any other. We think you're just what we're looking for, and this little boy we have in mind for you is darling. Of course, we all want you two to meet as soon as possible, but what's another four weeks? Compared to the years ... all those years you've wanted to adopt, it's just a minute out of an hour, right?"

"Oh, Mary, thank you, thank both of you for putting up with me. It's just that this is the most important thing I'll ever do in my lifetime, and it's making me nervous as hell. So, you're saying we can put it off until my work in this movie is over? Talk about having your cake and eating it, too!"

"Four more weeks, Bill. Just four more weeks. You'll love him. He's darling!"

## Chapter 28

# The Friday before the Monday

"Some men see things as they are, and ask why.
I dream of things that never were, and ask why not."
— Robert Kennedy, quoting George Bernard Shaw

I usually showered before I went to bed, probably hoping that I would get lucky and end up with another hot body in bed with me. Like wearing clean underwear in case you are in an accident, I wanted to be freshly scrubbed, smelling good, and have a desirable, smooth body. Ready for anything. "Cleanliness is next to godliness," I've been told, but for me, cleanliness was next to sexiness.

But on Friday, May 17, 1968, that spring day turned upside down in more ways than one. I was in the shower early that morning instead of at night because it just might be … hopefully … the most memorable day of my empty life. The appointment was for 10 a.m., which gave me less than two hours to get ready and down to the agency on Mission Street. I had to be clean, clean, clean for him. I cut the hairs in my nose, filed my nails – even the toenail that was turning a disgusting yellow. Cologne? No. Wash it off. The Burberry plaid shirt? No, too casual. The black shirt? No, too swarthy. The Brooks Brothers blue oxford button-down? Yeah. Loafers? No. Brooks Brothers cordovans? Perfect. Moisturize, deodorize, a little bluing in the hair oil to highlight the

Erin Sean

emerging gray among the brown, and I was out the door, sucking in the sunlight and sweet morning air.

Mary Davidson, my social worker, told me four weeks before, while we were still shooting *Bullitt*, that the agency had found what they thought would be the perfect little boy for me. He was just under two years old, so I wouldn't be burdened with his infancy, mixing formulas, and washing diapers. He had my coloring – blue eyes and brown hair – so we would be easily accepted as father and son. She knew that I was more than willing to take a black child or an Asian – especially Vietnamese – girl or boy – blind, handicapped, sick, or well. I knew I could love it as my very own, but Mary and Dorothy had thought it out much more thoroughly than I had.

Sailing into these unchartered waters of single parenthood was daunting enough. No use making it even riskier by flaunting it in strangers' faces. A single white man, hand in hand with a black boy? Uh uh. A single white man checking into a motel with a young girl? Call the police.

So out of the 850 kids to choose from, they had carefully chosen a little boy they were sure would be right for me, but their choice would make this day one of the worst ones I can remember. The spiral into darkness was about to begin.

Mary cautioned me before the door opened, "This is the way prospective parents first see a child they might adopt. Oh, did I tell you he will be two years old tomorrow?" We sat on folding chairs up against the wall in an auditorium, just off the concrete lobby. At the end of this very large, empty room was a fenced-in area, cluttered with bright-colored toys, limp dolls, fuzzy stuffed animals, and a small sandbox made out of a red plastic wading pool.

"You mustn't speak to the boy, Bill. Just watch him play and react with the toys and Jeanne, his social worker. We used to let the clients talk to the children, but you know, Bill, some of them are rejected, and these little tykes know when they are being turned down. I haven't told you this, but this little boy has been rejected by five couples already. He is …"

The door slowly opened. Jeanne held it open for a long minute until the thin child with her waddled through it, unsteady on his feet. He was dressed in a blue romper, white leather shoes, and a light blue knit sweater that matched his light blue eyes, luminescent against his dark skin. His head had been shaved and he stood, staring into space, looking very much like an alien, dazed by the crash of his space ship's hard landing. Then Jeanne, holding the little guy's hand, walked close by us and led him to the playpen.

Mary clutched my arm and gasped, "My God, Bill. I think he's black!"

She got no reaction from me. To this day, I really think this black woman was testing me. Both of us felt relieved, I'm sure, that I passed her silly test.

He stood at the gate to the playpen, staring at the yellow bulldozer, silver race car, and beach balls of different sizes scattered in front of him, but he wouldn't go in to touch them. They were unfamiliar objects to him, unknown in his foster home. A heavy chill began to envelop me. *He's not going to be the one for me.* That feeling of loss made me lonely and depressed. It was sad that he had no idea of what a toy was and didn't even show any interest in touching one. He just stood there. And I was sad for myself, frightened that if I didn't want him after all the effort Mary Davidson and Dorothy Murphy had made to get us to this point, they would give up on me, and I would never be allowed to adopt – ever.

Jeanne turned to us and shrugged her shoulders. There was nothing more to do. She took his hand and headed toward the door. It was over. Mary knew by my silence that I was dismayed.

"Not to worry, Bill. This happens quite often. Lots of people turn down the first child we show them. There has to be a real connection between the parents and the kids. We'll keep looking and the right one will show up. Just don't give up. We won't. We *never* give up."

"Mary, let me try to talk to him. Maybe I can get him to come out of his shell. I'm good with kids."

"Bill, we aren't supposed to let you talk to the children until you decide to take them. If you wanted him, he's yours to take home today, but he's been left behind before. You think that just because he looks a little retarded, he's dumb, but these kids are more than aware that you're turning away from them. If you talk to him, he'll think you like him and are gonna accept him."

Eventually, I wore her down, and she allowed us a space in the corner of the room to try to talk. I started jabbering about toys I had when I was a little guy like him. As I talked, I tried to get closer to him by sitting on the floor. I reached out for him, but he drew away. After I ran out of stories to tell him about my own childhood, we just stayed our distance, I, squatted on the floor and he, stood facing me. I was about to get up and surrender when out of nowhere he burst into a lengthy jabber fest of "La-la. Ga-ga. La-la. Ga-ga. Ga-ga. La-la" as if he had finally discovered a listener to his version of how the earth was formed, and at long last could share his discovery in every detail.

I took it as long as I could, but even though he seemed to enjoy his little rant, he never really tried to connect to me. No real eye contact. No touching. No smiles. Nothing. This was a strange child I could never call my son. Never play with. Never send to college. Never buy his first car. Never watch with pride as he grew into being a man. I rose to my feet and shaking my head said goodbye to Mary and Jeanne.

"Let's talk Monday, Bill. I'll call you."

My legs moved in slow motion. I opened the door and walked out into the cool San Francisco air. Standing still in the shadow of the building on Mission Street, I didn't think that in two days, my life would be soaring into a world full of love I'd never known and despair that would haunt me until I finally quit breathing.

## Chapter 29

# The Saturday and Sunday before the Monday

I had dinner alone at Denny's that Friday night. Maybe it was the wilted salad or the plastic-tasting dessert, but I twisted in the bedsheets all night with a frozen image of that little zombie kid with the shaved head and the blue-gray porcelain eyes standing there, staring into space. Never looking into my eyes.

*"Here we are, Saturday morning, May 18th, 1968, in sunny San Francisco, folks, and aren't we glad we live here? It is 8:03 and you're listening to KGO, the best station for news and music in the city. Good news! Good music! Good morning, San Francisco!"* The good news was that only one bomber and its crew were shot down during a raid on a Vietcong village in … blah, blah, blah.

The dreary news about the war went on and on, but not one single word about today being Aaron's second birthday. Would his foster mother bake him a cake with two candles on top for him to blow out? Would there be wrapped gifts? Toys? A stuffed teddy bear to hug? I knew there wouldn't. I almost tripped over the untouched, unloved toys I saw in the playpen, they were so real to me as I made my way to the bathroom.

My brother, Jerry, and Bill Randles unlocked the front door and walked into my kitchen. Jerry started the coffee and Randles laid out the still-warm rolls he had baked that morning. The comforting aroma of coffee and cinnamon seeped through the walls and into the bathroom where I was peering into two bloodshot eyes in the mirrored medicine cabinet.

Jerry: "Mornin'."

Randles: "Mornin'."

Me: "Mornin'."

"Well?" They both leaned over the old glass display case I used as a kitchen counter to separate the kitchen from the living room. Jerry, holding out a cup of coffee for me as Randles was reaching over with a warm roll on a paper towel, made his demand. "Details!"

"Like I told you last night on the phone. It's a no-go. No way! The kid belongs in a zoo."

"Which cage?" Randles cracked.

"You should see him. No hair. No vocabulary except 'La-la. Ga-ga. La-la. Ga-ga.' Smelled like urine. Never *once* looked at me. Mary thought we'd make a pair! I don't think so!"

We sipped our coffee in uncomfortable silence. Before we'd had two or three sips, Jerry refilled our cups. "I'm so sorry, Bill."

"Me, too," Randles quickly added.

"We thought we'd be drinking champagne this morning. Look. We're in our painting rags. We came to help you with the kid's room. Brought our own brushes," Jerry said as he came around the counter and put his arms around me.

"As long as we're here, let's paint the damn room," Randles piped up.

The next few hours seemed to fly by. With rollers and brushes dipped in Sears' Antique White, we magically turned the walls from a water-stained, brown wrapping paper hue to pristine, but warm and inviting, white walls, casting a vanilla glow. It had the feeling of home, comfort, rest. We pulled up the thin plastic tarps that covered the plywood floor.

"Good god, Jerry. I can hardly wait to lay some carpet in here."

Jerry fixed our tuna fish sandwiches while Randles and I washed the roller pan and the brushes, and then we pulled up chairs to the card table and opened a box of milk. Jerry was the first to speak. "You know I've been teaching for over five years now. Not that I'm an expert on kids, but one thing I know for sure. I know kids can change if they are loved. Seen it. Two years ago, the first time I had a sixth-grade class, there was this kid that everybody wanted to throttle. The little bastard would *not* shut up. Disturbed everybody in the class and even out on the playground. Little asshole!"

I stopped eating because I had never heard my brother speak of his pupils with swear words.

"Damned if Social Services didn't yank him out of his home … drugs and liquor. Mother's doing time for streetwalking. He got placed in a foster home. Three or four kids of their own, but they wanted to help if they could. The foster mother walked him to school every mornin' and hugged him in front of all the kids comin' in. The foster dad dropped in after school all the time just to see how the kid was doin'."

"What's your point?"

"Kids can change if someone really cares for them, Bill. The boy quieted down. Did his homework. Got along and became one of my favorites. No lie."

"But the kid has to *want* someone to love him. I tell ya, Jerry, this one I saw yesterday may be the right one for someone else. God knows who, but not for me, Jerry. I know it deep down. I feel sorry for the little guy, and Mary must think I'm an asshole, but it simply would *not* work out. The only thing … I'm so afraid they'll give up on me. I know there's some kid out there who really wants a home. Some little kid who wants me for his dad. If I were religious, I'd pray they don't give up on me. Guess we'll just have to wait and see."

We spent the rest of the afternoon at a gay bookstore, reading books we couldn't afford to buy and ogling the cuties strutting up and down Polk Street.

I spent that night cruising bars on Polk Street, not really horny, but trying to smother my brother's voice with jukebox music and black Russians. At ten to two, I was in Cloud Nine when the overhead lights came on and the bartender yelled out, "Last call!" The frantic quick searches left most of us as we were before the lights came on. Gripping a sweaty warm bottle of beer in our hands. It was to be another sleepless night in an empty bed. I slowly climbed up Union Street until I stopped at the corner on Larkin, hoping that at the last minute a car would pass me, the brake lights would come on, and the car would squat, purring like a kitten, waiting for me to saunter up to the open window and make a very quick judgment.

I slept in late Sunday and then caught the Hyde Street cable car downtown. *Why am I doing this?* I kept asking myself. Even though Macy's and the Emporium were open Sundays, I didn't have a pot to piss in as the saying goes except for $25 in cash, but that had to last me until the end of the month when the meager rents came in. Was I always going to be this poor? At thirty-nine, I felt like a financial disaster.

So, when I found myself opening the glass door to FAO Schwarz on Stockton Street it was as if some mythical beast were pulling me inside. I had no business being there. So what if that kid didn't get any presents for his birthday? First of all, he probably didn't even know it *was* his birthday. And he wouldn't miss a present he never got. I clutched my wallet as if the beast were trying to wrench it from my hand.

To save a quarter, I walked home. When I got there, it was growing dark. I heated a Swanson fried chicken TV dinner, and as I ate, sitting across from me on the card table was a new fuzzy brown teddy bear with chocolate brown button eyes. He seemed to be saying to me, "Now what?"

## Chapter 30
# The Monday

"Good morning. Mary Davidson speaking. Adoption Services."

"Hi, Mary. It's Bill."

"I was just about to call you, Bill. How ya doin'?"

"Not too good. I'm so sorry about that little kid, and I'm really worried. Are we still on?"

"Oh, Bill, don't feel bad. This happens quite often. The first one isn't always the right one. Dorothy and I went over all the files after you left. There are three or four more little boys we want to show you."

"Really? Three or four?" A wave of relief washed over me. A door that I feared had been locked forever was opening wide again and now I was free – free of wasting my time feeling sorry and guilty over that little zombie.

"Mary, I kept thinking about that kid, and ..."

"He has a name." Her tone was patronizing. "Erin Sean."

"Well, I was thinking how sad it was that Saturday was his birthday, and I didn't even have a card for him."

"He'll be okay." I sensed her biting her lip to avoid telling me to go to hell.

"I know. I know. But anyway, Mary, I bought a little gift for him."

"What!"

"I'd like to give him a birthday present, okay?"

"I don't think that's a good idea, Bill. As I told you Friday, these children sense when they have been rejected, and this would make two times that you saw him and then left him."

"Look, I was a teacher … for six years, and I was Santa Claus at Penney's once. I raised my little brother. I know kids. I know how to do it so he'll feel good. Hey, I'll just run in and hand it to him, sing "Happy Birthday," and beat it out the door. Okay?"

"It's against my better judgment." There was a pause so long that I thought my phone had gone dead. "But …" And then another long pause. "Okay." Another pause. "Jeanne can bring him back … let's see … around three this afternoon. Is that good for you?"

I found a cardboard box that the teddy bear barely fit into and wrapping paper I had saved from Christmas. What the hell! Snowflakes in May are good for birthdays, too. I didn't have any ribbon, so I just wrote HAPPY BIRTHDAY, AARON on the box and drew two candles on a small cake under the greeting.

On the stroke of three, I pushed the door open to the meeting hall where I had first seen the little zombie, and it looked dreary and faded as it had on Friday except now a folding screen stood in front of the playpen that stored the toys. Mary was sitting in front of the screen. She got up and met me in the middle of the cavernous room that was all beige, brown, and tan with dark stripes from the venetian blinds filtering out the afternoon sun.

"Hello, Bill. Good to see you." She saw me quickly taking stock of the empty room. "He's here." She pointed to the screen. "Jeanne is changing his diapers behind that screen over there. They'll be out in a minute." She took the box from me. "You know we found out why he's so dark. The foster mother has five of our infants and two children of her own … and an alcoholic husband." Mary lowered her voice until she was almost whispering in my ear. "She's been keeping the babies outside in a pen, naked, so all of them are almost burned to a crisp."

"Oh, my god!"

"That's probably why he doesn't know any words and acts so out of it. I am sooooo upset! Two-year-olds should have a vocabulary of about 20 words. More or less." Her body seemed to get rigid. "We're transferring all of the babies out of there today."

"I suspected something was really wrong with him. Didn't you?"

"She kept them clean and fed. That's about it, and we didn't catch it." Mary looked away from me and glanced toward the screen. "Somebody's gonna lose their job over this."

"I knew the minute I saw him that he wasn't the one for me. Mary, I want a kid who's bright. Happy. Aware of the world around him. I want to send him to college for Christ's sake!"

"Yeah. I know. Education's really important to you, being a teacher and all."

"I've been thinking about what a picky loser I must have looked like to you Friday. And I've been worried sick all weekend that you would give up on me ... thinking you'd never be able to find the right kid for me to adopt." I stopped because from behind the screen, Jeanne's voice, very agitated, kept getting louder and louder as she ordered Aaron to stop moving around.

I felt the tension rising – with Jeanne's exasperation, Mary's despair over one of her friends who might lose their job, and my ranting on about what a failure I thought I might be in their eyes. I walked around her with my back to the screen so she had to look at me. I felt I had to lighten things up.

"I really have to laugh at myself, Mary. Do that a lot. You know I just LOVED all the Shirley Temple movies. Still do." I raised my own voice to get over the racket behind the screen. "And I guess in the back of my empty head, I was thinking that it would be like a movie ... that I'd be sort of a white Bojangles, in an old, run-down orphanage looking over a lineup of poor little kids all in rags, when all of a sudden I'd spy this one really cute little kid. The music would start with a great drum beat, and we would hold hands while we tap danced out the door." I felt sheepish and silly even telling her this. "Into the sunset I suppose." Both of us grinned and the tension seemed to melt.

Mary looked up as she was holding the snow-flaked birthday package. "You spelled his name wrong, Bill. It isn't A-A-R-O-N. It's E-R-I-N, Erin Sean. That was on his birth certificate."

"But I thought E-R-I-N was a girl's name ..."

The screen moved slightly, and we heard more commotion behind it, and I remember Jeanne yelling, "Erin Sean, come back here! Come back!"

I turned away from Mary just in time to see him running toward me, and before I had time to realize what was happening, Aaron threw his arms around my legs so tight, so tight ... as if he would never let go.

It's very hazy to me, but I think I remember Jeanne saying, "I couldn't control him! As soon as he heard you talking to Mary, he started squirming ... just managed to pin his clean diaper on."

I stood paralyzed, unable to speak or move. The room seemed to be expanding and contracting, breathing deep breaths … and a warm blanket of white feathers fell over me. Mary or Jeanne, I don't remember which one, was speaking to me, but I couldn't hear them. I felt the tears trickling down my cheeks. I remember looking down and seeing through the blur a tiny wet spot on the top of his downy head just before he threw his head back and looked up into my eyes.

"La-la. Ga-ga. La-la. Ga-ga. La-la-la. Ga-ga. La-la. Ga-ga. La-la. Ga-ga."

I understood what he was telling me … hugging my legs, so I picked him up and cradled him in my arms.

## Chapter 31

# The First Five Days
# with Aaron

### Mary

Even though Mary had assured me it would be okay to take Aaron home with me that very afternoon, and as much as I wanted to, I had to put her off with the feeble plea that the nursery wasn't ready yet. "I need a few days to lay the carpet and get a crib, food, and diapers. You know."

"That all has to be done, Bill, I agree. How about this? Come back every day and pick him up for an hour or two so you can get acquainted."

I was relieved and thought it was a wonderful idea. Actually, I didn't even have enough money to buy him a week's supply of food, but that was the *last* thing I wanted Mary to know, and come to think of it, I had no idea what kind of food he ate. We had wrapped on *Bullitt*, but I hadn't been paid yet, so I just had a few coins in my pocket after spending so much for his teddy bear. I still had my Standard Oil, Sears, and Macy's cards so I could finish his room, but food for this toddler … no. I was already opening all the cans of soup I had stored in the pantry three times a day, and I hope I never have to have chicken noodle soup for breakfast again. Ever!

Tuesday, the first day of our time together, started badly. My front door-bell rang, and thinking it was one of my tenants with yet another depressing tale of no hot water or a clogged garbage shoot, I went to get the bad news. Instead of swinging the door open, I peeked through the peephole and saw a familiar hairy face with those sunken, watery eyes. It was that smart-ass bill

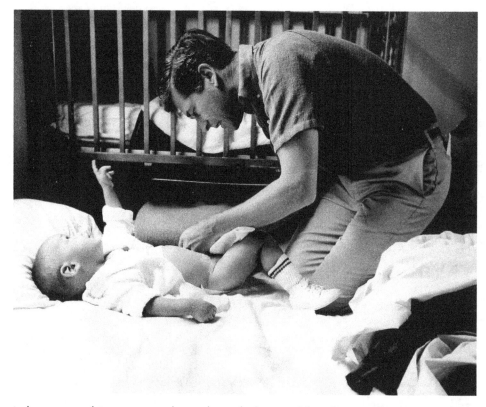

I slept on cushions next to his crib and changed his diapers there, too.

collector from the holder of the second mortgage. Five days earlier, I had made the mistake of opening the door just a crack so we could talk, but he shoved his sandal inside so I couldn't close it. His scent slipped through the crack in the door. Cigars, stale underwear, greasy hair, dry, flakey skin. I "accidentally" stepped on his foot and he pulled it back with a jerk. After a minute or two, I heard the door to the lobby close with a thud.

I thought he had given up hounding me after he limped out of the lobby, but he was back again at my front door, smelling up the lobby. Of all days! At 20% interest on the second mortgage, I was sinking into a whirlpool of debt and was forced to make a lot of hard choices. One of the choices I made that morning was to climb out the back window in the living room. Hanging from the ladder of the fire escape, I jumped six feet down onto the trunk of my old Lincoln parked below. I slid into the seat, twisted the key and backed the car out onto the street in a blind rush, just missing a UPS truck. Gunning the

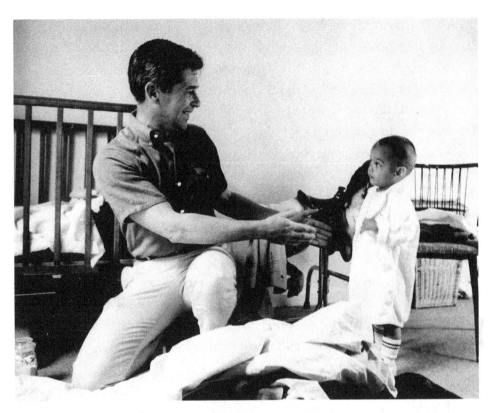

Diaper changing became routine.

motor, I roared by "Old Smelly" getting into his car and headed for the office of the adoption agency as fast as I could, smug that I had outsmarted him, and ecstatic that I was, at last, going to spend at least an hour alone with the most beautiful little boy in the whole wide world.

The '62 Lincoln was a four-door convertible I'd picked up for only $500 nine months before when I thought I needed it to impress Mary on her first visit to my house on Bernal Heights. After a good wash and wax, the car looked like a million bucks parked in my driveway. It was only five years old, but because of its nondescript dusty tan color and a couple of dings on the fenders, it was stored in the back of a car lot in Hayward. The lot was going out of business and the old gent in the office was ready to deal. He wanted $1,500 for it, but when I slowly counted out $500 in $20 bills one by one, laying them out, spread like cards on his desk, he grabbed the money and ran, as the saying goes. The Lincoln was mine!

It was May, and everything I ever remembered about springtime was in that car. To Aaron's delight, I lowered the canvas top into its cave. The trunk lid rose majestically, hinged from the rear, and slowly the canvas top also rose straight up, then collapsed, folding itself into its cocoon, snug under the descending lid. Aaron squeezed my hand and let out a torrent of gibberish, half babbling, half laughing with glee.

When I want to remember Aaron in the most endearing way, I always think about that first day when he stood so close to me as I drove slowly through Golden Gate Park with his left arm resting on my shoulder and his tiny hand on my neck, sometimes squeezing my right ear. The car seemed to float above the pavement, gracefully swooping in and around the trees and flowerbeds. We had no need for radio music because his steady stream of "la-la ga-ga" made my head giddy. The gibberish sounded more and more like, "You are my daddy. I am your little boy. You are my daddy. I am your son."

The car was afloat with sunshine and multicolored tulips that smelled like jasmine and roses. The wind falling over the windshield was a soft, tropical breeze. The purr of the motor was a trickling stream bubbling over smooth round stones. I was truly happy, feeling the warmth of being a family, a father with his son, completely content for the first time in my life.

After I returned Aaron to the adoption agency, I hurried home to finish laying the carpet in his room, one that I had stripped from one of the empty apartments upstairs. After that, I hauled in a Philippine mahogany chest of drawers I had bought 14 years before from the Trade Fair in Sausalito. Because it was contemporary, the top and sides were simple slabs, unadorned. To hide the stains and scratches, I covered the whole thing with a deep blue peel-and-stick shelving paper with a shiny surface. Blue for his blue eyes.

The next day, Wednesday, Pasek met us at David and Dennis' studio on Grant Avenue. Pasek immediately swooped Aaron up and held him the entire time we were there, unwilling to share him with Dennis or David. Declaring himself an uncle got a rise out of both of them, and they, too, declared themselves uncles. The family was growing.

On Thursday, Dad, Maude, and Aunt Ruth drove over from Oakland and met us at Blum's for lunch. We squeezed into the hot pink leatherette booth, and the waitress brought Aaron a booster chair. He got up from it immediately and stood by my side, as he did in the car, pushing his body into me so hard that I could hardly raise my hand to feed my face.

Dennis had hand-drawn some beautiful nametags for us with our names in rose and orange on a tan rice paper. I handed them out to everyone with a straight pin to fasten them on. "Grandpa," "Grandma," "Aunt Ruth," "Daddy," and "Aaron." Maude and Aunt Ruth were amused and put them on, but my father just sat, grimly picking at his food.

Frankly, I was hoping that at least Maude and Aunt Ruth would offer to do a little shopping for their new grandchild, but no such offer came. Instead, just as we were leaving Blum's, my father pulled me aside and firmly told me that what I was doing was crazy. "That kid is NOT my grandson, and you are, in no way, to ask this family for any money or anything else to help raise him. This is your choice, so now live with it."

I was deserted at the age of two, and I felt deserted now at forty. I had never asked my father to give me anything … never … so it was like a slash of a knife to think he had to warn me not to start asking now.

Actually, I owe a lot to my father because he was a role model for me. I learned from him the very essence of being a lousy father. He was distant and disinterested, everything I wanted to avoid. With Aaron, I would achieve everything I should have had with my own father. I would tuck my son in at night and kiss him before I turned out the light. I would sit him on my lap and read to him. I would cook his food, bathe him, kiss his boo-boos, comb his hair, take him to the doctor, play catch with him, teach him to swim, teach him to drive a car, walk him to school, talk to his teachers, help with his homework, encourage any talent he might have, play games with him, teach him how to hammer and saw, watch him graduate, help buy his first car, help him find a job and a home for himself.

Oh, yes, my father, the role model, taught me through his indifference how to be a real dad for my son, Aaron. The pain stops here.

Friday was the day Mary would deliver Aaron to me at my home on Larkin Street. Of course, I had lengthy, nightly phone calls with my brother about what happened each day with Aaron. He seemed as excited as I, but since he was teaching, it had been impossible to get together during the day so he could actually meet Aaron. You can imagine how befuddled and thrilled I was when he unlocked my front door early Friday morning and stood there beaming with a knocked-down baby's crib under his arm.

"I'm playing hooky today. I knew you needed this and Alison is sleeping in her own big bed now. It's got Aaron's name on it." He meant that literally. "I stenciled it on the headboard last night."

We had just finished assembling the crib when the doorbell rang. I felt the blood flushing through my head as I went to the door and peeped through the peephole just to be sure it wasn't the collector again. To my relief, I saw Mary's face, a smiling face that seemed to be glowing. I opened the door, and standing beside her was Aaron, still dressed in the blue rompers and the light blue knit sweater he had been wearing every day for the past five days. The only difference was that he was carrying his teddy bear in one hand and holding Mary's hand with the other.

"Here he is, Bill." Aaron let go of Mary's hand and ran over to me as fast as he could, and I picked him up, hugging him, kissing his cheek.

"Mary, this is my brother I've been bragging about. Mary, Jerry."

Jerry shook her hand and then motioned for her to step inside the nursery. She seemed pleased as she looked over the room, white walls, light grey carpet, the white-washed old shutters covering the window, a bright, shiny blue chest of drawers, and the 1915 World's Fair poster hanging over it. What she didn't see were the empty closet and empty drawers.

"I brought you this note from the foster mother. It was the least she could do."

In just two sentences, the note said he ate soft Gerber's baby food, but hadn't learned to chew solid food, and he never cried when he dirtied himself. Then Mary wished me well, told my brother goodbye, assured me she would keep in touch, and went through the door for what I thought was the last time that day, but I was wrong about that.

Bill Randles had packed a "care package" to accompany the crib. In it were cookies and brownies he had baked, and piled on top of them were six cloth diapers and a bunch of large safety pins, leftovers from Alison's baby days, I supposed.

Jerry left shortly after that, but on the way out, he pressed something into my hand and said, "This is from Randles and me. Pay us back when you can." A kiss on my cheek and he was out the door. I counted out $87 in assorted bills. I felt so blessed. So comforted.

I was holding Aaron as my brother closed the door, on the verge of giving a prayer of thanks for all my good luck, when Aaron looked at me, smiled a very big smile, and grunted. I smelled an odor I would be well acquainted with for the months to come. Still holding him, I got a bath towel and laid it on the carpet. I gently put him down on it, and he lay on his back, laughing, babbling, and kicking his legs in the air. I left him for just a moment, enough time to find a bucket to put the dirty diaper in, and a wet washcloth to wipe him clean. I was terrified that I might stick him with a safety pin, he was moving around so much, but I finished dressing him and carried him out to the Lincoln.

It was the first time I had been in a grocery store with Aaron, and it felt amazingly good. He rode in the cart as I piled it with Gerber's baby food, fresh diapers, Johnson's baby oil, Johnson's talcum powder, milk, and a few Swanson's TV dinners for me. I lifted him out when it was our turn at the checkout stand, and put him down at my feet.

The checkout clerk had just started bagging my stuff when we all turned to see what had just fallen with a loud clippety-clop onto the aisle.

"Hey, mister," a store clerk yelled at me, "Watch your kid, will ya? He knocked over this stack of Rice-A-Roni boxes!"

I couldn't stop smiling. He called Aaron "*your* kid." My kid! *MY* kid!

All the smiles and feelings of contentment were about to vaporize, however, because of what happened later that day. I faced nine months of sleepless nights, and if I did manage to sleep, my head would be filled with nightmares of distress and fear. There was no turning back at this point. No way out but to endure the best and the worst months of my life. My grin ended abruptly that afternoon when the doorbell rang again, and I saw Mary's face through the peephole, but it was grim, grim.

"Bill, I guess you didn't expect to see me again today, did you?"

I opened the door wider, beckoning her to come in, but she just stood in the doorway. "Something's happened, and Dorothy and I want to keep you informed. We don't want to keep anything from you." She glanced down at the bags of groceries at my feet. "Looks like you're busy, so I won't keep you."

"What's up? You look strange, Mary. What's happened?"

"Oh, it's probably nothing, Bill, and it probably won't change things. At least not right away, but someone has stirred up a hot mess at the agency."

"About me?"

"Yeah. Someone is … claiming you're gay and what's even more ridiculous, they're claiming you're planning an orgy in the nursery tonight."

I felt my face flush, and I held Aaron tighter.

"But Dorothy and I figured that you haven't had time to organize an orgy, so we aren't paying much attention to it," she said with a sly smile. "It'll go away, Bill, but we wanted you to know about it … to be prepared."

I was too stunned to say anything. I just stood holding Aaron, so she turned and walked out into the lobby. Then turning back she said, "We'll keep you posted."

I felt my left arm, the one holding Aaron become wet and warm, so even though I wanted to reach for the phone to call my brother or Pasek or Dennis, or even my cousin Ramona, I had to concentrate on changing another diaper. The five o'clock news was just starting with more news about the priests in Catonsville burning their draft cards, but my mind was not on the news. I put on one of the new diapers and powdered Aaron's bottom. It went much quicker than the first time even though he was laughing and kicking his legs again.

I warmed up the Gerber's spinach, chicken, and applesauce for him, and put a Swansons in the oven for me. It was our first meal at home together, but I found swallowing the food to be almost impossible because of the cold fear rising in my throat. Spooning the food into his mouth was a joy for me, but I kept flashing on Mary coming back and taking him away. The cold fear enveloped the little joy I was allowing myself to have and soon enveloped the entire room. He cuddled against me as we sat on the couch after dinner while I poured out everything to my brother on the phone. My poor brother, who shared everything with me, got the worst of the sharing deal. I was always in more trouble than he.

The phone rang just as I was filling the tub for Aaron's first bath. It was Pasek. After hearing what Mary had said, he said he'd be right over. I tested the water and it seemed just right for a toddler's bath. I undressed Aaron and lowered him into the tub. The minute his feet brushed against the water, he shrieked … crying, kicking, and flailing his arms. He was frightened and desperate to get away from the water. I pulled him up, hugging him and wiping the tears from his cheeks. He clung to me still crying, but not as intensely as when he felt the warm water on his feet.

I drained most of the water out until only a few inches remained on the bottom and then very gently lowered him down into the tub again. This time he started crying and kicking before he even touched the shallow pool. I quickly pulled him up and then put him down on the bath mat. I put a wash-cloth in the tub and wrung it out. Then as gently as I could, I tried to wipe him down with it, but he shrank away from the cloth and uttered the first words I had ever heard from him. "NO! NO! NO!" He looked at me through his tear-filled eyes, "NO! NO!"

## Pasek

Pasek, like my brother, Jerry, had a key to my apartment, so before I could wrap Aaron in a towel and open the door, he was standing beside me in the bathroom, looking at me as if both of us had lost our marbles. Aaron was sobbing and clinging to me with his damp arms around my neck, and I must have looked like a bomb had just exploded.

"What the hell? Did you drop him on his head or somethin'?" He patted Aaron on his wet head at arm's length, and then added, "Can I pour us a drink?" I nodded furiously. "I'll make it a triple." He went into the kitchen and came back holding two frosty goblets.

"He scared me shitless, Pasek. He freaked out in the bathtub like he was going to drown in six inches of water!" I grabbed the gin and tonic from Pasek's hand and gulped it down. "Then I drained most of the water out, down to just a puddle, but he screamed bloody murder when I tried to lower him down again! I tried bubbles in the bath, but when his feet touched the water ... Even the damn washcloth makes him start crying."

Pasek took the glass from my hand and put it on the toilet seat. Then he put his arms around both of us and just held us until I stopped hyperventilating and Aaron stopped whimpering. For several minutes we stood with Aaron snug between us. I wiped his tears and his runny nose with toilet paper after we both had calmed down.

"Okay now?" Pasek asked me. "Let's go sit on the couch. I brought you something." We sat close, and before I could adjust the pillows, Aaron crawled out of the bath towel and left me to sit on Pasek's lap. "Hey, I like 'em young, Young Man, but not THIS young!"

Pasek's eyes crinkled up with his smile that reminded me why I loved him, just this side of sex. I still think of him as the best friend I ever had, a comic with a wicked sense of humor, always laughing at himself, never making fun of anyone else.

He was caring, generous to his friends, and a talented designer of graphics like those he created for special events at the Cow Palace and the Civic Center Auditorium. His apartment, his clothing, his dinner parties, his seductions were always in the best of taste. I idolized him.

"I can't have a naked kid sitting on my lap. My reputation is bad enough already. He needs to be properly dressed." Then cooing to Aaron, "Wanna see what Uncle Pasek bought for you this afternoon?" He opened a shopping bag he had been holding and pulled out a baby blue flannel jumpsuit with rubber soles on the bottom of the feet. "It's for sleeping in, Big Guy, and they're called Dr. Dentons."

Between the two of us, we managed to get Aaron into the Dr. Dentons, and then he slid off the couch and ran around room, laughing and yelling, "La-la, ga-ga, la-la, ga-ga!" Pasek cheered him on. "Go, Big Guy, go!"

Like a family. Like nothing, I had ever felt before. My son in his Dr. Dentons and my best friend sitting beside me, sharing this moment, a moment I still cherish almost 60 years later.

After Pasek kissed both of us goodnight and left, I warmed a little milk for Aaron and sat with him on my lap while I watched the news about Robert Kennedy's campaign in California. Bobby's was an exciting campaign, and I was eager to vote for him, but I couldn't focus on him that night. I sat there cringing as I thought about Mary's threatening news and Aaron's terrified reaction to his bath. I felt as if I were being sucked into a vast, black hole.

Aaron fell asleep in my arms, and I sat savoring his body's weight against me, his tiny tummy movements as he breathed, the softness of the blue flannel, and the clean smell of my toddler. So clean! Even without scrubbing in a bathtub filled with warm water, soap bubbles, and a rubber ducky. No body odor. No stale breath. Even the poop in his diaper earlier that evening didn't offend me. I loved his clean toddler smell.

After the late news, I carried Aaron into the nursery and gently laid him in his crib. Then I pulled up a stool and sat staring at him through the wooden bars. "We'll beat this thing, Honey. I'll never let them take you away from me. Never. And I swear to you, somehow, I'll get you to love your bath. But like Scarlett always said, 'I'll think about it tomorrow.'"

Remembering my own fear of the blackness of a bedroom, I left the hall light on. It spilled a comforting glow into his nursery. Then I went to bed myself, exhausted from the stress and the intense frustration I'd felt all evening. Being exhausted didn't put me to sleep. I saw battles ahead. I felt the sheer panic of "them" snatching my son from my arms, calling me a *gay pervert* or a *filthy fairy*, not good enough to care for a child.

Around three in the morning, I did what any normal man would do in this situation. I slipped out of my bed, dragging my pillow, my sheets, and my blanket and headed for my living room couch, which I stripped of its seat cushions. Then I dragged the whole armful into Aaron's nursery. I laid the cushions next to his crib and bound them together with a tucked-in sheet. My pillow went down just opposite Aaron's sweet sleeping face. I lay down, pulled another sheet and a blanket over me, and then very carefully put my hand through the bars of the crib. Even though I don't think Aaron was awake, he took hold of my finger and held it.

## Ray

The nursery was out of focus in that bluish light that filters a room just before the sun rises over the city. It took me more than a moment to register where I was – on the floor next to Aaron's crib, lying on a disheveled mound of sofa cushions with my blankets and sheets twisted around me. That's where my groggy body lay shivering.

What jarred me awake was the sound of Aaron laughing and jabbering. He wasn't jabbering at me, though, and his exuberant giggling sounded as if he were in a private conversation with a very, very close and intimate friend. As if I weren't even in the room. *Hey, I've got a happy little guy!* But it seemed weird all the same.

His diaper was sopping wet and still warm from his early morning pee, so I quickly changed it, laying him on the floor because his sheets and blanket were soaked through. And instead of my usual morning routine of hot coffee and the *Chronicle*, it was now a new routine of heating the Gerber's baby food, washing diapers, and sitting with him as he jabbered away while perched on his potty. I patiently waited for his telltale grunt, but it never seemed to happen while he was sitting there – only after I pinned a dry diaper back on and was holding him as I tried to sweep the floor or clean up the sink. Then he would look at me, smile, and grunt.

The day buzzed by quickly. My attention was on Aaron as I answered the phone, cleaned the lobby, cleared a clogged-up garbage chute, did more grocery shopping, installed an electric outlet in Mrs. Mitchell's first-floor apartment, and tip-toed around our apartment while he took his afternoon nap. It seemed as though the sun had just come up when I realized the kitchen was darkening as the sun was setting.

I sacrificed my sacred hour of watching the evening news so I could have an early dinner with Aaron while we watched a new show on PBS for kids called *Sesame Street*. He was more interested in pouring his puréed mashed potatoes into his cup of milk, but I was totally amused by the show and excitedly phoned Pasek to tune into a kid's program that was almost as good as *Laugh-In*.

While Aaron spent part of our evening sitting on his potty with a ducky's head molded into the front of the seat cupping his tiny genitals, I quietly leaned over and started to fill the bathtub with warm water. This time I emptied half a bottle of bubble bath soap into the churning, running water.

I left Aaron sitting on his ducky potty as I went to see who was ringing my doorbell. It was one of my ex-lovers, Ray Williams, the realtor who found this 12-unit apartment house listing and performed some kind of real estate miracle loans so I could actually buy it.

When he was sober, Ray was a funny guy, quick to move, very bright, with a body of solid muscle and a belly so flat and hard you could bounce a dime off it. His cock was a lot bigger than mine, larger than most, and he was ready at any time to pounce on me, hungry for our bodies to grind together. Besides all that, he was an excellent cook, so why did we become "exes?"

After we'd dated for a few months, he moved in with me while I was remodeling a house on Crescent Avenue in Sausalito. I certainly didn't protest when he demanded to cook all the dinners, but his hard rule was that I absolutely had to stay out of the kitchen while he was wearing the apron and conjuring up a delicious meal. So, I'd sit in the living room, beginning at around 6 o'clock. He would make an occasional appearance in the doorway to see if I would like another drink. His glass always seemed to be full, and mine was usually sitting on the coffee table half-full. With each appearance, he would be a little giddier. Yes, a little drunker.

Dinner would finally be on the table by 9 or 10 o'clock. The table conversation was mostly one-sided with Ray chiding me for wolfing down my food as if I hadn't eaten in days. I was so hungry by the time we ate, it was almost painful, and as I gobbled my dinner, he would sit glaring at me with another drink in his hand, letting more and more bits of anger fly in my direction. His moving out after a few months was inevitable and a huge relief to me.

Thankfully during his "no cocktails until five" days, we were able to stay friends and managed to partner in a few real estate deals – he, the real estate broker, and I, the buyer or seller. I appreciated what he found for me in real estate, but I resented the way he would walk into my apartment as he did that night, out of the blue without a warning.

He immediately went into the kitchen and poured himself a drink, then returned to the bathroom where I was just about to lower Aaron into the Mt. Fuji of soap bubbles that filled the tub.

"I'm doing this as slowly as I can, Ray, because last night he almost killed both of us fighting to stay out of the tub. I don't know what the hell went wrong, but it scared the shit out of me."

"You had the water too hot," he said accusingly.

"Oh, for crying out loud, Ray. It was NOT too hot. It was something else."

I held Aaron's naked body up, his armpits resting on my hands, as his feet touched the bubbles. So far so good, I thought. I let him kick the bubbles, and at first, he giggled when they flew up into the air, but his kicking became more rapid. The bubbles blew away, exposing the water beneath his feet and he bent back into a rigid arch, screaming and crying, "No! No! No! No!"

"You gotta be hurting him, Bill!" I heard Ray roar.

"I'm NOT hurting him, Ray, but I have to get him in the bathtub to clean him! He has ta have a bath!" The old anger between us seemed to be boiling again.

In my frustration, I forcefully made Aaron sit in the water, quickly running a washcloth over him. His crying became a scream, and I pulled him out as fast as I could and wrapped a towel around him, then hugged him close to me. Both of us were dripping wet with flushed faces.

"Some dad! Reminds me of a lot of things my parents forced me to do. I still hate them for it." Ray poked at me as he twirled around heading to the kitchen to get another drink.

"Please get the hell out of here, Ray. I have my hands full without your drunken nagging." My stomach was tied in an angry knot. "Go home!"

He tossed his ice cubes from his empty glass at me. "See ya, *Daddy.* Don't call *me.* I'll call *you.*" He opened the door with a flourish then added, "If you're lucky," as he slammed the door behind him.

## Chapter 32
# God Bless the City Dump!

Before Aaron came into my life and became my family, I lived with two very close "family" members, Lillie Langtry (aka Lily) and Mammy Pleasant. The three of us slept in and on the same bed. That's how intimate we were. Mammy was housebound and never wanted to leave the apartment, but Lily loved to go wherever I went and was at the door the minute I rattled the car keys. She loved the Lincoln convertible, especially with the top down, where she could feel the gentle massage of air on her face, but riding in my 1949 Dodge pickup truck that I affectionately called "Old Rust" made her deliriously happy. Most of the time she rode in the cab with me, leaning against me to keep her balance. Occasionally, she'd jump into the trashy truck bed where she could bark at anyone or anything she saw, especially mutts like herself.

I don't think Aaron had ever seen a dog or cat before. They were just moving objects to him, like furry pieces of furniture on rollers. Maybe he saw them as he'd seen the other babies at the foster home. Distant in their cribs, noisy at times, crying and laughing, nothing to be afraid of, because he barely paid attention to Lily and Mammy. Ignoring them, he directed a steady stream of chatter at me, sometimes pulling on my shirt or sweater to make me bend down to look into his light blue eyes while he ranted on about god only knows what.

Both Lily's and Mammy's first reaction to Aaron was restrained curiosity. They spent a short time cautiously prowling around him, lingering on the scent of his body but never touching him. After deciding Aaron wasn't a danger to us, they retreated, still unsure, but very wary. Lily kept her distance, lying at the far end of the couch, her head cradled between her front paws, but her chocolate brown eyes lasered on Aaron's and my every movement.

Mammy curled her black body into a clam-shaped mound of fur at the sill of the French doors that opened onto our warm, sunny fire escape. Like candles in a window, her almond-shaped, acid-green eyes glowed as she stared at Aaron, prepared to run and hide if he ventured too close or to pounce on him as she did on little, gray mice. Never blinking.

Both animals climbed onto my bed that first night. When I couldn't sleep and moved into Aaron's room, they stayed in their spots on my bed. On the second night, they settled in, as usual, Lily sprawled at the bottom of the bed, and Mammy, in a ball of fur, claimed her spot near, but not on, the pillow next to mine. I left them there to go sleep on my loose couch pillows in Aaron's room. Just before dawn, when I tried to roll over on my couch pillows, I couldn't move my legs. Lily, sound asleep, covered them like a furry blanket, and a loud purring came from Mammy, who had chosen the top of my head as her warming pillow. There were now three of us yawning and stretching on the floor next to Aaron's crib.

Aaron awoke beaming, arms and legs thrashing in the air, giggling and blabbering to his invisible friend, and my cat and dog leaped to their feet to scurry out of the room. They were frightened by this exotic creature who was taking so much of me away from them.

I fed us all, changed Aaron's diaper, and cleaned the cat box. Then I picked Aaron up and carried him down the back staircase to the basement where Old Rust was garaged next to the Lincoln, ready for another trip to the city dump. Aaron sat in the cab with his teddy bear while I loaded up the truck, and Lily sniffed the cracked cement of the basement. Dusty piles of discarded clothing and broken chairs sat next to cardboard boxes full of things that smelled so bad I didn't want to investigate to see if anything was worth saving.

After cussing at Old Rust who wouldn't start, then pouring gas by the teaspoon into the carburetor, I could feel her shaking as her motor finally turned over. Poor Aaron whimpered in fright while Lily wagged her tail and barked. She jumped onto the seat, trying to nudge Aaron out of her chosen spot next to me. When I yelled at her to stop pestering him, she reluctantly retreated to her second-favorite place, next to the passenger door with an open window.

I can't remember any Disneyland ride more jarring or fun than driving that beat-up old Dodge as fast as possible through the city dump over the most cluttered, bumpiest dirt roads I've ever encountered. Aaron hung onto my neck so tightly I could barely breathe, and Lily kept slipping off the plastic seat cover, barking and yelping with joy as she jumped back up onto it.

I had just finished tossing the crap from my truck, cursing myself for not bringing gloves, when I looked at a pile of junk next to the pile I had just created and spotted it. It was cactus green and turned upside down so I could see scratch marks on the bottom from past summer trips to lakes or the seashore. I climbed over a chest of drawers to get to it and turned it over. What a treasure! The inside was clean, not marred or cracked. It was about four feet long, flat-bottomed, with a bit of rope hanging through a small, round hole in the bow. I heaved it into the bed of the truck, let Lily jump up next to it and headed home. Aaron was going to have his own little rowboat!

I couldn't get over my good luck finding a plaything for Aaron that was in such good shape and FREE! To hell with going right home! I drove down to Aquatic Park and parked outside the Maritime Museum. Lily jumped off the truck and ran circles around us as I led Aaron down to the sandy shore, with the plastic boat under my arm. I put the boat down on the sand and lifted Aaron into it. He was blabbering again, holding his teddy bear, sitting in something he sensed was his alone.

We stayed on the beach for an hour or so while I pulled the boat back and forth over the sand, gradually easing it into the small, breaking surf and then out a few more feet until it was surrounded by water. A scheme to end the bath trauma began to form in my mind.

That night after dinner, I brought the little green boat into the kitchen and scrubbed it inside and out. Then, while Aaron watched from his high chair, I poured warm water into the boat until two inches sat on the flat bottom. I floated a tiny, yellow rubber ducky on the water as I sat on the floor next to the boat, holding a plastic cup and washcloth. I soaked the washcloth and wrung it out a dozen times, letting the water fall onto the duck. Then I filled the cup and bombed the little duck with more water, all the time acting like a silly fool, thoroughly enjoying playing with the water and Ducky.

Old Rust parked across from the Wildflower on steep Greenwich Street

I emptied the boat, wiped it dry, took off Aaron's clothes, and gave him his teddy bear to hold while I sat him in the boat and wiped him down with the washcloth. He didn't cry. He didn't arch his back and scream, "No! No! No!"

I was receiving another wonderful gift from this little boy. He was teaching me patience. It would take longer than I would have liked, but dammit, I liked taking my time.

## Chapter 33
# Mama's Immoral Sons

Good thing that damn Princess phone had a 25-foot cord because I was on the thing most of the day and night – all the time I was wiping Aaron's dirty bottom and heating his Gerber's spinach, while I was shaving, and while I watched the news out of the corner of my eye. The phone hardly ever rested in its cradle.

Before Aaron, it was as if I were an actor playing a giddy playboy in a romantic comedy – sleeping in after cruising the bars for sex until two in the morning, eating pretzels and bananas at the crafts table on movie sets, or being pampered at a photo shoot in a new car parked on the Marina. Then ... *zappo* ... I'm co-starring in a domestic drama with a cat and dog circling around a new creature they have to live with, not even housebroken. The new role I play is overwhelmed with tenderness, surprise, responsibilities, a sense of urgency, and cold-in-the-belly fear.

And interwoven in all these push-pull must-do duties, while keeping my eye on Aaron, playing with him, hugging him, the phone kept jangling. Each time it rang, my blood ran a little cold, thinking it might be Mary Davidson calling to tell me that the cries of outrage were so loud now that I would have to pack up Aaron's clothes and his teddy bear so he could be put back into another foster home, a home with *straight* parents.

Aaron is awake and jabbering. I'm washing his bottom before breakfast.

The phone rings.

Pasek is breathless, reading me the *New York Times* review of *The Boys in the Band*. "Isn't it great, Bill? A play on Broadway about *us*! Finally! *Real guys!* Gay! Just like us! Takes place at a birthday party. Wouldn't ya just love to be in New York right now?" He gushed, "They get nude in *Hair*!"

I'm dishing up Gerber's oatmeal for Aaron, kibble for Lily, tuna for Mammy, and raisin bran for myself.

The phone rings.

"Hello, Billy. It's me, Aunt Ruth. How's my little daddy doin'? I talked to your dad last night, and Billy, I don't want you to think he doesn't like you just because you went off and adopted a kid. It's how the two of you think about the war. Know what I mean?"

I'm loading the washer in the basement with diapers and pee-soaked sheets.

The phone rings.

"Bill, it's Ann. I have a booking for you at 10:30 tomorrow morning. Macy's. Wear brown casuals and black socks. Blue or pink button-down. No whites."

*Oh, my god, I need a baby sitter*! The phone rings.

"Mr. Jones, this is Myrna Lee at the water company. Your April bill was not paid. Can you send us a check right away? You don't want to be delinquent for more than 45 days. There is a surcharge of $120 for turning the water back on."

"The check is in the mail."

I vacuum the lobby, halls, and steps. Ding-a-ling.

"Hi, Bill. It's Judd. When are we gonna meet the kid? Pasek says he's cute as hell."

I sweep the back steps and basement. The phone rings.

"Mr. Jones, your dog, Lily, is in my kitchen. I took her in because *you* let her roam around the neighborhood without a leash. Come over to my house and get her, and you'd better bring something with you to pick up what she left on my front walk."

Unlocking the front door to the lobby while carrying Aaron and pulling Lily on her leash, I hear the phone ring.

"Mr. William Jones?"

"Yes."

"This is Goodman's. Those kitchen tiles you ordered are in. When can you pick 'em up?"

I stack small bottles of Gerber's in the pantry and pick up Aaron's toys and Lily's mess of chewed-on shredded paper towels on the floor. The phone seems to get louder.

"Good morning, Bill. What's this I hear about you adopting a kid?"

I plant marigolds out front in a raised flowerbed and prune the rubber plant in the lobby.

"Bill, Ann again. The booking at Macy's has been changed to 11:30, okay?"

The goddamn garbage shoot gets clogged *again*, and I ram a bamboo pole down it to clear it.

"Mr. Jones, this is Mrs. Metcalfe in number one. I feel terrible about this, but I saw your darling white dog in the basement and she looked like she wanted to go out, so I opened the back door. I couldn't stop her and she ran down the street. I am so sorry!" I hear Mrs. Metcalfe sniffle.

Number five's sink isn't draining, so taking Aaron along with me, I use the plumber's snake and push a wad of hair down the pipes. The phone rings downstairs.

"Hi, Bill. It's me. I just got off the phone with Glenda, and you'll never guess what she did."

"What now, Jerry? Kill your kids because you're leavin' her?"

"Worse. She went to Byron and told anybody who would listen that the reason we're getting a divorce is because I'm a fag ... including Mother."

"That bitch!" I feel my heart beat a little faster. "First she won't let you even see Alison and Mark if Randles is around, and now this! Damn!"

"I haven't talked to Mom yet, Bill. Scared, I guess. Randles and I want to come over tonight. Is that okay with you?"

"Of course. Maybe we can call her together. I bet she's in a tizzy."

I felt a little relieved when I looked at the clock. It was almost six, and Mary Davidson hadn't phoned with more bad news. She was probably home by now. Out of the office. No news is good news!

Jerry and Randles opened my door with their key, and Randles, who hardly ever drank, fussed with a corkscrew and finally managed to open a bottle of wine they had brought. I was just finishing spooning Gerber's chocolate pudding into Aaron's mouth when Jerry handed me the phone and said, "Bill, please. You talk to her. I can't. I just can't bear to hear her cry, and you know she will!"

"Hey, maybe we can tell her that Glenda is looney, just makes things up, and wants everybody to think it's your fault, not her fault you left her. That she'd say *anything* to put all the blame on you and make herself look like a helpless victim. Mom'll believe that. When you two got married, she told me that Glenda was just like her mother ... nuts."

Randles lifted Aaron out of his high chair and gave him a little toss in the air, which brought out a squeal of delight from him. "I'll hold him while you two try to lie to your mother. Good luck!"

"Hello, Mama, how you doin'?"

"What do you think? How do you think I'm doing after what you two are puttin' me through? I'm rotten. Rotten because of you two boys!" I could hear her trying to stifle her anger and rush of self-pity tears.

"Mama, don't cry, Mama. Jerry's here, and he is so sorry that Glenda told you that big ..."

"Glenda told the whole damn town! She told 'em that Pearl's two sons, both of 'em, are HOMOS!" She was choking with rage. "Stanley Pierra came into the bar today and bought everybody a drink, and then stood there and yelled out, 'Here's to Pearl's two fruitcake sons!' Why the hell did you do this to me? Do I deserve this kinda thing? After all I've done for you!"

"Mama, please."

"You oughta be ashamed of yourself, Bill Jones!"

"Mama, I'm just trying to help Jerry here. You shouldn't listen to Glenda. She's ..."

"She told me that you went out and adopted a kid. A boy. Is that *true*? If that is true, Bill Jones ...," she controlled herself enough to empathize every word, "you are *immoral* and should be thrown in jail for doin' something like that! It's wrong, wrong, wrong, and you are not my son anymore! It's *immoral!*"

Jerry saw my face go white and took the phone from my hand.

"Hello, Mama. It's Jerry ... Mother?" He slowly put the phone on its cradle with a gentle click. "She hung up on me." I watched as Randles, still carrying Aaron, walked over and stood behind Jerry and gently stroked his neck and shoulder.

What might happen next? Should we just keep cool and wait for her to calm down, or should one of us write her a letter ... or phone her after a few days or weeks? If we asked our cousin Ramona, she could talk to Mother and help her through this, but buried deep under a pile of baggage in our secret closet, we had no one on our side to help Mother calm down

We were so shaken up, none of us could think. We stood together in the lobby like three silent mannequins unable to speak or think. We gave each other lots of hugs to go with the "good nights" and "I love you." Then Jerry and Randles walked out to their car, still stunned and dismayed.

I had something else on my mind. Another hurdle to leap. I brought out the plastic boat and put it on the kitchen floor. Then I poured a couple of saucepans full of warm water into it. I took off Aaron's clothes and let him hold his teddy bear. I flipped off my shoes and socks, took off my khakis, and stepped into the boat, cooing and giggling as I stomped on the water, splashing it all over the floor, the cabinets, the stove, the refrigerator, everywhere. Even a little on Aaron.

Next, I got out and knelt by the boat so I could take a plastic tumbler and pour water over the yellow ducky, never looking at Aaron, just pretending to enjoy the playtime. I felt his hand on my arm, moving with it as I dumped the water on the rubber ducky over and over. I put the tumbler in Aaron's hand, and he knelt down beside me, dipped it into the water, and splashed it against the duck, laughing, squealing with sheer joy.

We played with the water, bombing the poor ducky for a long time until Aaron leaned in and patted the water with the palms of his hands. I patted the water, too, for a while, then stepped back into the boat, jogging in it, splashing the water again. I took Aaron by both his hands and lifted him up and over the side of the boat, dangling his bare feet just above the surface of the water. He started to take strides in the air as if he were running, every once in a while touching the water, and giggling all the time.

He seemed to reach down with his feet, wanting to step into the water. I very slowly lowered him until he touched the bottom of his green boat, letting him kick the water and splash it with all his might. He was empowered, and as long as he was standing, kicking, jogging, he felt no fear. It wasn't until two nights later, on Friday, our first week anniversary, that he finally relaxed and sat down inside his boat to play with the ducky as he poured water on it over and over.

After I dried him off, powered his bottom, and pinned a fresh diaper on him, I put him in his Dr. Dentons. We cuddled on the couch while I read a book to him that had one word on each page with an illustration. "Dog. Cat. Food. Bed. House. Car. Mama. Daddy. Tree. Flower." I turned the page back to Daddy. I pointed at the word and said "Daddy." Then I pointed at myself and said it again. I pointed at Aaron and said, "Aaron." This pointing and saying Daddy and Aaron went on until I saw his eyes begin to blink and close. By that time, Lily had crept slowly up to be near us and rest her head on Aaron's feet.

After I tucked Aaron in his crib and kissed him goodnight, I tiptoed out to the kitchen and started to wipe up the wet floor. Bending over on my hands and knees, with soggy bath towels thrown in the boat, and my damp shirt and boxer shorts clinging to me, all I could think of was one word.

*Immoral.*

The phone rang, but I just ignored it.

## Chapter 34
# Wash Your Troubles Away

For the next five or six nights, we played in the water in the little plastic boat in the middle of the kitchen floor. One night, it had very little water but a lot of floating toys besides the yellow rubber ducky. The next night, it held the same toys and warm water up to his chest. The third was a bubble bath, and on the fourth, we blew bubbles while he sat in his boat, popping them in midair. He loved scooping up handfuls of soap bubbles and throwing them all over the kitchen floor. It was worth all the mopping up I had to do later to hear him squeal with delight, laugh as he spanked the water, and squirm happily as I wiped him down with a warm towel.

Tiny soft brown hairs were beginning to sprout over his shaved head, and I realized that I'd have to stock up on Johnson's Baby Shampoo soon.

After his bath, I put him in clean diapers and his Dr. Dentons. Next, it was our ritual to cuddle on the sofa with Lily and Mammy while we turned pages of books or magazines. I would point to a photo or drawing and say "motorcycle" or "table" or "lady" to try to get him to say it back to me. It always ended, as I kissed him goodnight in his crib, with my touching his chest and saying, "Aaron." Then I would put his hand on my chest and say, "Daddy."

The second week passed pretty much as the first, except more and more of my friends, both gay and straight, just "happened" to be in the neighborhood and dropped in on us. The minute they sat down, Aaron was tugging at them to lift him up on their laps or dragging Lily by her collar over to them so she could get petted. He would put his toys around their feet or stand in front of them, staring into their eyes as he hugged his teddy bear, speaking in his own language, "La-la, ga-ga, de-de, la-la," and expecting us to understand exactly what he was jabbering about.

Visitors who entered with smiles, trying to deceive me and cover up their skeptical and wary thoughts about this strange new relationship, left, hearts aflutter, with smiles that only infatuation can cause. Aaron cast the same magic on everyone he met. One by one, the friends who came under his spell fell in love with him, but some of my closest friends were refusing to associate with me because, to a lesser degree than my mother, they thought a gay man should not be raising a child. One close friend, Michael Vincent, even wrote me a letter saying that was how he felt.

"Hi, Bill. It's Mary. Mary Davidson."

I felt a chill flash through my body. Was this the phone call that would tear him away from me?

"Hi, Mary." I quickly added, "Everything's *super* here, Mary. He's taking baths every night now."

"That's wonderful, Bill. That *is* such good news. I'll be sure to tell Dorothy. She'll love hearing it. Anything else?"

"He's still on Gerber's, Mary. I've put solid food in his mouth, but he doesn't seem to understand how to chew it. Last night I put a little piece of bread in and moved his jaw up and down, but he won't do it on his own … yet."

"Don't feel pressured to bring him up to his age level, Bill. Just relax and he'll grow into it. What he needs now is to know you love him. The rest will take care of itself."

"Okay." I waited for the other shoe to drop.

"Just wanted to check in, Bill. If you have any *real* problems, don't hesitate to call me." There was a pause. "By the way, the complaint that was filed on the first day you had him, hasn't come up again, but we're afraid if the word gets out, we might be in deep doodoo. Ya know, Dorothy's a good Irish Catholic, but her biggest fear right now is that the adoption agency will have bricks thrown through the window by outraged *Catholic* women!"

"Good grief, Mary."

Playing in his boat on the roof of the Wildflower Apts.

"So, if the newspapers ... or any reporters come around, *don't* tell them what we're doing. Tell your friends *not* to talk about it. I know that's asking a lot, but until the adoption is finalized, and that will take about nine months more, it's terribly important to keep it out of the news. We can handle any personal complaints here at the agency. Okay, Bill?"

"Sure. Of course. Thanks. Thanks, Mary."

"Bill, we have every reason to believe that you and Aaron will be a legal family soon, and when that happens, no one will have the right to take him away from you ... ever."

"Unless I screw up as a parent."

"Right, but that'll never happen. I'll give you a call in a couple of weeks just to see if you need anything from us, Bill. Relax! And give Aaron a big hug and a kiss for me. Bye-bye."

That night after his supper and a few uneventful minutes of Aaron's sitting on his ducky potty, I sat him in his empty boat and pushed it slowly from the kitchen into the bathroom. He stood beside me, naked, holding his rubber ducky, while I put the boat in the bathtub. To my relief, it just fit inside with a few inches to spare. I lifted him into it and turned on the faucets so that just a tickle came to cover the bottom with warm water. He sat there as I handed him toy after toy, until he was surrounded. Then I turned the water on so that it poured in a little faster, raising the toys higher around his body.

We both lifted toys and dropped them in the tub, causing the other toys to bob up and down around him. He giggled and stood up, stomping and splashing, then sat down as if he were falling, causing the water and toys to go flying up over the side of the tub. He was happy. He was in a bathtub. He was taking a bath, and I was William, the Conquering Crusader.

Taking a bath in his green boat in the bathtub

## Chapter 35

# Assassination

The faint glow of dawn was just filling the nursery when the Princess phone next to me rang and shocked me out of troubled sleep. I recognized Pasek catching his breath.

"Bill ... Oh, my God. It's terrible ... terrible! I've been crying all night. You don't have the news turned on, do you?" Pasek's voice was raspy. "I know you need your sleep, so I waited to call you."

"Pasek, what's happened?" Pasek was always the silly and happy one, but it sounded like he was sick or hurt.

"Robert Kennedy was shot last night ... in a kitchen ... of some damn hotel in LA, and he's dying ... no ... dead." He blew his nose so hard that I knew he was crying.

By now I had gotten up from my bed on the nursery floor and had walked out into the kitchen, dragging the phone cord behind me, shivering in my boxers and shaking from Pasek's news.

I lit the gas under the coffeepot and then slowly opened the pantry door to look at the back side of it, my secret pinup space of the most sexually attractive men in the world to me. All movie stars except one. Pasek and I kept talking. He calmed down eventually and mused that the baby shower would not be called off because of this, but Dennis and David's fun decorations would be taken down, and Pasek would replace them with bouquets of flowers.

As we were talking, I was looking at the faces of men I dreamed of having next to me on my pillow. Paul Newman, Humphrey Bogart, Spencer Tracy,

Robert Walker, Montgomery Clift, Lew Ayres, Dana Andrews, Gene Kelly. It wasn't their bodies that stirred my soul and groin. It was the tenderness in their eyes.

Thumbtacked in the very center, surrounded by these stars, was an exquisite close-up of Robert Kennedy's face on the latest *Life* magazine cover. His eyes were filled with so much sadness, probably from his brother's assassination, but I also saw intelligence, compassion, and strength. He was more beautiful than any of the actors surrounding him. It brought tears to my eyes.

*    *    *    *    *

Pasek shared a large flat in a brick building on the corner of Hyde and Bay Street with another gay man, older than Pasek and me, but just as liberal. The traffic on Bay and the clanking of the cable cars on Hyde forced them to keep the French doors in the arched windows closed most of the time. Pasek had filled every available vase and coffee can with flowers that he later told me he had swiped from flower boxes in the neighborhood. Their fragrance filtered through every room, including the back porch overlooking the Bay and Fisherman's Wharf.

I climbed the stairs, holding Aaron with one arm and a paper bag full of clean diapers in the other hand.

"Bill, I think I should tell you something. First you should know that Michael and Bob love you as much as I do," he assured, "but they ... they are having a very difficult time trying to understand this ... this adoption thing."

"I know. Got a note from Michael."

"It has *never*, in the history of the world, crossed *anyone's* mind that a homosexual would ever even *think* about adopting a kid. Much less you, Mr. *Playboy*."

"I know, Pasek. I know. I can see it in people's eyes. They look at me like I've just decided to be a Buddhist monk or a brain surgeon, but no one ever comes out and says anything or asks me about it. It's the pink elephant in the middle of the room that no one wants to acknowledge."

Pasek squeezed my hand.

"Michael has this propriety thing about kids, Bill. He would *never* want one of his own, but he's of the old school, the old British school where the child *has* to have both a mother and a father, and *never* be raised by a stranger. And certainly not a gay male stranger." He hesitated, swallowed hard, and then went on. "We've talked a lot on the phone the past two weeks, and Michael thinks the gay life, your gay life, *our* gay life, will make Aaron … gay … and that's a fate worse than death to him. Go figure."

"Do you think Aaron will turn gay because of us, Pasek? To be honest with you, I've had the same thoughts. I get so scared thinking about it. I'd never forgive myself if he grows up to be gay … because of us. I'd rather die."

"First of all, that just ain't gonna happen, and if it does, so what? I'm glad you came early. Here. He handed me a stack of paper plates and napkins to put on the buffet table.

Gary Fusfeld and Ray Williams arrived together, lugging huge trays of cheese, sourdough bread, cold cuts, tiny sandwiches, chips, and pickles.

We had just finished lighting the last candle when the doorbell began ringing, and one by one, friends climbed the stairs, looking up at us smiling, each with a wrapped gift in their hands, except Mona who was struggling to make it, carrying a full, heavy case of Gerber's baby food.

Pasek and I met everyone at the top of the stairs, and I had been so occupied with greeting them that I had forgotten about Aaron until I heard him laughing and jabbering his *la-la* and *ga-ga* to a guest. I turned around to see one of our lesbian friends pick him up, and after hugging him, handing him over to her lover, who also hugged him. She handed him over to Dennis, and just as he was about to hand him over to someone else, the doorbell rang for the last time. I pivoted to see Michael Vincent and Bob Lanci coming up the stairs, but not looking at us.

When they reached the top, we all hugged. With serious looks, they handed me two small blue boxes from Tiffany's. One held a silver bell and the other a silver spoon. "The bell is for the little one to ring when he gets hungry," Michael explained.

"And the spoon's for him to eat what you dish out," Bob added.

I looked away from these expensive gifts to see Aaron being swooped up by one of the guests and tossed like a trapeze artist to another friend. Aaron was squealing in delight, and I didn't think he could get hurt, so I didn't stop them. When we all sat down, Aaron took turns climbing onto laps to touch faces or pat heads, leaving a trail of smitten faces.

Pasek rang the silver bell that Michael had given Aaron. "Bill's Aunt Ruth baked us a wonderful chocolate cake and sent it over. We're about to serve it with coffee, but before we do that, I think we would all like to hear a little about this adoption from Bill, don't you?"

There was a smattering of applause. I had been holding Aaron and put him down to run over to crawl up onto my brother's lap, then stood and looked at all my friends' faces. They were silent and intently looking back at me. Some looked as if they would rather be anywhere else but there.

"You're probably wondering about what's happening … me wanting to be a daddy. Well, so am I. Never thought it could actually happen. Anyone who really knows me like my brother, Jerry, isn't though. Guess you want an explanation, and I don't blame you."

All eyes were on me, and in bits and pieces, I tried to tell them all the crazy things I had thought of, and done, for the past 30 years … starting with the satisfaction I felt taking my mother's place raising my little brother, … about wishing I could be a father to some of the kids I was teaching in the fourth grade … about the nuns chasing me with broomsticks, and the pregnant girl who wanted me to take her baby. I even told them about my going to the Sexual Freedom parties in Berkeley so I could eventually have a baby the usual way. That got a lot of laughs.

I wondered if I should stop or tell the whole story. I was beginning to feel uncomfortable talking about myself so much, but I knew I had to finish.

"Years later, my dear friend Cora Lee, who's here today, offered to bear me a child. She believed I'd be a good daddy. That is, she's smarter than me and knew I could handle a toddler or older child, but who would take care of it as an infant? I proposed that my mother would probably do it for me, but after Cora Lee met my mother, the deal was off. Definitely off."

My brother Jerry began to snicker and my story drew some smiles, but I looked around the room and realized I had one more extremely important thing I had to face. Important for my survival.

"We're all still grieving over Robert Kennedy's death … and we hurt … at the sudden shock. I know a bunch of us have done a lot of crying. It's painful for us … everybody."

No one was smiling anymore.

"It made me think." I paused and looked at the sober faces in the room. "There's more than one kind of assassination. You can take a gun, and like a coward, shoot another human being. He drops dead." A feeling of sadness swept through the room.

"But there's another kind of assassination. One that's just as deadly. Friends can shoot down another friend's most cherished dream and kill it. Yeah, kill it. *You* have the power to assassinate a dream. Or – you have the power to support your friend's dream, and it will come true. It'll live." I looked into every eye and saw a few welling up with tears.

"I am asking each and every one of you – please, please do not assassinate my dream. Please give me ... and Aaron a chance. We need every one of you to make this happen. It can't happen without you."

At that instant, my own eyes welled up, but I saw through the blur that Aaron was now sitting on Michael Vincent's lap.

## Chapter 36
# Mame and the Grape Stem

Hey there, Mama Bill, I bet you don't remember the tickets we bought last November, do you?"

"*Mame*! Angela Lansbury! Oh, my god, Pasek. I did forget. Do you have the tickets?"

"Scotch-taped to the inside of my refrigerator door. You owe me $22."

"When are they for?"

"Saturday. Eight o'clock at the Curran."

"I've got to get a sitter!"

"Don't ask *me*. I'm busy that night."

"OK, I'll find someone. Maybe Michael and Bob."

"Don't push your luck with that, Billy Boy. Pick you up round 7:30. Okay?"

\* \* \* \* \*

Dennis Redmond had offered to sit for me at the baby shower, so I sheepishly asked him if the offer was still good. To my surprise, he said he'd love to spend the evening reading fairy tales to Aaron. I had Aaron fed, bathed, and in his jammies by the time Dennis showed up at seven.

I took one last glance at Dennis and Aaron on the sofa before I went out the door to get into Pasek's Volkswagen. How beautiful they were! I wanted nothing more than to tear up my ticket and run back to snuggle with the two of them. Pasek honked his horn impatiently, so I hurried out to his car, flopped in beside him, and slammed the door.

"What's *that* all about?"

"You know. Unrequited love. Dennis. I dream of the three of us together. Forever."

"Hopeless dreamer!"

Just before the curtain went up, I squeezed into a phone booth and called home to see if Aaron had gone to bed without a fuss. Dennis assured me, "Everything is hunky-dory. Hey, enjoy the show. We're doin' just fine. He hasn't stopped talking since you left. He can even out-talk *me!*"

Pasek and I melted into our seats on the balcony as the curtain went up on a street in New York City. It's 1928. Then magically, Mame's living room appears and Mame makes her grand entrance, gliding down a curved staircase. She is flamboyant, classy, dressed to the nines, and the center of attention. I project. I am Mame.

Mame's best friend, Vera Charles, a little tipsy, sweeps in on the scene, and it's obvious that they are old friends. Bosom buddies. Pasek nudges me with his elbow. He's projecting. He is Vera Charles. Then Agnes Gooch and little Patrick are ushered into Mame's wild, noisy cocktail party, filled with arty people who like to have as much fun as Mame. Agnes turns the orphaned child, Patrick, over to Mame to raise.

At the end of the first act, the foxhunt at Peckerwood had us bent over laughing, but even before the curtain fell and the house lights came up, I was out of my seat, racing for the phone booth.

Dennis tried to assure me. "Go back to your seat, Bill. Really. I know it's a little late, but we just finished the rocky road you had in the freezer, and he isn't sleepy at all. I'll try to get him back into his crib, but I can't stand it when he cries, so I keep bringing him back out here."

"Dennis, it's 9:30, and he should be in his crib asleep."

"Hey, guess what? I just looked over and he's asleep on the sofa with his head on Lily's belly. I'm not going to try to move him. He's out of it, quiet at last, so have a good time. See ya later."

The curtain rises for the second and final act. My heart has either stopped beating or is beating so fast I can't feel it. I am Mame. Aaron is Patrick. Pasek is Vera Charles, and we are bringing a child into our chaotic world of gay men who *love* to party. I am sitting in my seat, but feel I am the soul of Mame coming to life on the stage.

Then, distressed upon realizing Patrick hasn't turned out the way she thought he would, Mame sings "If He Walked into My Life," a song about her anguished self-doubts raising Patrick, questioning the very things I am questioning about myself. As I listen to the lyrics, I'm moved to ask:

Would I guide him with a strong hand or be too lenient? Would I be too permissive or too strict? Would I force Aaron to conform to my wishes or let him develop on his own terms?

I hear Pasek sniffle, and I know he's hearing the lyrics through my ears.

*Would my lifestyle be too wild? Would I let him have a normal childhood?*

I tap Pasek on the arm and he hands me a Kleenex.

*Would there be too many uncles and too many aunts in and out of our lives and not enough quiet family time? What family – his grandparents who abandoned me and couldn't bring themselves to call him their grandson?*

We blow our noses at the same time, almost drowning out Mame's last question, the very question I keep asking myself to this day.

*What if I fuck this up? What if he is fucked up by me? There won't be any second chances! My life with my precious son is NOT a rehearsal!*

Pasek wipes a tear running down his cheek and hands me several more tissues.

*     *     *     *     *

When I opened my front door, the lights were still on, but Dennis and Aaron weren't in the living room as I had expected. I tiptoed into the nursery, and Aaron was in his crib with Teddy in his arms and Snoopy as his pillow. The mattress that I had been sleeping on next to his crib was gone. I turned off the lights in the kitchen and living room, brushed my teeth, and made my way over to my bed where Dennis sprawled under the covers.

"Hi, Daddy Bill. Get undressed and come to bed. Close your damn bedroom door and lock it. Nobody's going to accuse *us* of having an orgy in his nursery!"

It was comforting to have Dennis's arm across my chest and to hear his deep breathing turn to a snore as quiet as a cat's purr, but it didn't help me sleep. I kept thinking of my little boy. *Am I doing the right thing? Will he grow up to be the kind of man I hope he'll be? I love him and can't give him back. Am*

*I being selfish? Will he turn gay because I am? Will he hate me later on? If he ever hates me, I'd want to die."*

My atheist heart then prayed, "Dear god. Help me."

The next morning, I heard Aaron giggling and talking to his imaginary friend, so I got up, leaving Dennis in a fetal position, wrapped in rumpled sheets. I fixed oatmeal for our breakfast since Aaron still hadn't learned to chew solid food and placed a bowl of bananas, oranges, and white grapes on the table.

Dennis came out of my bedroom fully dressed and was chatting away, mostly about a project he had been commissioned to do for a new casino being built in Las Vegas, when Aaron started flailing his arms and gasping for air, his eyes wide with terror. From that moment on everything was in slow motion. I floated to his side and lifted him out of his high chair, seeing a few grapes rolling around on his highchair tray.

"Oh, god, Dennis, he's choking on the stems!"

Aaron was pulling on my bathrobe, his eyes wide and overflowing with tears, looking at me for help. I tried squeezing him to my chest as violently as I could without hurting him, to make him cough the stems out, but it didn't work. My heart almost stopped beating.

I held him as tight as I could with my left arm, leaning him back, then put my index finger of my right hand in his mouth, pushing down as far as I could. He was gagging. I can still feel the warm, wet softness inside his throat. My finger touched the hard stem, and I went farther down past the stem until I could finally press it against the lining of his throat. Pressing and slowly pulling the stem toward the roof of his mouth took seconds that seemed never to end.

I finished extracting the stem from his mouth, and he reached up and threw his arms around my neck, and with desperate hugs, rubbed his tear-soaked face on both my cheeks. My face was flushed, and it took me several minutes to calm down before I could speak. I kept saying, "It's all gone now, Honey. You're okay. You're okay. Daddy's here. Daddy's here. Daddy's here."

Dennis looked stunned, and for quite a while he was speechless.

I got Aaron to drink some water, but he didn't want the rest of his breakfast. I dressed, and with Aaron sitting on my lap, drove Dennis to his studio. I decided to take the morning off and just spend it with Aaron and Lily.

I drove Old Rust out to the beach by the Cliff House, and we played in the sand building a fort until Lily ran through it. It was lunchtime when we returned to the apartment building, and Aaron seemed to have forgotten the trauma of our breakfast. He was hungry, so I reheated the oatmeal and scrambled an egg for him to swish around in his mouth before he swallowed it.

After lunch, I carried Aaron, some of his toys, and a bucket of paint with a paintbrush up to Mrs. Metcalfe's kitchen, finished painting the ceiling, then cleaned up and went downstairs to fix dinner. Mrs. Metcalfe asked me if I would mind if Lily spent an afternoon or evening with her, and I was more than happy to have Lily provide company for this delightful old lady since I had my hands full taking care of a toddler and a crumbling old tub of a building, ready to sink like the *Titanic*, taking us down with it.

That evening, I cooked two dinners, one you could chew and one you could swallow without chewing; Gerber's ground beef and mashed potatoes for Aaron and a Swanson meatloaf dinner for me. Aaron was on the kitchen floor playing with Lily. I picked him up and slipped him down onto his highchair seat. The television was droning on as usual about the upcoming Democratic convention in Chicago and how many square miles of the jungle we had destroyed in Vietnam with Agent Orange. It was during the weather report that Aaron took his spoon and started to bang it on his tray.

"What's up, Honey?"

He banged it again. Then he reached out to me with both arms.

"Are you finished, Honey? Wanna get down?"

I lifted him down and handed him his cup of milk. He pushed it away and came over to me and lay his head down on my lap.

"Hey, I'm not finished eating my dinner, Aaron. Are you sleepy?"

He crawled up onto my lap and looked up at me. He then patted my cheeks very gently with both his hands. Still looking at me with his intense, light blue eyes, he said, in the most casual way, one word.

It was a word I was longing to hear, born to hear. All the years of loneliness and feeling isolated vanished. It was a word I could give my life for. It was the word that pulled the aimless shambles of my useless life into a flaming ball as bright as the sun, and it wasn't the "love" word I wanted Dennis to say.

I'll cherish that moment – that word – as long as I live.

"Daddy."

L to R, TOP: Dennis, Jerry's daughter, Alison, Jerry, Randles; BOTTOM: me, Jerry's son, Mark, and Aaron.

## Chapter 37
# Is Wanting a Lover Too Much to Ask?

I met the Redmond twins, David and Dennis, at a garden party in Marin about six months before Aaron came into my life. They were identical, thick blond hair, styled and combed the same way. Their voices were indistinguishable. They were blue-eyed, with tanned, masculine faces, and dressed *casually chic*. Their Polo shirts differed, one pink and the other rust. David wore white tennis shoes, and Dennis wore tan ones. One of them handed me their business card that read Redmond Designs, Grant Avenue. I still could not tell which was Dennis and which was David by the time the party ended, but I thought they both were hot.

"Good morning. Redmond Designs."

"Oh, hi. My name's Bill Jones, and you gave me your card ..."

"I think you want to talk to my brother."

"Hello. What can I do for you?"

It sounded like the same person, and it disturbed me to think one of them might be putting me on.

"You can tell me which one I'm talking to."

"Dennis."

"Hi, Dennis, remember me? My name's Bill, and you gave me your card."

"No, I think David gave it to you."

"Whatever."

"Did he give it to you at Sutter's Mill? He hands 'em out there like Halloween candy."

"No. Yesterday at Frank Hamilton's. You know. Frank and Mason. On the lagoon in Belvedere."

"Oh, yeah. I think that was me. Are you the Macy's model?"

"Yeah." I felt that tingle in my chest remembering how sexy they both were, and it didn't matter which one gave me the card. I wanted to get skin to skin with either of them. "We talked about your studio on Grant, and I'd like to see it sometime. If that's okay with you."

"Sure. Whatcha doin' for lunch? Wanna join us?"

I had a booking at Macy's with their photographers that afternoon, so I put on my best *casual chic* and drove Old Rust down to Sutter and Grant, the corner Redmond's three-storied Art Nouveau building anchored, just a block away from the arch on Grant Avenue that defined the beginning of Chinatown. The small building was old, stately, and the elevator rickety, but it had floor-to-ceiling windows that flooded the Redmond studio with light, both sunlight and light at night, from the lamppost on the corner.

I pushed the elevator door open and stepped out into a room filled with magic. One of the walls supported a 20-foot-long mural of gold rush miners dancing wildly with each other in a saloon. It was being painted boldly, cartoonish, on weathered barnsiding boards. Dennis stood on a six-foot ladder, paintbrush and bucket in hand.

"Hi, Bill. I'll be down in justa minute. David, pour him a drink. This is gonna hang over the bar at Sutter's Mill on Kearny. What d'ya think?"

I looked up at the immense project and then down to Dennis's pressed khakis snugly stretched over his legs and crotch.

"Wow! Terrific, Dennis!"

The studio floors were worn, dark walnut planks, uneven, and glowing with wax applied hundreds of times over the years. Dennis's drawing table was in the corner where the two streets crossed below. Ten-foot windows on either side of his drawing table framed a cityscape of honking cars below and blue skies filled with drifting clouds above.

David's zone was near the elevator with two photographers' floodlights, one on either side of his stool, dispensing even white light that covered his large drawing table. On the wall behind him were black-and-white sketches of appliances, mixers, vacuum cleaners, knife sets, vases, stacks of towels and sheets – all ready for the Macy's ads in the *Chronicle* and *Examiner*.

The third artist who shared their studio was an architect, Judd Wirz. All three sat facing the middle of the room, where a round table was the focal point of their workplace. The table was top-heavy with vodka, gin, whiskey bottles, tonics, bowls of cut lime, beer bottles in a tray of ice, and glasses – highball, wine, tumblers. All just a short walk from their drawing tables. Drinking was a shared priority.

It took several weeks of intense staring before I could tell one from the other and even longer to distinguish David's voice on the phone from Dennis's. The only difference was that David was self-absorbed and matter of fact. Dennis more intimate and interested in what you had to say. Soon enough, I began to see it was Dennis whom I wanted.

After many lunches, cocktails, and dinners, one night I finally took advantage of Dennis's drinking me under the table. I drove him home to his apartment on Sacramento Street and invited myself in for a nightcap.

Before he had a chance to turn on the lights, I closed his front door and pulled him toward me. I could taste the liquor on his tongue, but it was his eager kiss that intoxicated me. I pulled away from him, just far enough so I could loosen his belt and unzip his fly while still kissing him. I felt his hands unbuckle my belt, undo the button, and slowly as if to tease me, unzip my fly.

It didn't matter if this happened because we were loaded or if we were just horny late at night. What mattered was that he seemed to want me and my swelling cock, as much as I wanted him. We unbuttoned our shirts so our chests could press together, skin to skin, all the while tasting each other's saliva. He led me over onto his leather couch in the bay window. We tugged each other's pants down and over our shoes, coming back up to embrace again, kissing as we explored each other's chest, butts, thighs, groins, finally cupping each other's balls, stroking them gently.

Dennis slid off the couch and onto the carpeted floor, pulling me down on top of him. He tugged at the elastic of my Jockey shorts until they slipped down below my waist, and I pulled his down, too. Except for our shirts and shoes, we were pressing our bodies together so as much skin could touch as possible. Neither of us spoke. We slowly moved our bodies, pressing, releasing, pressing again, until the slow dance became rapid thrusts. We were panting now, and Dennis forced his breath to fill my lungs. I returned the same breath into his lungs until we felt dizzy because no oxygen remained. We separated for the first time, both gasping for air.

I had longed for a night alone with Dennis in my arms for such a long time. It was finally happening, and it was more wonderful than I had dreamed it could be because I felt that ingredient that separates *having sex* from *making love*. I didn't dare say the L-word, and down deep, I was sad because I knew Dennis would probably never whisper that word to me. Maybe to some other guy, but not to me. Why does that one word thrill us? Why do men die for it? Why is that one word so crucial for our very existence? I can hardly define it. It has so many meanings. Love.

I drove him to his studio the next morning after he had fixed ham and eggs for us. As soon as we got into Old Rust, I said, "Last night was great, Dennis. Really, really great." I waited, hoping he'd agree. But he was silent, and I bit my tongue.

He was leafing through the morning paper quickly, looking for the Macy's ad with David's drawings in it. "Yeah. Oh, here it is. Full page."

"How 'bout dinner?"

"Can't tonight."

"Lunch tomorrow?"

"Didn't I tell you Tucker is coming back to stay for a week?"

"Tucker?"

"I've been up front with you, Bill, right from the start. I told you about Tucker when we first met at Frank and Mason's. Tucker and I have an understanding. He's my lover, even though he lives in New York. You just weren't listening."

"Tucker?"

My happy morning quickly dissolved with the depressing thought that Tucker, whoever that was, would be the one Dennis would whisper, "I love you" to. Not me. Not ever. It was fuckin' depressing.

## Chapter 38

# Mona

We were paired off as a couple in a commercial. Not as the principals, just "extras" as usual. They lined us up on a ramp leading to the Golden Gate Bridge in shiny new 1965 Fords, all the models in every available color. That day was outstanding for two reasons. One is that I met Mona, the third Ramona in my life who bowled me over with her wit and charm. The other is that it was the only time in the history of the Golden Gate Bridge that traffic was halted at both ends for filming a commercial while we drove in a single line across it. It had to be in one take, so dozens of cameras were stationed on both sides, attached to cables and hanging from the towers. I drove and Mona laughed at her own wit. It was the beginning of a long and eventful friendship.

She promoted herself constantly, giving our agent little gifts. "It's a silver whistle from Shreve, Ann. If you need me, just whistle." On location, she buttered up the assistant directors and quite often was picked from dozens of extras to do "special business" (when the camera focuses on the action of an extra, usually connecting to the "star").

I owed a lot to her for keeping me aware of any new movie to be shot in the Bay Area, and for suggesting me as her partner for anything "special."

But the thing, besides her beauty and style that made me adore her, was the laughter, uncontrolled laughter that we fostered in each other. Her wit was her real beauty to me. We spent hours on the phone talking and laughing.

But Mona deballed every man in her life, and I was constantly on guard, fearing I would be one of them. She had many affairs, using the men as long as they still paid her bills and were able to service her – until a better one came in sight. She married Calvin Scott because he knocked her up after a high school football game in the back seat of a Nash sedan. Then she dropped out of high school when it became a joke around school that she was getting fat and would *not* be the homecoming queen.

She tolerated Calvin as long as he catered to her every whim and took over as nursemaid to the baby boy born nine months to the day after he'd "borrowed" his mother's Nash. Mona would rather be out dancing, jitterbugging to Tommy Dorsey, than cuddling a crying infant with wet diapers who shut up only when she let him suck the milk out of her breasts. She quickly bored of Calvin, his overbearing mother, and his poor-paying job at a Texaco station.

By the time Little Cal was one year old, Mona was pacing the floor like a caged tiger, desperate to get out of their third-floor apartment and spread her wings to fly away to parties, travel, and new men. She felt imprisoned in her marriage and motherhood. Even though she was a knockout beauty with a perky face and tits, and loved fucking men, she was terrified that the only way she could make money was to sell her package to men she couldn't choose.

She wasn't formally educated, a high school dropout, but she was bright, able to take advantage of any situation with cunning. Besides her glamorous good looks, she had a fabulous, quick sense of humor. Her laugh was infectious, and laughing at her jokes was a trap you were only too glad to fall into.

When an unexpected death opened the cage door for Mona, she and Little Cal escaped in a flash for Los Angeles where she was sure Paramount or MGM had a trailer in a back lot with her name on it. Her Aunt Florence conveniently died in San Francisco and left a three-unit, brown-shingled apartment building in her will for the niece she barely knew. Mona now had a steady stream of rent money flowing her way, and it paid for Little Cal's caretakers and Mona's expensive clothes and hairdos.

Within a week of arriving in LA, she signed up at a talent agency that booked extras in the movies. She reveled in her new "glamorous" life, walking through the gates of every movie studio in Hollywood. Her small paychecks, plus the steady rent income, established a life she'd enjoy until the day she died.

Mona found men willing to pay her way if she would warm their beds while they traveled in Europe, men who were only too glad to wine and dine her in the flashiest watering holes in LA, and men who groveled at her feet if she would only be seen with them. They showed her off as a prize cow.

Things didn't change that much after she moved into her building next to Golden Gate Park in the Richmond District. She still did extra work in the movies, but those filmed in San Francisco, not Hollywood. Little Cal was growing up in private schools while she traveled with some sugar daddy in Europe or China, and she seemed to grow more beautiful as she matured, letting the silver threads of hair highlight her honey-colored coiffures.

*　　*　　*　　*　　*

"Bill, Honey, I need you to help me. Can you drive me over to Sausalito? I've got to clear out Cal's apartment." Mona's voice was agitated, and I knew immediately she was on the verge of crying.

"Why? What's going on, Mona? You sound …"

"It's my damn kid, Bill. I think he's dying. He hit a tree driving like hell on his motorcycle. He's over at Marin General. Doctor told me he's in a coma and not gonna make it." I heard her catch her breath and blow her nose. "How soon can you drive me over to Sausalito in your truck?"

"Gee, Mona, I'm so sorry." I tried to bring her words into focus while I was struggling to pick Aaron up out of his highchair with one hand, pressing the phone to my ear with the other. "So, why do you need a pickup truck?'

"I wanna clear out his apartment in Sausalito. If he's dying, I don't want to have to pay his rent, so I need to move his stuff out of there right away. You gonna help me, aren't you Bill?"

"Sure. Sure. But Mona, he may not die. You don't know for sure. How about waiting to see how things go?" I knew it was useless to reason with her, and it was also hard to say *no* to her.

I picked her up and drove her across the bridge, where we'd met three years before, to her son's garden apartment on a hillside in Sausalito. I felt a chill as we opened the unlocked door and walked in. It was a small studio with an alcove where a double bed waited for warm bodies. Her son had very little furniture. A table and a couple of chairs. A small TV with rabbit ears. Basic kitchen utensils, pots, and pans.

We began tossing everything in cardboard boxes, but when I opened the closet door, I stopped, surprised at what I saw. Half of the closet held skirts and blouses, a woman's shoes, a purse, fluffy sweaters, and a box of Kotex.

"Mona, look! He's living with a woman! I don't think we should take stuff out of here. Let's put it back." I looked at her and thought, *she's up to what she does to every man in her life – including her own son. He's a grown man in a relationship, and Mona is deballing him. Not respecting him or the woman who might be the love of his life.*

"Leave *her* clothes here. She can pick 'em up when she gets out of the hospital." With that, Mona carried out a box of cassettes and a small radio/cassette player in a cardboard box and tossed it into the bed of the truck.

"You didn't tell me a girl was with him when he hit the tree. Was she hurt? Broken bones? What?" Mona was not only disrespecting her own son, she hadn't been up front with me. Using me, and I didn't like it.

"She only has a lot of bruises. My kid's in a coma and dying!" She climbed into the seat, pushing Aaron, who was napping, out of her way.

"Have you met her? Have you talked to her on the phone? What's she gonna think when she walks into their apartment and finds it empty?" My voice was getting edgy, and Mona was acting petulant.

"I don't give a damn what she thinks. I don't know her and don't want to know her. She's living and my kid's dying. Let's get out of here. I've got Cal's things. That's all that matters."

"Does she have a name?" I snarled.

Mona glared at me and snapped, "Ronnie."

## Chapter 39

# Ronnie

I first fell in love with movies as a kid, immersing myself in others' adventures, tragedies, loves, and I'd lose myself in the plot. One night, after I'd put Aaron to bed, I watched Charlie Chaplin's *The Kid,* which introduced five-year-old Jackie Coogan. The film left me in tears because I became the Little Tramp and Aaron was Jackie – straight hair with bangs, arms stretched out for me, pleading to stay with me as the authorities pulled him away from me and dumped him in the back of a truck with *County Orphanage Asylum* painted on the door.

That scene played through my head every night when I tried to go to sleep after tucking Aaron in and kissing him goodnight – Aaron being taken away from me by force. The tears. The pleas. The desperation. That clip I saw was my very own nightmare. Where did the movie end and my life begin?

And the plot was thickening. Mary's occasional phone calls were less humorous, less encouraging, less sure that everything would be all right. Another character in the plot, the villain, was invisible to me, a character who was trying to destroy me, but one I was not allowed to fight out in the open.

"He's at it again, Bill." Mary sounded exasperated. "Dorothy's at her wit's end dealing with him, but he's spreading his lies to everyone in the department who'll listen to him, and I'm sorry to say, some of those dodos actually believe that BS."

"Wouldn't it help if whoever is doing this could come to see how Aaron and I are living here?" It wasn't the first time I had offered to take that chance.

Nightly routine

"I can't believe anyone would want to take him away from our home. He wakes up laughing in his crib for gods sake! Mary, if they take Aaron away from me, I got to be sure I've done everything that's possible to keep him. I'll go down fighting, but I can't fight a ... an invisible foe!"

Visions of stern men and women in uniforms, snatching Aaron from my arms, became my nightly agony before I managed to sleep. And playing with Aaron, desperate to be with him every minute during the day, was keeping me from insistent and frequent calls for repairs from the tenants.

Number three's sink was clogged daily. Number twelve's window wouldn't stay shut if there was the slightest gust of wind. Five's light switch in the kitchen was stuck, leaving the overhead light on day and night. The old iron pipes were rusted through and leaks were springing up everywhere. Everywhere. In all 12 apartments.

The phone rang just as I was putting Aaron on his potty for the third time that morning. It was Mona and she was crying.

"Hey? What's up, Mona?"

"Do you know how much they were gonna charge me for his cremation, Bill? Two hundred dollars! So, I told 'em to stick it up their ass. He's an adult. *Was* an adult. So let the county pay for it."

"Aren't you gonna have a service for him?"

"I don't know any of his friends. We were outta touch for a couple of years, you know. So, none of my friends knew him either. Why would I have a service for him? Who'd be there?"

"Just asking."

Mona and I had such fun talking on the phone almost every day, but this wasn't one of those days. I wanted her to hang up.

"I'm crying because I was a lousy mother, Bill. The last time we talked ... that's what the little prick told me. A lousy mother! I had him in the best private schools I could afford, and that's what he called me. 'Lousy'"

"Mona, Aaron's grunting. I gotta go."

"Hang on just a minute. Let him grunt. You gotta help me. Remember when we emptied out Cal's apartment and found some woman's clothes there?"

"Yeah, at first I thought maybe he might be a cross-dresser."

"Well, Ronnie showed up here and she can't pay the rent there. She needs a place to crash, and dammit, Bill, you need some help with that kid of yours."

Protesting, I shrank from her pleas. "I don't have an extra bedroom here for her. I don't even know her!"

"Her name's Ronnie, like I told you, and she'll be at your door any minute. I told her you'd take her in, so don't disappoint me … I mean don't disappoint *her*."

*   *   *   *   *

The doorbell rang just as Aaron grunted and tried to get off his potty by himself.

"Hang on! I'll be there in just a minute!"

The doorbell stopped ringing, but it was a few minutes before I was through wiping and cleaning Aaron's butt and finally able to grab the doorknob with a wet, soapy hand. Aaron was slung under the other arm with a dry diaper draped over his bottom. I remember being agitated as I swung the door open. Doorbells, the phone ringing, Lily's barking at every new sound, Aaron's constant needs, and chores I needed to do, but didn't, began to take their toll. I was feeling old at thirty-nine.

The bright midmorning light from Larkin Street glared through the cut glass of the lobby door, silhouetting the figure standing at my apartment door, a suitcase on the floor beside her. I managed to switch on the light in the entry, which illuminated a young girl's face, one I remembered seeing in a Rembrandt painting. Her eyes were large brown ovals, shaded by thick, dark eyebrows that matched her hair, which lay over her shoulders in two long braids. She had partially hidden her slim body with a man's dress shirt tucked into a black skirt that was full and hung below her knees, partially hiding her legs, which were encased in black cotton stockings.

The total image was one of quiet sureness. Her sad eyes looked directly into mine.

"Mr. Jones, Mona said you might need me to help you with your son and could put me up for a while until I find a job and an apartment."

"She said I needed help? Really!"

"I'm very good with kids. I don't eat much, and I won't get in your way." She looked like a little girl trying to convince herself of her worth, and hoping I would buy it, too.

"Come on in. Leave your suitcase in the entry." She followed me into the kitchen. "Hungry?"

Aaron's nanny, Ronnie

"Oh, no! Not hungry at all!"

I ignored her, poured a glass of milk and put a plate of graham crackers in front of her. She sipped the milk and nibbled on one of the crackers.

I sat across from her with Aaron on my lap. "Ronnie, isn't it? You were living with Cal?" I tried to get all the facts lined up. "I'm so sorry about Cal. Were you hurt badly in the accident?"

She pulled back the starched sleeve and slowly brought her arm up for me to see the stitches on her forearm, the white skin, dark blue around the wound and faded out to a reddish bruise.

"They just took the cast off yesterday. Thank god for that. Now it just itches." She looked at Aaron, smiling. "Would you mind if I put his diaper on? I love little kids, and he is sooo cute."

She leaned over me and picked him up, laid him on the kitchen table, talking and cooing to him all the time she folded the diaper around him, pinning the ends neatly in front of his belly. I sat, not knowing how I should handle a complete stranger taking over my motherly duties. And she did it so smoothly, so sweetly, so efficiently!

"Ronnie, I guess you *could* crash here for a couple of days until you get on your feet again, but you can see I have only two bedrooms. You can bunk down on the sofa, I guess. Put your things in Aaron's room."

"I sure appreciate it, Mr. Jones. I guess you know Mona cleaned out our apartment, so when I got out of the hospital the apartment was empty except for our bed and a couple of chairs. I was so lonely … and broke. I couldn't even pay this month's rent."

I remembered all too well that awful day I helped Mona empty the apartment but thought it better not to tell Ronnie we used *my* truck.

"I got in touch with Mona, but she … still grieving over Cal, I guess. She gave me your address and said she'd make all the arrangements with you. So, I got in my car and drove here. I didn't have any place to go to except here. I hope it's okay with you."

"Sure." What else could I say?

The next two or three days seemed to zip by. The apartment was cleaner than usual. A bowl of California poppies, picked from cracks in the sidewalk, appeared on the kitchen table. Ronnie parked her old red MG in front of our building, and on the second day, she asked if she could take Aaron with her when she drove back to Sausalito to pick up her cleaning deposit. I watched them drive off with mixed emotions: sad and a little jealous, seeing my son having such a carefree time with this loving, sweet girl. On the other hand, I was elated that I would have a couple of hours to myself to finally fix a dozen trouble spots in this tired, old apartment building.

Ronnie bought groceries with some of the money she got back from her reluctant landlord, money she could not afford to spend on us. As she cooked dinner, Aaron sat on the floor and watched *Sesame Street*, and I sat on the couch, catching up on my mail and the morning paper. I sat bolt upright when the idea hit me.

"Ronnie, can you leave the kitchen for a minute? I just had an idea and I want to show you something."

She and Aaron followed me out into the lobby and over to a side door with no number on it. "Wait here. I have to go back and get a flashlight and the key, if I can find it."

I finally found a ring of keys hanging in the basement, and after trying a dozen or so in the lock, I found one that worked. I pushed the door open, which was not easy, since it was blocked by scraps of lumber and paint cans. Ronnie held the flashlight, and we carefully stepped into a small, dusty, creepy, dark storeroom that reeked of rat urine.

"Ronnie, when this was built back in 1915, my apartment and these rooms were storerooms or workshops. I don't *really* know what they were used for, but I do know that during World War II when they needed housing, the owner slipped in bathrooms and kitchens and rented them out as apartments. When I bought the building last year, they were used as storerooms again. I plan to legalize them as soon as I can, but in the meantime …"

The next morning, while Aaron napped, Ronnie and I armed ourselves with brooms, mops, Clorox, and Dutch Cleanser. After we swept the cobwebs from the ceiling and walls, we opened the one casement window on the Larkin side and the small windows in the back, one in the filthy bathroom over the toilet and another over a rusty and paint-splattered kitchen sink that looked out into the light well, encasing the battered garbage chute.

I bought a used enameled kitchen sink unit from a salvage yard, a small gas stove at a garage sale for Ronnie, and a brand-new refrigerator for Mrs. Metcalfe in number three, which surprised and delighted her. Her old one cleaned up pretty well, and within a week we had a freshly painted, livable apartment for Ronnie, just steps away from our apartment and from Aaron's "nanny."

Thanks to Mona's intervention, my life began to smooth out. Ronnie became an extension of me, and Aaron was cared for 24/7. The three of us nourished each other. I was even able to go to the movies again with Pasek, but I didn't stay in the bars until they closed with him like before. I could have a nightcap with him after the movie if it wasn't too late, but Ronnie wouldn't leave Aaron's side until I came through the door, and I didn't want to jeopardize such a good thing by taking advantage of her.

The nightmares of Aaron's being torn from my arms persisted though because every time Mary came by or phoned, she was glum, talking about the arguments going on at the adoption agency over my sexuality. Several months had gone by, but there seemed to be no end to the demands, the urgency, of ending the placement. My life *could* have been wonderful. I was surrounded by caring friends and family, and everything seemed to be falling in place, if only …

Ronnie brought care and more security into my home. Aaron was becoming bouncier, more playful, and affectionate every day. He was feeding himself and chewing his food. If I wasn't hugging him, Ronnie was. If Ronnie or I weren't hugging him, Mrs. Metcalfe, Pasek, my brother, Randles, Judd, Dennis, or even the waitress at the Savoy Tivoli would gladly take on that warm, sweet chore. Life was good, if only …

The phone rang and it was Dorothy Murphy, the head of the adoption agency. "Bill, can you come down to my office today or tomorrow. We have to talk."

## Chapter 40

# Little White Lies

Dorothy Murphy sat upright behind the worn city-issued oak desk that separated us, and Mary Davidson rolled an office chair on casters next to me, then sat close enough to pat me on the shoulder if the conversation got too tough. Dorothy leaned in, looking straight at me over the thin frames of her bifocals. "Where's Aaron this morning, Bill?"

"Oh, good news on that, Dorothy. He's with his nanny right now down at Aquatic Park making sand castles. Yeah, we got a nanny! Ronnie. She moved into a small apartment next to ours a couple of weeks ago, and he loves her."

"That sounds good, Bill. Is she there every day?"

"Most of the time. Sometimes she does office work as a temp for money, but I'm giving her free rent and most of her food."

"I bet she loves him."

"Who wouldn't? I should bring him around, Dorothy. You should see him with hair on his head. He gets cuter by the minute."

"How old is Ronnie, Bill? Retired?"

"Oh, no. About nineteen, I think."

"Oh."

I should have said she was in her fifties, because Dorothy was getting that look of "Oh, damn!"

"She's really mature for her age, Dorothy." I needed to convince her. "Very reliable. Quiet. Loves taking Aaron out in her car to different playgrounds. She's a godsend, Dorothy."

"Sounds like you have everything in hand, Bill." She pivoted around in her office chair and looked out the window for a moment, then pivoted back to look at me. "I've asked you to come in today to update you on our problem and to ask you to do something I've never asked another applicant to do."

"Whatever you want, Dorothy."

"The outrageous complaint about our placing a child with you is picking up steam with some of the social workers here, Bill, and things are getting out of hand. Mary and I are both convinced that you are the best parent for Aaron, but we're looking at what might come down. We might have to face a court battle to prove that these charges are unwarranted so we can finalize the adoption."

"Oh, my god!"

"Believe me. We don't want to go to trial over this, but we might be forced into it." She got out of her chair and began to walk slowly around the room.

"Bill, the trial won't be just about you. It'll affect the whole idea of doing single adoptions. Single adoptions in other states, too. If we lose this one battle, hundreds of children, maybe thousands of children, will never have a home and a parent who loves and cares for them."

"Dorothy, I'm so sorry. What should I do? Get a lawyer?"

"Mary and I think we should be prepared to go to trial, Bill, and to start with, we want to lay a paper trail, so to speak. We think we'll need a professional evaluation of you. An evaluation by a psychiatrist." She paused, anxious to see my reaction. "We can't make you do it, Bill. It has to be voluntary on your part, but you know how important it is, don't you?"

I felt I was being backed into a corner. Fear began to numb me, and I was caught like a trout on a hook. It had been fairly easy so far because no one had asked me, face to face, if I were gay. I didn't have to lie. I just had to keep my mouth shut, but now Dorothy was asking me to talk to a psychiatrist. You can't lie to a shrink, and if I told him the truth, I would lose Aaron. My throat constricted, but I was able to get out a couple of words that Dorothy and Mary strained to hear.

"Okay. Whatever you think."

Three days later, I parked Old Rust on Sacramento Street and walked into an old Victorian that had been converted into offices. Dr. Hardy's office was in the back of the house in a room that had been the dining room, a dark-paneled space built of pine but painted to look like walnut. It still had the built-in buffet and the glass display case that once showcased a family's best china and crystal stemware but now housed leather-bound books and a detailed model of a wooden Chris-Craft speedboat. My kind of room!

"Bill, Dorothy has told me the background of your adopting Aaron. Aaron, isn't it? I need to tell you that this is a one-time visit, not the beginning of therapy, and it's important to everyone concerned that we don't play footsie here. No little white lies. Just try to relax. I'll be asking you some questions, and I want you to answer them quickly and without too much thought. Okay?"

"Okay."

"How old are you?"

"Thirty-nine."

"Where do you and Aaron live?"

"On Russian Hill. On Larkin. Larkin and Greenwich. I have a 12-unit building there."

"Aaron have his own room?"

"Yes. Yes, of course."

"Playmates?"

"Just me. Just me and Ronnie, his nanny." That sounded so isolated, so I quickly added, "He'll be enrolled at Phoebe Hearst Preschool when he's two and a half. In October."

"Sounds like you're rich, Bill. Tell me how *are* you financially? Paying the bills?"

"Most of them. The rents are still low, and the building is old and needs a lot of repairs, but I also model for Macy's, and I do extra work in films. So, I have enough to raise Aaron if that's what you want to know. Oh, yeah, sometimes I do handyman jobs for friends and other people. Need your office painted?"

What I didn't tell him was that I had to open the coin box on the washer in the basement that morning so I'd have enough for the parking meter. Sort of a white lie, I guess.

"Family? Do you have relatives close by?"

"Yes. My Aunt Ruth lives just a few blocks away on Filbert, and my father and his wife live in Oakland. I have a half-brother, Jerry, who's a teacher and lives in Hayward."

"Mother?"

"She owns a bar in Byron – in Contra Costa County – near Brentwood, Oakley, Tracy."

"I know the area. Do you see them often?"

"Mostly my half-brother, Jerry."

"Is he married?"

"No. He was." I thought Hardy would think he might be gay, so I blurted out, "He's got two kids."

"Is he your father's or your mother's son?"

"Mother's, but I raised him. I was eleven when he was born, and she was too busy working to take care of him when he was a baby."

I wanted to say "drinking" instead of "working" but thought this one little white lie would be okay. "Working" sure sounded better to me.

"What's your relationship with your mother at this time?"

"A little strained, I guess. She doesn't quite approve of me adopting."

I thought another little white lie would sound a hell of a lot better than telling him about my mother screaming over the phone that I was an immoral, queer pervert and would roast in hell.

"When did your father and mother separate?"

"When I was two."

"The same age as Aaron."

"Come to think of it."

"Which one did you live with?"

"I lived with some neighbors for a few years, then with my grandmother, then with an aunt, then with my mother when she remarried. I was eight."

"How was that?"

"Great because my stepfather's two kids came to live with us. A boy about four, Buddy, and a girl about six, Corky." What I didn't tell him was that I hated my stepfather, and Louie hated me.

"Did you get along?"

"I was *so* happy. We built a treehouse in our fig tree, and I read books to them. We went to movies with my mother and stepfather in Stockton and had Chinese dinners before we drove home. I felt like I had a family for the first time in my life."

I didn't tell him about the drunken fights they had, and that as a way to punish her husband, Louie, my mother would kick Buddy and Corky out to live with their mother, another alcoholic, in Stockton. I thought that by not telling him things like that, it would be the same as an innocent little white lie. No real harm.

"Who was your first sexual encounter with, Bill?"

"I don't remember her name."

"How old were you?"

"Five."

"I mean with another adult."

"Oh, I guess around twelve or thirteen."

"With?"

"Johnny Addington. He lived on a farm about a mile from our bar. We used to wrestle. Never got naked, but I guess when you're that young, things can happen even when you're fully clothed."

I felt I had already said too much and regretted that I hadn't lied about him being a girl instead of a farmer's son.

"Ever have a girlfriend, Bill?"

"Oh, sure. Lots of 'em."

"Tell me about them."

"Well, in high school I went steady with Verla Richardson for three years. Then in college …"

"Which one?"

"College of the Pacific in Stockton. I went with a girl from Antioch. Doris Alexander. And for a while, I dated a really beautiful girl, a Southern belle from Hercules. Emily Bond. She was voted "Sophomore Doll" her second year at Cal. My father and his wife flipped out over her. They thought Doris was brainless, but she wasn't. She was smarter than me."

"Did you have intercourse with those young women, Bill?"

"Emily and I used to get naked together and touch each other's … you know … privates, but she would never let me push it inside her. Not even the head."

What I didn't tell him was that after I had put my clothes back on, in a frustrated state, I'd drive over to the boathouse on Lake Merritt in Oakland, where the gatekeeper would finish what Emily started.

"You're almost forty now, Bill, so tell me about your sex life at this age."

"What do you want to know?" I asked, trying to look nonchalant.

"The usual." Then he tapped out each word with his pen. "Who? When? What? And how?"

"Actually, since Aaron came into my life, the only sex I've had is after he's gone to sleep and I get into the shower. I swear Dove soap is the best. We're goin' steady."

"So, you're not coming clean with me, heh, Bill?" He smiled broadly at his own sense of humor, making me feel like we might be buddies. "Pardon the pun. I'm sorry if I got us off track. Sometimes I can't control myself." We both chuckled, which eased the tension.

"I have a lot of women in my life as friends, and I have a lot of male friends, too, but I don't have anyone special … sexually. Let me put it this way. I'm an average kind of guy. One who really likes sex, hot sex, but who wants love more than sex. I've had sex with women and with men, too, so I guess you can say I go both ways."

"You consider yourself bisexual?"

Actually, the one girl I did finally fuck was Cora Lee Murray … accidently. The memory of it came rushing back to me.

"Yes, yes. I'm bisexual."

"And if you fell in love with another man, would you want him to live with you and Aaron?"

And for the first time that afternoon, I couldn't lie to Dr. Hardy. No little white lie this time. I didn't leave something to his imagination.

"Yes, I would. If he loved Aaron. If he loved me. If I loved him, and if Aaron loved him, we'd be a family."

There were no more questions about my sex life after that, and for the rest of the hour we talked about my favorite subject … Aaron.

"What are your thoughts on discipline, Bill?"

"I don't think it's good to just let kids run wild, but I do want him to make choices for himself. So far, I haven't had any trouble with him – like screaming in restaurants or running loose in grocery stores. He doesn't seem too eager to please me, but he cuddles up with me every chance he gets."

"Come on, Bill, what problems are you having with him? He's two. You've got problems."

I told him about the first week when Aaron wouldn't take a bath, and how I finally got him in the tub. I admitted the diaper changes were taking up too much time, and how frustrated I was that he had to be spoon-fed, completely passive about chewing his food.

"I'm trying to wean him away from Gerber's, so I'm making him mashed potatoes, squash, and peas and sometimes beans, but I have to take hold of his jaw and move it up and down to get him chewing. He won't do it on his own."

"You're on the right track, Bill. Just be patient and consistent. By the time he's a teenager, he'll be eating you out of house and home."

Aaron as a teenager! That thought buoyed me for a split second. "The other thing that worries me is that he still hasn't started to talk. What I mean is … he jabbers all the time, from morning 'til night, but not words like hello or goodbye. That worries me … but he does call me Daddy."

"Words are just around the corner, Bill. Then you'll wish he'd shut up. If he jabbers a lot now, he'll wear you out when he starts asking questions."

"Can I tell you something that really is beginning to bug the shit outta me?"

"Of course, Bill. What's beginning to bug the shit out of you?"

"Aaron being so damn happy in the morning."

"What?"

"I mean every morning around dawn, he lies in his crib and talks to imaginary friends. Not just talks to them but laughs at something he has just said to them or something they have said to him. I tell you it's making me feel something is wrong with him. It's a little weird, and I'm scared."

"You're scared because …?"

"Because when I go into his room, he just keeps up the jabbering and laughing. As if I'm not even there. I don't understand what he's carrying on about. It seems … you know … unnatural."

"Does he ever wake up crying or screaming, Bill?"

"Never."

"Nightmares? Bad dreams? Does he sleep the whole night through?"

"Yeah, he never wakes up during the night. I check on him all the time. No bad dreams."

"Sounds like you've got a very happy kid on your hands, Bill. Live with it."

I hoped my little frets wouldn't be held against me. Did I sound like an old nervous nelly? Whatever he would report to Dorothy would be a heavy weight, either to help us – or to end my desperate wish to keep my son forever. So much rode on this single hour I'd spent with Dr. Hardy. Had I told him too much? Should I have lied about my sex life? Did I come across as too strict or too lenient with Aaron? Should I have changed all the pronouns when I told him about sleeping with men?

By the time we shook hands and said our goodbyes, sweat was covering the back of my shirt, but I felt like a kid at recess. It was wonderful to leave his dark office and feel the spring sunlight bathing me. I drove directly down to the sandy beach at Aquatic Park to be with my little boy and his nanny. I needed to pick him up and hold him close to me.

## Chapter 41
# Disney and the Deprived Kid

I suffered through a whole week not knowing what Dr. Hardy thought of me and wondering if his evaluation would help us or destroy us at a court hearing. My life with Aaron hung like a bug on a spider's web, unable to move, escape, fight back. My poor friends, Ronnie, my brother Jerry, Randles, and especially Pasek, took the brunt of my anxious, wailing, and constant phone calls. I had everyone near and dear to me in a frenzy. Dr. Hardy was taking his fuckin' time getting back to Dorothy at the adoption agency, and it was driving me crazy with fear and anxiety.

On Thursday, exactly one week after my appointment with Dr. Hardy, the phone rang early in the morning, just as I was tying Aaron's sneakers. I took a deep breath and counted to 10 as I lifted the phone.

"Hello. Bill Jones speaking."

"Oh, is it really? Sorry, I must have the wrong number. I'm trying to call Henny-Penny," Pasek giggled. "The sky is falling! The sky is falling!"

"'Taint funny, McGee."

"Ah, come on, Billy. No news is good news, right?"

"I guess so, but it's been a whole lousy week, Pasek. Seven days!"

"You know what the real problem is here, Billy? They can really get you on only *one thing*, and I've got the solution all worked out to that *one* thing. Wanna know what they can get you on?"

"What problem other than the pedophile-serial-killer-pervert-vampire problem? You mean I have another problem I haven't heard about yet?"

"Your kid is deprived, Billy. It's that simple. He's a *deprived* kid." Pasek was wound up. "He's never been to Disneyland!"

"Disneyland? He's never been to a Colma cemetery or Milpitas either."

"We're going to clear your name, Billy. I've made all the arrangements. No one will ever accuse you of depriving Aaron again. Pack your bags, Billy Boy. We leave tomorrow morning."

"Pasek, you're drinkin' this early in the morning?"

"Hey, listen. Listen! Richard and his rich sugar daddy have invited us to stay in their beach house in Malibu for the weekend. They're on location in Utah. Can you believe it? If we start off at eight tomorrow morning, we should get there around four or five, and then we'll have all day Saturday at Disneyland! Don't you love it?"

"Pasek, what about your job?"

"I told them that I'm planning to have a sore throat and need to take Friday off. Yeah! It's okay with 'em!"

"He's only a little more than two years old, Pasek. He won't even know where he's at. Maybe in a few years, Uncle P."

"There you go depriving that poor little kid, Billy. Depriving! That's probably the only reason they'll ever come up with that's bad enough to take him away from you. Otherwise, you're a good daddy. I'll pick you up in the morning. Have some coffee ready in a thermos, will ya?"

"It's gonna cost a lot, isn't it, Pasek? The rents won't come in 'til next week, and all I can lay my hands on right now are the quarters in the washer and dryer."

"Oh, I forgot to tell you. Sugar Daddy works for Disney! It's a freebee, Billy Boy! Tickets. VIP! Won't cost us a nickel ... and food, too! Life doesn't get better than this! And just wait 'til you see the Malibu digs! Right on Broad Beach!"

Pasek rang the doorbell a little after seven the next morning. He was smiling ear to ear and was sporting a beanie on his head with two big, round black mouse ears sticking up like black sails on a pirate ship. He apparently thought it could hide his comb-over.

We took turns driving and holding Aaron, figuring Highway 1 on the coast would be more beautiful than 101 or 5; the only drawback was that it would take more time to drive it. I do love to drive, and the gentle dips and rises, plus the snake-like turns, and the glimpses of the sequined ocean between the cypress trees made me forget my fear, for a few hours, that Aaron might be snatched from me. Although I loved driving that coastal highway, I was envious of the time Pasek got to hold Aaron, afraid that even my best friend might take him away from me.

The house in Malibu was set back from the Pacific Coast Highway with just enough room for a circular driveway leading to a three-car garage and a solid walnut, burlwood entrance gate, centered in a high stucco wall that surrounded the entry courtyard. We walked over the shallow end of the swimming pool on a Japanese bridge that led to the double front door of the mid-century house designed by Charles Eames. When we entered, I saw two white grand pianos reflected off the tiled floors. I looked up to see a ceiling of a skylight and motor-controlled mesh curtains that dressed and undressed the view of the Pacific Ocean beyond the floor-to-ceiling glass windows. I was in awe!

*   *   *   *   *

At Disneyland, I slipped Aaron into his stroller as we went to the front of the ticket line. We smugly waved our VIP passes at the young man tearing off stubs and announcing, "Next!"

We had just swept through the gates and started to walk down Main Street toward the castle when I heard Aaron's familiar grunt. I grabbed him and his diaper bag and ran into the nearest men's room. After I had cleaned him, dried his bottom, and dusted him with Johnson's baby powder, we joined Uncle Pasek, who was sitting on the edge of a fountain with a big grin on his face, watching all the daddy types strolling past him. Our first ride was on the Dumbos swinging around in a lazy circle, but Aaron was not impressed.

I held Aaron on my lap as we rode on the Pirates boat through a jungle in a dark tunnel. Aaron's diaper felt moist and warm, so when we got off the Pirate's boat, I headed for the nearest men's room. Pasek was dying to take the thriller roller coaster ride through Magic Mountain, so I let him go on it without us, thinking it would be too frightening for Aaron. Pasek bitched that it wasn't as much fun as he thought it would be, probably because he had to do it alone.

From then on, every ride and show we took in was appropriate for toddlers, like the teacup and saucer ride, but I seemed to spend the entire day spoon-feeding Aaron, adjusting safety belts around Aaron, changing Aaron's

The deprived kid and his daddy at the beach house in Malibu

diapers, pushing him in his stroller, and carrying him – usually to the nearest men's room to change another diaper.

We rode the gentle People Mover, went underwater in the submarine, drove a car on the tracks of Autopia, stood in the Circle Vision Theater, boarded the Mark Twain to float down the "Mississippi," rode through the dark tunnel to see the Pirates of the Caribbean again, and rode Donald Duck on the elaborate Disney merry-go-round. Aaron didn't look at anything. His attention seemed to be focused on playing with my ears when he rode on my shoulders or rubbing Pasek's head, messing up his comb-over. He took almost no notice of all the enchanting sights on the rides or in the sights of the rides.

The storybook friends like Peter Pan and Cinderella couldn't engage him. He acted as if they weren't there. He was missing the whole experience.

I could see the frustration growing on Pasek's face. He wanted to go on the bobsled through the Matterhorn so badly, but after our free dinner, as the sunlight faded from the park, he was being led into another kiddy ride – the one ride that Aaron finally reacted to.

We settled in our padded seat on the caterpillar-like train of open boats, a seat that was just wide enough for two adults with a toddler standing between them. We entered a darkened tunnel, and like Dorothy seeing Oz in Technicolor for the first time, we floated out of the tunnel into a new kind of world, a world filled with the song, "It's a Small World," a song that haunts me to this very day.

Little people, very little people, popped up all around us singing the song. They sprang out of the tulip beds of Holland and peeped out of windows in Paris, doors of the Taj Mahal, and chimneys of miniature cottages in Ireland. They swung on tire swings hanging from dwarf trees and danced through tiny cobblestone streets leading to a dollhouse castle.

Aaron held on to our shoulders for balance as he jumped up and down. He was electrified, shouting, "La-la! Ga-ga! La-la! La-la! Ga-ga! Ga-ga!"

His blue eyes were wide, darting from tiny person to tiny person.

Pasek looked at me in amazement, and asked, "What the hell, Bill? What's got into him? Holy shit!" Aaron kept bouncing and yelling for the whole ride, even after we piled out of our boat and looked up to see fireworks exploding above us.

The lights in Disneyland were glowing as we walked away from. It's a Small World. Magic was happening all around us, and Aaron had come alive. He had connected with the whimsical elves. For the first time that day, he had seen something beyond his stroller, beyond looking up at the ceiling of a men's room, beyond me as I carried him. The twirling teacups we rode in hadn't done it. The Mickey and Minnie Mouse who gave him a balloon hadn't done it. It was these little friends of his, friends I had never seen before, maybe the imaginary friends that he talked to every morning in his crib that he recognized and was overjoyed to see.

It's a Small World was the birthplace of Aaron's contact with the real world. It shocked him into coming out of a very closed-in world of his own, and he began to look around, pointing at the colored lights, laughing at a dwarf called Dopey.

"Bill, it's almost closing time. What do you say? Can we *please* go on the Rocket Jets ride? Look, the elevator takes us up to where you get in, and it's on our way out to the exit. Okay? Okay?"

"I'd love to, but I don't know if they'll let us take Aaron with us."

"No harm in trying. Come on, give me a break!"

Our VIP passes got us waved through to the elevator, and we slowly rose to the launch pad, about five stories high. The elevator doors opened and an attendant showed us to the rocket-shaped pod temporarily secured to the landing platform. Pasek got in first, facing forward, straddling an upholstered bench-like seat. The attendant strapped him in with a safety belt and turned to me.

"This little guy is a little young for this ride, isn't he, Mister?"

"Well, the space is small. Just big enough for two adults, so I think my son can ride between us … like a ham sandwich." I flashed my VIP pass. "And it's tight enough so he won't fall out."

"Okay, but remember, I warned you not to take him."

"He'll be all right. Just strap us in."

It took several more minutes to load up the other pods on the steel arms that radiated out from the base of a tower that looked like a spaceship from NASA. It resembled a sprawling octopus that would swing us in a circle, around and around at a terrific speed, vertically and horizontally with our pod revolving at the same time. On the end of each arm, was another "rocket ship" pod, each holding two adults – with no toddler squeezed in between them. The ride was well named *Rocket Jets*. As we swung through the night air, the gravity pulled our cheeks down so much that we could hardly get our screams out. Aaron sat squeezed between us, unable to see anything except Pasek's back. In a flash, the ride was over, and all the adults staggered out of our pods, laughing and gasping for air, with me carrying Aaron. It was way past his bedtime, and he went limp as he closed his eyes, resting his head on my chest. For him. It's a Small World had been much more thrilling.

We filed into the elevator, and suddenly everyone stood in cathedral silence, all facing doors that would open eventually and allow us to talk again. Pasek was standing next to me and reached over to stroke Aaron's head. The elevator seemed to be slower going down than it was going up, and as we grew close to the ground floor, Pasek leaned over and kissed the top of Aaron's head. He staged-whispered to Aaron so everyone in the elevator could hear him, "You know, Little Guy, your momma would have loved that ride. Would've peed her pants. Nobody loved rides like that one more than your mommy did. Too bad she died this morning."

He patted Aaron's head again. The doors split open, and Pasek led us out through them, leaving the others standing in the elevator with their mouths open.

## Chapter 42

# Vietnam, Nixon, Joplin, and Me

My television set was like a peephole into hell, and it was on almost all day. Every day. "Hey, hey, LBJ, how many kids have you killed today?" seemed to drown out the Beatles and Aretha Franklin. It was number one on my hit parade and stuck in my head.

How could I replace Bobby Kennedy with this wimpy-dummy, Hubert H. Humphrey? He was LBJ's slimy mouthpiece, who, like Charlie McCarthy, moved his lips, oozing LBJ's words, defending his damn bloody war in Vietnam. He was heading for the Democratic Convention in Chicago, and if he got the nomination in August, there was no way I would vote for him. Nixon was even worse. Bobby was dead, and Eugene McCarthy was left groping in the dark. George Wallace's Ku Klux Klan sheet shadowed all the campaigns, even though he was running against Nixon as an Independent. America was on its way to hell.

The car ride back from LA took less time than the drive down there, mostly because it was Sunday and the traffic was light. Aaron slept most of the way, and I leaned back to take in the quiet views of the green hills, soft as a woman's breast, and the reflections on the slow rise and fall of the undulating Pacific Ocean waves.

"Pasek, I've been thinking about what I will do if the adoption falls apart."

"Like?"

"The first thing tomorrow, I want to see a lawyer. Know any?"

"I slept with one last year. I think I still have his number. Why?"

"I want to give you power of attorney for me."

"What for?"

"That way you can sell the building if I'm not around, then send me the money."

"What do ya mean, 'If I'm not around?'"

"I might be somewhere else. Like London, where they speak English."

"London?"

"Yeah, I'm going to kidnap Aaron and raise him in England."

"You won't have to do that, Bill. I know … I know it's gonna be okay. It's a feeling I have."

"But if … if they come after him, you'll do it for me, won't ya?"

"You don't have to ask."

*     *     *     *     *

As soon as I turned on the kitchen light, I saw the red button blinking on my Sony answering device. I left our suitcase and the overflowing dirty diaper bag in the hall. Carrying Aaron, who was asleep, I hurried over to the machine and pressed the message button.

"Hi, Bill, it's me, Mary. I hope you and Aaron had a great time in Disneyland this weekend. I envy you doing it." She paused for a second and then told me what she was really calling about. "Dr. Hardy would like you to come back and see him Monday morning, Bill. He sent us his evaluation and wants to explain it to you himself. Bye-bye."

Shit! I pressed the message button again. "Hello, Bill. It's Ann Brebner. Can you work Tuesday and Wednesday nights? They're shooting in the lobby of the Fairmont Hotel. If you have a tux, wear it. Otherwise, a dark suit will do. It's a fancy fundraiser scene with Julie Christie. Confirm this with me Monday."

Great!

*     *     *     *     *

Dr. Hardy was smiling as he opened his office door for me and motioned for me to sit down. "Coffee or tea, Bill?"

"No, thanks." I was taking deep breaths, trying not to blurt out something I'd regret, like, "*Will you get to the point and tell me what the fuck you told Mary and Dorothy about me?*"

"Bill, I want you to know how much I appreciate your being so forthcoming about how you honestly feel about yourself ... and about how you feel about being Aaron's parent. You could have painted a better picture of yourself, but you didn't. You couldn't."

I wondered if this was an elaborate buildup to just let me down. I wanted to stamp my feet, I was so anxious. He went over in detail what we had talked about during our interview over a week ago. I couldn't for the life of me figure out what he was leading up to. I felt sweat running down from my armpits and down my spinal cord, and it wasn't a hot day. He rose from his chair behind his desk and walked around it until he stood facing me.

"Bill, I have been counseling and treating family members for over two decades, and I am sure of one thing. Not everyone should be a parent. There are more fathers and mothers than you can imagine who are not emotionally qualified to bring up children. It's sad but true. And it's those parents who leave deep and lasting scars on their offspring."

I could hardly breathe. *Was he saying I was one of them?*

"And then there are the humans who were born to be parents. Parents who care about their children. Love their children. Sacrifice for their children. Give them opportunities to grow, flower." He held out his hand and took mine.

"And you were meant to be a parent, Bill. It's my opinion that you'll be a very good one, too. That's what I wrote on your evaluation. Good luck. I'll be in your corner."

As I walked down Sacramento Street to where I had parked Old Rust, I felt the warm blanket of sunlight wrap around me. I smelled jasmine. The sky was trying to be blue, but it was so bright that it turned white. Someone I hardly knew ... cared. Someone who could help me ... was on my side. I saw that my world could be good. Be full. Bring some love to the America that was going to hell.

\* \* \* \* \*

Ronnie turned down my offer to put sheets and blankets on my sofa and insisted her sleeping bag would be just fine for the two nights I'd be working on *Petulia*. I didn't like to leave our apartment just as Aaron was being tucked in, but I needed the money, and I knew he'd be happy knowing Ronnie was in the next room. I began to wonder if the small amount I'd be earning as an extra would be worth it to be away from him all night.

We extras were herded into a banquet room off the lobby of the Fairmont, where we were given vouchers to fill out and were told that the caterers would have chow ready for us in five and a half hours. In the meantime, the crafts table had been set up in a corner, loaded down with snacks of all kinds, coffee, tea, and milk, and a tray of apples and oranges. We sat at large, round folding tables with no cloths covering the cigarette burns, scratches, and stains of food and drink from past banquets.

Mona made her entrance, as usual, sweeping into the room dressed in a formal gown, with every diamond she owned draped around her neck, on her fingers, wrists, and ear lobes.

"Darling, my *favorite* co-star, how the hell are you?"

"Marvelous! As usual. Ask anyone."

"And how's our little nanny doin'?"

"Mona, I tell you, I owe you one with her. Aaron loves her, and she seems happy, too."

"She eating you outta house and home?"

"Not at all … in fact …"

The double doors swung open and the second and third ADs (assistant directors), came running into the room. "Fundraisers, we need you in the lobby. Bellboys and desk clerks, be sure wardrobe checks your uniforms before you come in."

We filed out into the elaborate gold-, black-, and red-carpeted lobby. The first AD placed us around the room as partygoers, travelers with suitcases, and registered guests. A wooden dance floor had been placed in the center of the lobby over the wall-to-wall carpet, and a scraggly looking bunch of hippies was sitting on the grand staircase.

After 30 minutes of standing in place, we got our directions. Mona and I were chosen as one of the dance couples. We stood and waited another 30 minutes while the sound and lights were being tested and adjusted on the stand-ins. Finally, Richard Lester gave the signal to the hippies on the staircase to start playing dance music. Julie Christie, George C. Scott, and Richard Chamberlain were led in and placed where the stand-ins had been.

The band was miked and amplified to burst eardrums, and a messed-up female with long kinky brown hair, parted in the middle, began screeching the lyrics to something I'd never heard before. Mona said she heard it was called "Viola Lee Blues," but it was like no blues I'd ever heard before … or wanted to hear again. I got my wish. After the band had performed the song once, they were instructed to pretend they were banging on their guitars and keyboards but not make a sound, and the singer was told to lip-synch the words, but not to really sing. The song was played back so you could barely hear it, but the dialog between Christie and Chamberlain was loud and clear.

It took two whole nights to shoot the scene. Between set-ups, Mona and I were herded back into the holding room to smoke, read papers, and gossip with the other extras. On the last night, Mona and I were joined at our table by the singer and three of the band members. They did something Mona and I would never do on a set. They drank. Not only did they drink, but they also passed a bottle of Southern Comfort around for everyone at our table.

"Jeez. My fuckin' throat's killin' me."

Mona turned away the bottle offered her, and asked, "Got a cold, Honey?"

"Naw. It's this fuckin' lip-synchin' I gotta do. Fuck! You try it for two nights!"

"My name's Mona, and this is my gay friend, Bill."

"Mona, for Christ's sake!" I hated when she did that. She thought it was cool and really "in," but it embarrassed me, and pissed me off.

"My boys are … we calls 'em, Big Brother and the Holding Company, and I'm their singer, Janis, with an "s" instead of a "c" and "e". I love singin' blues from my gut, and now I've been lip-synchin' from my gut. Fuck!"

I've thought of Janis with an "s" instead of a "c" and an "e" many times since then. I imagined Aaron growing older with a sore throat because all he could do is lip-synch with his la-la's, and ga-ga's, instead of real words. How frustrating not to be able to speak words or sing lyrics! Never to be understood. How depressing to never be able to sing … or say out loud,

"I love you."

## Chapter 43

# A Thousand Words

I had just put Aaron down for his afternoon nap when the Princess phone started ringing again.

"Hi, Daddy Bill."

"Hi, Uncle Pasek."

"Whaas cookin'?"

"Me. My social worker phoned me this morning and all hell is breaking loose. Did you know that there's something called the *DSM*?"

"Is that like the WPA or the PTA?"

"It stands for ... here I wrote it down. *Diagnostic and Statistical Manual of Mental Disorders, DSM.*"

"So?"

"Mary says that's the latest thing being thrown at her ... and Dorothy. Guess what? You and I are listed by a bunch of psychiatrists as having a mental disorder!"

"Well, I always knew you were crazy! I may be a big sissy, but I'm not nutty just because I like to suck cock!"

"Pasek, if we go to trial over this, they'll use it against me! Homosexuals are officially disordered – mentally. And guess what?"

"What?"

She told me that the asshole that's got his hair on fire about me adopting Aaron is a fuckin' psychiatrist!"

"You're kiddin'."

"It seems someone who knows me and knows about Aaron is going to this shrink, and spilled the beans!"

"Fuck!"

"Mary thinks I should make a statement in writing that I'm not gay."

"Fuck!"

"How can I do that, Pasek? I may be officially nuts, but I'm not a liar."

"Nobody's perfect, Bill. I'm a great liar. I do it all the time, but *you* can't even tell a little white lie. I should give you lessons on how to lie and get away with it. I tell every guy I meet that I've got a 10-inch cock, and I end up in bed with most of them. They don't measure it, and they never call me on it."

"This is more than trying to get in somebody's pants, Pasek. Seriously, how do I say I'm not gay in a written statement? It'll be produced as evidence in court."

"Just say – oh, yeah. Just say that *this* is the time that you *havta* say … I'm not queer. Don't ya see? This is the time … you're *forced* to say … Get it?"

"Oh, Pasek, isn't that sorta like a little white lie? Let me think on it!"

\*     \*     \*     \*     \*

Ronnie took Aaron to a playground, which gave me a chance to jump into Old Rust and shop for the Formica countertop I was installing in number ten. On the way back from Goodman Lumber, I was listening to the announcement that Pope Paul VI had reaffirmed the Catholic Church's opposition to all forms of artificial contraception, including birth control pills, which had come on the market in 1960. I wondered if Aaron's birth mother was a Catholic. Is that why she got pregnant? Did she know about the pill? She was only nineteen. Old enough to know about it, but maybe an *obedient* Catholic. The thought sickened me and I clinched my fists around the steering wheel.

Driving down South Van Ness, I was distracted by a man in a business suit sitting on a bench at a bus stop. Not distracted, overwhelmed … with a rush of hot surges as I got a good look at his face. He reminded me of our butcher when I was in grade school … a sexy Irishman with a tanned face, perfectly setting off his bright blue eyes and masses of dark curly hair. He delivered meat to my mother's restaurant, and once I followed him to the restroom. He closed the door, and I pressed my ear against it to hear him pee. I nearly swooned.

EVANDER CADE SMITH
ATTORNEY AT LAW
683 McALLISTER STREET
SAN FRANCISCO 94102

TELEPHONE
922-5200

July 30, 1968

Adoption Service
Department of Social Services
1680 Mission Street
San Francisco, California

Re: William Jones, Parent,
    Aaron Hunter Jones, Child

Gentlemen:

This office represents Mr. William Jones who is in the
process of adopting Aaron Hunter Jones through your agency.
Mr. Jones speaks very highly of your staff, especially
of Miss Dorothy Murphy and Mrs. Mary Davidson. These
two ladies have impressed Mr. Jones with their pragmatic,
humanistic approach in matching the proper lives as a
family.

As you know, Mr. Jones is one of your agency's single
parent clients. Your willingness to pioneer in this
field is highly commendable. Mr. Jones is appreciative
of his responsibility in this unique role. He is first
of all aware of the life he holds in his hands, his son
Aaron's. Secondly, he appreciates his responsibility
to the thinking people in your agency who have initiated
this program. Thirdly, Mr. Jones feels that he must
succeed as a model for future single parent adoptions.
Because of all these considerations, Mr. Jones has asked
that I write you concerning some untrue and irresponsible
charges made by some unknown, to him, individuals.

Supposedly some gossip monger has given your agency some
hearsay sewage material. The nature of it is to the effect
that Mr. Jones has been indulging in sex orgies and including his son as a participant! My initial flush was
to burn with disgust that a person would seek to harm
such an unselfish and beautiful relationship as this
parent and son enjoy. After calm reflection, I then
felt sorry for the demented soul who would go so far
in such a gross fabrication. It is obviously the rantings

Evander Smith's letter to the adoption agency

EVANDER CADE SMITH
ATTORNEY AT LAW
683 McALLISTER STREET
SAN FRANCISCO 94102

TELEPHONE
922-5200

Adoption Service
Department of Social Services
July 30, 1968
Page Two

of an ill person. Voltaire had this poor, sick soul in
mind when he said, "When you would hurt someone accuse
him of that which you feel innermost in your own soul."

If we were concerned only with Mr. Jones appreciating the
fact that there are vicious and sick people on the street,
I would then advise him to pray for them. But, respecting
the fact that your agency has the tremendous responsibility
of protecting this child, I feel this matter must have
a radical inquiry. I request that you furnish this office
with copies of all material relative to these allegations,
e.g., who, when, what, where etc. In addition to this ,
please furnish all departmental correspondence and notations
concerning the subject. We will, of course, wish to check
your file at a later time to personally verify everything
as to accuracy and completeness.

Upon receipt of the requested material, we will ask for
a hearing to confront the witnesses representing the
statements to be facts. We will cross examine the witnesses.
The entire proceeding will be reported by an official
court reporter so as to preserve the record for further
proceedings in Superior Court if necessary. Initially
this would be in the nature of a Writ of Mandate against
your agency should you fail to permit the finalization
of the adoption. Then suits for tort by interfering
with a family relationship as well as libel and slander
will be filed against the intermeddlers who initiated
the malicious and untrue gossip. These suits against
these conspirators will be brought irrespective of your
agency's final determination. You can, of course, appreciate
the fact that Mr. Jones cannot in good conscience permit
this scurrilous attack to go unchallenged. Your files
and some of your employees will by necessity be subpoenaed
to support the ingredients of Mr. Jones's suit against
these people.

I am enclosing a xerox copy of a letter dated July 28,
1968, that I received from Mr. Jones. This was requested

EVANDER CADE SMITH
ATTORNEY AT LAW
653 McALLISTER STREET
SAN FRANCISCO 94102

TELEPHONE
922-5200

Adoption Service
Department of Social Services
July 30, 1968
Page Three

by me as background material and not for publication to
you. However, this letter is the most beautiful expression
of love by a father for a son that I have ever read.
You will undoubtedly want to consider this plea for help
and its message of love in evaluating Mr. Jones's fit-
ness to be Aaron's father. I only wish you could find
a man with this much compassion for all the little orphans
to call "Daddy".

May I please have your timely response to this letter.
Foremost, Mr. Jones is obviously concerned over his child's
well being as reflected in your agency's plans. And, as
requested above, we require information about your agnecy's
informant (s) to help us in arranging for a confrontation
and suit. None of the acts against Mr. Jones by the tort
feasors are privileged communications between then and
your agency. Therefore, your agency must reveal the requested
information to us either voluntarily or by subpoena.

Sincerely,

EVANDER CADE SMITH

encl.

I slammed on the brakes and changed the station to music. Then I backed up to where he was sitting.

"Can I give you a lift? I'm going across town."

He looked up from the book he was reading and studied my face for a minute, then smiled. "Sure."

He climbed up into the truck and slid across the vinyl seat close to me with his knee leaning on the gearshift mounted on the floor. Even though both windows were down to let in the summer air, his aftershave cologne filled the small cab with a smell of soapy cleanliness, menthol fresh. All I could think of was how much I wanted to nuzzle his neck to smell his skin.

Each time I shifted gears, the back of my knuckles stroked his knee and the smooth poplin pants that covered it. Brooks Brothers, for sure. I glanced at his face and saw he was looking at my hand so close to his leg.

"I'm Bill. What's yours?"

"Evander. Evander Smith."

"Funny. I'm Jones and you're Smith."

"Stranger things have happened. Say, I don't have to be downtown for an hour or so. Can I buy you a cup of coffee?"

I was hoping he was going to suggest we pull over, unbutton our pants, and have a quickie, but the thought of sitting across from this handsome man, a chance to study his face, and maybe get to know him – become his lover – excited me even more.

Looking back on our time in the café, I know that he was toying with the same idea I had when we first sat down, but our conversation took an abrupt turn when he told me he was a lawyer. A gay-activist lawyer. It was a god send, an open door that I rushed through, spilling out my story of my love for my son who might be taken from me. He listened intently and then reached over and put his hand on mine.

"I have an appointment, and got to go, Bill, but we will be seeing a lot more of each other. I want you to write what you just told me and send me the letter as soon as possible."

He handed me his card and left, hailing a cab, probably not wanting to be seen on Montgomery Street in Old Rust, which amused me. I sat there for a few minutes thinking about him, this handsome, sincere, sexy man, but more than a quickie, more than a lover … I needed, desperately needed, a lawyer. An activist lawyer. That night I wrote the letter

I thought Dorothy Murphy was asking for ... but really poured it on ... using Pasek's suggestion as best I could.

*     *     *     *     *

July 25, 1968
2459 Larkin Street
San Francisco, CA

To Whom It May Concern
c/o Dorothy Murphy and Mary Davidson

It seems we are being sucked into some insane, sickening practical joke where the deepest of human emotions – that of love between a child and his parent – is callously bandied about in terms of stag-show humor.

It fills me with disgust and fear to think such viciousness is being taken seriously. I resent this Salem witch-hunt and talk of a lie detector test. I resent that the precious inner life of my child is at stake because of the unprofessional, unofficial, and unproven accusations of an obviously disturbed person (or persons).

I resent the gnawing fear that each hour with my son may be our last hour together. I resent the fact that he must sense this fear and cry each time we must part. I resent being the victim of this bizarre joke, which makes me uptight and not able to give my son a totally relaxed and confident environment.

I resent that the professional opinions of Mary Davidson and Dorothy Murphy are questioned in suh an unprofessional manner. I resent the fact that on my own volition and whole-hearted trust in Mary Davidson, I informed her BEFORE THE PLACEMENT that I had received outpatient therapy in 1961 and now that ancient history may be used against me AFTER THE PLACEMENT. As I told Mary, I went to Langley Porter because I didn't know which way my life was going professionally – and it depressed me. I was through with teaching and knew that my modeling career could never satisfy me – either emotionally or financially. In therapy, I discovered that I seemed to have a "will to fail." I had been abandoned by my parents when they separated. I was two, the same age as Aaron, my son. I felt unworthy and rejected and tried to prove my unworthiness in every way – in schoolwork, in business, and even in my closest emotional attachments.

That was almost nine years ago. By the termination of my therapy, I was working hard for myself, remodeling Victorian homes. Since then, I have bought and sold six buildings. The latest is a 14-unit apartment building worth a quarter of a million dollars. My net worth is a little over one hundred thousand dollars, although my annual income is still low. I am proud of my achievements and it is most important to me to feel that I am working to pass the fruits of my labor on to my son. By the time he is ready for college, he should be a moderately wealthy man.

I think it is just for me and my doctors to know what soul-searching I experienced at that time. It's not that I have anything to hide, but I don't think it is right to single me out from other adoptive parents. I cannot believe that professional social workers question other applicants' sexuality so unreasonably.

I find it disgusting and humiliating to justify myself. I have no need to, but *I feel that this is the time I must say that I am not a homosexual.*

If someone is slandering me, let him do it officially and quickly, so I can take the proper legal actions now before my son is harmed permanently by our separation.

Aside from the fact that we are being involved in what might easily get out of hand and become a personal, human tragedy, I am deeply saddened, as I'm sure you are, to think that the single-adoptive parent program is in jeopardy and that hundreds of children who could be placed in loving, healthy homes might never have that chance.

My home has been approved by two specially trained, experienced professionals. Their opinion, my reputation, and the future life of an innocent child are at stake. We must be strong in our convictions or this might reoccur in the next four months if another psychiatric patient accuses me of grand theft, rape, or treason. What more is to come? What other unnamed horrors are in store for those of us who want to light a candle in this darkened world of insane hatred and violence? I am prepared at this time to sue any person or persons who slander my good name, which jeopardizes the legal adoption of my son, Aaron Hunter Jones. You will be contacted by my lawyer, Evander Smith, within a few days.

Sincerely,
Bill Jones

*     *     *     *     *

Three days later I wrote to Evander Smith. It took me about six hours to type a three-page letter, and I poured out my soul to him, outlining the adoption procedure and the nightmare I was going through, but I have to admit that most of the letter was about Aaron, his nearness to me in every way, how my life had changed because this little boy loved me. Needed me. I begged him to do *everything* he could legally do to nail this bastard who was making our lives a living hell.

*     *     *     *     *

A week later it was my turn to host "the Group's" monthly charade and potluck. Pasek was the first to arrive with his ratatouille and last to leave after helping me clean up and wash the dishes. The group, Michael Vincent, and his lover, Bob Lanci, Dennis, and Judd Wirz, the architect who shared Dennis's studio, came together, and Gary Fusfeld made his grand entrance, fashionably late as usual.

Unlike the rest of us who were still wearing our cashmere sweaters, button-down collars, and khaki pants, Gary sported tight paisley pants of faded orange, coordinated with his rust-colored belt and shirt. He flung his straw cowboy hat across the room, and declared, "Pour Uncle Gary a drink! She's had a bitch of a day at the old Saks farm milking the cows."

Michael took a deep breath. "You think you've had a bad day? Try working with Alma Spreckels!"

Bob Lanci scoffed. "Or havta bus your own damn dishes when the busboy's off with a damn hangover!"

Pasek clinked a spoon on his glass. "Ladies! Ladies! No bitchin'. Dennis, you and Judd pour the drinks, and Daddy Bill and I'll get dinner on the table."

While we were still on the crème brulé that Gary brought, Pasek announced that all the uncles in the room had to give me their attention for the rest of the night. There would be no charades. He told them over their groans that I needed their input and advice, and that I would be reading two letters–the one I wrote to Dorothy and the one to Evander, and then Pasek would read the one Evander wrote to Dorothy. Silence.

I felt guilty taking up their time with my woeful letters, but they didn't seem as restless and bored as I thought they would be. It helped pique their interest when I told them how I met Evander and what a hunk he was. I was coy when they wanted to know how he was in the sack. Better to let their imaginations answer that. So, when Pasek began to read Evander's letter, everyone leaned in to hear every word.

Pasek finished by laying the pages of the letter down and slowly leaning back in his chair.

"Oh, good lord, and I thought I had troubles." Gary sighed.

Bob added, "I'd bus dishes for the rest of my life instead of going through that shit."

Dennis and Judd nodded their heads, and we all sat, drained, perplexed, wondering what I should do next, or if indeed there was anything else that could be said – or done.

Michael, the proper Englishman, pounced on the letters piled neatly in front of us, bounced to his feet, and threw the pages as high as he could. As they came fluttering down, carpeting the floor, he began to bellow, in his best Eliza cockney accent,

*"Words, words, words! I'm so sick of words! I get words all day through. First from him,"* and he pointed at Bob then at me, *"now from you. Is that all you blighters can do?"*

It broke the ice, and Pasek took over,

*"Don't talk of stars, burning above. If you're in love, …"*

We all shouted, *"Show me!"*

He stopped. "Oh, hell, I can't remember the rest of it!

Bob said, half laughing, "You know, Michael's right. Enough words. Don't write any more letters. Everything that had to be said has been said. No more words."

Dennis, who worked every day with drawings, layouts, and photos, added, "Yeah. A picture's worth a thousand words."

Judd spoke up, "Dennis might have something there. We need to show them a picture of Daddy Bill and his son, Aaron. Maybe at a playground."

Pasek sighed, "Too casual. Bill's got to look solid. Responsible. Daddy-like," He paused, "… not mushy daddy-like, but in control. In a business suit."

Everyone leaned forward to contribute.

"Dark gray."

"Too dreary. Dark blue."

"Bank of America executive!"

Michael leapt to his feet again, "I know just the photographer! Emilie Romaine. She's on Sutter. Does Pacific Heights, usually mother, father, and all the kids in white. White shoes, socks, dresses, suits, all white. Very chic. I did her office."

Gary extended his arm and let his wrist go limp. "Oh, no, not all white. Keep it blue to go with Aaron's eyes. And ladies, you won't believe this, but we just got in a lot of children's wear at the store. And guess what? There's a blue velvet romper and jacket that has Aaron's name on it!"

"He can still have white shoes and socks though, right?" Michael asked.

"And a white Peter Pan shirt, too. I was going to buy it with my discount anyhow. The whole outfit for his Christmas present, but what the hell?" Gary beamed. "Little Lord Fauntleroy."

There were a lot of hugs and air kisses at the door as they filed out, some laughing, and some humming "Show Me!" Gary went out into the lobby with Pasek, but turned back, smiling, and said, "No! Little Boy Blue!" as he blew me a kiss.

## Chapter 44
# The Thousand-Word Picture

The world seemed to be spiraling into hell all summer in 1968, especially in August when the Republicans nominated that sleazeball, Nixon. France set off its first thermonuclear bomb in Polynesia, and our shitty war in Vietnam got worse each day. The Democratic convention in Chicago was a bloody nightmare. Even worse was the daily dread that Aaron could be snatched from my arms at any moment.

*　　*　　*　　*　　*

I had just turned off the evening news when the doorbell rang. Aaron was still a little damp as I quickly pulled on his seersucker Dr. Dentons and took another swipe at his wet hair with his bath towel. I swung him up to straddle my neck and ride on my shoulders, which he loved because he could pull on my ears and pat the top of my head. I opened the door, and there stood Gary in a suit and tie, his work drag, holding a beautiful black shirt box with Saks Fifth Avenue printed in gold on the top.

"Hey, Aaron, Santa Claus couldn't wait to give this to you, so he told me to come over right after work today, and give it to you early." He gestured toward the kitchen. "Bill, make it vodka this time instead of gin, okay?" Then he lifted Aaron off my shoulders. "It's a special suit he made just for you, Master Jones, and Uncle Gary told him it had to be blue."

"Gosh, Gary, I didn't think you were serious. Thanks ever so much! So thoughtful of you. How much?"

"You bitch! It's *my* Christmas present for Aaron. Get your own damn present for him."

I hurried over to the counter that separated the kitchen from the living room to make a vodka and tonic for Gary. He plopped down onto the sofa, put the box on the cocktail table, and pulled Aaron up to sit on his lap. As I sat down beside him, he was lifting the lid off the box.

I pulled back the silver tissues that enfolded the royal blue suit, rompers, and jacket. When I saw it and felt the soft velvet, a warm wave started in the pit of my stomach and rushed to my throat. "Gary, I … I don't know what to say … how to thank you. It is beyond … my … god, it's beautiful! Something I could never afford." A vision flashed of my mother in her black velvet skirt that had made me teary-eyed because she had looked so beautiful so many years before.

Gary took a long gulp of his drink. "I get a discount, Sweetie. And the buyer's a friend of mine. A *really* good friend if ya know what I mean."

*     *     *     *     *

Two weeks later, Emilie Romaine, the socialite photographer, with the prodding of Michael Vincent, found an hour she would donate to "The Cause" so long as I paid for the printing and paper costs. Pasek dropped off a striped tie he wanted me to wear, as well as a pair of white knee socks for Aaron to go with the white shoes Michael and Bob had bought him. We must have been a sight when I drove Old Rust into the Sutter Street Garage, looking like a millionaire and a millionaire's son slumming it in a dented, rusty, and dirty old Dodge pickup with a cracked windshield.

Aaron was picking up a few words, which made me very happy. He loved motorcycles and would squeal, "Mo! Mo! Mo!" every time he saw one. Lily was Lee, and no meant no, but in the garage elevator, he came up with a word I'd never heard him use before. Besides that, he put two words together. The elevator was crowded and I was holding him, standing in the very back. A short woman of a certain age, with dyed red hair, turned around and faced us. Her face was caked with makeup, her fake eyelashes were long and black, so long that they stroked the inside of her eyeglasses, framed by clusters of plastic jewels.

"Oh, aren't you just the cutest little fella?" She reached up and pinched his cheek. He pulled away. "Wasa, wasa, wasa. I could just eat you alive!"

Aaron looked straight at her and said, "You ugly." My face turned crimson. Just then the elevator doors slid open, and I pushed our way toward them as fast as I could.

* * * * *

Emilie Romaine's studio on Sutter Street was large, painted totally black, the only light came from floodlights on tripods and from a spotlight reflecting on an oversized, silver umbrella. A 12-foot-wide roll of elephant-colored paper hung from a steel rod overhead and continued down to seamlessly cover the floor beneath our feet. Not one to waste a minute, she rapidly shot one candid photo after another with a mammoth camera mounted on a wooden tripod.

She was a kind and patient woman, who was able to comfort and amuse children, which won their respect. That's why she was in demand by the Pacific Heights families. Aaron loved her sense of fun, the jack in the box, the yellow balloon that fluttered out of control. As the hour went on, he became hyper, running around the studio, playing hide and seek in the dark corners. I found myself scolding him and demanding he behave, which was new to him. The sterner I sounded, the more he teased. It was a game for him in an exciting new playground, but I was feeling the pressure of what needed to be done and the little time left to do it.

Emilie finished taking all the candid shots she wanted and let me know our time was almost up. Michael had briefed her on the importance of our portrait and what we were striving to show our antagonists, so she put a chair on the muted paper and told me to sit and hold Aaron. He squirmed and tried to get off my lap so he could run and play, but I tightened my grip on him so he couldn't get down, and then he decided to crawl up on my shoulders for a piggyback ride. I panicked, firmly holding him close to me so he wouldn't move around so much.

He stopped squirming and looked up at me to see if I was serious. I grinned and winked at him, and I could feel his body relaxing, as he rested his head on my shoulder. Emilie took her last picture, and said, "Bill, I do believe we got it."

A week after the shoot, I went over the contacts with Emilie to choose those I wanted to be printed. I was thrilled with the ones of Aaron, but I was *not* happy at all with the ones of the two of us, especially the last few sitting in the chair. I looked so stiff and formal and wanted to do them over, but Emilie was impatient with me.

"It's exactly what Michael told me you needed, Bill. You realize, don't you, that I did this work for nothing. Free! And, Bill Jones, I can't afford to give you another hour." She took her red marker and circled a picture, one that I especially disliked, and said firmly, "This is the one you're getting!"

A few days later, I picked up the prints and dropped the one Emilie had chosen off with Dorothy Murphy's secretary. I was too disappointed in it to see Dorothy's reaction, which I thought would be the same as mine, but it wasn't.

"Hi, Bill, it's Dorothy. Mary's here with me and we both *love* the photo of you two. In fact, Mary tacked it on the bulletin board right after you left it here yesterday, and it's causing quite a commotion. Some of the workers in other departments are making trips over here on their breaks just to see it! Wait a second. Here's Mary. She wants to talk to you."

"Hi, Bill, it's Mary. I put a sign under the photo that just says *Bill Jones and Aaron*, and you'd be surprised at the reaction it's getting. The ones on our side, and that's *almost* every person in this department, think it's great. Fabulous! It's stopped any wavering … any questioning. It's made the goal of single adoptions viable. I wish I had thought to do it before this. Here. Dorothy wants to say something."

"Bill, if it comes to a court battle, and I hope it doesn't, the publicity alone might ruin the program. But if it does, we're ready for it. Dr. Harper's position is that you will make a good parent whether you are straight or gay. He wants to make a point that the current view that homosexuality is a pathology is wrong, wrong, wrong. The letters from you and Evander Smith are compelling, and, Bill, I don't know if your photo could be used as evidence in a courtroom, but it sure has won our case here at the adoption agency!"

It relieved me – a little – to hear this, but it would take me much longer to appreciate Emilie's photo. Now it hangs in my entry hall with a spotlight on it for every guest to see. I had it enlarged and printed on canvas, and it looks like a Renaissance painting.

Below the portrait, stands a fountain I bought in Carmel that has been flowing steadily since 1996. Just under the photo is a small wooden plaque someone sent me after our adoption became national news. The poem pasted on it reads:

Not flesh of my flesh,
Nor bone of my bone,
But still miraculously
My own.
Never forget for a single minute,
You didn't grow under my heart
But in it.
            —Fleur Conkling Heyliger

I cherish the photos Emilie Romaine took that day. Especially the one I didn't like. Each time I replenish the fountain with fresh water, I look at Aaron's face and those beautiful, contented blue-gray eyes. I think I know what he was thinking. I think he was happy that I loved him even though he had just pushed all my buttons. But I remember all too well what I did to make him calm down. I had to be the stern daddy and show him who was boss. But when he relaxed and leaned against me, I was the happy one.

## Chapter 45

# Dodging the Bullets

August and September of 1968 were black and bloody, every day full of threats and disappointment. All kinds of wars polluted the daily lives of Aaron and me – Vietnam with LBJ's daily kill count on the news, olive drab helicopters, Agent Orange, and coffins lined up at American airports as far as the eye could see.

There was a political meltdown with our hero, Bobby, assassinated. Then George McGovern and Eugene McCarthy were defeated at the bloody war-like Democratic Convention by that shadow and echo of LBJ, the little weasel, Hubert H. Humphrey. He would run against "Tricky Dick" Nixon, and for the first and only time in my life, I refused to vote. *That'll show 'em!*

Outside the Miss America pageant on the Atlantic City boardwalk, feminists crowned a live sheep and threw their bras, girdles, false eyelashes, and hair curlers into the "Freedom Trash Can." Barbra Streisand proved big noses can be gorgeous in *Funny Girl*, and Tammy Wynette was on every music station singing "Stand by Your Man."

It was a mad world outside our apartment, but I tried to create a world inside that was calm, fun, educational, and with a sprinkle of fairy dust – as "normal" as possible. With a print machine, I had left over from teaching, I labeled everything in the apartment on three-by-five cards – chairs, tables, windows, doors, pictures, mirrors, sinks, toilets, rugs, beds, toys – *everything*.

Aaron loved the books I read to him, and his vocabulary grew. I printed each word he could now say and taped them to the wall next to his potty.

Since he was still in diapers, and I was the parent anxious to potty train him, I let him sit on his potty as long as I could keep him there by reading the words on the wall. In between words, I would give a little grunt, hoping he would get the idea, but mostly, all he ever did was pee. When he did, I would jump back, because it always shot straight up into the air, raining down all over the tiled floor and me.

Any soldier can tell you that no matter how deep the foxhole, a bullet or a piece of shrapnel can find its way to your body, and one San Francisco quiet afternoon on Russian Hill, in an apartment that was barricaded and safe, a bullet whizzed toward me, toward Aaron, Mary, Dorothy, and the entire single-parent program.

"Hello, is this Mr. Jones? Bill Jones?"

The voice was unfamiliar, but I acknowledged it. "Yes. Who's this?"

"I work for the *San Francisco Chronicle*. I'm a reporter, and I just got a very interesting call about you, and I need to verify it."

I felt a chill descending from my throat, down into my lungs, down into my groin, a chill that froze my brain and tongue for a second or two.

"I'm busy right now."

"Look, Buddy, I can verify it through other sources, but I'd like to give you first whack at it. It came from a very reliable source, and if it's true, and I think it is, it's going on the front page. Now, would you like to make a statement?"

"I don't have any statement to make, and I ... I don't even know what you're talking about." My thoughts raced ahead. Dorothy had told me several times that if the rumors got out, we could expect protests from "religious" groups marching back and forth in front of the adoption agency. I had been so careful and warned my friends to keep it secret, but what would Dorothy think of me if I talked to this reporter? I felt trapped.

"Look, Bill, May I call you Bill? I got this call from a psychologist who's married to a chick who works at Social Services in the adoption agency for god's sake. Now can we stop beating around the bush? What's your story?"

I swallowed hard, and then I started to beg. "I know what you're talking about, but hear me out first, I'm begging you not to print the story ... not until the adoption is finalized at least. You know, you know, there're hundreds of kids in foster homes in San Francisco – older kids, handicapped kids,

Chairs, tables, toys, books, dishes; everything in our home wore
a printed label.

mixed blood. They'll stay in foster homes or be … institutionalized if … if
Dorothy Murphy's program fails, and you … you would make it fail by telling
the world about it. We desperately need to keep this quiet until we can prove it
works. Know what I mean?"

I was beginning to sound like my father, *"Ya know what I mean?"*

"It's not just the single adoption plan that's at stake here. My life is hanging on a thread right now. I … I might even lose my son." My throat had
defrosted, but now it was so thick I could hardly get the words out. "So, I'm
begging you to do what I suppose is impossible. Don't let the news out, *Please*!"
Don't print it yet!"

I heard no response from him, but I could hear typewriters clicking behind
him. "What's the name of the broad that runs the agency, Bill?"

"Dorothy, Dorothy Murphy."

"You gonna be home the next few minutes, Bill? I have to check on something here, and I'll get back to you, okay?"

Aaron's growing vocabulary

My phone conversation must have awakened Aaron from his nap because I heard him calling me. I no sooner got him seated on his potty than the phone rang again.

"Hi, Bill. Here's the deal. Number one, you don't talk to any other paper, okay? You don't talk to any TV reporter, okay? The *Chron* gets the story when the time's right, okay? This may be the worst decision I've ever made, but …"

Just then Aaron started yelling from the bathroom, "Daddy, come, Daddy!"

"That your son, Bill?"

"Yeah!"

"I'll make this quick so you can go take care of him. Got a pencil?"

"Yeah."

"Mildred Hamilton. Write that down. She'll be gettin' in touch with you, and she'll want to sit down with you, okay?"

"But …"

"Here's our deal, Bill, and my word's as good as yours, dig?"

"But now you're saying you still want to report this, right?"

"Mildred Hamilton is a *feature* writer here, and says she'll do it."

"But I told you why it's so important to us that it doesn't get in the papers, it would kill us!"

"Hang in there, Buddy. Mildred's piece will only be in the *Chron after* the adoption is finalized, okay? I give you my word that we'll wait 'til the coast is clear, and it won't harm you or anyone else. But the deal is that you give me the story in case it becomes news before we can do Mildred's feature. In fact, if you know Mildred's work, it'll be the best thing in the world for you and Aaron, for all those other kids, for Dorothy Murphy, and especially for her single adoption program.

"I understand. Thank you from the bottom of my heart."

"Now go take your son off the toilet, Bill, and Bill …"

"Yes?"

"I was adopted in 1934, and one thing I know … I love my mom and dad. Bye for now, Buddy."

## Chapter 46

# The Paper Doll and the Village

Hillary Clinton had it right. It does take a village to raise a child. If Ronnie hadn't moved in and become Aaron's nanny, staying with him while I repaired the Wildflower Apts. or worked as a movie extra, I couldn't have supported us. If my brother and Randles hadn't helped me paint and wallpaper the empty apartments, I would have lost rent money, taking the time to do it by myself. If Pasek hadn't encouraged me and held my hand, I would have folded in depression and drowned in feelings of failure – fighting an unseen antagonist.

My village seemed to grow, and although I got all the credit for raising Aaron, I knew I couldn't do it alone. I guess I realized it the night Pasek and I were mugged outside the Paper Doll, our favorite gay bar on Union Street in North Beach. Ronnie stayed in my apartment with Aaron until I came home a little before dawn. I'd spent half the night filing a complaint at the police station and going to the emergency room at San Francisco General Hospital with Pasek, whose nose was broken when he was pulling one of the thugs off me.

The evening had started off so well. I didn't go out at night much anymore, so it was a treat for me to smell the popcorn in the movie lobby and smoke a cigarette in a bar without a diaper bag under one arm. Ronnie agreed to feed, bathe, and put Aaron to bed so Pasek and I could see *Barbarella*, the erotic outer-space movie starring Henry Fonda's daughter, Jane. We got a hamburger at the Grubstake on Pine Street afterward, and then drove over to the Paper

Doll for one drink so I could get home before ten when Ronnie would want to go back to her own place.

The Paper Doll was packed, as usual on a Friday night, the bar lined with hopefuls, thinking it would be smart to make out with a hunk that you could sleep in with Saturday morning, and if it was really good – Sunday morning, too. Pasek even had breakfast menus according to the sexiness of his partners. A cup of coffee for the Hoh-Hums, and toast and juice added for the Okays, but for the Here's-My-Number-Let's-Stay-in-Touch, eggs, and bacon. If it was truly a Knocked-Out-of-the-Park … pancakes!

Being a model for Macy's ads was an advantage and a disadvantage. The advantage was, of course, you got eyed the minute you walked in the door of a gay bar. The disadvantage was being a model that guys recognized can be intimidating, and it takes more time and courage for them to actually try to make contact. I loved the attention and the sly looks that were quickly hidden. But unlike my "bachelor" nights when I could be choosy, hanging around and drinking until the last call, my nights out with a babysitter waiting for me, were very short, and not much help in finding relief from being on-fire horny. Or as Pasek called it, "having blue balls."

Pasek bought us gin and tonics. Then he moved away from me, inching down the bar to stand next to a handsome dark-haired man, whose temples were distinctly gray. Pasek used his usual pickup line just as Mama Cass finished singing "Dream a Little Dream of Me," I heard him say to the man, "Er, excuse me, Sir. You see, I just got in town and I think I'm lost. I'm hoping you can give me directions."

The man smiled, took a glance at him and said, "Sure. I live here in Frisco. Where'd you want to go?"

"I was hoping you'd give me directions to, well, to your bedroom."

Just then the atmosphere changed as a spotlight flooded the stage in the back corner of the room, and my attention was redirected. An older white guy stood behind the bass, a black man held a saxophone, and a lanky, young man, sporting a Beatles haircut sat at the grand piano. He leaned into the microphone. "Ladies and gentlemen, Ann Weldon!"

A gorgeous woman came out from behind a screen and stood leaning against the black piano. Her face was radiant, the color of coffee and cream, and her body filled a butter-colored chiffon dress. The bass set the rhythm, the piano set the tune, and the sax introduced one of the mellowest and fullest voices I've ever heard. She started to sing "You Make Me Feel Like a Natural Woman." I wanted to stay as long as she could still keep singing, but Pasek tugged at my sleeve and whispered, "Come on. It's past your bedtime. We gotta go right now, Billy. I got the directions to his bedroom!"

I left the Paper Doll walking backwards with Pasek guiding me, not willing to take my eyes off her, and savoring every note she sang. The only relief I felt after we walked out the door was that the warm October night air was clear and fresh, not hazy with cigarette smoke. Pasek had parked his Volkswagen down an alley across the street from the bar, and as we neared it, we saw three dark figures opening the door, and he exclaimed, "They're going through my glove compartment!" We ran toward them. "Hey, guys, what the hell you doing in my car?"

A fist hit my face and a shoe left a dirty print on my khakis at the same time. I toppled over to the asphalt. Looking up I saw two thugs above me, and heard them cursing, "Fuckin' cock suckers! God-damn queers!" They punctuated each curse with a kick to my sides and stomach. I covered my head and face. Then I heard Pasek yell at them to stop kicking me. One of them yelled back, "Whatcha goin' to do about it, *homo*?"

I staggered when I got to my feet. The faces around me were flushed red, their eyes dark, squinting. One raised his arm ready to bash me with a flashlight. Pasek ran toward him and struggled to take the flashlight away. The thug swung around and hit Pasek in the face with it. He sank down on his knees, holding his nose that was gushing blood. I heard the clatter of footsteps, and they were gone.

"Jesus! Now there's blood all over this cashmere sweater my mother gave me last Christmas! And that guy hit me with a flashlight? Fuckers!"

I reached into Pasek's pocket and pulled out his keys and a hanky to stop the bleeding. We sat in his car for just a minute to stop panting, and then while driving him to the hospital, he pulled everything out of his pockets.

"Oh, hell! That guy was husband material, and he's gonna think I'm a flake. He gave me his phone and address, and now I can't find it! Bill, after you take me to the hospital and we report this to the cops, will you drive me back to the alley so we can look for that matchbook he wrote on? Please?"

After we stopped at a police station to report the mugging, we had to wait a long time in the emergency room for a nurse to clean Pasek's nose and face. Ronnie, who was very understanding, agreed to sleep on my sofa until

I got home. When Pasek reminded me, I drove us back to the alley where it happened, and we crawled around in the dark alley at three in the morning where the pavement was still damp with blood. Our only light was from books of matches, and it was becoming obvious we were on a useless mission until Pasek, still on his hands and knees yelled out,

"Eureka!"

# Chapter 47

# Merry Christmas, My Lai

A blast of trumpets sounded and a CBS SPECIAL REPORT banner unfolded across the screen. *What now, for god's sake!* Aaron was holding a book and tugging at my pant leg, but I left the TV on, hoping he was more interested in cuddling and reading than watching it. Walter Cronkite looked solemn, as he always did when he commented on the war.

"A classified document and film have come into our possession, and although it was stamped CONFIDENTIAL, after hours of deliberation, it is the decision of the CBS News Department to share it with you, as fellow Americans, who have the right to know facts about the undeclared war we are now waging in Vietnam."

I was holding Aaron on my lap, turning pages for him to look at the illustrations, hoping that would be enough to distract him.

"I regret to tell you that what you are about to see will disturb you, and I regret, even more, reporting that there has been an elaborate cover-up by the United States government to suppress this news for almost a year."

Lily circled near my feet, and finally settled down with her chin lying on one shoe. Mammy lay curled beside us on the sofa.

"In South Vietnam, there are many small villages, made up mostly of rice farmers and their families. My Lai is one of those villages. On March 16th of this year, a platoon of US soldiers, called Charlie Company, massacred more than 500 Vietnamese civilians in this village."

The camera moved over the landscape of sprawled bodies seeping blood; faces and gory limbs were thoughtfully blurred out by the CBS news team. Revulsion, as if I were going to spit up something, started in my stomach and crawled upward. The camera moved from the bodies near their burning homes to a ditch next to a dirt road, where more bodies lay.

Then the words Cronkite said blurred too, but I did hear a few very clearly … "Lieutenant William Calley led the charge, and personally executed dozens with an automatic weapon. His victims included a two-year-old boy, who lies crumpled in the ditch." The camera panned down on the tiny body.

I held Aaron so close to me that he whimpered. The limp body of the little two-year-old boy in the ditch, like the others, showed a digitized face, but what I clearly saw was Aaron's face on that discarded body. Revulsion surged through me. I got up and carried Aaron close to me as I trudged over to the TV set, tempted to kick in the glass tube. Instead, I stooped over and yanked the cord out of the socket.

We went back to the sofa and I read each page, pages that Aaron loved to turn, but sometimes it was difficult reading the words as anger welled up inside me.

*　　*　　*　　*　　*

The thought of Aaron being thrown in a ditch and blasted with a machine gun festered in my mind, and the vision of it came and went at the oddest moments. A couple of days after the news of My Lai, Pasek, Aaron, and I went shopping for a Christmas tree at the Guardsmen lot. The invigorating smell of cut pine was strong, and a portable radio was playing Christmas carols, loud, tinny, and filled with static.

I found a tree that was symmetrical and full but a little too tall, so I asked one of the guardsmen to saw off a few inches from the thick bottom of the trunk. He laid it on its side and I could smell the sap oozing from the trunk as he cut it, but when I bent over to breathe in its fragrance, I envisioned blood dripping from the stub. My Lai … Christmas carols … Aaron and Lily running through the trees on the lot … helicopters spraying Agent Orange … here comes Santa Claus! Rice fields. The ditch by the side of the road. Then gently slipping the tree into the bed of Old Rust.

"Pasek, I think I'm going nuts."

"So, what's new?"

"I can't stop thinking about what that creep, Calley, did in My Lai.

Killing … shooting that little boy. I just can't stop thinking about it."

"Yeah, me, too. But you know … you have to dump it somehow. Nothing you and I can do about it anyway. It's Aaron's first Christmas for god's sake. You *can* do something about that. What's more important than the first *whatever*?"

Pasek helped me erect the tree on its stand and string the colored lights. Then he hurried off to a cocktail party, leaving me to hang the ornaments and aluminum foil like icicles. *Sunset* magazine said to hang the small ornaments toward the top and the large ones at the bottom, which I dutifully did. However, they didn't warn me that cats love to lie under the tree, belly up, and swat at the shiny balls hanging from the lowest branches.

I had turned the sound up on the TV to be able to hear *Julie Andrews's Christmas Special* while I gave Aaron his bubble bath. As soon as I could coax him out of the tub, I wrapped him in a towel and made a beeline for the sofa in the living room so we could watch the show. My eyes diverted to a spread of glistening shards of glass under the tree, reflecting the blinking, colored lights above it.

"Mammy! Damn you!"

Lily rose and walked slowly into the kitchen with her head down and her tail drooping, thinking she had done something to displease me. I heard Mammy meowing, and when I found her, she was busy trying to lick the tiny slivers of the ornaments from her fur.

"Mammy, now look what you've done!" She kept licking. The scene was definitely not a classic Rockwell painting of a typical American family at Christmastime. Aaron was shivering as the towel slipped off him, and I grabbed Lily's brush to clear Mammy's thick black coat before she swallowed any of the shards. Lily peered at us from around the kitchen counter, afraid to leave her safety zone, as I rushed past her to get a broom and dustpan to sweep up the mess under the tree before Lily, Mammy, or Aaron could step on it.

Julie was singing her last song, and I heard as I dumped the sparkling bits and pieces from the dustpan, *"You better watch out. You better not cry. You better not pout. I'm telling you why. Santa Claus is coming to town!"*

I grabbed Aaron's Dr. Dentons and headed for my little family. As I was pulling the leggings over Aaron's feet, I heard her finish the song, *"He sees you when you're sleeping. He knows when you're awake. He knows when you've been bad or good, so be good for goodness' sake!"*

I hoped Santa hadn't seen me get so mad at Mammy. That was me being bad, but something good, very good, came out of it. I hadn't thought of My Lai for at least 30 minutes.

## Chapter 48
# Signatures

"Merry Christmas, Bill."

"And a Merry Christmas to you too, Mary."

"Dorothy and I are still laughing about Aaron calling Santa, Daddy."

"I guess I got carried away about always telling him the truth. Do you think I screwed up?"

"Oh, no, Bill. Not at all. Everybody understood. Everyone was laughing *with* you. We've never seen so many big smiles at a Carriage Trade event before. There's no right and wrong way about teaching our kids about things like Santa and the Easter Bunny. As long as our kids know we love 'em. That's what matters."

"It was funny, wasn't it?"

"Eh, yes, yes, it was really funny."

I knew by her distracted response that she had really phoned me about something else.

"Bill, I wish Dorothy wouldn't ask me to do her dirty work all the time, but here I am again with bad news. A petition's being passed around at the agency. It says that because they have reason to believe you are not just a single man, but actually a single *gay* man, you should be denied the adoption."

"Christ! A petition?"

"You'll never know how much it pains me … us, when we have to tell you more dreadful stuff like this, and just before Christmas, too."

"So, what's next? I've written my letters and I've seen a psychologist. I had Evander write you a letter. We did the portrait. I'm running out of counter-attacks. What'll we do, Mary? It's eating me up."

"Look, it's not come to a head yet, and the week between Christmas and New Year's a washout. If this was just another adoption we would have finalized it by this time. We kept praying that things would cool down and these troublemakers would go find something else to bitch about, but they're acting like dogs in heat. There's no stopping them!"

I had never heard Mary speak like that before. *Dogs in heat?*

*          *          *          *          *

Pasek came over that night with a bucket of Kentucky Fried Chicken and a six-pack of Anchor Steam beer. Between dusting the crispy bits of chicken off my sweatshirt and wiping Aaron's runny nose, I told him about Aaron's thinking Santa was me in Santa drag, about the petition, and Mary's calling them dogs in heat.

He loved the Santa story, but the idea of a bunch of conservative busybodies passing a petition around to tear Aaron from us made his face flush red and his eyes narrow. "Fuckin' assholes! I'd like to drown them all in a gunnysack as my uncle did to a litter of kittens. Into the fuckin' Mississippi River!"

"Pasek, I'm scared. Really scared. What should I do?"

"Sue the fuckers!"

"Sue 'em? Over what?"

"Over saying you're gay!"

"But I am, Blanche, I am! And it could be proved so easily."

"You got witnesses, pal. Me. And your brother, Randles. There's more, Bill, a lot more."

"Then what? Ever hear of perjury, Pasek? One lie, just one, and they can prove I'm gay, that you're lying 'bout it, and you go to jail!

"Yeah, I guess you're right. Five minutes with you and anybody'd know you're a flaming faggot. Hey, how about that lawyer you tricked with?"

"If you mean Evander Smith, we didn't trick."

"Maybe not, but he liked you enough to write a letter for you. And didn't charge you a cent, right. Phone him … now!"

I took Evander's card from my wallet and dialed his number, but a recorded message said he would be out of town until the first of the year and asked that we not leave a message because the machine would handle only 10 calls. Then a quick "Happy Holidays" and a click.

"Pasek, I'm being put on hold ... until next year! First Mary and Dorothy, and now Evander. What'll I do? What'll I do?"

"Celebrate, dammit, celebrate! OK, it might be the last Christmas for you and Aaron, but get your head out of your ass, and let's get goin' on this Christmas feast!"

I found myself shifting gears again, closing doors that led to dark corridors, and opening the ones to rooms lit with the glow of Aaron, my son. *My son.*

"Twenty people! You know, Pasek, Woolworths is already having a sale on Christmas stuff. Santa hats are half price!"

## Chapter 49
# Shifting Gears for a Happy New Year

The week between Christmas, 1968, and the New Year, 1969, rolled by like a ball of molasses and set me on edge. I had to watch myself and not take my anxiety out on Aaron or Pasek. The signed petition hung over my head, like a guillotine blade about to drop, and I was counting each hour until I could ask Evander what we should do, but he wouldn't be in his office until January 2nd. The final papers should have been processed months ago, but Dorothy felt trapped and didn't want to rock the boat. It was a hell of a week.

Depression set in, and all I could think about was how terrifying the past year had been. The year 1968 will be remembered in history books a churning, violent year of assassinations, American soldiers murdering toddlers, tear-gassed riots at universities, the election of Nixon, a slimy "used-car salesman," the racist Governor George Wallace and Black Power, a serial killer called Zodiac, and drugs seeping into our music, into naive minds, into desperate, lonely lives. And for Pasek and me, a mugging outside a gay bar.

I shift gears.

Aaron blossomed into my life, giving me a chance to be reborn, and if we could succeed with the single parent adoption, thousands would follow us. Martin and Bobby left us with ideals. Kennedy said, "It is better to light a candle than to curse the darkness." And King's *I Have a Dream* speech lit more candles. The students who rioted were bringing Black Studies into the universities. Wonderful pop songs were written about peace and justice. Dick and Tom Smothers, Cecil Williams, Walter Cronkite, Eartha Kitt, Joan Baez, The Summer of Love, the Broadway musical *Hair*, *The Boys in the Band*, the Catonsville Nine, and the love from the "Group," especially Pasek, were all lighting candles.

You just had to shift gears to see it.

Aaron was coming out of his dark shell and showing a real sense of humor – at my expense, of course. One of the things he loved to do was to slip out of the towel I was drying him with and run through the apartment stark naked, making me run to catch him. He'd be giggling the whole time, jumping up and down on the sofa, crawling under the table, and barking at poor Lily or Mammy. When we went to the beach, I never made him wear a bathing suit, and he was growing up without shame. His nakedness brought him joy.

New Year's Eve, a night Pasek and I usually spent in gay bars or gay parties, kissing as many guys as would let us, was different for me this year. I wanted to spend it with Aaron, even though he would be put to bed around eight o'clock, unable to welcome 1969 with me at midnight. Pasek pleaded with me to ask Ronnie or even Mrs. Metcalfe to babysit for me so we could go to a party Michael and Bob were giving. I didn't even consider it because I planned to tiptoe into the nursery at midnight so I could kiss Aaron on his cheek.

Aunt Ruth had put a $50 bill in the tie box she gave me. I could think of so many ways to spend it, like paying the PG&E bill, but I shifted gears again, and instead, bought a case of champagne. Twelve chilled bottles for my 12 tenants. I "borrowed" something special from a prop table in the photo studio at Macy's, a beautiful long, wide, red ribbon made of silk with the gold numbers 1969 attached to it. At first, I thought I might put it on the front door to the lobby for the tenants to see, but then I had a better idea.

I waited for a decent hour on New Year's Day to deliver the bottles of champagne, allowing my tenants to sleep late. The first one was Mrs. Metcalfe, who answered the door in her flowered cotton bathrobe, covering her flowered nightgown that hung down to her flowered slippers. She looked at me, wondering if I was annoyed that she kept Lily with her all night. Then she looked down and saw Aaron holding the heavy bottle, and she gasped.

"Well, I never!" She looked back at me, smiling. "That's the cutest thing I ever saw!" She stooped over and took the bottle from Aaron's hand, then kissed her other hand and patted him on the head with it. "And a happy, Happy New Year to you too, my little dumpling."

Aaron was beaming as we knocked on number two. Aaron stood with a bottle in his hand, naked, except for the ribbon draped diagonally across his chest with 1969 sparkling on it.

The door opened. "Thelma, throw on something and get out here quick. You won't believe what's standing here at our front door."

## Chapter 50
# The Sky Is Falling!

After Aaron had delivered the bottles of champagne and delighted the tenants as a New Year's baby, we bundled up, and I pulled him, Teddy, and his monkey in his Red Flyer down Hyde Street to the Buena Vista. We ate their special clam chowder, washed down with a Shirley Temple and an Irish coffee, the drink Buena Vista introduced to San Francisco. After our lunch, I pulled Aaron and his buddies back up Hyde Street, not the thing you want to do, considering the steepness of the hill.

We went through our usual routine of eating separate foods for dinner, Aaron's bath in his green boat, then chasing the little rascal, still wet from his bath, around the apartment until I could catch him, towel dry him, put him in his jammies, and finish off his day by reading two or three books to him before I tucked him in bed. Routine is comforting.

January 1, 1969 was the last happy day I had for the next six weeks.

I didn't sleep the night through and kept waking to look at the clock. I could think only of phoning Evander and trying to figure out what time he would be arriving back at his office, what time I could possibly phone him, and what I needed to tell him. It was one long thought, punctuated with dollops of unconsciousness, repeating in my aching head, for the whole night. Seven o'clock would be too early. Eight o'clock might be too early, too. Surely he would answer the phone at nine.

The second the clock read nine, I dialed his office number. A recording of his secretary's voice greeted me.

"This is the office of Evander Smith. He is out of the office until January 2$^{nd}$. Please do not leave a message unless it is an emergency. As of January 2$^{nd}$, you can leave a phone number, and Mr. Smith will return your call as soon as possible. We wish you all a Merry Christmas and a very Happy New Year."

"Evander, please call me as soon as you get this message. The sky is falling! Oh, yeah. It's Bill. Bill Jones. You've got my number."

Aaron spent most of the morning, first chasing Mammy through our apartment, then attacking Lily with the aid of Teddy, yelling at them in ear-splitting war hoops. Every time they found a quiet place to curl up and snooze, Aaron would sneak up and pounce on them. I was so focused on waiting for Evander to phone me that I hardly heard the commotion. Reading the *Chronicle* didn't take my mind off the Princess phone either. I was pinning Aaron's diaper on when the phone rang around 10:30. I sat him on the bathroom floor and ran to pick up the receiver.

"Hi, Bill. Sorry it took so long to get back to you. What's up?"

"Oh, Evander, Evander, I can't tell you how happy I am to hear your voice!"

"Bill, you sound distraught. Can you calm down a little bit, and tell me what's the matter?"

"There's this petition, and the adoption should have been finalized in October, November at the latest, and I don't know what to do. I'm so scared, Evander. So scared!"

"Sit down, Bill. Are you sitting?"

"Yeah."

"Now take five deep breaths. Let me hear them."

Five deep breaths later, I was able to tell him about the petition in the adoption agency and how troubled Dorothy Murphy was when it was taped to her office door. At first, she thought it would sabotage the whole single-parent adoption plan, but the petition statement made it clear that it supported the single-parent adoption plan she had devised, but also made it plain that a *gay* single parent would not be tolerated. If Dorothy continued to support me, they threatened to send the petition to the mayor and both newspapers.

"Bill, this is a matter of *civil rights*. You may have wondered why I took your case and never billed you for my time and the letter I wrote."

"Well, one of my friends thinks you want to get into my pants. Frankly, I was hoping you did."

There was a burst of laughter from Evander. "No, Bill, that's not the reason, but come to think of it …"

"Just joking, Evander."

"Oh sure. Well, I don't have much time to chew the fat with you this morning, Bill, as much as I'd like to, but the fact is, I've been looking for a case like yours for a long time."

"What do ya mean?"

"Hang onto your hat. A *civil rights* case that we could make a federal case of and finally put an end to all this damn prejudice and harassment we've been going through – longer than the Negroes have suffered – for once and for all!"

"A federal case! Really?"

"Bill, I have three or four very wealthy gay men, and a wealthy lesbian, who are eager to put their money where their mouths are and take a case like this as far as we can go. Because it really is possible to sue in federal court if somebody's rights under the US Constitution are being violated. In Aaron's and your case, it's your right of equal protection under the law, protected by the 14$^{th}$ Amendment to the Constitution that would give you a right to sue, starting with the city."

"But, Evander, what about Aaron and me? The adoption? Doesn't it take years for a case like that to finally make it to Washington? By the time you get it there, Aaron will be in another foster home! What's worse is that Dorothy Murphy told me last month that if I hadn't taken Aaron, the next step for the agency was to institutionalize him."

"You've got friends you haven't even met yet, Bill, and you've got me. We will *not* let you down. Aaron *will* be your son. I give you my word."

I found it almost impossible to take five deep breaths. "The sky's falling, Evander. The whole damn sky is falling down around me … Aaron and me."

"Bill, I know how anxious you must be about this, and I'll get to it as soon as I can clear up some other cases demanding all my attention right now. Things have piled up here in the office while I was away. In about a week or so I can … hey, gimme Dorothy Murphy's number, will ya? Just try to relax. I'll contact her and go see her if I have to, in a week or so."

Another week went by, and the cloud above my head got darker each day. I had to stop dwelling on it when Aaron wanted to play. Because I was so preoccupied, he would tip something over or pull Lily's tail to get my attention. He wasn't the one acting badly. It was me, but all I could think about was the pickle I was in. Pasek gave up asking me to go to a movie and threatened to kick my ass if I didn't come out of my depression lickety-split. He also declared that the dumps I was wallowing in were *boring*. His cruelest accusation.

Boring to him, but I was on fire inside. I decided to call Evander again after two weeks had dragged by. His secretary answered the phone.

"Yes, Mr. Smith is involved in a trial in Fresno and cannot be reached for a few days. Please leave your number, and I will pass it on to him the next time he calls in. Do you wish to leave a message?"

"Just tell him that Bill is suffering from a concussion because the sky fell and hit him. He'll know what it's about."

I pulled my gloom in around me and waited. Another week went by and when the phone rang, I jumped up to answer it. It was Mary Davidson, sounding serious and disturbed.

"Bill, your lawyer was here just as we were leaving last night. He and Dorothy went into her office to talk, and I was *not* invited!"

"I didn't even know he was back in town, Mary."

"They were in there for about 15 or 20 minutes, and he left without even saying *hello*' to me."

"That doesn't sound like him."

"Then Dorothy came out of her office looking like a truck had hit her. She walked right by me without saying, 'goodnight' or 'see you in the morning'. Just stared ahead and walked out. Bill, what's going on?"

"I have no idea. Honest, I haven't spoken to either one of them for about three weeks. I'll call Evander right now and find out. Then I'll call you back, okay?"

I dialed Evander's number immediately but got his answering service with a message he was back in court and a request that I leave a short message and my phone number. I no sooner put the receiver on the hook, than it rang. One ring and I had it to my ear.

"Bill, Mary. Did you get him?"

"Couldn't. He's back in Fres ..."

"He's suing Dorothy and me! She just told me! And she's calling a meeting this afternoon. That's the soonest we can gather all the workers who signed the petition and the soonest the city attorney could get here. She asked me to ask you to be here, too. Two o'clock."

"Shall I bring Aaron?"

"Not yet. Not yet."

The "not yet, not yet" could mean only one thing. It was just a matter of time before they would take him away from me. I could barely walk over to Ronnie's apartment to ask her to take Aaron for the rest of the day. Sirens were sounding in my head, and my heart was racing, but I managed to drive over to the Social Services Building.

Mary met me in the marble lobby, looking drained and frantic.

"Bill, everyone who signed the petition is in Dorothy's office. We're waiting for the city attorney to get here. I've got to go in, too, but she wants you to stay with her secretary outside her office, so she can call you in if she has to. Okay?"

"Sure. Sure. Okay."

From where I was sitting, I could hear voices behind Dorothy's office door, but I couldn't make out what was being said, even though every once in a while one of the voices rose above all the others. About a third of the cubicles in the outer office were empty, the occupants probably in Dorothy's office. Within a few minutes, two gray-haired men in pinstriped suits, carrying leather briefcases, hurried past me and knocked on Dorothy's door. It opened right away, and they almost ran inside. The door banged shut, and I was left sitting across from the secretary, who seemed too occupied with her paperwork to even look up at me. The workers still in their cubicles were also intent on looking at anything but me.

I leafed through a *Sports Illustrated*, a *Ladies Home Journal*, two *Time* magazines, and a *Life* magazine dated June of '68 with Bobby Kennedy's soulful face on the cover. I ripped it off and stuffed it in my jacket pocket. The office was deathly still, but sporadically the silence was punctuated with the rat-a-tat tat of typewriter keys. The sound was jarring and distracting. I kept looking at my watch. The hands barely moved.

The door to Dorothy's office creaked open for just a moment, and a rush of voices, all speaking at the same time, came spilling out, too garbled to understand. Then someone grabbed the handle and slammed the door shut again. A man's voice rose above the others. Then it was very quiet. The door opened wide and the two lawyers walked out. One of them glanced at me and walked away, but the other stood in front of me, looking down. He reached out his hand, and I stood to shake it.

"Mr. Jones?"

"Yes."

"How do you do?"

Then he quickly walked over to the other lawyer, who was impatiently waiting for him, and they left together. Dorothy's door was still open, and I could see 10, maybe 12 workers around her desk speaking almost in whispers to each other. One by one, they came out and had to walk by me. Several looked directly at me with looks that sent chills down my back. The others wouldn't even glance my way as they marched back to their desks and swivel chairs in their tan cubicles.

Dorothy stood framed in her doorway and beckoned for me to come in. Mary sat beside the desk, wiping her eyes.

"How much of this are you aware of, Bill?"

"All I know is what Mary's told me … that Evander was here, and that the two of you are being sued. Believe me, I didn't put him up to it. I did tell him to go after whoever it is that's out to … You know I'd never do anything to hurt either one of you. You've been so good to me. You've changed my life. I, I guess …"

Dorothy led me to a chair next to Mary's and pulled her own chair around so the three of us were close. "Bill, I don't know what to say. We're both overwhelmed by what Evander is threatening to do."

"What?"

"A lawsuit. It just starts with Mary and me, then everyone who signed the petition, the San Francisco Adoption Agency, the San Francisco Social Services, Mayor Alioto, the California State Social Services, and Governor Ronald Reagan."

"You're kidding!"

"I'm dead serious, Bill, and so is Evander Smith. He's out for blood, and he has all the money in the world to take this all the way to the highest court in America!"

"He said something about civil rights to me, Dorothy, but I told him that it would take too long and that the finalization was past due. I'm desperate, Dorothy. Maybe I should get another lawyer. What do ya think?"

"He's given us two weeks to present evidence that you're an unfit parent, Bill, and if there's no evidence, he's gonna sue us – everybody – right up to the governor!"

"For what? Because some of the workers here think I'm gay? He can't be serious!"

"Our attorneys think he might have a case, Bill, an outstanding civil rights case. In all the years I've been here, nothing like this has ever happened. I'm sick about it."

"Please don't blame me. Please don't."

Mary, who had been dabbing at her eyes all this time, finally spoke. "Bill, I'm just speaking for myself now, but I feel you and I have a bond, and a little boy who loves you is that bond. You can count on me to be your friend to the end, whatever the end may be."

I reached over to take her hand just as Dorothy put her arm around my shoulder.

"That makes two of us, Bill. Somehow, someday, we three will sit down and wonder what in the world were we all so worried about."

Mary chimed in, "You know, Bill, this too will pass."

By the time I got home, Ronnie had already fed and bathed Aaron. She was chasing him around the living room, naked and wet from his bath. He was yelling and laughing, delighted every time he slipped away from her again. Ronnie left as soon as she got him to step into his jammies, giving me just enough time to down a gin and tonic. Aaron and I crashed onto the sofa with books, Mammy and Lily curled up next to us. *This too will pass. This too will pass.*

*   *   *   *   *

January was coming to an end, and February loomed. My Lai and Bobby's assassination were behind us. Martin Luther King was also gone, and in his place were the Black Panthers. Unfortunately, Nixon and the Vietnam War were still with us. But more important, so was Evander's threat to sue the bejesus out of the whole damn San Francisco Adoption Agency. Thankfully, Pasek came over every night when he got off work to console me, even though I bored him silly, endlessly going over the events and high drama of that office meeting.

"You gotta get laid, Billy Boy. You need to throw your legs up in the air and moan and groan! That's how I get through shit."

"You won't believe this, Pasek, but I haven't even jacked off since New Year's Eve."

"I don't believe it!"

"Believe it!"

Just then the phone rang, and it was a familiar voice.

"Hi, Bill. Evander here. I have to apologize to you again for being out of touch. This case in Fresno, I can't really talk about it, but some really heavy stuff is coming down on some, yeah, more than one politician here, and it's gonna crack this state wide open." He paused, realizing I couldn't care less about his case in Fresno. "Sorry about that. It's driving me crazy. Okay, I'm back with you. What's been happening? Dorothy doing anything? Anything movin' along?"

"Two days ago she had a really big meeting with her staff and a couple of lawyers from the city attorneys' office. I didn't hear what they were talking about, but I was sitting outside her office and got glared at by *everyone* leaving after the meeting. Boy, they looked pissed off!"

"Great!"

"Great?"

"Yes, great!"

"Evander, tell me why everybody being pissed off at me is great?"

"Because it's workin', Bill, it's workin'!"

Pasek tried to take the phone from my hand, and we struggled to possess it.

"Gimme that damn phone! I wanna talk to that asshole!"

I pushed him back down on the sofa and motioned for him to zip his lip, which he reluctantly did.

"Evander, how can it be working? No one's talking about drawing up the final papers. I'm getting looks that could kill from some of 'em at the agency. What good is a lawsuit that'll take years, and then be too late for me to keep Aaron? What am I missing?"

"Do you know what a deposition is, Bill? When you sue someone, and they fight back, both parties get to sit down before the trial and have their lawyers question all concerned under oath, question them about anything that might come up in the trial. Understand?"

"Well, sure, but …"

"Bill, who gives the final say about legalizing the adoption?"

"Well, I guess Dorothy Murphy."

"Right. Has she done that yet?"

"You know she hasn't."

"When should she have done it?"

"About three months ago, according to Mary."

"Right. And what's stopped her from doing what she should have done, heh?"

"Well, she's been pinned to the wall, I guess. She's been threatened by somebody in her own office. Threatened with this petition for one thing."

"Right. She's afraid her idea of single adoptions will go down the tubes because a few dumb bastards in her agency will go off and blab to the papers that you're gay."

"That's about it, yeah."

"Well, don't you see, Bill? I've given her the ammo she needs to shoot 'em down. It's the depositions."

"Depositions?"

"Yes, the depositions where every single blowhard who signed that shitty petition could be asked, by me of course, just how far their prejudices reach. We know they don't want gays to have the same rights as straight. How do they feel about Negroes adopting white children? Jews adopting Christians? Unwed mothers? Abortions? None of 'em will want the world to know what miserable lowlifes they are as Americans who *should* believe in equal rights."

"But you're suing Dorothy and Mary and …"

"That's how lawsuits go, Bill. You sue everybody. In this case, everybody from your social worker, right up every step in the ladder to the governor. You dump shit on everybody's head, and see who comes out clean."

"Evander, give me a minute." I could almost hear clinks as the pieces, one by one, seemed to fall into place. "If you're giving Dorothy the power to force the troublemakers to shut up by scaring the pants off 'em, threatening them with depositions, that means she can finalize the adoption. Right?"

"Right!"

"But that means you're giving up a case you wanted to take to the courts."

"Another case will come along. Someday the court will finally come around and give every American, black and white, gay and straight, the same damn rights."

"You really think this will work?"

"If Dorothy is as smart as I think she is, yeah. She can make this happen, and you know, once the papers are signed, no one can take Aaron away from you, unless, of course, you *are* an unfit parent. And that's where we got them tied and fried. We've got 'em against the wall. Nothing to do with your being a *gay* parent. They have to come up with sure-fire, rock-solid evidence that you are an *unfit* parent. Maybe I'm sticking my neck out here, but I'll bet all this year's fees that they can't find that kind of evidence."

"I've got my fingers crossed."

"Give 'em, ah, 10 more days, Bill, and I'm sure – beyond a reasonable doubt – you'll be Aaron's daddy for keeps. Now keep me posted, and for god's sake try to relax. Have fun with your little boy. Go out and be with friends, maybe that Pasek guy." He blurted, "Bye now. Gotta run."

I put down the phone and turned to see Pasek slouched on the sofa, rubbing Lily's tummy, frustration written all over his face.

"Pasek, why don't you ever ask me to go to the movies with you anymore?"

## Chapter 51

# Judge Levin and Quiche Lorraine

I opened the *Chronicle* on the morning of February 13, 1969, and saw on the front page a photo of three businessmen with their suit pants rolled up to their knees, wading in the newly constructed Vaillancourt Fountain on the Embarcadero. The caption read *It's Gonna Be Another Hot One!*

My first thought was *nice legs*! But I had more on my mind than to dwell on anything sexual. I had spent the whole day before cleaning the house, ironing Aaron's Peter Pan shirt, and shopping for quiche pans and ingredients like Gruyere cheese, nutmeg, and white pepper. I still can't figure out why it called for white pepper. Black tastes the same, but the thirteenth was a red-letter day and it called for white pepper. Everything had to be perfect.

Actually, this day, a day I had been dreaming of for over a year and a half, began 10 days before when Mary phoned me, breathing very quickly, at times gasping for air.

"Bill, it's happening! I wish you could have seen what's been going on here for the last two days! Dorothy's ecstatic, and so am I!"

"What, Mary?"

One by one they've been knocking on Dorothy's door, and guess what?"

"What?!"

"Crossing their names off the petition! Every last one of them! And Dorothy has all the papers ready. We made an appointment for you to sign them on Thursday, the thirteenth. Judge Levin. He's done thousands of these, and we're sorta hoping he doesn't realize it's a single adoption. He's a really nice old guy, but who knows? If he ever has a *question* about it, we would be in deep trouble. You know what I mean? Oh, gosh, I almost forgot. You have to make out a check to the San Francisco Social Services Department for $167."

Pasek, my brother Jerry, and Randles were the first to arrive. They had no sooner shut the door when Maureen McCurry, a gorgeous extra I had met on the *Bullitt* set, knocked on it. Her marriage to Walter Hill, the first AD on *Bullitt* hadn't lasted a year, but she swept in, flashing that wonderful Irish smile, her white complexion emphasizing the wide brown eyes and wavy auburn hair. Even Pasek was bowled over by her looks and style.

Jerry asked me, "Who else is driving down with us?"

"Ronnie, of course, and Ray Williams, if he's sober."

Everyone nodded their heads.

"That makes seven and a half, counting the kid. Let's take Old Rust," Pasek declared. "Ronnie and Maureen can sit up in the front with you, and we can put a blanket down and ride in the back. We manly men can rough it. Right?"

Randles asked, "Who else is goin'?"

"Well, Michael, Bob, Gary, and Dennis are all working. My dad and his wife, Maude, and my other half-brother, Russell, his wife, Sandi, and my Aunt Ruth – the triple chocolate cake one – are all going to meet us there."

"What about Mona, Bill?"

"Maureen, you know Mona. I think she's getting her pedicure today, but Ann Brebner will meet us there. Isn't that something? Ann Brebner!"

The phone rang, and I picked it up. "Hi, Ray. Where the hell are you?"

"Signing escrow papers, but I'll meet you there. What's the judge's name?"

"Levin. Gerald S. Levin. On the second floor. Listen, we're leaving now, but I'll tell you what I have to tell everybody. Now listen, Ray, this is *really* important. Mary and Dorothy have both warned me that if the judge reads the document and finds out it's just a single man adopting, he may or may not sign the papers!"

"What the fuck?"

"I know. I know. I'm scared to death, but that's why Mary and Dorothy won't be there. They're afraid if they show up, the judge will know something's fishy, cause they usually don't go to the judge's signing of adoption papers."

"Don't worry about me, Billy Boy. I'll be there as soon as we finish here and have a little toast to celebrate, and trust me, I won't say a word about you being a fag." With that, he hung up.

Ronnie carried Aaron out of the bathroom washed and combed. His blue velvet rompers were wiped clean of food stains, and his white shirt, shoes, and socks were spotless.

"Just number one," she announced.

"Okay, let's get goin'. Jerry, will you please bring that blanket from under Aaron's crib? Our appointment's in just half an hour. Out, everybody! Out!"

Before I closed the door and locked it, I gave the living room the once-over to be sure the table was set and the flowers on it, with no toys on the floor. We all piled into Old Rust and rode off to City Hall.

Evander was still in Fresno, and another lawyer, Jay Conner, took his place to record the document. He was young, good-looking in a rumpled suit, and grinning ear to ear. My family and friends stood in a group, like tourists from Ohio, on the bottom step of the grand staircase rising from the rotunda floor, introducing themselves to each other.

Jay called us together to make a tight circle around him. "We have a few minutes before we go up to Judge Levin's chambers, and I have a couple of things I want to share with you. First of all, I'm going to read the document the judge will be signing. I want you to know we aren't trying to pull the wool over his eyes, but we're hoping *he* doesn't bother to read it, cuz if he does, and objects to an single adoption by a single man, he won't sign it, and we'll be back where Bill started 18 months ago."

There were more than a few gasps and groans.

"Here goes."

A. JAY CONNER
683 McAllister Street
San Francisco, California
Telephone: 922-5200
Attorney for Petitioner
SUPERIOR COURT OF THE STATE OF CALIFORNIA
FOR THE CITY AND COUNTY OF SAN FRANCISCO
ADOPTION OF AARON HUNTER JONES,) NO. 14423

a Minor)                    JUDGEMENT OF ADOPTION
_____)
The petition of WILLIAM WOODFIN JONES for an order of
This Court adjudging that henceforth AARON HUNTER JONES, a minor,
Shall be the adopted child of the petitioner came on regularly
This day for hearing. A. JAY CONNER appearing as attorney for the petitioner; and the petitioner and the minor child having appeared before the Court and the Court having examined them each separately; and the Court having heard the petition and evidence in support thereof and the matter is submitted, the Court finds:

I

That all the averments contained in the petition of WILLIAM WOODFIN JONES are true; that WILLIAM WOODFIN JONES, a single person, is an adult more than ten years older than the unmarried minor.                    (4.)

II

That no consent to adoption by any parent is required because the child has been relinquished for adoption as provided by law to a licensed adoption agency, the Department of Social Services of the City and County of San Francisco, State of California; that such agency has filed herein its report and consent to this adoption and has joined in this petition; and that the State Department of Social Welfare has waived the report required to be made by it.

III

That the petitioner has executed an agreement that the child shall be treated in all respects as the lawful child of the petitioner.

IV

That the child is a proper subject for adoption and the petitioner's home is suitable for the child; and that the interest of the child will be promoted by his adoption by the petitioner; now therefore;

IT IS ORDERED, that AARON HUNTER JONES, be
adopted by WILLIAM WOODFIN JONES and that these
persons shall thereafter
sustain toward each other all legal obligations of parent and
child and shall have all the rights and be under all the duties
of such relationship including all legal rights and duties of custody, support, and inheritance.
IT IS FURTHER ORDERED, that the child shall hereafter
bear the family name of the petitioner and shall be known as
AARON HUNTER JONES.
Dated: FEBRUARY 13, 1969
GERALD S. LEVIN
JUDGE OF THE SUPERIOR COURT

Except for the few gasps and gulps at me being referred to as *a single person*, and my Aunt Ruth giggling at Aaron being referred to as *the unmarried
minor*, everyone was intent on listening to Jay read the order and trying desperately to make sense of all the legalese in spite of the echoing noise and commotion in the rotunda.

All 14 of us managed to squeeze into one elevator to the second floor. Jay
knocked on Judge Levin's office door, and we filed in behind him. Jay and I
stood in front of the judge's large walnut desk, and the rest crowded in behind
us with Ronnie holding Aaron, who was licking a yellow lollipop.

The judge glanced up from a pile of papers on the desktop and looked
amazed. He began to chuckle. "What in the world is this?" he mused. "I've got
to tell you, I've never had so many family members in my chambers before just
for an adoption! Usually just the mother and father! Who are the ..."

Jay quickly interjected, "Your Honor, this is the father, Mr. Jones, and
he is eager to have you sign the order. Eager. Very eager. The interviews and
placement have taken more than 18 months, Sir."

I bent over and signed the document as fast as I could and then shoved the
paper over to where the judge was sitting. He signed it, looked up at the row
of beaming faces, rose from his leather chair, and came around his desk to pat
Aaron on the head.

"And this must be your mommy, eh, Little Man?" he chuckled, looking straight into Ronnie's eyes. She was speechless and looked back at him with a weak smile, tight-lipped.

Jay looked at me, jerked his head and gestured with his eyes that the document Levin had just signed was still laying on his desk. I knew he wanted me to pick it up while the judge was talking to Ronnie, but I was too afraid of doing something illegal, of messing things up to the point of no return. Jay gave me a disapproving look, knowing any minute the judge would return to his chair and expect Ronnie to sign the document, too. I felt helpless and trapped.

We heard a loud banging on the door. It swung wide open, and Ray Williams staggered in, a little wild-eyed, shaking everyone's hand like he was pumping water out of a well. He headed for the judge and Ronnie.

"Well, well, so you're Judge Levin? Didn't you and your wife buy that Queen Anne on Pacific and Webster?"

Jay pushed me aside and grabbed the document. He took hold of my arm and rushed us toward the door. Pasek and my brother nudged all the women and my father toward the door, and Randles pulled on Ronnie, who was still holding Aaron. As we rushed out, Ray was still pumping Judge Levin's hand, asking him if he was ready to move into a brick mansion on Broadway that he'd just listed.

I grabbed Aaron from Ronnie's arms and ran down the grand staircase with Jay, too impatient to wait for the slow elevator. Jay was determined to record the order as soon as possible in case the judge took a second look at the copy we'd left and put the brakes on the recording.

I paid a small fee to the Recorder's Office, and Aaron was my son. Simple as that.

We piled in our vehicles and drove back to our apartment – now our HOME – to celebrate. I had my untried and virgin quiche Lorraine, all four pans of it, and a salad Randles had made waiting in the refrigerator ready to serve because I knew Ann Brebner had to get back to Brebner Casting, and Pasek had to get back to his job. Ray Williams had stocked my refrigerator with several bottles of French champagne, and my Aunt Ruth arrived with her secret recipe Triple Chocolate Kahlua cake with a sign sticking up on toothpicks that read JONES AND SON – ESTB. 1969.

My head was swirling, and the champagne was just being poured. I hadn't had a drink, but I felt a little drunk. Ray poured a glass for everyone except Aaron, who was trying to maneuver a stemmed champagne glass full of milk up to his lips.

Pasek stood up, and I thought he was about to make a toast, but instead, he opened an envelope and announced, "One of Aaron's uncles couldn't be here today, as much as he wanted to, but Uncle Michael Vincent has sent a note he wanted me to read to the new daddy. Here goes."

*If it's true that adversity introduces you to strengths you never knew you had, then you must be the reigning champ of anyone I have ever known, or known of, in my life. Congratulations to Daddy Bill, and may he and Aaron live happily ever after. Love, Uncle Michael.*

Beautiful toasts came from around the table, even a short, "Good luck" from my father. No one even mentioned the quiche.

We got a lot of hugs and kisses at the front door as I stood holding Aaron, thanking each friend and member of my family for being with us on one of the most important days of our lives. I turned around to see Pasek coming from the sink in the kitchen area with a tea towel in his hands.

"They're all washed, and ready to dry," he said as he handed me the towel. "I've got to get back to work before they realize I haven't been there all morning!"

I opened the door for him, and we stood, embracing each other with Aaron squeezed between us for a long, meaningful minute. When he drew back from me, I saw a tear on his cheek.

"Bill, remember that Christmas Eve when your half-brother beat you to it when he announced your dad and Maude were about to become grandparents? Remember you were so excited and eager to tell him the same thing, but you kept quiet? Remember that Christmas Eve? Remember what I said to you?"

"How can I forget? Anybody can ... oh, you know ... wanna come back for dinner? Lots of left-over quiche!"

## Chapter 52

# A Valentine for the
# Human Race

I was exhausted by the time Pasek left, and as he walked out the door, the phone started to ring. Word travels fast among *my* gay and straight friends. Everyone wanted to hear what happened in the judge's chambers and wanted to congratulate me on *finally* being a daddy. One by one, the "Group" phoned, wanting us to go out and get plastered to celebrate, but this was the day I had been waiting for most of my adult life, and I was determined to celebrate it my own way. Ronnie was sure I'd be going out that night with Pasek and the guys, so she knocked on the door and asked when I'd need her.

"Thanks, Ronnie, but I won't need you. Tonight's our first night as a legal family, and we've made great plans for it. Wonderful plans! Dinner of Gerber's baby food and a Swanson's TV fried chicken for the daddy. A bubble bath with every toy that floats. Jammies, and all of us, Lily, Mammy, the kid, and me on the sofa. I'm reading him *The Little Prince* again cuz he likes the pictures and then to bed. I could sleep for a week!"

Just as she was about to leave, she turned and came back to kiss Aaron. "This has been one of the happiest days of my life, too. When the judge thought I was Aaron's mother, I almost cried I was so happy. Night, Bill. See ya in the morning."

After I tucked Aaron in bed and made sure Teddy, Monkey, and Snoopy were tucked in beside him, I leaned over and kissed them all goodnight. I decided to stay with him until he fell asleep. I grabbed a couple of pillows from the sofa and lay down beside his crib, holding his hand through the bars of the railing, just as I had done when he first came into my life nine months before.

The phone kept ringing, but I was too tired to answer it. My answering device could hold only 10 calls, but at least I could call those 10 back the next morning. Sleep, a deep sleep, spread its motherly arms around me. For the first time in nine months, I didn't lie awake, thinking of ways I could escape with Aaron from the threatening claws of the "monster."

At first I didn't hear the doorbell, but it was insistent, and I gradually awoke, thinking it was part of a dream. My left arm was numb from lying on it pressed against the floor. When I managed to get up, my head, groggy, I staggered to the front door, thinking it must be a tenant with a plumbing problem. After all, it was past midnight. Damn!

When I opened the door, I couldn't think of what to say. Standing there, looking very sheepish, was a man about my age, in a suit and tie with a large red ribbon tied around his waist. He had dark, wavy hair and wore horn-rimmed glasses that circled his brown eyes, so brown they looked black.

We stood, looking at each other eye to eye, both trying to see the shape of the other's body, if there was hair on the wrists, the texture of the skin, without being obvious.

I was first to speak. "Can I help you? Are you looking for one of the tenants?"

"Eh, no. I was sent here for you. You *are* Bill Jones, aren't you?"

"Yeah."

"And you have a friend by the name of Pasek, don't you?"

"Yeah."

"Well, I met him and some of your friends tonight at the P.S. bar."

"Yeah?"

"They're celebrating you becoming a father. Just today, right?

"Yeah."

"Well, they showed me a photo of you and your son, and I got all excited."

"Yeah."

"Yeah. I'm Peter, and I'm here from Raleigh for a few days on business."

"Yeah?"

"So, Pasek drove me here and tied this ribbon around me cuz he knew you'd like to meet me. He said what you needed was someone like me to, you know, welcome you back to the human race, whatever that means."

"I think I know what he meant. Do ya wanna come in? I have to warn you though, it can be only for a couple of hours, and then we'll call a cab. Sorry, but my son wakes up around dawn, and I can't let him see a stranger here."

"Sure. I understand. Where's your bedroom?"

\*    \*    \*    \*    \*

Later, when I woke up, I reached down and put my hand around my cock. It was still semihard, and the sheet was moist next to me. I lay smiling and rolled back and forth thinking of Scarlett O'Hara, smiling to herself the morning after Rhett Butler carried her upstairs to have his way with her. The endorphins were still surging through my veins when I heard Aaron giggling and talking to his invisible friends.

It was Valentine's Day. I showered quickly before I went into the nursery and lifted Aaron, wet diaper and all, out of his crib. I scrambled eggs for us as he nibbled on a piece of bacon. He was beginning to eat solid food, which delighted me.

I answered the calls on my answering machine, then made two very important ones. The first one was to Mary Davidson and Dorothy Murphy. Valentine's Day wasn't a holiday for them. They were winding down the week's work that Friday. Dorothy told me that they had already started several preplacement interviews and paperwork for single adoptions. Both male and female applicants, and because the door was finally open, she had no reason to think the adoptions would be as difficult or take as long as mine had.

The second call was to Pasek.

"Hi, Daddy. What's cookin'?"

"Me, thanks to you! Wow, what a night!"

"Well, Honey, your mother knows what you need in hard times. How *did* you like the Peter present I sent you last night? He was sure lookin' good to me, and I almost took him home myself, but you know me. Selfless. Sacrificing everything for my family."

"Yeah. I can hardly wait to see the bill. In the meantime, besides blowin' a great big kiss on your pecker for giving me Peter last night, I wanted to ask you something very personal."

"What, Billy?"

"Will you be my Valentine, and can I borrow $50 from you? Pay you back when the rents come in. Honest."

*　　*　　*　　*　　*

After I changed Aaron's diapers for the second time, we got in Old Rust, dressed exactly as we were in the portrait, and headed for the glistening white See's candy store on Polk Street. Aaron was too short to see the bins of chocolates in the display case, but the dazzling array of red cellophane-wrapped, heart-shaped boxes made him giddy with excitement, and he went back to gurgling, "La-la!, ga-ga!, la-la!" as he pointed to them and tugged on my pant leg. I bought a small heart-shaped box for Aaron and the largest one they had left on the shelf for Dorothy and Mary.

I hadn't been in the adoption agency since the day the city attorney held the meeting in Dorothy's office with all the workers who had signed the petition, so I felt nervous and sweaty as Aaron and I walked through the outer office toward Dorothy's office. Mary saw us and looked surprised. She left her cubicle and joined us as we knocked on Dorothy's door.

Dorothy was standing behind her desk and dropped into her chair when she saw us come in.

"Bill! What a surprise!" Then she saw Aaron standing beside me holding a large heart-shaped red box as wide as he was tall. "Come in! Come in!"

I gently pushed Aaron toward Dorothy and told her, "Aaron wanted to give you and Mary something for Valentine's Day, Dorothy."

"How sweet!" She took the box from Aaron and placed it on her desk on top of a pile of folders, then plucked him up onto her lap. She gave me an exaggerated scowl, adding, "And *fattening*!"

Mary chimed in, "Aaron, this is a lovely gift from you, but don't you think it's too much candy for two old ladies like us? Maybe we could share it with you and your daddy."

Dorothy put Aaron down and stood up, looking straight into my eyes, and said pointedly, "And the rest of the staff out there in the office." Then she looked at Aaron. "Would you like to share it with more people, Darling?"

I think I gulped. I know my face turned a rosy pink shade. Mary lifted the lid off the box and offered Aaron his choice. His choice was to take two at once and pop them into his mouth. Mary then handed him the box to hold as she opened the office door and led him out. Dorothy and I followed.

The social worker in the first cubicle stopped her typing and paused, looking over the box several times as she decided on the piece she finally took. She thanked him and smiled.

The second one kept typing until she realized Aaron wouldn't move on until she acquiesced and took a piece. She stared at Aaron, and then in spite of not wanting to, she smiled at him. "Will it be all right with you if I take two, Aaron? I have a little girl at home who would love a piece."

The third social worker turned in her chair to look at him very closely, almost touching her nose with his. "You are the sweetest little guy, you know? I see some chocolate on your cheek. Can I kiss it off?" Aaron just looked at her, not saying yes or no. She kissed him and took a piece out of the box. "Thank you, Aaron. I bet your daddy's very proud of you. You're a good boy!

I took over from Mary and continued walking up and down the rows of cubicles with Aaron, offering his candy to each person, whether they smiled at him or not. At each desk, I looked down and tried to make eye contact.

*Have you been on our side all along? Are you our friend or are you one of the assholes that put us through hell for nine months?*

Some looked back and smiled. Some refused to look at me, but I knew they could never take him away from me. Only one or two didn't thank him profusely for making Valentine's Day so memorable. A few kissed and hugged him. He was the star attraction that day, and I felt as if I were 10 feet tall, so proud of him, and so pleased with myself.

They could see that Aaron had changed into a happy, sweet, well-behaved little boy who was outgoing and lovable. He was healthy, well dressed, and looked contented, part of a family with a parent who cherished him. It showed.

I told Pasek that evening, "It was more than just facing the enemy and offering a piece of candy. It was … love and forgiveness. Pasek, ya know how isolated we feel as gay men? Like no one will ever really love us for what we are? How we feel about the police cracking down on us, and the navy putting guys like us in the brig? Know how we feel to be always the last one picked for a team? Well, today, walking up and down those aisles with Aaron, my *son*, Pasek, my *son*, I finally felt like I was a part of the human race. Not queer. Not different. Just another parent with just another kid.

It's the most wonderful feeling, Pasek. Wonderful! I hope to god you'll feel it, too, someday. You must! Just another human in the human race. Wonderful!"

Aaron and I never celebrated our Adoption Day on February 13th after that day. Instead, we celebrated it on Valentine's Day every year, and I always try to do something on Valentine's Day in remembrance of it. Starting on a rain-soaked Valentine's Day in 2004, for a month I officiated at more than 450 same-sex weddings in the building where Aaron and I became a family in 1969. San Francisco's City Hall, a classic beauty, will always be very, very special to me … especially on St. Valentine's Day.

Dorothy Murphy and Aaron on our fourth Valentine's/Adoption Day visit

## Chapter 53
# The Invitation

Larkin Street was level, so Aaron could ride his trike and pull his wagon up and down in front of the building, but Greenwich dropped down from Larkin in a steep decline, so I had to stay with Aaron to be sure he didn't roll down to Polk Street and break his neck. Kids raised in apartments don't have backyards to play in, but Aaron, like millions of other city kids, adored the sidewalk in front of our home.

The April rains came and came and came, leaving Aaron house-bound with not much floor space to play on. I had laid a wooden floor in the living room, which took a beating from Lily's toenails and Aaron's toys, but all I could think of was the soft red and blue Turkish rug I had played on at my Aunt Ruth and Uncle Elzie's. It had roads for my toy cars woven into it, but Aaron had no such thing, and I was constantly picking up toys that cluttered the living room and kitchen.

The only way to give him more play space was to take over the two-car garage facing Larkin. I grabbed a crowbar and knocked the sheetrock and studs out in the pantry to make a floor-to-ceiling doorway. Luckily, the garage doors had opaque glass in the panels that provided light, and on the Greenwich side, two small windows could be opened for fresh air.

I painted the walls and ceiling white, and then I glued sheets of Masonite to the cement floor. My childhood dream of landscaping such a large space came true. I painted gray roads, twisting and turning through green fields with bridges crossing bright blue rivers, leading to a harbor and an ocean. I laid out red squares for future houses and stores that would become a town.

Aaron now had his own backyard and his toys had a place.

"What a cool place to have a dance party, Billy," was Pasek's reaction when I showed him Aaron's new playroom.

"Yeah. I hadn't thought of that. I guess we could dance in our stockings so the floor wouldn't get all scratched up. I'm painting airport runways tomorrow."

"Speaking of parties, when are we gonna have one to celebrate what you've done? You wouldn't even let us take you to dinner the night the adoption was final. Remember?"

"Funny. I've been thinking about that too, Pasek. It's overdue, but when I start thinking about who to invite, my mind goes off the rails. The Group, of course, and everyone who came to the baby shower. Then, I start thinking of all the straight people I know, and, well, family members."

"Wow! Picture it. All us sissy uncles and your family. What a hoot!"

"Yeah. And I'd even like my brother's ex-wife to come. And Jerry's kids, of course. Oh, god, my father and Maude! Russ and his wife. Dorothy and Mary from the agency. My mother won't come, but my cousin Ramona will, and the other cousins might, too. Aaron's gay uncles dancing in their socks – cheek to cheek – and my stepsister and her husband dancing in their socks! In the same room! See why I get so discombobulated?"

"Bill, even if everybody in the whole damn party starts pointing at you and yelling that you're gay, nobody can take him away from you. Nobody." He paused for a second. "Who gives a shit, anyway?"

"Would you do it if you were me, Pasek?"

"Bill, do you remember the Christmas Eve you spent in Oakland with your dad and his wife? Christmas before last. You came back to the city and were almost in tears because your stepbrother one-upped you and announced that he and Sandi were going to have a baby?"

"Yeah."

"You took a bottle of champagne with you to celebrate when you told them you were about to adopt a kid. Remember?"

"Yeah."

"And you brought the champagne home with you, didn't you?"

"Still have it."

Before the 180 guests arrived

"Because your dad's *favorite* son beat you to it. Making him a granddad. Right?"

"Yeah, right."

So, let's show the old man who's the best son after all. Let's give a party that'll go down in history! Fill up our glasses with that damn champagne, and show 'em all what really matters. Gays give a great ... *party*!"

"Will you design the invitations, Pasek?"

"I already have."

## Chapter 54
# Not Newsworthy

"I keep forgetting to tell you guys something. A couple of weeks ago, this woman from the *Chronicle* came over to interview me. Aaron and me. She brought a *really* cute photographer with her. I could've eaten him alive."

Gary giggled, "I hear you used to be good at that before you became Mother of the Year."

"Fuck you, Gary."

Pasek looked at me with a hurt face and chided, "Dammit, Bill, how come you didn't tell me? A couple of weeks ago? We talk on the damn phone every day!"

"I wanted to surprise you guys. I thought her article would be in the paper within a couple of days, but after the first week, I knew it wasn't going to be printed. At first, I was a little embarrassed to tell you that I was interviewed, but it wasn't worth a space in the paper, and then I just sorta forgot to tell you. Sorry."

Gary came out of his stupor and managed to ask, "How juicy was the photographer? Get his number?"

"No, and he was straight, straight. Kept saying he'd like his daughter to play with Aaron someday. He took a couple of shots of Aaron with Ronnie, and I think he took one of me when I went to pick Aaron up at Phoebe Hearst, but I'm not sure. He didn't want any posed pictures."

Gary asked, "What's the reporter's name, Bill? I know a lot of those cats at the *Chron*. Terrence O'Flaherty's a good friend of mine."

"I wrote it down. Here. Here on this cocktail napkin. Mildred. Mildred Hamilton, but I guess Mildred and her cutie-pie just wasted a couple of hours on us. He even took a photo of the portrait Michael's friend did for us. "I liked Mildred a lot. She sensed I didn't want to talk about my sex life, and she was gung-ho about single adoptions. In any case, the paper wasn't interested in it. I never heard from her after the interview, so I guess she was too embarrassed to tell me that it wasn't newsworthy and they wouldn't print it."

Pasek tried to reassure me. "What does that damn *Chronicle* know about important things like a single guy adopting a bald kid? The front-page head-line last week was all about which was the best coffee in town!"

"Yeah. To hell with the *Chronicle*! Who cares? Oh, how 'bout the party on Saturday, the 14th of June?"

"Let me mark that here in my pocket calendar. Hey, did you know that that Saturday, the 14th is the day before Father's Day?"

Embarrassed that I had only looked for free Saturdays that month, I snapped back, "You think I'm dumb, but beautiful, don't cha? Of course, I knew."

## Chapter 55

# The Terribly Wonderful Morning After

I could hear Aaron jabbering away to himself in the nursery, and I knew I should leap out of bed to change his diaper and cook his oatmeal, but I seemed to be sewn to the sheets. It took a tremendous effort to open one eye, much less two. In the blurry morning light, I was able to recognize my Princess phone on the nightstand, but I had to squint and blink a couple of times until I could focus on the tall shapes looming like smoky skyscrapers behind it. Three champagne bottles and one of them was half full. My head seemed to have bloated up four times its normal size, and I was dry-mouthed. Parched.

I could hear my blood banging on my eardrums, and I was dying of thirst. My mouth and brain were dry, and I had the worst hangover of my life. The dry brain tissue seemed to be cracking like mud baking in the sun. It was too painful to open my eyes, so I decided to lie there in my misery and reconstruct the night before. The night of The Party.

It started out so beautifully. All of Aaron's uncles had pitched in and not only decorated the entire apartment with real and fake flowers but also had brought heaping plates of finger food and arranged them on my dining table, using fresh yellow daisies as a tablecloth.

Pasek stood beside the table, bowing like a maître d' showing off the ship's Caribbean buffet. "Call *Sunset* magazine and tell 'em to get a photographer over here immediately!"

All the uncles had rented penguin suits except Uncle Gary, who showed up in a paisley maroon smoking jacket with a pink and orange ascot and dark red tuxedo pants. Aaron, in his blue velvet romper suit, and Lily, with a collar festooned with white and yellow daisies, ran excitedly through every room, not knowing what was about to happen but thrilled to be a part of it.

Uncle Ray and Uncle Randles were setting up the bar and glasses, when Uncle Jerry, now known as Uncle-Uncle to distinguish his relationship as Aaron's *true* uncle from all the other uncles, asked me, "Did your dad ever get back to you?"

"Yeah. When he phoned, he told me my party was too fancy for him. He wasn't about to go out and rent a tuxedo just to come to a party, and that was that. Forget it! I haven't heard from him or my step mother or Aunt Ruth since then."

"You told him that "Black tie *optional*" meant just that, didn't you? That he could wear his old brown suit and a necktie?"

"Of course. That's all I expected of him, but I didn't think he'd want to drive to a party in the city at night, *especially* to please *me*. I really wanted Aunt Ruth and Maude to be here. Oh, well."

Uncle Michael and Uncle Lanci were loading the turntable with LPs in the livingroom when Uncle Gary called from Aaron's playroom, which he had morphed into a darkly lit disco complete with a revolving mirrored-ball. "Hey, I need that Bee Gees album out here for dancing!"

I was busy trying to calm Aaron and Lily down. The phonograph in the livingroom was playing *What the World Needs Now*, and I whispered to Aaron, "That's true, isn't it, Honey? That's what the world needs now – love, sweet love." I picked him up, held him in a hug, and kissed him, then glanced at my wristwatch. "Oh, my god! It's almost nine!"

A wave of panic swept over me when I looked around, saw we were alone in the livingroom, smelled the clouds of pot drifting out of the darkened, disco playroom, and heard the door-bell ringing as if someone were leaning on it.

"Pasek, Gary, Michael, dammit! Lanci, Jerry, get out here! *Stop* what you're doing in there!"

I opened the front door and started to grin, a grin I wore for the rest of the night. There stood my ex-lover, Dennis, with his twin, David, and behind them, looking a little lost, was my step mother, Maude, my Aunt Ruth, and to complete the picture, my stoic father in a new gray suit, sporting a new bright blue tie!

I had no sooner ushered them in than the doorbell rang again. Aunt Ruth and Maude hurried over to Aaron and took turns holding him. For the next hour or so, I didn't leave the front door, greeting all my old tricks and lovers, oohing and aahing over all the gowns and cocktail dresses my cousins and aunts and lesbian friends wore, feeling like movie stars.

I lost track of who was gay and who was straight. I prayed to myself that some of my gay friends wouldn't put the make on my half-brother, Russ, or one of my straight cousins.

I was shocked to see so many of my family filing in. Aunts, uncles, cousins, and my young stepsister, Corky, with her middle-aged husband.

After most of the church-going side of the family poured themselves glasses of nonlethal punch, they all seemed to declare it a family reunion and took over my bedroom to gossip, and to get to know my stepmother, Maude. My father hadn't seen my mother's side of the family since they'd divorced over 30 years before.

Most of my gay buddies dipped into the champagne and brandy punch before meandering back through the pantry to Aaron's disco playroom to dance and smoke weed. My tenants and friends from Glide Church and men and women I worked with as movie extras and in modeling jobs seemed content to stay in my livingroom, sizing each other up, and showing off their finery.

Every few minutes someone would gently remove a warm, empty plastic glass from my hand and just as gently replace it with an icy-cold full one while I was welcoming new guests.

Lying in pain the next morning, I remembered Pasek ushering everyone back into the living room. The uncles circled, refilling empty glasses with champagne from the bottles. Then Pasek stood up on my cocktail table and asked for everyone's attention.

"Unaccustomed as I am to public speaking ..." That got a big laugh from anyone who knew him.

"We are gathered here in this sacred church to unite in matrimony, Bill Jones and his faithful dog, Lily ..." This time everyone was laughing.

"Oh, hell, you know why we're all here getting plastered. Most of us don't even know each other. Hopefully, that will change before this night is over.

But we all have one thing in common. Something we are proud of. Something that has made us remember that good things *can* happen even in the middle of a bloody, useless war." He took a breath. "We all know Bill Jones." I felt my face flush, and I knew it wasn't the liquor.

"Most of us have dreamt of something we really wanted to do. Or a place we wanted to see. Or a project we wanted to give to better the world. But unfortunately, a lot of those dreams never came through. Bill had a very simple dream. He wanted to be a daddy. And we're all here tonight to congratulate him on making his dream come true."

There was applause.

"Ronnie has to put Aaron to bed now, but before that happens … Bill, hold Aaron, will ya?" I took Aaron and put him on my shoulders so he could be seen in the crowded room.

"Here's to Daddy Bill Jones and his son, Aaron Hunter Jones." Applause. "Let's drink to that!" Everyone drank, and I caught a glimpse of my Aunt Eleanor, the teetotaler, sipping a very small sip from her wine glass. Another wonder!

The rest of the night was hidden by a thick fog in my aching head. I pulled the sheet up over my head, embarrassed when, unfortunately, I did remember trying to kiss *everyone* on the lips when they went to leave. Oh, my god! Even Uncle Albert and my cousin Lorry!

The last time I got that drunk was on my twenty-fourth birthday, and my lover at the time, John Something, had decided to go back to his old lover, realizing my youth and inexperience didn't provide him with the hot sex he thought he'd have with me. So, I drank a pint of vodka and collapsed onto my birthday cake.

Now, I was trying to forget a dreadful conversation that took place in the kitchen at the height of the party. It was with one of my cousins' husbands, a slimy old letch, whose breath of whiskey and cigarettes spilled over me as he rasped in my ear, "I've never seen so much gorgeous pussy in one room in all my life, Billy. All these goddamn broads, movie stars, and models. Jesus, I envy your life. I bet you get a piece of ass every night, don't ya? No wonder you never got married. If I had all the ass you're gettin', I'd be damned if I'd get hitched either."

The Princess phone started to ring like an alarm, startling me, but helping me shake myself free of the nasty words coming from his nasty mouth. I picked up the receiver on the fourth or fifth ring.

"Hello. Hello? Pasek? Ouch! My head!"

"I know what you mean. I had a hangover too. But Billy, It's gone now … the hangover. Gone! Gone with the wind!"

"What did you take?"

"It completely flew out the window when I opened the paper, Bill!"

"The paper?"

"You mean you haven't seen the Sunday *Chronicle/Examiner* this morning? You're kidding!"

"I'm just now crawling out of bed, for god's sake."

"Wait 'til you see what's covering the whole front of the Sunday "Women's Section." You won't even remember you had a hangover, Bachelor Father!"

I picked up the Sunday paper lying in front of my apartment door and opened it up to the Sunday "Women's Section," gasped, and brushed a few cocktail napkins off the sofa to fall back down onto it, forgetting my throbbing head. The hangover disappeared.

## Chapter 56

# Father Is a Bachelor

### Father's Day Feature Story – June 14, 1969
### By Mildred Hamilton, *S.F. Chronicle/Examiner*

*'ll bet you a cigar that the biggest Father's Day grin is on the handsome face of William Jones – San Francisco's first man to adopt a child as a single parent under the Department of Social Services.*

*Today is his first Father's Day after finalization of the adoption and he and button-nosed, blue-eyed 3-year-old Aaron Hunter Jones are celebrating as a joyful duo.*

Those were the first two sentences of her article, and the rest of it filled the entire page! It covered my entire journey, 18 months of sleepless nights, and the joyful days being with Aaron. She ended her story with this:

*Jones looks back at his pre-Aaron days. "I was working 12 to 14 hours a day. I was unmarried. I had no children. And I was asking myself, 'WHAT am I doing?' Now I know. My life really is beginning at 40 ..."*

A side bar notice in addition to Mildred's article that Father's Day started a long history of single adoptions:

*Adoptive Parent: Requisites*

*How does a single person qualify as an adoptive parent?*

*"The requirements are the same as they are for couples," according to the San Francisco County Department of Social Services, 585 Bush St. "Basically, they call for loving and caring for the child as if he were your own, having enough money to care for another member of your family according to your standards. This does not mean you must be wealthy."*

*And you must be a stable individual who has a fairly full life without a child. In a single-parent situation, the department also looks for an extension of the family — brothers, sisters, parents — to secure the child's future if something happened to the adoptive parent.*

*Recent changes in legislation have permitted a few single-parent adoptions after comprehensive investigations. "All things being equal," the department says, "a home with two parents is better, but one good stable loving parent can give a child a good home."*

*   *   *   *   *

After leaving the paper on the cocktail table for a week so I could read it to Aaron each night after his bath, I carefully folded the entire Sunday edition and put it in his cedar chest along with other historical editions of the Chronicle I knew he would love to see when he was a father himself — or a grandfather — to share with his own family. The only difference in the stack of newspapers was that I had written something to Aaron, scrawled over our story, the morning after the party. It read —

**Aaron, my son —**

**This is the way the paper was delivered to our door this morning — and me with a hangover that just wouldn't stop. Boy, did we celebrate last night — 180 guests!**

**ANYWAY — I'm so proud and happy to be your Daddy.**

**I love you.**

Mildred's article was picked up by the Associated Press, and I was sent clippings of it, enclosed with heart-rending letters from Spain, England, France, Italy, Hawaii, and Australia. But it was the response from American television and radio shows, wanting to hear our story, that took us on another kind of adventure. Under great pressure to appear "normal" and to encourage more adoptions, I sheepishly went back into the closet — for a while.

## Chapter 57
# To Tell the Truth

New York City in muggy August is exhausting. Hot and wet. You sweat and then are chilled when you walk into a blast of air conditioning. The stifling air chokes you with exhausts from a thousand taxies and dumps its black soot on windowsills and the collar of your starched white button-down. I loved it. Aaron tolerated it.

We stayed with John Rose – "Rose" to his gay friends – in his townhouse that included his dental office on the Upper East Side. Rose could go from his kitchen sink, and in a few steps, be in the white rooms where he scraped, cleaned, and polished teeth. You didn't need laughing gas while you were in his chair because he told one joke after another. Patients loved him.

We'd had an affair-ette when I first arrived in Manhattan and kept in touch. I gave him a "Rose" party when he and his grumpy lover, whom he referred to as "Smiley," stayed with me on Bernal Heights before I moved onto Russian Hill. He was handsome in a puckish way, with dark brown curly hair and pale, white skin. He *hated* the sun but bought a new 1959 green metallic Chevrolet convertible because he liked the Buck Rogers look with the huge horizontal fins that flared out over the trunk.

He insisted we stay with him even though Goodson-Todman had paid for a room at the Biltmore for two nights when they flew us in to appear on *To Tell the Truth*. They also gave me $35 a day to cover expenses. It sounds like a small amount now, but in 1969, it was a lot of money. Especially for me. Since

Rose insisted on cooking for us and even lent me his car to drive out to Fire Island after the show, it was money in my pocket.

Rose was there to pick us up at Idlewild, and the next day I pulled Aaron, sitting on a pile of pillows in Rose's shopping cart, all through Central Park. He loved the zoo, especially the monkeys and the elephants, but both of us were sopping wet with sweat when we came upon a fountain spraying water high in the air. I took off Aaron's clothes, and he ran naked through it with the water falling like rain over him. He was happy and giddy, and I was content to sit in the shade and cruise the daddies coming out of the zoo with their children skipping around them. Everyone was in shorts to keep cool, and as much as I hated summer in the Big Apple, I was thankful for it and its heat, granting me the sight of men in shorts.

The next day, we went to the Seagram Building, a smoky brown jewel set back from Park Avenue, graciously, generously giving the city a large open public plaza with two dark rectangular pools of water that reflected the buildings around them. When the building was constructed in the late '50s, the architect, Meis van der Rohe, had insisted on this open space, the first in any American city. I loved that building more than any other in New York.

I reported to Laura McPherson to be briefed about how *To Tell the Truth* was played. I was to be one of three contestants, all claiming to be Bill Jones, the first single man to adopt a child in the United States. Gary Moore, the host, would read my sworn affidavit that I was, indeed, that person. The three "daddies" would sit in a row, facing the panel and asking us questions, trying to decide which one of us had adopted the child.

The next day, Aaron and I arrived at the television studio where Laura took Aaron by the hand and led him up onto a stage, closed off from the audience by a curtain. The panel that day was Garry Moore, Peggy Cass, Kitty Carlisle, Bill Cullen, and Orson Bean. Orson was 10 days younger than me and delicious to look at. I was extremely nervous but sure they would never choose one of the other two contestants – Number One looked like a skinny, long-haired, out-of-work actor, and Number Two looked like a garbage truck driver who had borrowed his short cousin's suit to be on the show. To my dismay, the other two got most of the questions from the panel. I was asked only two questions.

"Number Three, if I didn't have to live in New York, I'd move to San Francisco in a split minute. It's like the Emerald City of Oz, don't you think? Magic. Where do you and your son live in San Francisco?"

Answer: "In a storage room on the ground floor in my apartment building on Russian Hill."

"Number Three, there are some magnificent stores in San Francisco, aren't there? Where do you buy most of your son's clothes?"

Answer: "My brother gives me a lot of his son's hand-me-downs, and also the Salvation Army has a really good selection. And toys, too."

The entire panel voted for the other two except for Orson Bean, who leaned forward and said, "I vote for Number Three. I sensed love in his answers."

Then Garry Moore stood up and said, "All right then. Let's see who the real daddy is. Open the curtains!"

The curtains opened slowly and there was Aaron, standing alone on the stage, looking a little bewildered.

"Aaron, who's your daddy? A million people want to know. Go to your daddy, Aaron."

He stepped down from the stage and ran over to the desk where the three of us were sitting, stopped for a second to look at the others and then climbed onto my lap. The audience gasped and then clapped. The panel was clapping, too. My mouth was dry, and I felt a trickle of sweat run down my spine.

*     *     *     *     *

Think of Fire Island as a long pencil. Cherry Grove, the Pines, and others were small neighboring communities, separated by class and in Cherry Grove's case, sexual orientation. They were within walking distance of each other, about a mile apart, and shared not only the wide, sandy beach facing the Atlantic Ocean, but also the lack of roads, electricity, sewers, water heaters, street lamps, and house numbers on the flimsy beach cottages. Instead of numbers, the houses were named.

Visitors and guests had to look for the houses by names at Cherry Grove, the only all-gay enconclave on the island. The "streets" were boardwalks with names like Beach Walk and Lewis Walk. That's where Grandma's House, the house Aaron and I stayed in, was located.

Grandma's House was just one of the campy names painted on driftwood and attached to the cottages. As you'd walk along, the names of the cottages made you smile. Besides Grandma's House, USO (servicemen welcome), Peter's Inn, Hard Times, Seaman's Rest, Fanny Hilton, Hell's Belles, Dames at Sea, Head Start - USA, MGM, Twin Piques, Camp Us, Tri Us, Boys in the Attic, and White Swallow were a few others.

The Pines was not totally gay like Cherry Grove but boasted celebrities, most of them gay and "with-it" straights primarily from the theater world, with houses designed by in-vogue architects. Otherwise, Fire Island was straight, straight, straight and had to live with the embarrassing stigma of being a wild "gay" summer vacation spot, although the Grove and the Pines were only two small sections.

Driving to Sayville where the ferry would take us to Cherry Grove, my head was swirling with memories of the summers there in 1959 and 1960 when I was a model at the Rice-McCue Agency. Walking down a boardwalk around sundown, the cocktail hour, you would hear something I have never heard anywhere else – peals of laughter coming from every house. Sometimes screams of laughter. Sometimes rolls of chuckles. Peering in the windows and open doors, you could see in the candle and kerosene lantern light, gay men in shorts and open shirts, bent over, holding their sides laughing.

I also remembered one painful Sunday night on the beach when Wyatt told me he couldn't have dinner with me the next evening. In fact, he would be sleeping with Chita Rivera that night! We had been dating for just a short time, but I was sure I had found "Mr. Right." I was sure we were meant for each other. We even were booked at the Rice-McCue Agency, as "real" persons, not as "fashion" models.

We were the ones who did the breakfast cereal and insurance salesman ads; both from rural communities we'd been anxious to leave. The thing that drew me to him, complete with visions of a house in the suburbs with a white picket fence, was that both of us wanted more than anything, more than money, success, or fame, was to be parents. We both dreamed the impossible – to have children. Wyatt had the maturity and insight that I aspire to even now. He once told me as we were making his bed in the morning, "You know, Bill, I want to be on the cover of *Life* or *Time* someday ... but not as a model. I want to be on the cover because I achieved something or because I have a talent. Don't you?"

It wasn't just that a guy I was head over heels in love with was going to be naked with someone else. I felt rejected and the pain of losing the treasure I thought I had just found, hurt me so much that I cried for weeks. It wasn't just the pain of losing Wyatt as a lover. In the '50s and '60s, the word bisexual was a powerful no-no. The gay community thought of bisexuals as traitors, and the straights were sure they were dirty faggots. I had no idea what bisexuals like Wyatt thought of themselves, but it must have been confusing. I couldn't bear the thought that I had given my heart to a damn bisexual!

*　　*　　*　　*　　*

Boarding the Sayville ferry, I was glad to find seats on the bench next to the railing so Aaron could look down at the water and the white wake breaking from the bow. A guy flopped down beside us with his overnight kit and a large bag of groceries on his lap. "Hi, my name's Josh, what's yours, and what's the story on this little kid? I guess you know everybody on the dock was talking about you two."

"My name's Bill, and this is my son, Aaron."

"Divorced?"

"No."

"Excuse me for asking, but did your wife die?"

"I think his mother might still be alive. You see …"

"Jeez, does she know you're bringing her kid to Fairy Island?"

"Josh, I am not married, and yeah, I'm a single gay guy like you."

"Then how in the hell did you get this kid? Did you knock some dame up?"

"No, I adopted him."

"Bullshit!"

"No, really. In San Francisco. Last February."

"That's bullshit. It's against the law, isn't it?"

"It was … until last February in California."

"Jeez!"

"I'm not bullshitting you, Josh. Do you ever watch *To Tell the Truth*? We're on it. Watch it next Tuesday."

A blast of the arrival horn stirred cheers from the crowded upper deck as the ferry bumped against the dock with its rustic gay bar, jammed full of dancing and laughing men. I carried Aaron and our bags off the ferry and walked past the bar, looking for Grandma's House, and was bewildered by the changes I saw.

The last time I had been there was in the summer of 1960 as a guest of Peter Bailey, who leased Grandma's House every summer. Just nine years had passed, but now the beach shacks were no longer naked on the sand dunes. They had been updated, painted, and securely closed off with fences and gates.

Peter loved to do brunches and they were spectacular. I still think of him every time I see the words "crepe," "soufflé," or "brulé." He was an executive at Bergdorf's, very fashionable and chic, and also the best cook in New York. Eventually, he wrote several coffee table books on hosting and moved on to summer in the Hamptons. He was a few years older than me and was good-looking and in shape, almost bald, which only made him only more distinguished and sexy-looking.

Keeping it simple and clean was his motto, and Grandma's House was an example of that philosophy. Unlike the changes I saw in other houses on the boardwalk, it had no pretentious high fence and entrance gate, isolating it from others. It did have a new electric line that leashed it to a wooden electric pole. He had kept the house for the last nine years – unadorned with cluttered gimcrack Victorian trim. It was a shoebox, painted yellow and white with a simple pitched roof, and it looked proud to be still standing level on pilings over sand dunes that dropped down to the beach.

Peter carried our suitcase into the guest bedroom. "I'll get to watch you and Aaron in my office at the store, but you know, the rest of our little tribe coming to dinner won't. Too bad *To Tell the Truth* will be shown on a workday."

"A guy we sat next to on the ferry couldn't believe I'd adopted him. Now, for the rest of the weekend, I guess I'll have to go through the same drill with everybody I see. Peter, save me!"

"If anyone drills you here, Bill, I'll spit on their paella."

"I really appreciate your inviting us out here – especially after the way I carried on – crying on your shoulder the last time I was here."

Peter confessed, "I know it's hard to believe, with me being so absolutely gorgeous and all, but I've been dumped, too. *Several* times. And it hurt! I'm sorry, but what happened to you two on the beach that night?"

"We had a wonderful Saturday and Sunday all alone on the beach, away from the Grove. Then after dinner, Sunday night, we were walking on the beach, and he told me not to fantasize about a future with him. He told me he wasn't completely satisfied being in a gay crowd … that he was bisexual … that he had a date with Chita Rivera the next night … that he'd be sleeping over. I can't remember if I hit him. I know I felt like doing it, but now I don't think I did. All I remember is that I was bawling my head off, and the next morning when we drove back to the city, neither one of us said a word."

"As a matter of fact, only a few weeks ago. I saw him and his wife sharing a banana split with their son on Madison. I think his kid's about the same age as Aaron."

"Wife! What was his wife like? It wasn't Chita Rivera, was it?"

"Relax. No, it wasn't Chita Rivera, Bill."

* * * * *

Burke McCue, my agent, was one of the dinner guests that night along with Joel Rice, his business partner, and Billy Livingston, Joel's longtime companion. Joel and Billy had a house in the Grove, too, but it was a mansion compared to Grandma's House, with a large inground swimming pool that overlooked the Atlantic.

Burke looked like your friendly Irish neighborhood cop, strong features, bright blue eyes with heavy brows, and a smile that announced he was about to tell another one of his over-the-top stories. He had been a hoofer in Broadway musicals until he met Joel and surrendered to the *business* world of show business.

Burke smiled that Irish smile. "I kept hearing about the 'meat rack' all these years, but until last night, I was too scared to go there after the bar closes. Ya know, I bet you've heard a hundred stories about how the Sayville cops sneak up on those guys in the dunes, and surprise, surprise, the gays get tossed in the hoosegow, and Sayville cleans up on fines for us gays doin' it in *public*."

Billy Livingston growled. "I'd be up for a murder rap if Joel ever poked his nose around that meat rack. It's gross."

Joel smiled to think his lover would kill him in a jealous rage. "It's not always in the bushes on the dunes, you know. Every night's different." He caught Joel's glare, and quickly added, "I've been told."

Burke continued, "Well, mind you, Tom was like me. Both are too chicken to ever go there, but last night after a couple of drinks, we decided to toss it to the winds. So, we went to the bar late and got the word. It was going to be on the beach between here and the Pines. We crawled up the dunes and climbed over the snow fence where we could watch. It was a full moon last night and we watched all the shenanigans. You've never seen anything like it. Shorts down around their ankles, blowin' each other and god knows what else. You could hear them gruntin' and groaning over the waves!"

Joel was on the edge of his chair listening to Burke. "I bet you went down on the beach, didn't you, Burke?"

"Well, we were getting pretty excited and might have joined them, except that all of a sudden a whole bunch of flashlights came on, and the police were shouting, 'You perverts! You're all under arrest! Hands up! Stay where you are!' I heard Tom saying, "Oh, my goodness!"

Burke continued, "Every damn guy there yanked their pants up and started to run in all directions … real fast!"

Billy blurted out, "For god's sake, Burke, did you get caught?"

"No! You know me. I got dancer's legs, and I leaped right over that damn snow fence and ran like hell, but I realized Tom wasn't behind me. I snuck back to the fence. The moon came out from under a cloud and I saw him down on his knees looking for his dentures. We were whispering, sort of a stage whisper, I guess, and I'm in a panic and here's me asking him, 'Bessie, Bessie, you OK? Bessie, you hurt?"

Then Burke lapped his lips over his teeth and mimicked Tom. "No names, please! No names!"

\*     \*     \*     \*     \*

One of Peter's "young executive" houseguests that weekend was Jim Reynolds, a wholesome man with auburn hair, whose constant smile caused his blue eyes to squint. From within that squint, his blue eyes beamed happiness with himself and the life around him. Aaron chose Jim's lap to sit on after dinner, and Jim couldn't stop smiling. I began to envy Aaron. Jim's quiet, paternal playfulness with Aaron was stirring feelings in me that had nothing to do with being paternal. It dawned on me how much I wanted a lover to share Aaron's and my life, but it didn't seem right to think of passionate lovemaking and caring for a child, too.

Peter had assigned the double bed in the guest room for Aaron and me and the single bed for Jim. Aaron eventually left Jim's lap and climbed up on mine where he dropped off to sleep. I carried him to our bed and tucked him in after slipping a waterproof sheet under him.

I said goodnight to Jim and Peter and went outside where the shower was hooked up to a large steel oil drum, painted black and sitting on an eight-foot high, four-legged platform. The black paint absorbed the sun's heat, and if we used just a little bit of water at a time, enough warm shower water lasted for each day.

I spun around when I heard Jim say, "It'll save water if I get in there with you, Bill."

After our shower, with towels wrapped around our waists, we moved Aaron, cradled in the rubberized sheet, still out like a light, over to the single bed. We muffled all the sounds that humans make when their bodies try to climb into each other, but even if we both had yelled out, "Oh, my God!" when we shot into each other, Aaron would never stir from his deep slumber. Knowing he wasn't aware of us in the next bed thrashing around didn't stop me from worrying and feeling guilty, and that guilt feeling stayed with me the next day.

Jim spent the entire day with us: at Peter's brunch, swimming in Joel and Billy's pool, making sand castles on the beach, and watching the annual volleyball game between the Grove and the Pines.

The news about a gay guy who had adopted a child spread like lightning through the Grove and the Pines, and it wasn't hard to pick us out of the sweaty crowd. Celebrities were not a rarified item on Fire Island, but they were given the courtesy of being ignored for the sake of their privacy. Not that Aaron and I were celebrities, but we were an outstanding rarity for the Island, and we were treated with the same courtesy; we were stared at for a brief awestruck moment, then ignored so we wouldn't feel intruded upon.

Tennessee Williams was one of those celebrities, and to my amazement, he was one of Peter's dinner guests the next night. After dinner when I had put Aaron to bed, the twin bed, we sat and told stories about our first inkling that we were attracted to men ... the usual conversation after, before, or during most dinners with gays. I tried not to sneak intruding glances at Williams that night, but I wanted to see his reaction to the confessions.

Tennessee wasn't like the rest of Peter's extroverted friends and guests who never let a moment go by without filling it with bitchy remarks or dirty jokes. He didn't avoid the rest of Peter's guests, but he preferred to sit back and observe and listen to us chit-chat. He was mostly silent, but his intense glare seemed to quiet the rest of us, creating actual, occasional quiet moments in the house.

One of those rare quiet times shattered when Peter's neighbor came flying in, slamming the front door behind her. Her peroxided straw-like hair was standing on end like porcupine quills. Her flabby body was shaking under the muumuu that flapped around her mammoth breasts. She wore flame-red lipstick that was smeared and eyeliner and mascara dark enough to draw attention away from her powdered jowls. She flopped down on a chair after circling the room like a dog looking for a place to relieve itself.

"Jesus fuckin' Christ! What a fuckin' bitchy time I've had for over an hour chasing that shitty thing. Little shit!"

Peter brought her a drink and tried to calm her down, but she was hell-bent on screeching, "I'll kill that fucker if it takes the rest of my life! Thanks for the drink, Pete, old boy, but get rid of the damn ice!"

Almost in unison, everyone in the room, except Tennessee, leaned forward and asked her who she wanted to kill.

"That fuckin' moth that I've been chasin' with a swatter for over an hour. That's who! Look at me! Sweaty fuckin' armpits and sweat running down my tits!"

Peter offered to go next door and spray insect killer everywhere, but she held up her hand, a ring on each finger, and told him to go to hell. There would be no pesticides sprayed in her house.

"Ya know it wasn't just the swattin' and running after the damn thing. It's what happened in the fuckin' bathroom that really pisses me off!"

There was another chorus, "What happened in the bathroom?"

"I chased the goddamn moth into the bathroom, and ya know what?"

"What?"

"It flew into the fuckin' toilet bowl! Down into the water! I could see it flappin' its wings trying to get out, so ya know what?"

"What?"

"I decided to sit down and piss on the little fucker! So I pissed and pissed, and you know what?

"What?"

"The little fucker flies right out from between my damn legs!"

The howls of laughter came in waves for a long time then finally subsided. The room became quiet when Tennessee cleared his throat. We stared at him when he spoke in that soft southern drawl from his chair in the corner.

"Was it the same moth?"

## Chapter 58
# Aaron's Wings

On our return flight to San Francisco, Aaron had to sit on my lap since he was flying free and the plane had been oversold. I hope anyone who reads this never has to hold a squirming, diapered toddler on their lap for five hours as I did, but luckily the stewardess took him up to visit the pilots several times. The first time he came back wearing a large pin sprouting bronze metal wings with AA in red letters in the center like the body of a bird. The producers of *To Tell the Truth* used American Airlines for their guests, and I'm glad they did. The seats were wide and the stewardesses were attentive to Aaron.

After lunch, Aaron dropped off for his afternoon nap and I closed my eyes, trying to recall as much as I could about the week in the city and the weekend on Fire Island – Aaron on top of the Empire State Building; Aaron running naked in the Central Park fountain; Aaron coming down from the stage to show the world who his daddy was; Rose's green '59 convertible, top-down on the way to the island; Jim's chest and thighs; swimming in Joel's pool, volleyball in the Pines; Jim's blue eyes; gathering tiny white pebbles on the beach with Aaron. Jim's smile, kiss.

New York City is dazzling, masculine, but the view of San Francisco's skyline as Pasek drove us home from the airport was soft, pastel, feminine as it slowly engulfed us, stirring my heart. And I could hear the word *home* drifting all around me. *HOME* ... where Aaron could sleep in his crib again, take a bath in his boat again, and be potty trained again.

I dumped a suitcase full of dirty shirts, underwear, socks, and a plastic bag full of wet diapers into the washing machine. I read several sharp notes from tenants, complaining about the lack of water pressure, but my answering device was filled with messages from friends who had seen us on *To Tell the Truth*. I was home, and Aaron was ready for new adventures.

Seeing things through Aaron's eyes made me open my own eyes wider than ever before. The Renaissance Faire, as my three-year-old son was seeing it for the first time, brought the jousting knights and the ladies in waiting who followed in the queen's procession alive. They stepped out of the pages of dusty books and surrounded him, filling the air with sounds of flutes and mandolins.

He had never seen a horse before, much less one draped in tasseled tapestry, carrying a knight in shiny, aluminum-foiled armor that blinded the eye reflecting the noonday sun. My heart beat faster as I saw it for the first time – the way my little boy was seeing it.

\*     \*     \*     \*     \*

I bought 12 small pumpkins for the tenants and a large one for Aaron. Pasek and Gary came over the night before Halloween, and we carved all 13 into ghoulish faces. When we lit the candles inside, Aaron cast the magic spell of a child bringing them to life. I turned off the lights and the four of us huddled together on the floor, giving each pumpkin a name and whispering their stories to Aaron. Carved pumpkins can bring the magic.

My brother's kids and Aaron went trick-or-treating together in Hayward, where Jerry and Randles lived. Russian Hill, where we lived, had almost no children, but in Hayward, the streets were flooded with little witches and princesses, cowboys, and ghosts. Aaron was an astronaut, and Mark and Alison were the crew of *Star Trek*. After our kids had crammed enough candy into their mouths to make them hyper and giddy, Jerry and I secretly flushed the rest of their loot down the toilet. Look out for the meanies on Halloween! They can be dressed in costumes to look just like daddies.

The annual New Car Show in the Civic Center Auditorium offered something for everyone. Since I couldn't afford a new car, I went straight to the classic car display. Pasek and the Group were potential buyers, so they took turns sitting in the driver's seats of the shining new cars, but the star of the show made Aaron go ga-ga as he crawled under the ropes to take possession of it.

I had taken him to see the movie *Chitty Chitty Bang Bang*, which he loved, and there sat the full-sized movie prop in all its brassy, wooden-bodied, wings outspread glory. He dashed to it, running under the display ropes before I could stop him. He climbed up onto the running board and sat in the driver's seat, unable to look through the windshield but in total control, as the auditorium ceiling split open for him and his winged car took off into the blue sky. After all, he was wearing his magic wings pin with two A's on it, just like the two A's in his name.

Aaron could drive Old Rust when he sat on my lap with both our hands on the wheel. He could sit on the pilot's lap and drive the big jet airliner. His pin with the wings on it, which he insisted on wearing every day, gave him the magical power to take flight in Chitty Chitty Bang Bang. For a split second, I saw it through his eyes, and a thrilling shudder racked my body. Magic. Wings.

I took photos of Aaron in and on his dream car as quickly as I could before the security guards ordered him off of it and scolded me. Now I knew what I wished Aaron could get for Christmas. Damn the cost!

## Chapter 59
# Aaron's Acid Trip with Claude
## *Hair* – 1969

Like a jealous lover, I was hurt to think Pasek had friends outside our group that I didn't know about, but he *did* have other friends. One of them was a school buddy from St. Louis, who was in town for a few months working as a stagehand on the new musical *Hair*.

Pasek was aflutter as usual when he phoned late one Friday night. "Jonesy, boy, do I have good news!"

"You finally nailed that married guy in the paint department?"

"Not that good. But damn good! Remember me telling you about Ben, the guy I went to art school with?"

"No."

"'Member? I told you. The first guy who ever let me fuck him? You know … remember … standing up in the supply closet."

"No."

"Well, he's in town and we had lunch today, and guess what? He's gonna get us in to watch a dress rehearsal tomorrow. Eleven. Isn't that great? Can you make it?"

I think I might have sounded a little annoyed. First of all, who was this Ben person that Pasek knew, and I didn't? Second, I had been so busy taking care of Aaron that I hadn't kept up with what shows were in town and felt completely out of it.

"Not that I'm picky, but just which show are you talking about?"

"*Hair*, Jonesy, *Hair*! The first Broadway all-singing, all-dancing musical with naked bodies all over the stage! Can ya believe it? And we can see it free, Bill, free!"

"Oh, *that Hair.*"

"Well … well … well? Do ya wanna go or not?"

"Ah, Pasek, you know I do, but I can't, dammit. I don't have a … a babysitter."

"What kind of a daddy are you anyway? Are you going to deprive Aaron of the cultural arts? Of the theater? Who needs a babysitter when we have the whole Curran Theater to ourselves? Bring him. He'll love it!"

"Gosh, Pasek, I don't know. Maybe I should …"

Pasek interrupted me and announced, "I'll pick the two of you up tomorrow morning at 10. No suit and tie, but a couple of diapers just in case."

It was cold and windy the next morning and thinking the theater wouldn't be heated for a rehearsal, I dressed Aaron in long pants with a thick undershirt, a shirt, and a sweater to keep him warm. Then to be sure, I put the new brown tweed overcoat and matching cap on him that I was planning to give him as a Christmas present.

*    *    *    *    *

It was strange to walk through the stage door and then directly through the wings to where Ben, Pasek's fuck buddy in the supply closet, was hoisting a piece of scenery up into the vast layers of drops and rigging. Pasek introduced us on the fly, since it was obvious, by the sight and smell of Ben's sweaty sweatshirt that he was too busy doing his job to chat with us.

We were tempted to sit in the front row, all the better to examine the nude bodies when they appeared, but it would be too obvious, and besides, we didn't want them to ask us to leave because we brought a three-year-old to an "adult" show. Pasek led us up the stairs to the first tier, where we sat dead center in the first row with a great view of the entire ornate theater and the rows of red seats below us.

An iron pipe banister was raised a few inches above the solid railing in front of us, which allowed us to see more of the stage and orchestra pit. It also provided a barrier in case you lost your mind and decided to leap to the stage to be a part of the production.

Up to that time, a Broadway musical wasn't a Broadway musical to me unless it had a chorus of pretty girls and chorus boys in tight pants tap-dancing up a storm. *Hair* changed all that. I left the theater, humming some of the poignant songs, even though earlier I walked in through that stage door begrudging the time wasted to watch a bunch of hippies doing their rock and roll thing.

But I was amazed and overjoyed watching this show. The main character, Claude, could have easily been one of our group of friends, a solid, good person with good intentions. Each musical number was not only delightful to hear and see, but it also developed the characters and advanced the story. *My story … discarded people who wanted peace and love in the world rather than the sordid mess we found ourselves in. It was for free thinking, free love, and antiwar to a fever pitch. My kind of entertainment!

It was hard not to stand and applaud at the end of the first act, but we felt self-conscious about being the only two there watching the show. Aaron ignored the entire first act, including the bare-assed cast emerging through holes in a gigantic dark sheet that covered the entire stage. I brought a toy jeep and several plastic soldiers for him to play with, and he spent most of the time on his knees, using his theater seat as a battlefield where his soldiers shot each other and his jeep could run over the bodies. It was a little disconcerting to know he was reveling in a play war while I was being completely turned on by an antiwar musical.

His dispassionate tolerance of what was going on below us on the stage came to an abrupt stop. He brushed his toys off his seat and sat down to watch and listen. Something had caught his attention and he leaned forward, mesmerized.

Pasek and I were caught up in it too, a little fearful of what was unfolding, but needing to experience it also. Claude had been seduced into the hippie clan, and they lit tokes, the smoke fogging the air around them. It started serenely enough with a song called "Walking in Space," but as they smoked and then began to swallow pills, the music changed. The lights changed. Claude and his new friends were on an acid trip, and Claude was the center of his own nightmare.

Strobe lights flashed to the beat of the loud music. At that moment, Aaron stood up and grabbed the banister. Nuns appeared and began choking

Buddhist monks in yellow saffron robes. Aaron began to jump up and down. Vietcong soldiers in black pajamas shot the nuns. Aaron squealed and pulled himself back and forth in a trance, yelling, "La-la, ga-ga, la-la, ga-ga, la-la, la-la," to the beat of the drums. He was lost in it, his eyes wide, and his feather-light hair flowing like whipped-up waves as he twisted and turned.

I nudged Pasek's arm to get his attention so he could see how wildly Aaron was reacting. We both found it amusing and turned back to the show where the cast was singing "Dirty Little War." The whole thing, which was listed in the program as "The Trip Scene," lasted about 20 minutes, coming to an end with the brilliant song "Good Morning Starshine," and a billboard-sized cock and balls descending from the loft above the stage, undoubtedly lowered by Ben, Pasek's old fuck buddy in the supply room.

It slowly dawned on me during a session with one of my therapists years later that what I saw when Aaron went on his own little acid trip that night was the writing on the wall, and I wish to god I had thought more about it then. I would learn soon enough that the little boy I loved more than I loved my own life, was what would be called later, for lack of a better term, a "crack baby."

Years later, a troubled and concerned social worker at the adoption agency, against the rules that could have had her fired from her job, slipped me a page from Aaron's file. It told, in a matter-of-fact tone, about Aaron's birth. His teen aged birth mother was dropped off at the entrance to San Francisco General Hospital a little before dawn on May 18, 1966. She was in a stupor and both her pale arms were black and blue with needle marks. After her prolonged labor, Aaron was immediately taken away from her and spent the next three weeks in intensive care, where he went through a torturous withdrawal from the heroin in his bloodstream. The young girl who gave him life never saw him again. A dirty little war.

## Chapter 60

# November of '69 – Baby Buggy, War, Boys in the Band

My '62 Lincoln Continental sat six comfortably and six more if they were willing to ride on the trunk lid, which seemed as wide and long as an aircraft carrier. Of course, the baby buggy I had picked up at a garage sale to carry Aaron, sandwiches, and iced beer took up a lot of room, too. But this anti–Vietnam War march through the streets of San Francisco was going to be a very long one, and the Group, along with many of my tenants, were determined to go on it with me.

Pasek drove Old Rust, overflowing with friends and protest signs, and I drove the Lincoln with Aaron on my lap to the starting point in Union Square. The exuberant feeling of finally being able to give Nixon hell for prolonging and expanding the carnage spread through the crowd, and the event, so serious, so imperative, became a joyful, buoyant party in spite of our intent. As we walked, our hearts grew lighter to see thousands of people with signs and banners in front of us. When we looked back down Market Street, thousands more kept joining us like streams flowing into a river from all the side streets, Spear Street, Stockton, 5th, Mason. I felt like I was walking on air.

I had put a sign on the front of Aaron's buggy that said, I THANK GOD EVERY DAY THAT MY SON IS NOT VIETNAMESE! Over the carriage canopy, I'd attached an enlarged photo of a Vietnamese child whose lower jaw had been blown off. It was my way to venerate My Lai and the two-year-old who had been shot and killed by Lt. Calley.

The November weather was perfect. Cool air, bright sun, only a few puffy white clouds. It made me think of the excitement in fall when school started after a boring, hot summer. Somehow, this protest against the slaughter in jungles far away was beginning to make me feel happy to be alive, alive in this city, on this day with my friends and my little boy in his buggy, who wore his cowboy hat and was shooting at make-believe Indians walking beside us with their protest signs.

I could have pushed the buggy all the way to the Golden Gate Park, but my friends nudged each other aside to take a turn pushing the buggy. Even strangers began to ask if they could take a turn. After the rally in the park, Pasek, Aaron, and I rode a streetcar back down Market Street – empty now and littered with bottles, cans, and drifting paper – to Post Street where we had parked the truck and convertible. Then we drove back to the meadow in the park and loaded everyone, including the baby buggy, to return to the Wildflower Apartments.

The next morning I got a call from a magazine called *Family Health*. "Hello, Mr. Jones, I hope I'm not interfering with your work or time with your son. My name is Betty Klarnet, and I'm a writer. I live in New York, but the magazine I write for, *Family Health*, is based in Boulder, Colorado. They're very eager for me to come to your wonderful city to interview you.

I read about you in the *New York Times* and was blown away. Then my publisher phoned to tell me you were going to be on *To Tell the Truth*, which made me so excited about doing your story. My editor is an advocate of adoptions, and the idea of being able to adopt as a single person is something he's been championing for years now."

"Yeah, we have hundreds of kids here in San Francisco who need homes. It had to happen sooner or later. I'm sure the adoption agency here would be more than happy for you to spread the news. When were you …"

"If it's okay with you, the photographer and I could be there day after tomorrow. We need to spend at least four days with you and Aaron. We don't want to interfere with whatever you're doing, so we would just tag along and stay out of your way."

That's what happened. Betty with her recorder and notebook, and Douglas, whose face was always hidden behind a camera, were with us from the time we got out of bed until I tucked Aaron in at night. They left after three days, and I never heard from them again.

The featured article for the December issue of *Family Health* was about us, with a cover photo of Aaron and me at a playground. The story was told in such a loving and thoughtful way that I spent money I didn't have to buy 25 copies for the Group and other friends. I even sent one to my mother. I thought Betty and Douglas had abandoned us, but they actually had poured their hearts and souls into this article.

November turned out to be a red-letter month of '69. Dennis Clooney, my friend from New York, the lead in *The Boys in the Band,* came to our apartment for Thanksgiving dinner with the entire cast, thanks to Pasek, who got all gushy when we went backstage after the show. Once he heard they were living in hotel rooms and had no plans for a Thanksgiving dinner, except to eat in restaurants, you couldn't stop him. What surprised both of us was that even though the play was about homosexual friends celebrating a birthday, only a few in the cast were actually gay. So, besides the Group and the cast, we hosted their wives and girlfriends, too.

It's the Thanksgiving I remember most vividly. Luckily, the storeroom I had converted into an apartment was big enough to place enough card tables in a long train to seat a lot of crazy and funny people. Aaron sat at the head of the table in his high chair, wearing a Pilgrim hat, and the rest of us were the Indians with a turkey feather stuck in our headbands made up of one of my many neckties. Show people seem to be always *ON*, and one jab led to another until some of us were wiping away tears of laughter.

The dinner was a potluck with Pasek and me cooking two turkeys, and we were amazed how many delicious side dishes could be put together in hotel rooms. Aaron got bored with the jokes he couldn't understand, so while I looked away, he slid down under the tray of his high chair and went to look for Lily and Mammy, who were crouching under his crib.

That's where I found them. Curled up, arms, paws, legs, tails, fur, and skin into a mound of sleeping comfort-givers. I gave thanks for that sight. *My cup runneth over.* I was sure things could never be better than this, but on that day of thanks-giving, I had no idea what was in store for us in December.

## Chapter 61

# December of '69 – Mike Douglas, Death's Cold Breath

"Mr. Jones, would you mind holding your son for a minute so I can talk to you? I'd like to sit in his seat so I don't have to raise my voice over the engines. My name is Beth, and I'll be your hostess for this flight."

I pulled Aaron over to sit on my lap and gathered up his toys. She tenderly touched Aaron's arm and asked him his name. Never shy, he spoke up.

"Aaron."

"And who is this lovely little guy?"

"Teddy."

"Does this adorable monkey have a name, too?"

"Monkey."

"I know who this is, Aaron. Let me guess his name. Is it Snoopy?"

Aaron looked amazed that she knew Snoopy's name.

He held the stuffed dog up to Beth's mouth so she could kiss it, which she did.

"Do you live in Philadelphia, Mr. Jones?"

"No, we live in San Francisco. We're flying to Philadelphia to ..." My ego *begged* me to say, "Be on TV ... The Mike Douglas Show," but it would look like I was bragging, so I just said, "... do some business."

She seemed really anxious to talk to me, and I thought maybe I sat in the wrong seats or something was wrong with my ticket. Sue Horwitz, Mike

Douglas's assistant, had sent me the plane ticket and hadn't included one for Aaron, since toddlers under two flew free. Then I remembered that Aaron had turned three in May, seven months before! I had very little cash on me and was sure the airline would demand I pay for a ticket for him immediately.

"I can see you're worried about the noise you heard when we took off from San Francisco, Mr. Jones. That's why I'm here to tell you everything will be all right when we land. The loud noise you heard was a tire blowing, but we have many more wheels and tires to land safely when we get to Philly. Don't panic when the pilot tells us all to get into 'crash positions.' It's just a precautionary move. No more threatening than the lifeboat drill you take just before a cruise ship leaves the harbor."

"Blew a tire?"

"Nothing to worry about. Captain Hayes is one of the best pilots at TWA."

"Blew a tire!"

"Now, Mr. Jones, when the captain makes that announcement, be sure your safety belt is as tight as it can be. Okay? Take your shoes off, your glasses, and any jewelry, like your watch, then put your son on your lap, hold him tight and bend over as far as both of you will go. Okay? I have to go now to talk to each passenger, but I'll be back soon with drinks. Dinner will be served in about two hours."

She was in a hurry, but she turned around and asked Aaron if he would like some ice cream. Then she said, "Take care of Teddy, Monkey, and Snoopy 'til I get back with the ice cream, okay?"

*Blew a tire!*

It could have been the air conditioning, but for the rest of the flight, I felt the cold breath of death enveloping my body.

I took the instruction letter from Sue Horwitz, and on the back of it, quickly wrote out my last will and testament, giving Pasek the task of being the executor so he could sell the Wildflower, Old Rust, and the Lincoln. If Aaron survived me, as much as I knew Pasek loved him, I knew he couldn't take on the daily grind of raising Aaron and still keep his demanding job. So, I wrote to my brother Jerry, asking him to raise Aaron for me. He was the devoted father of Mark and Alison, a teacher, and in a long-term relationship with Randles. They would be the perfect parents for Aaron.

"This is Captain Hayes speaking. We are descending and will be landing in Philadelphia in approximately 10 minutes. I am sure the landing will be soft and very safe, but just as a precaution, follow the instructions of our hostesses and assume the crash position. It's been a pleasant flight and we're on schedule. Your bags will be on turntable number four. Thanks for flying TWA."

It was an icy December night, clear with no moon or clouds. I was able to lift my head enough from my bent position to peer down at the lights below us. Scattered white and yellow lights first from rural patches, then becoming denser in the checkerboard pattern of suburban housing. Looming ahead were the flickering multi-colored neon lights of the low-rise city I'd read about in the sixth grade. Then they came into view – long rows of blinking lights lined up on each side of several runways.

We flew over the airport and made a wide circle over Philadelphia as the wing on my side of the plane dipped steadily, pointing to the array of stop lights, neon signs, headlights, and taillights crisscrossing on the streets. I held Aaron a little tighter, and he began to squirm.

As the plane dipped to approach the runway, I bent over as far as I could with Aaron and all his friends in my arms kissing the top of his head. The clean scent of his fine hair filled my lungs as I inhaled what I thought might be my last few deep breaths.

"Daddy loves you, Aaron. Daddy loves you, Aaron. Daddy loves you, Aaron."

The jet engines were almost silent, and I could hear a gush of wind. I felt the thud of the flaps lowering on the wings, then heard the screech of the rubber as the tires hit the runway. At the same time, the jets roared so hard in reverse that they shook the plane. We lurched forward as the brakes, flaps, and jets yanked the plane back violently from the speed it took to glide onto the tamarack.

"Welcome to the City of Brotherly Love, everyone," Captain Hayes soothed over the loud speakers. I quickly raised my head, and Aaron scrambled to get away from my clutches just as everyone burst into prolonged applause. I turned to look out the window to see if there was any snow on the ground and gasped when I saw what was lined up in between the terminal and our plane as far as I could see. Up and down the runway was a jukebox of red, green, white, and blue blinking lights. Side by side, bumper to bumper, a line of ambulances, fire trucks, tow trucks, police cars, motorcycles, white coroner vans, and TV news vans, poised, waiting bravely to save us from a fiery death. Or remove our bodies.

I wouldn't swear to it, but I am almost sure I saw the look of disappointment on some of the faces. Skidding in on the belly of the plane would have been an awe-inspiring tale to tell at Christmas dinners.

I learned my lesson when we flew to New York to do the *To Tell the Truth* show in August. Two lessons, actually. One was to dig into my empty pockets and buy enough disposable Pampers for the two days in Philadelphia instead of lugging around a plastic bag of wet and dirty cloth diapers. The other was to "suggest" that the *Mike Douglas Show* pay me for being a guest. My reasoning? I was a member of AFTRA, the union for TV and radio actors. It was a bold move on my part, and it took a desperate man to make it.

They didn't blink, and I received a check for over $100. It meant that I could buy that special Christmas present for Aaron, the one I couldn't afford. It lured me to the display window at FAO Schwarz every time I went downtown to shoot an ad for Macy's. I knew it would thrill Aaron to find it under our tree Christmas morning, and I wanted it for him so badly that I had been tempted to do something dreadful – ask Pasek for another loan.

A slab of stucco the size of a ping-pong table had fallen off the Greenwich Street side of the Wildflower, and the repair had wiped me out financially. Fortunately, no one had been walking beneath it when it shattered on the sidewalk. This would be Aaron's and my second Christmas together, but the first one as legal father and son. It had to be special!

As soon as we arrived at the airline terminal, I took Aaron over to the enormous window framing the TWA jet we had just left, so we could look down on all the emergency vehicles flashing their colored lights. His vocabulary was growing, mostly single syllable nouns, and for some reason, he was fascinated with motorcycles. When he saw them on the streets, he bounced, waved his arms, and pointed at them, all the time shouting out, "Mo! Mo!" When he saw the line of police bikes with their blue and red lights flashing, it was as if a bolt of lightning had struck him. He couldn't stop saying, "Mo! Mo! Mo!"

To save some of the daily expense money Sue Horwitz had sent me, we ate dinner at McDonald's before I checked into our room. Because of the time zone difference, it was hours after Aaron's bedtime, but like clockwork, he had fallen into his usual deep sleep on San Francisco time. Normally, at 10 o'clock at night, before Aaron came into my life, I'd be dressed in my latest cashmere sweater and tightest pants, on my way out the door to stalk the gay bars until I ensnared a trick for the night. Maybe I was getting old or maybe it was because I wasn't so desperately lonely anymore, but that insane horny drive seemed like a dream of my past. The love of my life was curled up on one side of our king-sized bed with his arms wrapped around his closest friends, Teddy, Monkey, and Snoopy. As much as I would have loved to prowl the dark streets of Philadelphia that night, I smiled to myself knowing I'd rather be right there, in that hotel room with my little boy who stirred my heart, not my body. He was my "Mo!"

## Chapter 62
# Titty Titty Bang Bang

I couldn't have survived the next few weeks without Aaron's young nanny. Ronnie would pick up Aaron at childcare and cancel any of her plans if I had a booking or a project in one of the apartments. December of '69, after we flew back from Philadelphia, was overwhelming. Luckily, I was booked at Macy's to shoot ads almost every other day. Macy's checks from the ad department gave me money to buy new clothes for Aaron at Penny's, food for us at the Searchlight, Xmas decorations, a tree for Christmas, and cheap presents for what seemed like hundreds of friends and family. I felt the tingle of edging closer to Christmas morning when at last, Aaron could see what I bought for him.

I couldn't avoid seeing our creepy president and his sly sidekick, Kissinger, on the nightly news, pretending to actually care about the slaughtered bodies of young Americans in caskets, filling army cargo planes, landing on American soil daily. It wasn't easy to turn my head away, but it was the holiday season, and I had to focus on my responsibilities that had nothing to do with Vietnam.

Because of all the news coverage and the two TV shows, the adoption agency was getting piles of letters for me that needed to be picked up and answered. I spent hours at night after I tucked Aaron in, stuffing envelopes with my form letter and licking stamps. Pasek helped me on the nights we went to the movies so I wouldn't feel guilty about leaving the apartment with stacks of letters still to be answered. He dragged me off to see movies all the time, insisting that most of them had subliminal gay themes.

Since I was the only one of the Group who owned a pickup, six of us, plus Aaron and Lily, went Christmas tree shopping together with Michael's Rolls Royce following Old Rust to a lot on Mission Street. It took hours longer than it should have because we were so picky. The trees were too tall, too short, too wide, or too scrawny, crooked trunk, not pine or not fir. Never go shopping with a gaggle of opinionated gay men! Pasek and I delivered the trees, trying frantically to remember who bought which tree. It was past Aaron's bedtime when we finally got back to our apartment, so after giving Aaron a quick bath and reading him a short book, I tucked him in, and Pasek and I decorated the tree.

The next morning, when Aaron saw the tree, he walked slowly over to it, his eyes in a wide trancelike stare. He stood there for a few minutes, quiet, taking it all in, then spread his arms and started jabbering to the tree, "La-la, ga-ga. La-la, ga-ga!" He walked around it, discovering each shiny ornament and light and carried on a conversation with the tree as if it could understand every word he spoke.

I had learned the hard way not to have any balls or lights within Mammy's striking distance the year before when she batted at them like punching bags. This year, the floor under the tree was clear of shards of glass and made a perfect place for Aaron to use as his private cave. Several times, I found him lying on his back, staring up through the maze of pine branches, bedazzled by the reflections of the colored lights on the mirrored ornaments. He was adventuring into his magical world, and I wished I could join him.

On Christmas morning, I reached into Aaron's crib to pick him up, and to my amazement found him dry. He was still in his blue flannel pjs when he wiggled out of my arms and ran into the living room to see "his" tree. He skidded to a stop when he saw what was piled under and around it. I grabbed the phone and barked, "Pasek, get over here quick! He hasn't found it yet. Hurry!"

I let him pull all the bright packages out to the middle of the room, except for the huge box wrapped in Santa Claus paper, I was pleased that he didn't start tearing into the packages. He was enthralled just moving them around and stacking them, not knowing that there were toys inside for him from all his "uncles" and "aunts."

By the time Pasek arrived, I had Aaron changed into his blue velvet romper suit and had prepared coffee and waffles for us. We decided to wait until all the guests arrived to let Aaron open their gifts to him, but I was too excited to wait that long for Aaron to see what "Santa" had for him in the biggest box.

He didn't know how to open it and found its size intimidating. We couldn't convince him that it would be all right to tear the wrapping off until Pasek made a lunge for the bows and ripped them off, tossing them in the air. Then I began to rip pieces of the Santa paper off the top. Aaron finally got the idea and began to tear very small bits off the sides. We let him take his time until a large swatch of the paper fell to the floor and revealed a picture of a pedal car printed on the side of the cardboard box. He took a minute to study it, then pointing to the picture, repeating, first softly, then more rapidly and loudly, "Titty Titty Bang Bang! Titty Titty Bang Bang!"

"You'd better believe it!" chimed in Pasek, as he cut the taped seams open so Aaron could peer inside the box. Two glass headlights stuck out from the

Christmas night

gold plastic radiator, staring back at him. I tipped the box until the pedal car with the gold body, black fenders, and red spoked wheels rolled out. Aaron didn't say a word but crawled inside to sit in the driver's seat. He looked solemn, seriously down to business, examining all the dials and buttons on the dashboard.

He found a lever and pulled on it. Yellow and red striped wings slipped from under the running boards and spread out like flat umbrellas on either side of the car. Still, without a word, Aaron walked into his bedroom and came back out wearing oversized goggles, got back into his car, and began to pedal it around the room. He would pedal it a few feet. Stop. Get out and examine some part of it. Give Teddy a ride for a few feet. Stop. Trade off Teddy for Snoopy, and drive him for a few feet more. He sat in the car, took short rides, or got out, and acting as a scientist, explored every inch of it to evaluate its worth, even after the first guests arrived with hot dishes and bowls in their hands.

After dinner, all the "uncles" and "aunts" helped Aaron rip off the multi-colored wrappings of the presents they had given him, but it was Chitty Chitty Bang Bang that he wanted in his bedroom that night. He fell asleep gazing at it.

We sat, spread over the sofa and the floor around the coffee table for hours after I put him to bed, smoking, drinking, and trying to top each other with far-out stories. I had one I'd been dying to tell all day and finally butted in to tell it.

"After dinner last night at my dad's house in Oakland, I was driving home …"

"Sober, I hope," Michael sneered.

"Obviously sober, Michael, if you've ever had dinner at my dad's house. *Anyhow,* I was driving up Broadway …"

"Is this gonna take long, Bill? I have an appointment next Tuesday."

"As I was saying, Gary, I was driving up Broadway and Aaron had his head on my lap, sleeping …

"This story's making *me* sleepy, Bill."

"Oh, I thought you had already passed out as usual, Ray. Now let me finish my damn story!"

"The neon lights from the strip joints must have awakened him cuz he stood up on the seat beside me and got really excited, pointing at all the posters of naked women and saying, 'Titty! Titty! Titty!'"

Ronnie gasped and clucked, "Good Lord, Bill!"

"Not *only* that! He had a hard-on that pushed his rompers straight out!"

I finally had everyone's attention.

"Jesus, Bill, never gave it a thought before, but I think Aaron's straight!"

"I know, Pasek, I know! Isn't that great? A gay man raising a straight kid?"

Pasek rose and pulled me up to face him, then looking me straight in the eye with his hands on my shoulders, asked, "Where did we go wrong, Bill? Where did we go wrong?"

## Chapter 63

# 1970 – A Bridge Over Troubled Waters

On May 4, I drove Aaron to the nursery school, and as soon as he was safely inside, I jumped back into Old Rust to listen to the news.

"… Glide Church. Reverend Williams, can you tell our audience why you and members of your church … and hundreds of others, are here – marching into City Hall?"

"We're here to ask the Board of Supervisors, respectfully, to ask them for a resolution denouncing this horrific action by President Nixon, the bombing of a peaceful nation, Cambodia."

"Do you expect …? Reverend Williams … please stay one more minute … sorry, ladies and gentlemen. Cecil Williams just left and went into the rotunda.

I drove from Phoebe Hearst to City Hall and parked in a yellow zone, eager to join Cecil and the protesters. I found Cecil and some of Glide's members standing at the bottom of the vast marble staircase that rose from the floor of the rotunda to the second floor where the Board's chambers were, behind massive paneled double doors. The stairway was jammed with more protesters, and thunderous chants of "Resolution! Resolution" echoed off the marble walls.

Over the shouting and chanting, a bullhorn at the top of the stairs sounded a blast. We all quieted down. Then we heard screams from the crowd at the top of the stairs as people were being pushed away from the chamber's door and onto the stairway. Whoever had the bullhorn growled into it, "This has been declared an illegal assembly and you have five minutes to leave City Hall or you will be arrested and taken to jail."

I turned to Cecil and said, "We're gonna stay, aren't we?"

He grabbed me by the shoulder and scoffed, "Bill, I've been thrown in jail 11 times. It's no fun, I tell ya. I don't wanna do it again!"

I protested, "But Cecil, it's like letting them win. It makes us look like cowards … running away!"

"We've made our point, Bill. They know damn well we want a resolution, and we'll get it. It'll be on the front page tomorrow." He gave me a little push. "Now find as many members of the church as you can, and tell them to get the hell outta here!" He turned away from me. "You go that way and I'll go to the left. Go!"

The voice on the bullhorn warned us once more to leave or be arrested. Then like the Rockettes in Radio City, a blue line of the Tac Squad, helmets, visors, and nightsticks, all in one line, slowly descended the marble stairway, swinging their long, black sticks. The chants dissolved into screams and cries from the top of the stairs. I looked up and saw a woman holding her hands in front of her face to shield her from the blows. Like a human lava flow, they came staggering down the steps, leaving patches of red blood on them, a spotty trail the Tac Squad stepped on.

A logjam of human bodies struggled to get out through the brass and glass Polk Street entrance doors. I headed for one of the archways on the periphery of the rotunda floor that I thought might lead to a hallway that was connected to the Van Ness Avenue entrance. Panic was all around me, crushing me, and I breathed it in. I felt fear. Icy fear.

The Tac Squad finally reached the bottom step, separated in the middle, half to the left and half to the right. In a flash, they moved deftly to the periphery of the rotunda where they quickly circled around us, prodding us with their clubs to move toward the Polk Street doors.

I stood on my toes to see if I could spot Cecil or anyone else I knew, but all I could see was an ocean wave of hair and caps, protest signs with peace symbols, and a cutout of Nixon's face with a Hitler mustache and dark hair hanging over his forehead.

I felt the blunt end of a night stick rammed into my vertebrae, and a voice commanded me to move toward the entrance. A woman standing in front of me, unable to move because there were bodies jammed together in front of her, shuffling one half-step at a time to get out. I had to apologize to her for stepping on her heel. Then I felt the night stick again and the voice growled, "*Move*, friend!"

Over the din of screams and yelling, the voice kept telling me, "Move! Move, friend!" And with each command, I felt the impact on my back that grew more painful as we neared the doors. I thought I'd be out on the sidewalk any moment, free at last, so when he jabbed me again and ordered me, "Move, friend! Move!" I turned around and faced him, looked him straight in the eye, and said, with as much control as I could muster,

"What in the world makes you think we're *friends*?"

He glared at me and shouted, "Put your hands behind you, Smart Ass!" He cinched handcuffs on me so tight, I was sure the skin on my wrists was cut open. Then he pulled my arms up behind me until I was forced to bend over, crouching until my head almost touched the floor. He yanked on my arms, bending me over, then pulled me up the staircase, two steps at a time. At the top, he pushed me into a corner behind a column where a dozen or so fellow protesters, all handcuffed, were being hidden from the TV cameras. Some of them had blood running down their faces from wounds on their foreheads or scalps, under hair matted with blood.

We were herded down the back stairs and into waiting police vans where we sat on fiberglass benches facing each other. The doors were locked and there we sat for over an hour, our hands behind our backs, staring at each other. Eventually, conversations began, mostly about how brutally we had been handled, but I agreed with the rest of them that if the supervisors made the resolution, it would be worth it. I hoped Aaron would be proud of me.

A woman about fifty sat directly across from me. She wasn't hand cuffed. She sat upright, eyes straight ahead, not looking at me in particular. She was dressed neatly in brown slacks and jacket, wore a beret, and had a small aluminum suitcase

I broke the silence. "Miss, you weren't inside City Hall with us, were you?

"How can you tell?"

"No handcuffs. No bruises. How did you end up in the van with us?"

"I was just walking by. Minding my own business, when this nasty policeman told me to keep moving or he'd arrest me!"

"What were you doing in front of City Hall? Protesting?"

"No! I was working! I sell Fuller brushes, and nobody's gonna tell me I can't walk on a sidewalk! Nobody! Not even a damn policeman! So, he told me I was under arrest, and here I am. I got rights!"

I liked her. "Good for you, Lady. If I could, I'd shake your hand."

The skinny long-haired man sitting next to her agreed, "So would I. So would I."

With that, they turned to each other and had an intense conversation about civil rights that I was left out of. He was wearing a press badge issued by the *Berkeley Barb* and had a worried look on his face. He leaned in and whispered something in her ear. She drew back, searched his face and eyes for a minute, then reached into his shirt pocket and withdrew a half-smoked, hand-rolled cigarette. She looked to see who was watching her, then popped it into her mouth, chewed it, and swallowed it just as the van lurched forward. They drove us a few blocks and then parked in a dead-end alley, still hiding us from any news media.

Eventually, they drove us to the city jail and courthouse on Brannan Street. We were mugged, fingerprinted, then led into a windowless room where we were told to drop our pants and underwear and bend over. An overweight cop spread our cheeks to see if we were smuggling dope or weapons into the jail.

I couldn't help smiling thinking of this cop's dinner conversation that night at home with his wife and kids.

"How did it go today at work, Dear? See any trouble?"

"Yeah, Daddy, tell us what you did today? Did ya shoot any bad guys?"

The thought of *his* kids made me think of Aaron with a pang in my gut. I turned to the cop who had been purveying my asshole, and gasped, "I gotta get out of here. I'm supposed to pick up my son at daycare at five, and it's after three now! How soon can I leave? What do I have to sign so I can go home?"

"You're charged with a felony, buddy, and your bail's $5,000. You get one phone call." My hand was shaking as he pushed a phone to me. I was just barely able to get my trembling finger in the dial hole. I felt sweaty, hoping I could dial Pasek without making a mistake.

"Hello. Michelle's Dry Cleaning. Can you hold for a sec?"

I hung up, and when I put the receiver down, I felt crushed. Why didn't I ask them to phone Pasek for me? The look on my face must have registered with another cop standing next to me. "I shouldn't do this, but go on. Try it again."

I focused as if my life depended on it, and dialed the seven digits slowly and carefully. Pasek picked up the phone and I could hardly make my voice louder than a whisper. "Pasek, you won't believe where I'm calling you from. I'm in jail! Can you pick Aaron up for me at Phoebe Hearst? And I need someone to bail …"

The cop put his finger on the cradle, took the receiver from my hand, hung it up with a bang, and taking me by my arm, led me into the drunk tank. It smelled of vomit and urine and sweat. About 10 of us were locked in that unlit cell. Most of the men were disheveled, with varying growths of beard and eyes that seemed to glow in the dark. I sat as far away as I could from them at a place no one else wanted … next to the toilet without a seat or lid. Hours crept by, and all I could think of was being on my sofa with Aaron on my lap with him turning the pages of the book I was reading to him. Lily and Mammy curled up next to my thigh. So warm. So cozy. My home. My home. I wanted to go home!

I tried to close my eyes and my ears to the squalor around me, but sleep was impossible with the steady stream of cussing, ranting, and crying filling the cell. If only I had something to read! The desk clerk had taken my wallet, watch, chewing gum – everything – to be returned to me *if* my bail was paid. I turned my head away when one by one, the men in the tank sidled up to the toilet to take a leak. Normally I'd get turned on by the sight of a cock so close to me, but I felt repulsed and looked away.

One desperately drunk prisoner, whose lips were cracked open with pus and blood caked on them, crawled on his hands and knees to the stained toilet and grabbing the rim of it, lowered his head down to the water level, slurping up the water. I hurried to the bars that separated us from the room where a policeman sat at a table a few feet away and I called to him.

"Sir, there's a very sick guy here drinking out of the toilet. Could you bring him some water? Please. I think he's dehydrated."

The cop just glared at me for a moment, then broke out into a broad grin. "So, the hippie wants water for the drunk, eh? That's a hoot! Go fuck yourself. And get outta the country if you don't like our war."

At 4:30 in the morning, I heard the cell door opening. "Jones! Come on, get goin'. Somebody dumb enough paid your fuckin' bail."

"Are they here to pick me up?"

"He came last night and paid it, but he left after a couple of hours sittin' on his can."

The desk clerk handed me my belongings in a large brown envelope, but when I opened it on the sidewalk outside, the few dollar bills were missing from my wallet, along with the change I was counting on to phone Pasek. The city streets were nearly empty and the sky above the buildings was beginning to lighten as I walked back to where I had parked Old Rust near City Hall. A parking ticket sat under the windshield wiper. In front of my truck was a yellow newspaper dispenser. I read the bold headline filling the page under the *San Francisco Chronicle* logo. **Four Students Killed at Kent State!** Below the headline was a photo of a young girl kneeling down on one knee next to a dead body. Her hands were in the air and it looked like she was screaming.

\* \* \* \* \*

My lawyer, Evander Smith, read the felony charges to me, and my mouth dropped open. I was stunned. Unable to process what I heard, I could only say to him, "But policemen don't lie! They don't! Do they?"

"Here it is, Bill. Officer Yeargain writes that you were on the top step facing him, threatening him. He says several people attempted to take you away from him, but you refused to go. He claims you ... quote, 'drew his right fist back to hit me. At that time I then gave the suspect a butt stroke to the neck.'"

"You're kidding me!"

"Get this. He spells neck – k-n-e-c-k. Here, read it yourself. Threatening to hit a police officer and resisting arrest. Oh, yeah, disturbing the peace and inciting a riot!"

I covered my face with my hands and rocked back and forth in misery.

"Your only hope, Bill, is that I can negotiate with the DA and get the felony dropped to a misdemeanor ... like spitting on the sidewalk. Let's hope Yeargain doesn't show up for the hearing. If he's a no-show, the charges might be dismissed. Otherwise, we're in for a jury trial, and I hate to tell you this, but you'll be stone cold broke with my fees and the court's fees. I hope you're a *very* rich man, Bill Jones. You're looking at six years in jail and a $6,000 fine. That doesn't include the $250 a day for a jury trial."

Lady Luck was with me on the day of the hearing, and Yeargain was in a dentist's chair having a molar pulled. Karma was indeed working. He shouldn't have told lies about me. I went free, but the lawyer's fee was $500, an amount I wished I had.

I went to Cecil and asked him if the church could help me pay for it, but he told me the church would go bankrupt if it bailed out all the members that got thrown in jail – for whatever reasons. He did ask me to speak about my experience as a jailbird, and the rough treatment we had to deal with.

*    *    *    *    *

At the podium, with a microphone in front of me the next Sunday, I blurted out my sad tale, very aware that *all* my friends and my brother Jerry, and my other half-brother, Russell, and his wife, Sandi, filled the first two rows of the church pews. When I finished, I sat down on the edge of the platform facing the congregation.

I heard some giggling from the section my friends were sitting in, and was puzzled. Why were they whispering to each other and on the edge of their seats looking at me? Had I made a fool of myself? I looked down to see if my fly was open. It dawned on me that they were also staring at the woman sitting next to me. I turned to look at her, and although she looked familiar, I couldn't place her

I looked back at the crowded sanctuary and was surprised at an unfamiliar sight. Standing out like a beacon in a stormy night were two dark-suited men, with starched white shirts and black ties, standing in the aisle at the back of the church watching us. They looked like two penguins in a gaggle of multi-colored parrots.

I touched the woman's thigh to get her attention, and asked, "Do you see those two guys in the dark suits in the aisle? They give me the creeps. They sure don't belong here."

The woman looked at me, smiled, and replied, "Oh, don't worry about them. They follow me wherever I go. Boring. I call 'em Moe and Sack-a-Rocks."

Cecil took the mike in his hands and announced, "We are so honored to have a dear friend of Glide here with us today. She's a brave hero to us who know her, and a glittering, talented star to all of us. She puts her money where her mouth is and has come through for Glide so many times I've lost track of 'em."

He looked down very fondly at the woman sitting next to me and breathed into the mike before he handed it to her, "Brothers and sisters, let's hear it now for one of our own. Come on up here with me, Jane Fonda. Tell us about your vacation in Vietnam."

The whole congregation roared with applause and laughter. Everyone got the joke except the two men in dark suits.

## Chapter 64

# Raindrops Keep Fallin' on My Head

It was almost painful to leave Aaron off at the center the next day. He looked at me, half sad and half frightened, with his lower lip trembling. There was a question in his eyes, and I bent down to hug him again. "No, Honey, don't you worry. Daddy's gonna pick you up at five o'clock. Just like always. I'm so sorry about yesterday. But Uncle Pasek took you home for me, and did he play with you and read one of your books to you?" He nodded. "You had fun with him, didn't you? See you at five, Sweetie."

I went straight home and closed the door behind me. I looked around and took in all the sights I could only long for when I was incarcerated in that other world. I'd erased the chipped and stained bench in the drunk tank by remembering my green velvet sofa and the gray wall of iron bars by visualizing the white panels behind the sofa. I'd hummed the songs of *Sesame Street* to muffle the sounds of grown men crying and farting. It was so comforting to sit at my breakfast table and do nothing but stare at Lily and Mammy, savoring every second of being home.

I picked up one of Aaron's crayons and started to doodle over the want ads of the *Chron*. Then thinking of the protest at City Hall, I drew a large green peace sign that covered the page. Green for the environment. Remembering the pitiful men in the cell with me, I filled in one of the upper spaces with a black crayon. The other space, I left white. Black men. White men. My mind wandered back to Glide, Jane Fonda, and the faces looking at us from the pews. Such a mixture of color! I filled one of the bottom spaces brown for all the brown skins and the last one in yellow, for the Asians. Drawing seemed to calm my aching soul, and besides, I thought it very clever and wanted to show it off. I scotch-taped it to the mirror in the entry as proof I was still human and could think abstractly. We jailbirds are no dummies.

Pasek took it home with him that night and phoned me the next day.

"Uh, uh. I've been cleaning up your design, Bill, and it looks pretty good. I think it would make a good button for Glide. People come from Indiana and they want a souvenir to take home from that crazy, hippie church in San Francisco."

"You mean sell them at church?"

"Why not? They cost only pennies to make, and I bet they'll pay a dollar for one. It might pay Evander's fee. What do ya think?"

"I love the idea! Can you show me what you did with it? I'll take it down to Cecil to see what he thinks. I love the idea. Hope he does, too."

Pasek had added the word "GLIDE" to my design, and Cecil gave us his blessings. The first batch of one hundred buttons cost about $20 and was sold out on the first Sunday after the nine o'clock service. There were none left for eleven o'clock.

Glide sold them by the thousands for years. They paid for a lot of bail money and lawyers' fees, to be sure. As usual, I was first in line, and I still have the button. I gave Evander a button too, proudly smiling along with Glide's check for $500.

## Chapter 65
# Let It Be

Carol, Aaron's second nanny, and her boyfriend, Chic, stopped living in sin and tied the knot. At the engagement party I gave for them, they broke the news to me that they would be moving out of the Wildflower Apartments as soon as they were married, but it all happened so fast that I wasn't able to find another nanny before they moved out. I didn't realize how much I relied on having someone living across the hall to take care of Aaron if I got a booking, an extra job, or even more important, a chance to go out and raise Cain for a few hours at night.

As usual, Pasek saved the day.

"Remember when we went out on the Neptune Society's boat to toss Michael Pollard's ashes out under the Golden Gate?"

"Yeah, poor Michael. What did he die of? Do ya remember?"

"Jeez, Bill, I never asked, but I hope it isn't catching. He was great in bed. And so young, too. In his twenties. Mid, I think."

"I sat next to his mom and felt terrible. She cried the whole time we were out there. I wanted to hold her hand or put my arm around her, but there seemed to be a wall between us."

"I know whatcha mean, Bill, but I talked to her a couple a days ago, and she needs a smaller place she can afford now that Michael's not there. She's retired, and, I think she might be just what you need to take over the little nanny studio. Aaron's never had a granny nanny."

Helen Pollard moved into number A, a few days before Halloween in 1970, and helped us carve 14 pumpkins, one for each of the 12 tenants, and one *for* Aaron, plus one for herself. She was motherly and soft-spoken, a sweet, gray-haired woman who had lived with her gay son, and whose smile barely hid her grief in losing him. Aaron took to her immediately.

She loved making costumes for him, and whenever he was available in the afternoons, they would have an "Afternoon Tea, Milk, and Cookies," and as if she were playing with a live-sized doll, she would dress him in the costume de jour – Indian, astronaut, fire chief, lizard, Smokey the Bear, Royal Canadian Mounted policeman, sailor, Superboy with a cape, a knight, a devil. Whatever. He adored her. He called her Grandma, and she loved it.

$$* \quad * \quad * \quad * \quad *$$

Two important things happened before Aaron was five. He took a book from my hands one night as we were cuddled on the sofa, and slowly sounded out the words he didn't know, and easily read the words I had printed on three by fives and taped to the wall next to his potty. He could read! His being able to read was one of the two things that gave him comfort and joy for the rest of his life. The other was music.

On Thursday nights, I let him stay up with me past eight o'clock to watch *The Waltons* together. I felt it was crucial for him to see how a "normal" family looked. Aaron had many "uncles" and "aunts," a "grandmother" nanny, my frequent modeling partner, Nancy's three kids, who were like brothers and sisters to him, and me, Bachelor Daddy. But his family wasn't the Norman Rockwell family. The Waltons were, and I wanted him to experience that kind of family.

When *The Waltons'* theme music came up, he would jump up on my lap to watch it and try to stay awake until it was over, an hour later. Sometimes, just to stretch out our goodnights to each other, he would yell out to me from his bed, "Goodnight, John-Boy!"

And I would call back, "Goodnight, Grandpa!"

"Goodnight, Ellen!"

"Goodnight, Mama!"

"Goodnight, Grandma!"

And so it would go on, and on, until I would finally say, "Goodnight, Aaron. It's time you and Teddy got some sleep. Go to sleep!"

I had to tell you about our Thursday nights so you would appreciate what happened one night at a formal dinner given by Frank McGinnes, a lovely man I was "dating," and his father, with whom he shared a large brick home in Pacific Heights. Frank's father was gay, also, and it bothered me a little that their home was like entering a couple's private domain.

Even though their relationship was clearly not incestuous, it was also very clear they were like one person in their behavior, their beliefs, and their sense of elegant class. They loved giving formal dinner parties, and they shared in cooking the gourmet menus and creating exquisite table settings. The flowers and candles, the fine bone china, and the silverware were exotic and completely different from the way Aaron and I lived. I knew Frank and I were not on the same plane, but I hoped our affair would last. It was like looking through a window into another world.

Frank and his dad both seemed to like Aaron, and even though he couldn't share our conversations at the table, he was quiet and well behaved. Their living room was formal with oriental rugs, antiques from different eras, and a mixture of oil paintings, both classic and contemporary. The highlight of the room was a large black Steinway piano holding court in front of a bay window that looked out at Alcatraz and Treasure Island.

After discussing the movie *Carnal Knowledge* and tearing apart *The Owl and the Pussycat*, the conversation became intense, as every conversation did in the seventies when we got on our soapboxes over the war in Vietnam. Aaron asked to be excused, and I helped him get down off the two phone books used to stand in for a high chair.

In the middle of a heated sentence about our giving up and pulling out of Vietnam, I stopped to listen. Embarrassed, I apologized to Frank and his dad for Aaron tinkering at the Steinway and was just about to get out of my chair to scold him, when Frank said, "Wait, Bill! I think he's trying to play something!"

It was hit and miss plunking, some notes repeating, trying, and failing, but everyone at the table leaned forward to listen and reached the same conclusion. He was finding the keys and playing the theme of *The Waltons*!

## Chapter 66
# Everything Is Beautiful

Several wonderful things happened just before Aaron's fourth birthday, the Wizard of Oz one. One day out of the blue, he tugged at my pant leg and looking up at me, clearly said, "Pee-pee!" Oh, the joy of hearing that word! I rushed him to the bathroom and lowered his diaper, a *dry* diaper, and sat him on his ducky potty.

Quite often when Aaron urinated sitting on his potty, and even though a hollowed-out yellow duck's body cupped over his penis, his stream would shoot straight into the air, drenching me and raining back down on him. I tried to teach him to push down on his tiny cock to direct the stream into the pot, but it was awkward for both of us in that position, so I painted a stool that I had built in my high school woodworking class and put it in front of the toilet for him to stand on.

Unless I was standing behind him to help him push his penis down toward the bowl, the stream shot up or to the left or to the right, but never where it should go. It was an ongoing battle, but both of us were thankful that most of the time it saved him from wearing a wet diaper. It was bad enough when we missed his potty time and I had to clean his bottom and toss a smelly diaper in the laundry basket. I could hardly wait to have him tug at my pant leg and say, looking up at me, "Ca-ca potty."

The other wonderful thing that happened was that Pasek brought his mother and sister, Laverne, out from St. Louis for a two-week visit. Pasek gave them his bedroom on Bay Street, and he slept on my sofa – when he wasn't sleeping over at a trick's place. He had told me many times how much he loved his mother and his sister, but when I met them, I have to admit I was a little shocked. Mostly shocked when I first met Laverne.

Pasek was handsome, except for his thinning hair, and he had a twinkle in his blue eyes, especially when he gave you that toothy, happy-go-lucky smile.

He was well-developed, strong, and graceful. His sense of humor, mostly Polish put-downs aimed at himself, made me laugh. His clothes were Brooks Brothers and Cable Car Clothiers, always a clean shirt, and cordovan shoes, polished and buffed.

I could see right away why he adored his mother. Not chic like him. Not educated or talented like him, but in her own right, outstanding, glowing with love for everything and everyone around her. Her voice was soft and gentle, like her movements. Where Pasek was tall, over six feet, she was only a little over five feet. She wasn't trim like Pasek, but not fat either. Pleasantly plump and dressed simply from Sears Roebuck.

I was sure Laverne couldn't have possibly been my best friend's sister. She was as tall as he, but gangly, all hanging arms and skinny legs. Her cardigan sweater, blouse, and skirt were multiple shades of pink, turquoise, and beige and looked like they had been lifted out of the discard bin at the Salvation Army. She had the vocabulary of a twelve-year-old. But it was obvious right away that she looked up to her younger brother and not only respected him but was overwhelmed with gratitude for any attention he gave her.

I could feel in my gut the sure-footed caring among the three of them, and I learned from his mother and sister why they absolutely adored Pasek. It also explained why Pasek, even though he was tops in his field of events design, never seemed to have much more money than I did. Pasek's father had died when he was ten, leaving his mother to care for her two children by taking in laundry, doing housework around the neighborhood, and occasionally babysitting. She managed to help Pasek put himself through college and support her slightly retarded daughter at the same time.

Pasek, his mother told me in confidence, sent her his paycheck, and after she took out what she and Laverne needed to pay the mortgage and to live on, she returned the rest to him. My jaw dropped. I was dumbfounded, and a little annoyed to think he never shared that information with me. I blabbered every detail of my life to him, boring him silly, I'm sure. I felt a little betrayed like he was cheating on me. I wished *he* had told me instead of his mother.

His mother baked Aaron's chocolate birthday cake and spread green frosting over it. Pasek drew a large O and a Z for the top in white frosting, and I put four green candles on the cake with the letters – D for Dorothy, T for Tin Woodman, L for Lion, and S for Scarecrow under the candles. I bought a roll of yellow crepe paper, laid it on the floor and with a black marker, made it look like the yellow brick road. All the "uncles" and "aunts" showed up, and we wore green hats leftover from our St. Patrick's Day corned beef dinner party. We all sang "Somewhere Over the Rainbow" before "Happy Birthday to You." Aaron blew out his candles without any help from the rest of us, looking pleased with himself and grinning from ear to ear.

Pasek's mom and sister hovered over Aaron, pulling him up on their laps every chance they got. They even gave up an afternoon of sightseeing with Pasek to take Aaron to a playground. As it turned out, I benefitted from their mothering him the most.

Laverne was spoon-feeding Aaron ice cream with his breakfast when the phone rang. It was my agent, Ann Brebner.

"Bill, can you get away overnight for an extra call in Santa Cruz on the boardwalk? They'll pay you travel time as well as for special business. They're shooting all night in the pinball gallery."

"Absolutely!"

When I hung up, I realized I'd accepted the booking like a boor, just assuming Aaron would be taken care of by his two new admirers. I apologized profusely to them, but their eyes lit up, and Pasek's mom gushed,

"Oh, Bill, that would be so nice for us! I'll fry a chicken and make a pie. It'll be wonderful to do that for my children … and for Aaron. Don't you worry about a thing? My son was going to drag us off to some show about a beach blanket, but Laverne and I would much rather stay here with Aaron, watching your color TV. She can give him a bath and I'll read to him. I'm so happy!"

I got to the location in Santa Cruz late afternoon and signed in, then headed for the craft's table. Mona had gotten there before me and was holding court, laughing at her own jokes, telling the other extras about the crazy men she'd met in the crews of the movies she had worked in.

As the sun sank behind the hills, it grew darker, and the crew began to set up the lights and reflectors. A closed truck pulled up in front of the pinball gallery, and the driver and his helper came around to the back of the truck. They swung the doors open and adjusted a ramp from the floor of the truck to the pavement. The vehicle inside the truck started up, its motor roaring and its taillights glowing fire red. The white backup lights came on, lighting the ramp. Slowly, very slowly, the odd car was carefully backed down until it was in view. My eyes opened wider and with the other extras and crew, I crowded in to get a closer look.

It was painted glossy black, customized, every detail perfected … a Jag XKE hardtop, the rear of it sporting a hearse's body. A Jag sport-hearse! It was hard to believe. I unfolded my voucher and looked at the name of the movie. *Harold and Maude*. Names of a man and a woman. I assumed it was a love story. We were called inside to take our places, where I was directed to be hitting and jerking a pinball machine back and forth. That was my "special business."

My "group" had seen *Rosemary's Baby* and talked about it for weeks after, completely shaken up and disturbed by it, so you can imagine what I felt when I saw Ruth Gordon walking toward me. I thought I was hallucinating. Then I did something that still makes me blush. I can't explain why I did it, but just as she was inches away and about to pass me, I dropped to my knees and bowed my head to the floor! She kept walking by me and I stayed there until I felt someone tapping on my shoulder. It was the first DA (director's assistant).

"Hey, Buddy. Don't *ever* let me catch you doin' somethin' like that again!" Some embarrassments never go away.

It was still haunting me by the time I opened my front door the next morning. Pasek's mom and sister were dressing Aaron and tying his shoes as I walked in, looking tired and bleary-eyed. He ran over to me and hugged me, cooing, "Daddy! Daddy! Daddy!"

The two women grinned at me as if they could hardly wait to tell me something. Laverne leaned over and whispered something in Aaron's ear, then gave him a slight hug.

Pasek's mom was looking at me, beaming. "Good mornin'. So good to see you. Laverne and I've been waitin' for you to come home, cuz we've been teachin' Aaron how to put words together to make a sentence." She patted him on the head. "Haven't we, Little Honeybunny?"

I shook my head, and groaned, "I hope you won't give up. It seems impossible, doesn't it? I've been trying to get him to put just two words together, but he's still saying MO for motorcycle and Lil for Lily and Mam for Mammy. I don't know when he's gonna get around to telling me, 'I gotta go pee-pee' or 'I'm hungry!'"

"Sit down, Bill, Aaron's got something to tell you, don't you, Honeybunny?" She led Aaron over to me and said, "Aaron, what do you wanna tell your daddy?"

He stood in front of me with his hands on my knees, gazing at me with his blue-gray eyes, and said, as a matter of fact, "I love you."

It was the first complete sentence he ever spoke to me. Three words. Then my throat constricted and I teared up remembering how I felt the first time Aaron called me Daddy. Like the song says – everything *is* beautiful.

# Chapter 67
# The Age of Aquarius

How would you feel if you and the one you loved the most were in a car wreck, and the car began to fill with the stench of gasoline, smoke, and flames? Your loved one is trapped by just one finger clamped between two pieces of steel, and the only way you can save him (or her) is to cut off his (or her) finger before the gas tank explodes?

I have to plant that thought in your head so you can understand how I felt when I was Aaron's caretaker for weeks after his unbearably painful operation. I not only felt his pain, but my innards felt like shards of glass were blasted through them each time we had to go through the "procedure." Because he was my son, and I alone had to care for him, I was forced to be the cause of the pain he felt.

It started one morning as we were getting ready for me to drive him to Phoebe Hearst. His vocabulary had been expanding, and he was stringing words together to make sentences.

"Daddy, ca-ca potty,"

I quickly led him into the bathroom and sat him on his new "big boy" potty chair, which straddled the toilet seat. I handed him a book and said, "Call me when you're done, Aaron, and I'll come wipe your butt."

I took advantage of his being out of the living room, and turned on the TV, hoping to find the latest news of the bizarre Sharon Tate murder. It was gory and yet mesmerizing, like a highway accident you drive by as slowly as possible so you can take in all the details.

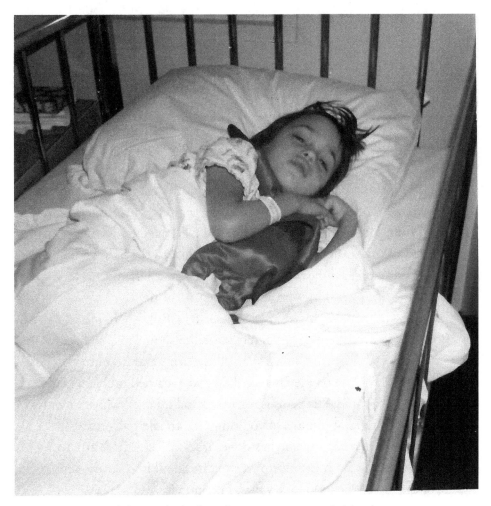

Mt. Zion Hospital the night before his operation, with Monkey

I sheepishly snapped the TV off and hurried to the bathroom when Aaron urgently called me, "Daddy! Daddy!" He was looking down toward his thighs as I took sheets of toilet paper to wipe him.

"Hey, Big Guy, I'm so proud of you! Look, no pee-pee on the walls or on the floor! You're doin' great. Just a couple of accidents now and again. You're my Big Boy." As I lifted him off his potty seat and buttoned up his pants, I could see tears welling up in his eyes. "Hey, what's the matter, Honey? Are you sad about somethin'?" He shook his head.

I sat at the kitchen table to glance through the morning paper. I turned the last page and was surprised to see Aaron standing in front of me. He stared at me with a worried look on his face, tears running down his cheeks, and clutching his privates.

"Daddy, pee-pee hurts!"

"Come here, Honey. Let's see. Did you scratch yourself?" He shook his head slowly. "Did you fall down and hurt it?" He again shook his head slowly.

He let me unbutton his pants, and as I pulled them down, he let out a cry. "Ouch, Daddy! Pee-pee hurts!" He was crying now, looking at me, pleading with me to make the pain go away.

I pulled his underpants forward so they wouldn't rub up against his penis when I lowered them. He quickly covered his genitals with his hands, not to hide them from me, but to comfort them, to make the pain go away. I pulled his hands away and turned him toward the window so the light would be better. What I saw panicked me. I pulled his underwear and pants up very slowly and carefully, then picked him up and headed for the door.

His pediatrician shook his head with disbelief. "Bill, I have to apologize to you. It never occurred to me to examine his genitals. He looks so healthy, and come to think of it, we gave him his shots in the arms and his buttocks. Guess we never looked at him completely naked. We've got a real problem here."

"What is it? My god! His penis is really red and it looks swollen, too. Did I feed him something that did it? Do you think it's an allergy?"

"No, Bill, it's nothing anyone has done. It's a defect. His urethra. See his urethra? Its opening is on the side of his penis. Should be on the top, in the middle of the top of the head, like yours. Like mine."

Like a fog evaporating into clear air and sunlight, it dawned on me why Aaron had so much trouble urinating straight into a toilet bowl. He was pissing up into the air because he was built that way, not because he didn't understand how to control it. I immediately felt guilty on two counts. I had blamed him unjustly for not aiming, for not holding his penis down, and I had stupidly thought it wasn't "proper" for me to examine his little cock and balls. It was enough that I kept them clean.

The doctor wrote a prescription for me as he dialed a number. "Sam, I'm sending a Mr. Jones and his son Aaron over to see you at your Mt. Zion office, and I'd appreciate it if you'd take a look at this. It's a displaced urethra. In my opinion, it should be operated on as soon as possible. The little tyke is in a lotta pain. I'll check if they have a room."

Mt. Zion did have a room and first, we visited to the laboratory where Aaron was punctured by a large needle in his arm, sucking his blood down into test tubes. Then we went to Aaron's room. It had one hospital bed that Aaron jumped up and down on a few times, but no TV and nothing to read. I shared his tasteless, institutional dinner, and then to pacify him, sat on the bed with him and made up stories.

A little boy named Aaron was always the good boy in my stories, and a neighbor brat called Adam was always the bad boy in their adventures. Adam caused his parents and teachers heartaches and embarrassed them. Aaron, on the other hand, was the pride of his parents and of the whole neighborhood. He always did the right thing. My stories must have been as dull as our meal with the canned string beans because he fell asleep with his head on my lap. They wheeled a cot into the room for me to sleep on, placing it next to Aaron's hospital bed, knowing I could comfort him if he woke.

I tried to sleep, but I rolled and tossed, envisioning the surgeon's scalpel slicing across Aaron's penis. The blood spurting. I sat bolt upright then put on my clothes and went outside the hospital to pace back and forth on Divisadero. The heavy traffic, speeding by with headlights blinding me and taillights flashing red, reminded me it was in the dead of night, and in just a few hours it would be dawn and he would be in surgery.

"Oh, I'm glad you're here, Mr. Jones. I think you can do this better than I, especially if he wakes up. The surgeon wants us to empty his bladder as much as possible before he goes into surgery, so if you don't mind, will you take him to the toilet?"

I was grateful she asked me to help. I needed to be needed. Aaron had been slightly drugged after dinner to help him relax and sleep, so he was limp as I carried him down the hall to the bathroom and stood behind him, helping him hold his penis down so he could hit the white porcelain target.

I took off my shoes and plopped down on the cot next to his bed after taking him to the bathroom one more time a few hours later. I had no sooner closed my eyes than I was aware of a muffled commotion in the room. I opened my eyes and was amazed to see the white room in a bright yellow glow. The sun was just coming up, and its beams spotlighted two nurses bending over Aaron. He began to whimper, not knowing where he was or who these women were.

"Daddy? Daddy?"

One of the nurses was giving him an injection, and the other was wiping his genital area with a yellow cleansing liquid that left a stain as if she had sprayed him with iodine.

"I'm right here, Honey. Daddy's here."

Aaron looked panicked, "I wanna go *home*! I wanna go *home*! No! No! I wanna go *home*!"

"Aaron, Honey, we'll go home right after ... after the doctor, the doctor, remember the nice doctor? He's gonna *fix* your pee-pee so it won't hurt anymore. He's gonna *fix* it so it ..."

The nurse came between Aaron and me pulling a gurney, which she placed next to his bed. The intern helped her slide him onto the gurney, then covered him with a heated blanket.

Aaron was sobbing, and I was choking up when he started screaming, "No! No! No! I wanta go home! No doctor! No doctor! No!"

They pushed it down the hall toward swinging doors. I hurried to catch up to them and grabbed Aaron's hand, holding it while I tried to calm him down. We reached the doors. One nurse and the interne backed into them, pulling Aaron's gurney in after them.

For a brief second, I watched them roll him through the doorway. The doors swung back into place, blocking my view, but Aaron's screams shattered the quiet hospital hallways and came through the doors loud and clear. His screams broke my heart. What he yelled out at the top of his voice would stay with me for the rest of my life.

"I want my Daddy! I want my Daddy! I want my Daddy! I want my Daddy!"

*   *   *   *   *

Two hours later, the swinging doors opened, and the surgeon walked over to me. "Mr. Jones, you've got a healthy little boy waiting for you in Recovery, but I want you to stay here for several hours after he comes out of the anesthesia. You can take him home tomorrow, but I have to warn you, you're in for, for the worst thing you can imagine, for a week or, or maybe more when you do a procedure to help him heal. I suggest you go back to the room and wait for the nurses to wheel him back to his bed. He needs rest, and I bet you do, too."

"Yeah, I feel like the walkin' dead. Tired! What's this procedure?"

"As the wound heals, and the urethra grows accustomed to its new location, there will be a great amount of bodily fluids draining, and unfortunately the drainage will dry on the opening, forming a crust, a crust that you will have to remove so your son can relieve himself."

"You're kidding!"

"The nurse will demonstrate the best way to do it before you take him home. By the way, Mr. Jones, I heard him ask for Teddy just as I left Recovery. Is that your wife? Teddy?"

Aaron came out of the anesthesia about an hour after he had been wheeled back into the room, groggy, but not in pain. He wasn't hungry even though it was late in the afternoon and he hadn't had anything to eat since the "food" they had served him the night before. I asked the nurse if he could skip the dinner, and instead, bring him a couple of dishes of ice cream. When Aaron saw the ice cream, he was suddenly ravenous.

An attendant wheeled a large, white plastic tub, nearly full of warm water, into the room, then left quickly. The nurse asked me to help her as she removed the dressing taped to the head of Aaron's penis.

"This is going to be very painful, Mr. Jones, so I want you to hold his arms, and if you can, his feet ... hold them down."

We lifted him into the tub of warm water, letting him squirm a little until he quieted down. He was crying but never took his eyes off me, as he kept saying, "I wanna go home. I wanna go home."

The nurse bent over him, and as carefully as she could, put her hands down into the warm water and loosened the tapes that held the bandages. She slowly pulled them off and dropped them into a metal container. Then she stepped aside so I could look at his tiny penis. It was red, swollen, and blood floated out of the incision. My stomach felt like a black-belt karate master had kicked me just above the groin.

"The pus hasn't formed yet, Mr. Jones, but it will, and you'll have to put Aaron in a warm tub like this to remove it. Understand? He won't be able to urinate because the pus will harden over the urethra."

"Oh, god!"

"Yes. I know how hard this will be for you, not to speak of how painful it'll be for Aaron, but it has to be done two or three times a day and at least once every morning at around three or four ... a.m."

"Jesus!"

"It'll take both you and your wife to do it for the first few days, but eventually, maybe before the week's over, she can do it by herself without you helping her."

"Christ!"

My radio alarm woke me at three a.m. a day later, announcing that a female tennis player by the name of Billie Jean King had challenged some loud-mouthed male tennis champion to a duel/match. A duel with tennis rackets. It occurred to me that no one would want to watch a match like that because obviously, the male could make hash of a poor female on the courts. It wasn't fair to her.

I filled the green boat with warm water, then carried Aaron from his crib to the bathroom. He could hardly open his eyes he was so sleepy, and I had a problem holding him up as he sat in his tub, keeping him from slipping down, going under the water. The pus and blood had formed, covering the head of his penis and urethra with a hard crust that seemed glued to it. As gently as I could, I put his penis between my two fingers and waved it back and forth, hoping the flow of warm water around it would dissolve it, loosening it from the opening. After a few minutes, it was obvious that that "procedure" wasn't going to work, and I would have to peel it away with my fingers.

Until then, Aaron had been fairly relaxed, luxuriating in his warm tub, and trusting me not to hurt him. As I plied the crust away that was clinging to the skin, he howled with pain, screaming as loud as he could, "No! No! No!"

"I'm so sorry, Sweetie. So sorry! It'll be over in just a minute! Please don't scream, Aaron! You'll wake the tenants!"

With the last tug, pulling some of the hardened pus out of the urethra, he jumped to his feet, screaming, crying, with droplets of blood falling into the water. Then a stream of urine shot out, down into the water, a mixture of yellow urine, red blood, and white lumps of pus. I grabbed hold of his tiny wet body and held it close to me, not caring if it soaked my bathrobe with the pink water. I only wanted his pain to stop, maybe because I was feeling what he was feeling.

We repeated the "procedure" every few hours for what seemed a lifetime. Each time I finally managed to get the pus off his urethra, the dammed-up urine was released in a torrent, a geyser of yellow that discolored the water in the tub. The pain I inflicted on him made him scream and sob, but he stopped crying so hard as the urine gushed out. It was a relief for both of us. I would lift him out of his tub, get down on my knees, and pat him dry with a towel, and he would lean into me, needing me to give him comfort. He hugged me, his way of thanking me for taking care of him … even though I had to hurt him to do it.

It took over a week before Aaron's penis stopped discharging the pus and the swelling went down. For most of that time, we were isolated. Occasionally one of my friends would drop in, bringing a casserole or a pint of rocky road for Aaron, but when I offered them the opportunity to peel away the crusted pus in the warm water, or even to take a look at the festering, they scurried out, their faces ashen. Even my brother Jerry, and my dearest friend, Pasek. Ashen.

Pasek phoned once or twice a day, always asking, "Is the coast clear yet? Can Aaron come out to play today, Mrs. Jones?"

Aaron was finally able to stand on his stool at the toilet in his bathroom to urinate, but his preference was to use it in front of the urinal that I had installed in mine. My bathroom walls were covered with one-inch mirror tiles from floor to ceiling, and he couldn't stop grinning at his reflection while he peed effortlessly into my urinal, never missing it once.

## Chapter 68

# OUT NOW!

Aaron's baby buggy had wheeled him through several anti–Vietnam War peace marches, but the one in April of '71 was going to be a really big one, and that called for a bigger wagon to carry him and our ice chest, crammed with beer and sandwiches. Luckily, I found the answer to my prayers in a garage sale before Christmas.

It was a child's pedal wagon that looked like a half-scale surrey with the fringe on top sung about in *Oklahoma!,* a canvas top with yellow fringe, two yellow wooden seats, and four bright red wheels. With the top down on my '62 Lincoln, it fit snugly into the back seat with Aaron and all our junk piled in it. We spread a blanket over the large flat trunk lid so four adults could ride on it to the start of the march. Four of us squeezed into the front seat, and off we went on the morning of April 24th to save the world.

It took over four hours to march from downtown to the meadow in Golden Gate Park, and we were a little disappointed at the beginning because it seemed as though there were only a few hundred of us, but as we passed each intersection crossing Geary, thousands more joined us. At the corner of Geary and Hyde, Pasek grabbed my arm and gasped, "Oh, my Gawd. Look! Jesus! There's goin' to be trouble!"

The San Francisco Police were noted for their support of the war, with decals of the American flag on their patrol cars and motorcycles to let the world and the antiwar protesters know which side they supported. Policemen were lined up, blocking Hyde Street on either side of Geary. I stopped pushing

Aaron's wagon in the middle of the intersection and thought briefly that I should turn around and go home. It wasn't long ago that I spent a night in the drunk tank after I was arrested in a peace demonstration, and repeating that was frightening, even more so with Aaron in the carriage.

Filling Hyde Street for a block on either side of our march behind the cops were hundreds of men in uniforms. Their faces were stern, many of them carrying American flags. It was a river of pressed khaki pants and jackets, rumpled jumpsuits in green and tan camouflage, and sailors in their whites and dress navy, a dozen or so police officers in their blue uniforms in front of them. Ready, I thought, to pounce on us, club us into paddy wagons, and probably take Aaron into child custody.

They began to slowly fill in the street directly behind us, just as the Tac Squad had quickly surrounded us in the City Hall rotunda a year ago. I began to feel shaky and nauseous. Pasek, my brother Jerry, and all of our friends seemed paralyzed, unable to move quickly. We stared in disbelief as the soldiers, sailors, and marines quietly lined up, crossing Geary in a single line from one sidewalk to the other, with hundreds of them filing in behind the front line.

Then the men in uniform behind us did something that made us break out into applause. They unfurled a banner stretching the width of Geary and held it in front of them. It read, *Servicemen for Peace* in blue, and then in larger red capital letters, OUT *NOW!*

We grinned with pride for these brave men who were defying all the hawks in uniform. That took guts, but we had a few signs of our own that Pasek and Michael Vincent had made. Michael and Bob Lanci held a large one that read, *FIGHTING A WAR FOR PEACE – IS LIKE FUCKING FOR CHASTITY.* And Pasek's sign said, *IF YOU WERE BEING RAPED, WOULD YOU AGREE TO A GRADUAL WITHDRAWAL?*

By the time we reached the crest of Geary, we stopped to look back at a vast sea of bobbing heads, signs, flags, and banners waving above them. Thousands had turned out again, determined to be nothing but a headcount, but a headcount that might impress the idiots in Washington, DC. We ended up in Golden Gate Park, but instead of staying to hear speeches we could give ourselves, we got on a Muni bus to go back to where I had parked the Lincoln. A parking ticket covered the peace symbol on my windshield.

## Chapter 69
# Thanks to the Wild Idol Inn Murders ...

The morning after Frank's dinner, I looked up music schools for children and found the one I thought Aaron would love. The Yamaha Corporation ran a keyboard school for kids! I picked up Aaron from daycare that very afternoon and drove directly to the Yamaha school to register him. We had a choice of one, two, or three days a week for an hour's class, and being the excited, eager daddy that I was, I signed him up for three classes a week.

After his first class when I went to pick him up, the instructor met me at the door looking exasperated. "I almost called you, Mr. Jones, to come pick Aaron up a half-hour ago, but I hated to think I had failed to control him, and, ah, failed you, too. He may have had eaten something with a lot of sugar in it before the class. I don't know, but he never settled down. He disturbed the other kids, who are here because they want to learn to play keyboards. Maybe you should talk to him tonight."

"I certainly will!" Then I gave Aaron my sternest glare. I could feel my face blush. "I'm so sorry about this, and, and I apologize to you and the whole class. It's really sorta strange, you know. He's usually happy, well-behaved, you know? This isn't like him, but I'll have a long talk with him tonight, and if you're okay with it, he'll be back on Friday."

Even though I ranted and raved at Aaron that night about how lucky he was that we could afford to enroll him in the keyboard school, and how he should appreciate this opportunity because all the poor children in China were starving for music lessons, it didn't do much good.

He cringed at my scolding and backed away from me until I stopped pacing back and forth. I looked and saw his eyes begin to tear up, his way of acknowledging that he had done something that displeased me. He didn't say he was sorry, but as I sat down, he came over and put his head on my lap. That was enough for me.

The next Friday, he hesitated but walked into the classroom and took a seat at one of the 20 keyboards that circled the room. I went into the instructor's office and read magazines until the class ended, and the instructor, holding Aaron's hand, came for me.

"I don't know what to say, Mr. Jones, but ..."

I thought, *it worked! It worked! He showed them how good he was!* But that was not the case.

"Mr. Jones, Aaron crawled under his keyboard, and sat there, very quietly, mind you, but sat under that keyboard for the whole hour. Let's face it. The Yamaha School is not for him. At least for now, that is."

Of course, being the alpha male that I am, I couldn't just accept it and keep quiet, letting time alone give Aaron a chance to evolve. I scolded him as I drove us home in Old Rust. When I parked across the street from our apartment house on the steep slope of Greenwich, he took advantage of the tilted cab and slid down to me, resting his head against my arm until I raised it to put it around his shoulder.

I bought him a simple keyboard, and he was delighted with it. He sat at it for hours, plunking the plastic keys. He eventually found the keys to "Happy Birthday" and some of them to "London Bridge Is Falling Down."

I found a very short, upright, apartment-sized piano in a consignment shop on Clement Street for $15, and with the help of Pasek, my brother Jerry, and Randles, we piled it on Old Rust and drove home, singing "The Old Gray Mare, She Ain't What She Used to Be." We rolled it into Aaron's nursery in our ground floor apartment, and Aaron went wild.

A private music teacher I hired went wild, too. He refused to sit at a piano that was that out of tune, so I hired a piano tuner. Then he said it was impossible to focus on teaching in such a cramped space, next to a child's bed. So we wheeled it into the living room each time he came over.

He had more patience with Aaron than I expected, but finally, when he threatened to jump out the window if he had to spend one more hour frustrated by Aaron's refusal to learn, we agreed to call it a day. I wasn't really concerned since our windows were just a few feet off the ground.

I assumed that Aaron was just rebelling, being a "bad boy." It annoyed me, and I'm afraid I often wore a cranky face when he climbed up on his piano stool to tinker with the keys. I swallowed my resentment and tried to shift gears. It was difficult for me not to make decisions for him, but I knew he had to find the right time, himself, to allow someone to teach him what he desperately wanted to know.

*   *   *   *   *

Another thing that concerned me was the fact that Aaron had *substitute* grandmothers, in fact, a lot of them, but my mother, Pearl, Aaron's *real* grandmother was not in his life. Oh, yes, he had Grandma Helen Pollard, Grandma Aunt Ruth, Grandma Maude, and Grandmother Witchcraft, but not Grandma Pearl.

Christmas of 1970 changed that. It was the first Christmas since Aaron came to live with me that his real grandmother, Pearl, spent with us. I wouldn't have invited her, still smarting over her snarling that I was a queer and immoral for adopting a child, but my brother asked her to come to his house on Christmas Eve for dinner, as he had every year. She finally accepted, even though she detested the thought that he had left a wife and their two small children to live in homosexual sin with Bill Randles. Now she had to eat the turkey Randles roasted, the dressing he made, and the pumpkin and mince pies he baked!

When I was a student at the College of the Pacific, I had countless conversations with God in the Morris Chapel, pleading with him to save me from being a homosexual. After two years of therapy off campus, I came to realize two things very clearly – I was born to be gay and it would take time to accept it, and secondly, my mother and father should never have been parents. The poor things were born that way, damaged souls, messed up, not capable of caring about anyone but themselves. I began to feel sorry for them, as strangers, not my parents. I knew by the time I was eighteen that I had to find love in a family I would have to create for myself. It actually freed me.

Unfortunately, my brother Jerry didn't realize the same thing until he was almost dead from AIDS in his fifties. He tried every way he could think of to make Mother love him. He bought her gifts, worked in her bar, took her on trips, and painted her house inside and out. He saw to it that his kids puckered up to kiss her "hello" and "goodbye," he phoned her once a week, and sent her cards signed, "With all my love, your loving son, Jerald."

She didn't speak to either of us for a couple of years after Jerry's ex-wife, Glenda, outed Jerry and me, loud and clear, to anyone who would listen to her in Byron. That didn't stop Jerry from sending Mother cards and pleading with her to have a family reunion with us and our children. I didn't miss her as Jerry did. My life was full without her. But Glenda's outing us as gay caused nothing but grief for my mother, a central figure in a town that was one block long. Her bar, The Wild Idol Inn, anchored the center of it, and her regulars, mostly farmers, blistered her with taunts of birthing not just one, but **two** perverts! Fags! Queers! She lived in shame daily and turned further away from us.

That is, she totally rejected us as her sons until the morning of October 5, 1970.

"Jerry, Jerry, turn on CBS! It's terrible! Terrible!" I was too upset to talk. "Just turn the damn radio on, Jerry. They're talking about Mom's bar in Byron, *right now!*"

I could hear him muttering to himself about being late for work as he walked over to the radio to turn it on. But when the newsman said, "There's been a shooting in Byron at the only bar in town with three executed, shot in the back of their heads, two men and one woman," I heard him catch his breath. Even though Mother was in her seventies, she still worked, tending her bar, happy to joke and gossip with her regulars, even after closing time, and the killings had taken place after midnight.

I dressed as fast as I could, drove Aaron to school, then drove to Hayward where Jerry and his lover, Bill Randles, lived. He phoned his principal and was able to get a sub to take his class. We ran red lights and broke speed limits, rushing to get to Byron, gripped by what we were imagining, guessing what horrible things must have happened to our mother. Even though I felt abandoned by her and unloved, she was still my mother. Jerry and I were both overwhelmed with grief and shock.

We were standing on the sidewalk outside the Wild Idol Inn in a state of shock, being questioned by one of the policemen, when a chartered bus with RENO BOUND painted in bright yellow across its side drew up across the street from the bar. The police hadn't identified the victims – two men and a woman – yet, except that all three were seniors. No matter how much we begged, they wouldn't release the names while the detectives recorded the murder scene. The block was teaming up with cops, police cars, and three ambulances. Cars with PRESS signs on their windshields and white vans with CH 4, CH 7, and CH 5 painted on their sides were parked erratically, blocking most of the street.

The door of the bus swung open and a few women, most of them elderly, began the slow descent to the pavement. Jerry grabbed my arm and yanked on it, turning my body toward the bus. Our mother stepped off the chartered bus. She hadn't taken more than a couple of steps before we both ran to her, hugged and squeezed her, showering her with kisses, and babbling, "Mom! Mom! You're alive! We thought you were shot! Murdered!'

She drew away, befuddled, and asked, "What the hell's goin' on?"

What had gone on was mad, bizarre, a story you wouldn't believe if it were in a movie. Luckii Ludwig wrote a book about it, titled *Coincidence,* published in 1977 by Vantage Press.

Luckii wrote, *In the early morning hours of October 5, 1970, in a village bar about fifty miles from San Francisco, three people – a bartender, his wife, and a solitary drinker – were murdered in cold blood. This is the story of a number of separate crimes committed on the same night, with five men meeting by coincidence at the only bar of a small town.*

Two half-drunk losers carrying guns decided to rob the bar, and after they had just shot the three victims, three more strangers came staggering into the bar with a kidnap victim, where they agreed to wait for the kidnapped man's wife to bring them $50 in ransom money! In their drunken crime wave, the five left a trail of evidence that quickly led them to be arrested, jailed, tried for murder, robbery, kidnapping, conspiracy to commit theft, burglary, and possession of stolen property. The two killers were to be executed, but the death penalty was abolished, and they are in prison for life. The kidnappers served several years in prison before they were paroled.

It took the deaths of three of Mother's friends, and Jerry's and my shock and grief thinking Mother was dead to finally make her realize how much she was missing. The two sons who seemed to care about her, and Jerry's children, her *real* grandchildren whom she had abandoned along with Jerry and me, could now be allowed in her life.

My stepsister Corky's two adopted girls and my adopted son were now grudgingly accepted as a part of her dysfunctional family, but for her, the adopted ones would never be her *real* grandchildren. As bad as that seemed, we managed to salvage our "family" through the tragic, bloody murders of three innocents and the incarceration of five misfits.

## Chapter 70
# Bill Jones's Son, for Sure!

I lay in bed at night, perplexed and anxious. I struggled to understand why Aaron had fun playing with other kids and was well-behaved with me and other adults, but when he was in a situation where he was being taught something, he constantly rebelled and not only hurt himself but hurt me, too.

I did my best to control my temper and be patient with him, but I didn't want to ask Dorothy or Mary for advice, because that would mean I was failing as a parent, and the shame I would feel admitting it would be unbearable. I talked it over with Pasek and Jerry, but none of us could understand what was going on. Aaron was lovable and loving. He never seemed to get in trouble at home or out with friends. He had a cute, vivacious way of charming you, and a mischievous sense of humor that I loved, but I knew that something was wrong, terribly wrong in the Jones household.

Aaron was only four and wouldn't be five, qualifying him to start kindergarten, until May of the next year, 1971. In desperation, I walked Aaron to the Sarah B. Cooper School, which was on the other side of Russian Hill and down the Lombard Steps, only three blocks away from our home. He would be going there next year, and I was hoping against hope that they would let me start him in kindergarten one year ahead of the five-year-old kids. The principal shook her head immediately to that idea but offered me something even better.

The city provided daycare there at Sarah B. Cooper from eight in the morning until five in the afternoon! Even after Aaron started school, he could still be taken care of until I could pick him up at five. Sometimes good things come so quickly as if you're being drenched in a rainstorm of lucky pennies. I felt like I'd just won the sweepstake. This would allow me even more time to work on the apartments than when I had been driving Aaron to Phoebe Hearst or out to the French school on Geary.

One outstanding teacher at Phoebe Hearst, Dottie Kay, took a special interest in Aaron. He liked her, too, and I dote on the many photos she took of him and gave me, one in particular that I flipped over. Aaron had climbed into a cardboard box, a refuge, just as I had done so often when I was his age, feeling abandoned and lonely. This one photo was unique. Most of the others showed him playing quietly with the other toddlers or beaming a happy smile running through the playground. This photo bonded him to me in a way I only dreamed could happen. Feeling alone and lost, Aaron and I both took refuge in our cardboard boxes. He was Bill Jones's son for sure.

## Chapter 71

# Old Rust, the Lincoln, and a Dream Die

Aaron was only four and wouldn't be five, qualifying him to start kindergarten, until May of the next year.

The preschool childcare center at the Sara B. Cooper School was a godsend. They took care of Aaron from eight until five, which gave me time to work on my apartment building and do odd jobs for friends, but because I had to pick him up by five, my availability for modeling or doing extra work was limited. Helen Pollard didn't drive, so I couldn't ask her to pick him up for me if I had to work late. My friends weren't always available even if it were an emergency. I was pretty much locked in, and it was hurting me financially not to be able to take some of the photo bookings or do "extra" work.

I began to think about finding a job. Ugh! At forty, it would be a challenge. I didn't want to teach again, even subbing, and although I was remodeling houses and apartments, I had almost no knowledge of electricity and plumbing. If I needed an electrical outlet, an extension cord, cleverly concealed in the drywall did the job. The Department of Public Works didn't know I existed. Their damn permits were an expense I couldn't afford anyway. I boldly hooked up sinks and toilets, then called a real plumber when the leaks became sources of small wading pools.

I'm a sucker for a sob story, especially if it's from a lady friend, and that's how my Isetta got totaled. I should have said, "No!" when Sandy, a friend of Lanci's, asked to borrow Old Rust, but I didn't. My mistake. She had been following a truck that was hauling a flagpole, hanging over its tailgate by about 12 feet, and Sandy absurdly thought that if you put your foot on the brake pedal, Old Rust would stop dead in its tracks. She returned my dear old pickup to me, missing its windshield and back window. I had paid $100 for it years before, and new glass was going to cost four times that, so I sadly drove it to a junkyard where I was offered $2.50 for it.

The loss of my truck was devastating, and I was forced to use my beautiful Lincoln Continental to pick up sheetrock and lumber from Goodman's. It worked as well or even better than Old Rust because with the top down it had even more space over its aircraft carrier trunk lid and back seat for me to pile stuff onto.

I loved that car. It was the car I drove Aaron in every day for the week before he came to live with me. The drives through San Francisco and Golden Gate Park were dreamlike with Aaron standing on the seat very close to me with his hand on my shoulder for support, except when we went around corners or came to a stop, I braced him from falling with my right arm firmly holding him in place. I was the protector and he was my Little Prince. The Lincoln didn't have seatbelts, but who needed them anyway?

The Lincoln had overflowed with loads of serious protesters when we drove to peace marches, and it also had carried our friends to Glide Church, picnics in Golden Gate Park, and our bikes to Marin County. Now it was both a family car and a workhorse.

Three jarring incidents happened to Aaron and me in the Lincoln that made it easier for me when I had to say goodbye to it. I laugh about it now, but at the time, I was so upset I was shaking.

It was a beautiful summer day, and I put the top down to drive over to Sausalito so Aaron could visit Enid, his "Grandmother Witchcraft." After our visit with Enid, who sketched his profile and made up a bizarre story to entertain him, we got in the car to head home.

Lily jumped on the seat beside Aaron so she could hang over the passenger side door, enraptured by the wind slapping against her nose and flapping her ears. I was distracted when the radio kept switching stations on its own. Since cars were lined up behind us, I couldn't stop working on it. I was driving and monkeying with the radio dials just as we were slowly leaving Sausalito, going over the last hill, when I realized Aaron and Lily weren't on the front seat with me!

The car behind me kept honking its horn. Honk, honk, honk! Irritated, I glanced in the rearview mirror to see the asshole honking his horn so aggressively. What I saw made me gasp. Aaron and Lily had crawled over the front *and* back seats and were sitting on top of the trunk lid, Aaron with his arm around Lily, smiling, his hair blowing in the breeze, and Lily, leaning against Aaron, with her nose high in the air, catching all the new smells in the wind.

Panicked, I slowed down to a gentle stop. If I had jammed on the brakes as I was inclined to do, they both would have been thrown forward and maybe off the rear deck onto the pavement. As the other car passed me, I looked at the driver and mouthed, "Thank you! Thank you!"

I was mortified and determined to be a more responsible parent. The next time Aaron rode with me, I made sure he sat on the bench seat and didn't stand up or move around. Little good it did. I was driving down Larkin Street the next weekend and sped up a little to get through a yellow light before it turned red. I made a left turn into the Broadway tunnel faster than I should, and Aaron slid away from me on the slick leather seat. He grabbed the door handle for support and the door swung open, dragging him with it in a wide arch. Out he went! I jammed on the brakes, stopped in the middle of the intersection, and ran to him, choking out his name, "Aaron!"

He was sitting up, looking bewildered, but not crying. He had landed on his feet and the movement made him automatically start to run. If he hadn't run, he would have fallen over and skinned his knees and hands – or worse. I felt sick to my stomach the rest of the day and too ashamed to admit it to anyone. Even to Pasek, my father confessor.

Several weeks after that, Aaron and I were driving on Highway 80 through Berkeley, when the right rear end of the car suddenly fell to the pavement, causing a screeching, grinding sound as we came to a stop on the side of the highway. Through the dust cloud, I caught a glimpse of the rear right wheel and tire wobbling past us into a clump of weeds. The loose lug nuts had all unscrewed, leaving me with a three-wheeled Lincoln Continental. A highway patrolman called AAA and I was towed to the closest garage, in a Volkswagen dealership.

They made me an offer I couldn't refuse – my Lincoln as down payment on a brand-new light blue Volkswagen microbus. I was forty-two years old, and this was the first new car I had ever bought. I was dizzy with excitement. It had three rows of seats. No more crowded friends squeezing into two seats.

And not only did it have seatbelts, but by taking out the third row of seats, I could make a wonderful open space for my trips to the garbage dumps and to Goodman's for supplies!

At a garage sale, I found a foam rubber mattress upholstered in dark blue Naugahyde that fit perfectly on the flat floor in the back. Now Aaron and Lily had a safe and comfortable place to play or nap, and I had a car with a warranty, giving me peace of mind about repair bills for the first time in my life.

As much as I loved my city by the bay, I felt an obligation to get Aaron into a more family-oriented neighborhood and school system. Sausalito was the first hometown I had felt proud to be from, but it had the same touristy vibe as San Francisco, and I wanted Aaron to have more than that. Every weekend, I'd load Aaron and Lily with their toys into the blue bus, and away we'd go across the most beautiful bridge in the world to Marin County to look at "open houses."

Ross was my first choice for raising my son. It was nearly perfect. A small town tucked away from busy highways, bars, and commercial buildings. The homes were large, shingled, unobtrusive, and reeked of gracious living, tradition, and stability. It also reeked of quiet, discreet wealth. In other words, a place I could not afford, but that didn't stop me from dreaming. I was obsessed with the idea of raising Aaron in a place like this.

It was 1971 and I didn't have a savings account, but still dreamt of buying a home in Ross that could cost as much as $125,000! But my addiction to our weekend jaunts over the bridge to look at open houses could not be cured. Sometimes I'm appalled at my own frenzied obsession to find whatever I'm looking for, whether it's a piece of furniture or a perfect campsite for a vacation, but then I find solace remembering how desperate I used to feel wanting to adopt a child. I was obsessed and I adopted a child. Someway I'd find a way to buy a house in Marin.

I thought I had found the answer to my prayers just a block away from the central part of Mill Valley. It would have been Shangri-La, a dream home I had fantasized about all my life. The *FOR SALE* sign that hung over the steps leading up to it was weatherworn and dangling by one thin wire. The building had been empty and deserted for a long time, probably because installing a new kitchen and bath would be too expensive. It was a long, two-story brick structure with a row of very large windows facing the street. It had no garage, but the interior of the second floor was as large as a small warehouse with a beamed ceiling and a walk-in fireplace. Aaron could ride his tricycle from one end to the other. It had been the town's library before they built a new one on the flats.

I found an unlocked door in the rear, and for weeks, I drove over to Mill Valley every chance I got so Aaron and Lily could run and play in it – and I could dream my dream. The town was asking $27,000 for it – cash. I calculated the cost of putting in a basic kitchen and bath and building walls with doors for bedrooms on the first floor. It needed new electrical and plumbing systems throughout. The cost of paint alone for the interior would be hundreds of dollars. I looked into loans for this project, loans I couldn't afford – the final nail in the coffin of my dream home. I grieved over losing the old library for a long time, and have kept track of its life since then. The last time it was on the market, the asking price was over five million dollars. So, besides losing my dream home, the dream of buying any home flew out the window. My dear Old Rust was gone, the Lincoln was gone, and my dream of raising Aaron in the suburbs was gone, too.

## Chapter 72

# Two Years in Kindergarten

<p>

Aaron and I were walking down the steps next to the curving cobble-stone Lombard Street on our way to preschool childcare one autumn morning, one absolutely only-in-San-Francisco kind of morning when I finally came to my senses. The morning fog had mostly dissipated, and sunlight washed over the pastel buildings that blanketed Telegraph Hill, high-lighting the phallic Coit Tower. A dim hum of city traffic lent the panoramic vision in front of us a hint of excitement, of all dreams being possible.

Aaron looked at me as if I had lost my marbles when I burst out with,

*Zip-a-dee-doo-dah, zip-a-dee-ay*

*My, oh my, what a wonderful day!*

A white cruise ship floated out at a snail's pace across the placid blue bay toward the Golden Gate, surrounded by a tiny fleet of sailboats with spinnakers billowing out in rainbow colors. A flock of gray pigeons squatted on the steps in front of us and scattered, flying out in all directions when Aaron jumped down a step toward them.

I squeezed Aaron's small hand, happy to be there, walking my son to school in a city so beautiful that everywhere you looked should be on a picture postcard. The warming sun was offset by a gentle, cool breeze, and I was aware that *this* was our home. If I believed in God, I would have thanked him (or her), my heart overflowing with gratitude for giving Aaron and me San Francisco to live in, work in, and love in – that gave me a son, a family. This

Aaron's kindergarten teacher, Marilyn Diamond, celebrating *Twelfth Night*

city breathed and you could feel its heart beat. It was alive and we were at home in it. Better than an old shingled bungalow in Ross any day!

September was the next page in my calendar, and I had written in large letters with a red felt pen – Kindergarten! Helen Pollard dressed Aaron in his navy-blue sailor suit for his first day at school. He looked damn cute in it, and Mrs. Diamond, Aaron's kindergarten teacher, swept him up in her arms after we came through the door.

"And who's this handsome sailor coming into my class? How'd I get so lucky?"

Aaron pushed away enough to look at her face for a second, then he looked at me a little wide-eyed as he tried not to grin. Obviously, he was thrilled with the attention but not sure how to handle it. Before I could introduce us, he turned, looked straight at her, and announced that he was Aaron Hunter Jones and that he was five years old, a big boy now, and old enough to go to school. Then he wiggled out of her arms and walked over to a pile of wooden blocks that had been stacked neatly. He was about to push them over when I caught him and held his hand, pulling him in close to me.

"Hello. You must be Mr. Jones, the man I've been hearing about, adopting this little boy. I'm Marilyn Diamond. Glad to meet you. Both of you. He's darling."

I began by apologizing. "I'm sorry about the blocks, Mrs. Diamond. Sometimes I don't know why he does things, things like that. I ..."

She interrupted me. "Mr. Jones, er, ah, may I call you Bill? I'd rather you call me Marilyn. He's just a boy doing a boy thing. Not to worry. He's not a hellion. Believe me, I've been teaching for years and years and I know a hellion when I see one."

The classroom was swarming with parents and children, creating a din that was hard to speak over, but Marilyn Diamond managed to get everyone's attention. She told us a little about herself and how much she loved children, probably because she and her husband didn't have one ... yet. She lived in Mill Valley and was excited every morning as she was driving over the bridge because she would be in a classroom with children she loved. In all the years she had taught, there wasn't a child she couldn't love.

With that to reassure us, she herded the parents to the door. Some of the children were holding back tears, some were bawling, and others, like Aaron, were standing in stunned silence. I should have been used to leaving Aaron in the care of teachers and daycare workers, but this was the first day of school. It was a beginning for him and it was the end of his baby years for me. I looked around at some of the mothers who were dabbing their eyes with hankies, and I felt a lump growing in my throat. I turned to leave and was in the doorway when I heard Aaron's worried voice yell out behind me, "Daddy, come early!"

I kept walking and didn't turn around, just waved my arm so he would know I heard him. Outside the cool breeze had grown to be a chilling wind, and I trudged back up the Lombard steps thinking about all the errands I had to do that day, and how the day wasn't as happy as when I was holding Aaron's hand and singing. I was also bummed out because I didn't have a hanky in my pocket.

*     *     *     *     *

Marilyn was about 10 years older than me and had never dyed her long silky hair. It lay in silver layers, pulled back into a magnificent ponytail that flowed down over her shoulders. Its softness complemented her soft pale skin. Her eyes were kind, with minuscule lines appearing around them only when she smiled, which was most of the time. Her clothes were simple and plain, but the fabrics were rich in deep colors and woven on looms from around the world. She wore large clunky necklaces she had bought from street artists in Europe and Asia.

I looked forward to the mornings when I could spend a few minutes talking with her before the first bell rang. She and her husband, who was also a teacher, traveled abroad every summer. They went to the ballet and the opera, took in all the new exhibits at the museums, and both gifted cooks, entertained artists, writers, and musicians in their home in Marin.

Aaron and I were invited to join them several times during that first year, and I still remember the smell of roast beef simmering in a dark burgundy sauce coming from the kitchen … and the laughter.

I doubt Marilyn ever invited another child from her kindergarten class to her home, but it was obvious from the first day that Aaron had charmed his way into her life. I drove Aaron over to Marin to have a "special" dinner with the Diamonds during the Christmas vacation. She was secretive, but enthusiastic when she invited us, and I was more curious than Aaron when she said only the two of us would be there.

She had roasted several ducks and made a mint sauce to enhance them, but the "special" reason for our dinner was a magical pistachio cake she had baked just for us. The frosting was green whipped cream with a live poinsettia decorating the center of it.

She put the cake in front of Aaron and removed the poinsettia with a flourish.

"Aaron, before my family sailed to America on a big, big steamship, they lived in a country far, far away from where the winters are colder than the inside of your refrigerator. When Christmas was just a few days away like it is now, all the mamas would spend the whole day in their kitchens baking pistachio cakes in ovens heated by lumps of burning coal. When the cakes were done, the mamas would put them on the windowsill to cool them."

"Why?"

"Why? Because they were too poor to have an electric icebox. That's why."

"Why?"

"Why? Because only kings and queens could afford iceboxes. That's why."

"Could a prince buy an icebox?"

"Only a *real* prince who finds a silver coin from the castle in his piece of pistachio cake, but first he has to eat all his vegetables at dinner. If he finds the coin in his dessert, then, and only then, he's the prince who can wear the gold crown and have enough to buy his mama, er, ah, his royal family, an electric icebox."

She carefully sliced the greenish cake and served the pieces on plates with poinsettias hand-painted on the rims. We all took tiny bites for fear the magical coin might chip a tooth.

Aaron stopped chewing abruptly and looked at each one of us wide-eyed, and his smile, almost hidden in green whipped cream, grew wider. He reached into his mouth and pulled out a silver coin the size of a half-dollar, licked it clean, then stared at it, as we all applauded. Marilyn's husband bounded over to their piano and started to sing a Gilbert and Sullivan song about a minstrel, and Marilyn opened a hatbox with a flourish to pull out a gold cardboard crown she had made that somehow just fit Aaron's head.

I don't know any other parent as lucky as I to have Marilyn Diamond for Aaron's first year in school. And I was astounded to hear her carefully appraise his progress during that first year, and suggest Aaron was not prepared to move into the first grade. He had severe problems we needed to sort out, and she wanted him to repeat kindergarten with her. Having been a teacher, I knew some children were held back, but I'd never heard of a child repeating kindergarten.

I was flabbergasted.

Marilyn had mentioned several things to me about Aaron during that first year in kindergarten that I found more amusing than worrisome. I should have been more concerned, considering how much trouble we had had when he disrupted the Yamaha keyboard class by refusing to participate. And I had tossed aside the snide remark one of his private tutors had made about jumping out the window if he had to give "that kid" another lesson.

So, when Marilyn told me Aaron was hiding under the table instead of joining the others learning to sing the "ABC" song or clapping hands in time to songs like "Farmer in the Dell" or "Mary Had a Little Lamb," I just smiled and shrugged my shoulders.

But at the end of the school year when she took my hand, looking straight at me, and said, "Seriously, Bill, I'm worried about him," I paid attention.

She was concerned that as smart as he was, by the end of the year he still had no concept of numbers. In fact, he couldn't add two and two. He couldn't draw a circle or a square, and his refusal to hold hands in a circle with the other boys and girls when they did group activities like dancing the hokey pokey caused a disruption in the classroom that Marilyn had to contend with over and over.

She wasn't exasperated with him, but more like a devoted mother with a handicapped child, she was fiercely determined to get him ready for the first grade. I knew she was asking me to trust her judgment and not think she was doing it just because she adored him and wanted him near her for another year. I agreed that he needed more time before he moved on.

The next three months of his school vacation zoomed by despite all the craziness around us. California Indians claimed Alcatraz Island as their territory and occupied it for nine months, inspiring Pasek and me to spend a day making tuna fish sandwiches to send them. Passenger planes, a Pan Am, a TWA, and a Swissair were skyjacked by the Popular Front for the Liberation of Palestine, a cause I approved of until they did the skyjacking, taking hostages, and causing so much terror and grief. The Supreme Court's decision that the Mitchell Brothers' pornography was "free speech," prodded the *New York Times* to call San Francisco the "Smut Capital of the United States" and the "Porn Capital of America." Pasek and I thought that was cheesy of the *Times* but giggled over it for weeks after, proud to be in a "capital" city!

South Africa was boiling over with apartheid, and Poland had riots over the price of food. A Superior Court judge in Marin County was murdered in the parking lot of Marin's Civic Center, and worst of all, causing all of us *real* grief – Janis Joplin died and the Beatles broke up!

On the positive side, besides all the modeling I did for Macy's, I nailed two national commercials – one for the new Ford Pinto and one for its competition, the new Chevy Vega. I took Aaron to the community pool in North Beach once a week and taught him to swim and dive, just like my Uncle Elzie taught me at the Sutro Baths when I was Aaron's age. Also, that summer my brother Jerry, Randles, their two kids, Dennis, Aaron, and I went to the Ice Follies at Winterland. Two very happy families, albeit with gay fathers, thrilled by the ice skaters with their flashy costumes, sat in the audience surrounded by other happy straight families. I felt proudly "normal."

As it got closer to the time for Aaron's school to open, I began to feel anxious. I couldn't bring myself to think Aaron could have "problems." He was polite and well-behaved. Everyone who met him seemed to like him. His sense of absurd humor was contagious. I found myself laughing at his antics, his dancing around the living room naked after his bath like a clown, the faces he would make at himself in the mirror, and the costumes he loved to wear. I knew he was bright when he started to sound out words in the children's books I read him when he was only three and a half. What I hadn't paid any attention to was his inability to add or subtract. Numbers just never came up. His vocabulary grew day by day, probably because my friends and I never talked "baby talk" to him, always using adult language. Looking back now, perhaps a little too adult at times.

I hoped that Marilyn was mistaken. Maybe he was just going through a phase. After all, when I transferred Aaron to the childcare at his school the year before, the director at the Phoebe Hearst Preschool wrote me saying, "He should have no difficulty making an adjustment to a new school situation. He is an amiable, mature child and handles himself well in all group activities." My thoughts, exactly – unless I forced myself to face certain behaviors.

He was a delight to be with but had trouble focusing or paying attention. It was hard for him to sustain any activity for very long. Sometimes I would try to teach him how to hang up his clothes, fold towels, or put away his toys in the boxes or drawers I had made for them, but he seemed to forget these instructions almost immediately. I chalked it up to his immaturity or sometimes to his deliberately not minding me, which, of course, led me to become Father Scolder. What I didn't see at that time were the telltale traces of something I would put a name to much later in his life.

Aaron was becoming more rambunctious during his second year in Marilyn Diamond's kindergarten class. He was quiet and attentive when she took him aside to be alone with her, but when she tried to include him in group activities, he became agitated and instead of crawling under a table or a desk as he had done before, he would run around the room or deliberately sit in another child's chair. I met with Marilyn and the principal, but the only thing they suggested that might be bringing on this kind of behavior was allergies.

Aaron's pediatrician recommended an allergist, and I made an appointment immediately. At first, we tried to eliminate certain foods like chicken and peanuts from his diet, but after a month of not finding any difference, the doctor decided to go a more painful route, injecting him with samples of different things he might be allergic to. Aaron had to lie on his stomach while the doctor injected his back with dozens of tiny pricks in rows, each one making him twitch with pain, and the doctor and I watched as some of the spots began to take on a pink, agitated shade.

## Chapter 73

# Aaron's Allergies Break His Heart

You learn something new every day. Aaron was allergic to the red dye used to make potato chips irresistible! He was allergic to 16 other food items plus the dust balls under his bunkbed, Acacia trees, pollen, hay and weeds in the fields, citrus fruits, and the worst thing possible – he was allergic to cat and dog fur! I gasped. Mammy and Lily were like a little sister and brother to Aaron, and I almost broke into tears when the allergist told me that they would have to be removed from our home. Aaron did start to cry. Uncontrollably at first, then he forced himself to stop so he could negotiate with the doctor.

"I'll be a real, real good boy if you don't take Mammy and Lily away from me." He looked at the doctor to see if he would change his mind, but the doctor just pointed at the resulting chart and shook his head. Aaron picked up the pace. "I'll keep my room clean and I'll pick up my toys. I won't play with my food anymore. I promise! And I'll go to bed when my daddy tells me to. I won't let my eyes get red and watery. You'll see! I'll mind my daddy better!" His voice was urgent and I could see tears welling up in his eyes again.

I took his hands in mine and tried my best to console him, "No matter how bad we feel about Mammy and Lily living somewhere else, they couldn't stand it if they knew they were hurting you. They'd be very, very sad, Aaron. They'd rather die than hurt you."

He pressed his lips tight and looked at me with so much anger in his eyes.

"Mammy and Lily never hurt me!" I had never seen him so angry, and I was a little frightened of my little boy. He pulled away from me and ran to the door of the doctor's office. I went after him, but he stopped at the door and turned around. Looking straight at the doctor, he almost screamed, "You, you, you bad man! You, you go to H-E - double chopsticks!"

I apologized to the doctor and tried to take Aaron's hand so we could walk back to the car together, but he pulled his hand out of mine and stalked away from me. He was mad at the world, but I hoped he would accept it eventually.

That night after Aaron's bath, when we four were cuddled on the couch reading a book together, Aaron put his arms around Lily's neck and tried to hug Mammy at the same time. The hug became a tightening squeeze until Mammy succeeded in escaping from his grasp, and as soon as she jumped off the couch, she hid under the coffee table where she licked her rumpled fur until it lay flat again. Lily was getting restless, too, as Aaron's hug around her neck got tighter. It had been an emotional day for both of us and Aaron was exhausted, ready to be tucked under the covers, but he demanded that I let both Mammy and Lily sleep at the bottom of his bed, something we had never done before. They usually curled up together under his bed, more than content that way, but considering the pickle we were in, it was a demand I couldn't refuse.

I get this eerie feeling every once in a while that someone "on the other side" is watching over me. Otherwise, how did I, as a single (closeted gay) man ever manage to adopt Aaron? Who brought Evander Smith into my life when I needed his help so desperately? How did I go from being the poorest gay guy in San Francisco to being the landlord of the Wildflower Apartments on Russian Hill? Who sent Pasek up the steps of my houseboat that Easter? How did I ever finish college with a degree and wind up with friends so loyal and loving? It had to be "one of them."

Sure enough, it happened again. The next morning as we were eating breakfast, someone knocked on the front door so quietly I almost missed hearing it.

"Oh, hi, Mrs. Metcalfe. Everything okay in your apartment? What can I do for ya?"

"Well, you know how we old ladies are. Lily usually scratches on my door every morning and we spend the day together, and I was afraid she might be ill or something cuz I haven't seen or heard from her for two days now."

I could see by the worried look on her face that she was not just concerned, but desperate to know if Lily was well. My sweetest and oldest tenant was anxious to see Lily.

"Come on in! I have something to tell you about Lily and Aaron and I just had an idea that might solve all our problems. How 'bout a cup a coffee?"

I wish now I had taken a photo of Mrs. Metcalfe's broadening smile when I asked her if she would take Lily in as her roommate, and let Aaron and me visit her for just a few minutes every day. Her smile pushed the flesh of her pale cheeks up and caused her eyes to become like crescent upside-down quarter moons

I promised to pay for Lily's food, vet bills, and toys she bought for her. It was important that Mrs. Metcalfe didn't spend a dime to care for Lily because I knew she was barely living on her Social Security. She had no idea how much she was doing for Aaron and for me, and I was forever grateful. My cup did runneth over that wonderful morning.

Aaron went to school that morning, smiling a smile as big as Mrs. Metcalfe's. He knew that as soon as he opened the lobby door that afternoon, he could run up one flight of stairs and knock on number one's door, and his dog, Lily, would answer it, wagging her tail furiously.

Pasek loved to play with Mammy, so, without my asking, he suggested that Mammy come live with him. That way Aaron could check in on Mammy whenever we ate dinner at Pasek's at least once a week. He loved Lily, too, but he could leave Mammy alone in his apartment for long periods of time as long as she had food, water, and a cat box to call her own. He had a nine to five and knew it would be a hardship for both Lily and him if he took her, too.

The sad part was that Lily and Mammy would be separated for the first time in their lives, but at the homes, they were going to they would receive more time and attention than when they lived with Aaron and me. Now, when Aaron was in school, I could take Lily out to the dumps with me or take her for a walk. She just couldn't visit us in our apartment, now cleaned within an inch of its life, and off-limits for dog and cat fur.

I tried my best to keep our apartment an allergy-free zone, but I had absolutely no control over what happened when he was at school or playing at a friend's house. I'm sure during lunchtime he stuffed potato chips into his mouth and ate an orange in exchange for a carrot stick.

Despite all my efforts to keep Aaron allergy-free and vaccinations to do the same, Aaron's behavior in the classroom didn't improve. It was the school policy to give every child in the San Francisco school system a hearing test, and when Aaron took him, we were all surprised to find out he had mild impairment in his right ear and a 75% hearing loss in the left ear. The doctor thought it might have happened before he was born.

That cleared up one problem I had with Aaron. When we were at home, I had to tell him several times to wash for dinner or to comb his hair. I had dismissed it as his being too engrossed in whatever he was doing, but when he was in the car with me, sitting to my right, he seemed to deliberately ignore me when I spoke to him, and it became an ongoing reason for scolding. It never occurred to me that he hadn't heard a word I had said!

He wasn't the rude, dismissive little boy I thought he was. He was my son, and when I realized how wrong I was, all I could do was take him in my arms and tell him that I loved him.

After I worked on her first campaign for mayor, Dianne Feinstein's husband, Bert, gave this puppy to Aaron because it was non-allergenic; Aaron named him "Bertie."

## Chapter 74

# Aaron's *Wild Duck*

The summer between Kindergarten 1 and Kindergarten 11 was jam-packed with adventure and fun, a relief from the calls I got from his school about Aaron's "problem." Just knowing that he had allergies and his birth mother was a dope addict could be the cause of his "problem" helped me talk with Marilyn Diamond and the principal very openly without feeling guilty or angry.

That summer was fun for both of us. We went to the California State Fair in Sacramento with my dear cousin, Ramona – another Ramona in my life – where Aaron got to pet a goat, hold a chicken, and put his tiny hands around the teats of a cow. We entered Aaron's "school bus," the '57 Isetta, in a Golden Gate Park car show, and he won a ribbon. Then I found a used speedboat in Napa that I could barely afford. I attached a tow bar to the bumper of my Volkswagen bus, paid for the 17-footer in cash (and coin), and trailered it back to San Francisco, where I found a berth for it in the Marina Yacht Harbor across from the new Safeway store.

Enid Foster, my "Grandmother Witchcraft," named it the *Wild Duck* because she said she had always thought of me as being a wild bird, constantly looking for a place to build a nest. I found that it was safest to take the *Wild Duck* out on the bay in the morning when the olive-green water was inviting and undulated in quiet waves. By early afternoon, the winds agitated the rolling waves until they fell, then rose high and spit white foam. It was an exhilarating experience swooping up to the tip-top of a wave in the *Wild Duck*, then flopping down to the bottom of the next wave with a heavy thud, like riding a roller coaster without paying the admission, but it was too dangerous for me to take a chance with such precious cargo.

I usually held Aaron on my lap so he could steer the boat. He loved the wind on his face, his light hair blowing back on me. On weekends, I took Pasek and other friends over to Sam's in Tiburon for breakfast, or to Angel Island for a picnic. Each time we piled in, put on our lifejackets, and shoved off, my heart started racing and I felt the world was mine. Captain Jones.

I loved the smell of the saltwater spraying over us, the feel of the warm morning sun on my face, the bucking of the wild beast beneath me, separating us from the icy, deadly water. The beast, my *Wild Duck*, sped in swoops and sharp curves, bouncing from wave to wave like a stone thrown to skip over the water. Then when it was time to go back to the docks, it slipped smoothly, quietly into her waiting berth. Berthing her and tying her lines was like the enzyme rush after orgasm for me. I'm a Cancer, a water sign. I am a water baby.

We finished that golden summer in August of 1971 by going to the Renaissance Faire in Marin County where Aaron, in his plastic breast shield and helmet, fought another knight about his age in a sword fight. The swords were long silver balloons, and the first one to pop would lose the battle. I was taken back by Aaron's aggressiveness in the sword fight and was relieved when it finally ended. During the duel, his face took on a ferocious scowl, and even though I had seen him look like that before when he was playing "Army" or "Monster Battle," this time it didn't look as if he were just play-acting.

Aaron's balloon sword was the first to pop, and he graciously bowed to his opponent as he had been instructed to do, but as we left the arena, he declared, "Daddy, next year I'm gonna bring a safety pin!"

## Chapter 75

# Life Isn't a Goddamn Fairy Tale

I worked hard to keep the Wildflower Apartments rentable. I also worked things out so I could have a nanny for Aaron, which came in handy when my balls turned blue from inaction, and I could go out at night to be a slut for an hour or two at a bar, or if it came down to the finish line, at a bathhouse for a clean and safe quickie.

But something new came creeping into our days, a mysterious, ghostly problem within my son that I couldn't see or touch or understand. By the time he walked into his first-grade classroom, it was evident my dream of having a normal life with a son who was normal was teetering on a cliff, and if I wanted to save that dream, drastic steps would have to be taken, but I was baffled, not knowing what those steps would have to be.

I kept in touch with Mary Davidson and Dorothy Murphy at the adoption agency, mostly when Aaron and I would show up every Valentine's Day with a gigantic heart-shaped candy box to officially celebrate our "Adoption Day," and unofficially to rub the staff's noses in the fact that Aaron was growing up to be not only polite and charming but also very happy, outgoing, and healthy, an adopted son of a *single* man, a *gay* single man.

I became very involved with the Carriage Trade, an organization supporting adoption, and eventually became the president, much to Mary's and Dorothy's delight. But I hesitated to talk to either one of them about the problems the school was having with Aaron because it would be like, you know, admitting I was a failure as a parent.

Unfortunately, Mary, whom I felt closest to, left San Francisco to move back East where she was offered a job as the director of a large city's adoption agency. I missed our "what's up?" phone calls to each other. I missed her diplomatic "suggestions" about parenting, love affairs, and cooking tips. She was the one person in the agency I would feel comfortable with as I poured my soul out. But I needed the insight only Dorothy could give me now, so I made an appointment to see her.

She seemed to want to talk to me as much as I wanted to talk to her. After I described, the best way I could, the problems that had come up about Aaron, she closed her office door and locked it. She didn't go back to her desk but instead drew up a chair to sit closer to me.

"Bill, I'm so glad you came in to see me. I was about to call you. You know, in 1966 when Aaron was born, we made 225 placements, and after your adoption was finalized in 1969, and the word got out about single-parent adoptions, we made 379 placements, almost twice as many. All the single-parent adoptions were with children over two years of age ... just like Aaron. And we have been seeing problems with these children. Almost all of them!"

I drew in a deep breath of air, "Oh, my god! What's goin' on? You saying single parents are causing it?"

"You know, Bill, I really don't believe that, even though some of my staff still do. I've been reading reports from clinical labs, and doctors are beginning to think alcohol and drugs can affect fetuses. All kinds of problems after they're born. Maybe even smoking a cigarette can up the ante. Can you imagine?"

"Well, Dorothy, I guess you knew that Mary asked me about that during one of our interviews."

"Asked you about what?"

"Asked me if it bothered me that Aaron's birth mother was a dope addict. I thought she meant "morally," you know ... was I judgmental about her taking dope? I told her, 'not a bit,' and that was all that was ever said about it."

Dorothy leaned back in her chair and after a while asked me, "Bill, have you heard the term 'crack baby'?"

I nodded.

"Aaron was taken away from her as soon as he was born. You know, her arms were covered with needle marks, and poor little Aaron suffered so, put

Three bachelor daddies and their sons from SF, Mill Valley, and San Jose

in intensive care and went through withdrawal from *her* heroin. Poor little guy! Poor little guy!"

I offered what I knew. "All I know is that she was nineteen and very pretty."

"Bill, I can't let you see her name or address, but I've got Aaron's file here, and I'll read you some of it, okay? The birth mother was nineteen and the birth father was twenty-nine when Aaron was born. She was 5'5", weighed 115 lbs. with light brown hair, dyed blonde, and had green eyes. She graduated from high school. Her ancestry was Italian, German, and Dutch.

"She had three siblings, but her mother, who had married five times, had given up two of her children to be adopted. Aaron's birth mother married a sailor when she was fourteen, but her husband was shipped out four days later, never to be heard of again. She lived on the streets until she moved back in with her mother and stepfather at the age of sixteen. She was addicted to barbiturates, dioxane, Nembutal, and heroin."

I was trying to take notes as Dorothy flipped through the papers in the file, but I was so confounded by all this new information that I could barely write legibly.

"It says here that she was involved in a Juvenile Court battle just before Aaron's birth. I can just imagine! She did come back to our agency with a formal request to get him back in 1967, one year before he went to live with you. She had no job. No way to support the two of them, and I spotted needle marks on her arm. I remember that very well. Then about the time Aaron was released by the courts to be adopted in 1968, she came back again with a 'mannish female companion' to try to get him back, but her second request was also rejected by the court."

"Aaron's birth father was 5'10", medium build, dark olive skin, brown hair, and eyes. He'd only gone through the eighth grade. His ancestry was Spanish and French. He'd been adopted when he was a teenager after living in one foster home after another."

Dorothy closed the file and dropped it in a filing cabinet drawer, ending our time together, but she took my arm to stop me from leaving.

"Bill, before you came and saw Aaron and decided to adopt him, Mary and I were convinced Aaron would eventually be institutionalized. We were overwhelmed at the time with hundreds of children we couldn't find lasting homes for. Even foster homes were scarce. It was a nightmare – believe me. We could see that Aaron wasn't developing at a normal rate, and we guessed something like this could happen. He's going to be all right and you're going to be all right, too. Hang in there, Bill. I'm so glad you came in to see me."

My meeting with Dorothy didn't exactly provide a happily-forever-after ending, but I understood a little more now, and I could see Aaron and me living "hopefully" forever-after. And that's better than any kick-in-the-ass fairy tale!

## Chapter 76

# The Next Twenty-Five Years

**1974**

Aaron's medical and therapy bills were beginning to pile up, and I knew I'd have to find a way to increase my income. I soon learned how hard it is for a person over forty to qualify for a job.

"You're overqualified, and you'll get bored."

"You've had little or no experience in this field."

"Are you willing to leave town?"

"Minimum wage. That's it."

I didn't want to teach again, and the only jobs at advertising agencies were starting in the mailroom. Bob Lanci talked Enrico into letting me wait on tables at Enrico's, and I liked dealing with the customers, but working in the kitchen was repulsive, so the job lasted only two days. Ann Brebner tried to talk me into taking classes to become a professional makeup artist for the movies, but it seemed too sissified for me.

I believed I was unemployable, and I would have to go on working for and by myself, so I searched the want ads in the *Chronicle* under businesses for sale. I hoped that the $500 in cash I had could be a down payment. Maybe for a sidewalk hot dog stand! At least I could close it in time to pick up Aaron after daycare.

What I did find was a tiny massage parlor that had a former barbershop in the front and a sauna, showers, and lockers in the rear. I tortured the poor, old, arthritic, alcoholic masseur with negotiations until he reluctantly reduced his price from $10,000 to $2,000 and … with a $500 down payment, rent at $175 a month.

With the help of some friends, we cleaned and painted the place, using my Sears charge card for the paint and carpet. I opened THE SUTRO BATH HOUSE on Valencia Street in May of 1974. It was the smallest, least profitable gay bath house in San Francisco, and after one year, I was $17,000 in debt!

Before adopting Aaron, hoping I could find a way to impregnate a woman to have my child, I talked my way into being the only gay man at the Sexual Freedom League parties in Berkeley. I got as far as hugging a naked woman, but my body said, "No!" to anything more intimate. What I did realize was that many straight couples were devoted to being "swingers," and other than a few private parties and nudist camps, had no place to go once or twice a week.

Cornered by the threat of bankruptcy, I closed the bathhouse to gay men on Thursday nights and tried something new … straight couples only. I created a "private club membership" in case the police came down on me, which, of course one sergeant from the Mission Street Station tried to do by storming through, asking the women if they were "ladies of the evening." The women and their husbands dressed and left as soon as they could. Going to Dianne Feinstein at City Hall and asking for her help did NOT help.

"Oh, yeah. I know the sergeant very well, but I'm not going to ask him to lay off trying to clean up the Mission."

"But Dianne, you know me. You know I'd never run a whorehouse! And the Sutro isn't one. Basically a gay bathhouse. Just naked people having fun, private fun."

Then Dianne said something that ended our friendship.

"Bill, go into another business!" She looked angry. "Businesses like yours are bringing *hordes* of gay men into this city every weekend!"

What ended the police harassing me was my speaking directly to the chief at the Mission station.

"Why you here, Mr. Jones? You own the Sutro Bath House, right? Want to tell me what's happening? Why one of my cops is knocking on your door every night?"

"The same thing that's happening in gay bathhouses all over town, including the Liberty Baths just down the street."

"I understand women go to yours. So …?"

"Just to be upfront with you, Chief, there's fucking and sucking, masturbating, oral sex, anal sex ... group sex ..."

He heard enough and called the sergeant into the office.

"Sergeant, you are never to set foot in any bathhouse unless the management asks you for help. Understood? Mr. Jones, here's my card. I've written my home phone number on the back so you can call me any time, night or day if any of my cops bother you again."

The business took off and I kept adding couples' nights, then added one night for women only. Gay men were finally allowed in with the couples and they brought women friends with them who were open to "free love." My bills were being paid on time! Armistead Maupin wrote a chapter about the Sutro in his San Francisco Column, "Tales of the City," and its interior was reproduced for the television series.

## 1977

One of the largest gay bathhouses in the city, at Folsom near 6<sup>th</sup> Street, went belly up. Two buildings, each two stories tall with a courtyard in between them, had been a complex of gay shops and a magnificent gay restaurant for a number of years under absentee management – the owners living in LA. Absentee management does not work, and it closed, only to be reconstructed as a bathhouse with a 20-person hot tub in the open courtyard. Bad management reduced it to a dark, empty place where horny drunks could stagger in for a dollar after the bars closed.

My premise on Valencia was overcrowded, and I leaped to buy the lease with an option to buy 1015 Folsom. I refinanced the Wildflower Apartments to buy the lease and one of our regulars, a contractor, got me a reasonable loan to remodel it, constructing a roof over the courtyard with a retractable Rollamatic skylight that was 60 feet long. He built a platform under it with a revolving stage, good for sunbathing during the day with the skylight open and closing to watch male and female strippers at night after our cabaret shows.

## 1978

Aaron's security at the S.B. Cooper School with his Special Ed class and childcare came to an abrupt end when he had to leave and register at the Marina

Middle School for the 6th grade. He couldn't cope with going from one class-room to another for different subjects, so he found a place to hide and didn't go to any of them. Mirabai Baker, a wonderful child psychologist, helped me look for residential schools for him. Over the next three years, he went to a new one each year.

Mayor George Mosconi and Supervisor Harvey Milk were assassinated.

## 1979

The Sutro Bath House became a fun news item in the *Chronicle*, and we were never the headline of bad news, partially because I developed my PR skills. I was struggling to pay 19 salaries, make repairs, buy supplies, meet the rent and utilities deadline, and take home enough money for Aaron's doctors' bills and food for our table.

I had to use my wits to get free publicity since I didn't have enough money left over for newspaper ads, and there were four gay newspapers to run ads in. I thought just for a lark, and hoping a few people might see it and show it to their friends, I would get the *San Francisco Chronicle* to place an ad in their Want Ad section under "Employment."

**Wanted to hire – Nude string quartet to play at the Sutro Bath House. No fatties or weirdos need apply.**

The *Chronicle* turned me down flat. "Not our cup of tea," I was rudely told. So, I put an ad in the *Bay Guardian*, a hippie offshoot street paper. It read under "JOBS" …

**NUDE STRING QUARTET – To play Wednesday nights. Apply at Sutro Bath House. 1015 Folsom St. No fatties, weirdos, or dopers. Must be well strung.**

To my delight, it was chosen as the AD OF THE WEEK, blown up dou-ble-size and highlighted in a large rectangle in the middle of the Want Ad section. I immediately mailed off copies to 10 friends, asking them to mail it to Herb Caen, the reigning king of gossip columns at the largest, most revered newspaper in Northern California. So, the paper that had refused my ad ran this item in Herb Caen's March 9, 1979 column … titled …

THESE FOOLISH THINGS. **The Sutro Bath House on Folsom has hired a nude string quartet, the result of an ad in the *Bay Guardian* which stipulated, "no fatties, weirdos, or dopers." The foursome, three men and**

**a woman, opens April 4ᵗʰ as "The Well-Strung Quartet," although the girl, a violinist, confesses, "I'm really more high-strung." Names are off the record because they have jobs in straight orchestras.**

And, yes, a young, talented string quartet played at the Sutro Bath House!

## 1981

AIDS. Unknown. Undetected. One businessman I worked with ended up in the hospital with very bad flu-like symptoms, and I had to wear a hospital mask to visit him. He seemed to recover and went home, but he quit his job and I never saw him again.

Aaron was accepted at Sunny Hills, a residential treatment center and school in San Anselmo.

## 1984

My two years' struggle to keep the bathhouses open, declaring it wasn't *where* you did it, it was *how* you did it, was over when Feinstein closed all the bathhouses. I exercised my option and sold the building in a double escrow, giving me more than enough to pay all my bills and give bonus paychecks to my 19 employees. I was drained fighting the politics of AIDS, especially Feinstein, who stupidly decided it wasn't HOW you did it, it was WHERE you did it.

At the same time, Ray Williams found a buyer eager to buy the Wildflower and I moved back to Sausalito, my "hometown," and bought the largest, most expensive "floating home" (houseboat) ever built. It was at the end of the Issaquah Dock, facing the city, three stories high and 4,000 sq. feet of living space. For the first time in my life, I had money, lots of it. Enough to pay cash for a 40-foot yacht I named after my mother, *The Pearl of Sausalito*, a motorboat, and a 1976 Cadillac convertible. Unfortunately, I turned the rest of my money over to my accountant to invest for me. Invest, he did. He invested in buying himself a horse ranch, an airplane, and computerizing his business. It took six years to recover some of it when he needed to refinance his ranch, and I was one of the lienholders.

Aaron turned eighteen. Sunny Hills made an exception of him and offered an extra year there in their care, but he left, much to my chagrin, and deeply disappointed staff members who were sure he was evolving and almost ready

*Phil Donahue Show* (1985); Aaron is in front, on the left

to live a fruitful life. He was placed in a group home but soon left it to live with members of a rock and roll band.

In order to continue paying my bills, I advertised in gay magazines as a bed and breakfast on my houseboat. I loved playing host to all kinds of gay men, then lesbian friends of the men, then straight couples who enjoyed gay people.

## 1985

In 1976, I joined a support group of gay fathers and from 1985 to 1986 I was their president. All had been married or lived with the women who bore their children. I was the only single father in the group and had heard every sad story the men told, but I also empathized with their wives, knowing how the women they left behind must grieve. I invited Amity Buxton and two of her

Pasek, one month before he died (1986), with Don Miller, his Sausalito houseboat roommate (1963)

friends to come to our support meeting and tell about their pain in finding out their husbands were gay and how they worked through it, understanding and forgiving them. Amity became our "hotline" for the wives to call for advice and consolation. She went on to write a book about spouses who were deserted by their gay husbands or lesbian wives titled, *The Other Side of the Closet*.

Aaron and I were on the *Phil Donohue Show* defending gay parents in New York City.

## 1986

My brother and his lover, Bill Randles, were diagnosed with AIDS and my invaluable, irreplaceable "best friend" – Polly Pasek – died.

The nurse who phoned me was on the verge of tears, and in hesitant whispers told me how much the staff at the clinic adored him and his optimism

—and his sense of humor. More than any other patient, Pasek was sure he would be cured, but on the night he died, he asked the nurse to put the "beautiful" color-changing bubble light on his nightstand so he could watch it as he fell asleep. He knew.

I left my houseboat after the nurse hung up and went down the gangplank to my runabout. I didn't want to deal with phone calls or knocks on my door, so I shoved off and headed toward Sausalito through the fog over the still waters. About a mile from shore, I dropped anchor and lay on the bottom of the boat so I could look up into the mist and concentrate on memories of the best friend I ever had.

I remembered driving Pasek to the airport when he left his job as an event designer in San Francisco to take a better one as a display man at the Chicago Art Museum. All the way to the airport, we were kidding each other and laughing, telling each other what a relief it would be living so far apart and at last having a better chance to find husbands who wouldn't be put off by *our* relationship. To our own surprise, and shocking all the departing passengers in the terminal, we embraced each other, our wet cheeks touching, and for the only time since we met, we kissed each other on the lips and he said, very casually, "See ya."

We flew back and forth to see each other until he took on another, a more prestigious job in Memphis as the head of a new art museum being built on the banks of the Mississippi. He was caught up in the razzle-dazzle of Memphis high society for a year and I was busy trying to succeed as the owner of a very small gay bathhouse.

Pasek's mother turned deathly ill, and he had to leave his wonderful job in Memphis to care for her and his slightly retarded sister in St. Louis. The next thing I knew, he called to say that he had been diagnosed with Lou Gehrig's disease and was told he might die. He apologized for not having the current fashionable AIDS virus, "But one can't be choosy, can one?"

I called a Group meeting, and we raised enough money to fly Pasek back to us for a two-week visit. Each of us hosted and entertained him for a couple of days, holding a series of dinners, day trips, museum goings, cocktail parties, and theater outings. His base was with me on my houseboat where I could tend to his more basic needs ... showers, shaving, dressing, one time providing privacy with a porno tape and lotion, and, yes, eventually wiping his butt.

In the middle of the night toward the end of his stay, I woke to his calling my name. I threw back the covers and rushed to the guest room to see what he wanted. He looked at me in a plaintive way and said apologetically, "Billy, my right foot is crossed over the left one, and I can't move it off. Hate to bother you."

"Pasek, listen to me. I don't want you to go back to St. Louis. Who's gonna take care of *you there? Stay here with me, will ya?*"

He shook his head.

"Pasek, I'll hire a real hunk to be your nanny ... so I don't worry about you if I have to go shopping ... or go see someone ... or ..."

"Bill, I shoulda told you sooner, but I've reserved a room at a clinic in upper New York state where they almost guarantee they can cure Lou Gehrig's disease ... really."

I drove him to the airport and couldn't have cared less whom we shocked. I kissed him goodbye on the lips again.

I was lying on the bottom of my boat, remembering that vivid, sweet sadness as I was saying goodbye for the last time to Pasek, my dearest friend, when the mist rose, dissipated, and I was blinded by the midday sun.

I wrote his obituary and ran it in the Bay Area Reporter, the leading gay newspaper.

## Bill Pasek
### 1931 – 1986

*Bill was diagnosed with ALS this last February in St. Louis, where he had returned to care for his invalid and dying mother. He was a gifted industrial designer in San Francisco and St. Louis as well as a designer at the Field Museum in Chicago.*

*He got us out of the bars and onto skating rinks, steam train excursions, kite flying picnics, house trailer trips, a baby shower, and lethal competitions at charade parties.*

*Bill was the one phone call you could make from the sixth floor at the Hall of Justice, the one who held you when your lovers left. His money, time, energy, and love were always at his friends' disposal, as was his self-effacing, never bitchy, Polish wit that made all of us love him so much. We all laughed with Bill and at Bill. He laughed the hardest.*

*In September, 20 of us brought him back to San Francisco for a 16-day vacation. He asked that we all meet him on crutches, walkers, and wheelchairs so he wouldn't feel so self-conscious!*

*It was two weeks of intense caring and fun and then he returned to the East to die. A big part of each one of us went with him and died, too. Bill is planning a big reunion potluck dinner for the Group right now. Until then, we will practice our charades techniques and keep him alive by remembering him and laughing.*

*There will be a West Coast Memorial aboard* The Pearl of Sausalito *at 11 a.m., Sun., Nov. 16, Please phone 332-2270 for details.*

## 1992

I was low on cash again, so at seventy-four, I decided to go back to work, the only work I knew – real estate. I sold the houseboat for twice the amount I paid for it and bought a 24-unit apartment house at 325 Larkin Street, right in the middle of Civic Center. City Hall and the auditorium were being retrofitted for earthquakes, a new public library had been built, and a new Asian Art Museum opened, converted from the old library. I installed a 50-foot flagpole on the balcony of the top floor and ran a large Rainbow flag up for everyone in Civic Center to see. Gold letters over the entrance proudly stated its name, RAINBOW FLAG APARTMENTS.

## 1993

My mother and brother both died in agony, mother with festering bedsores and Jerry of AIDS and a broken heart over his son's early death. And to this day, I live with the ghosts of so many I loved.

I can feel them pushing against me. I can smell them, hear them. Bill Randles died in Davies Hospital on Castro in the AIDS ward. Jerry, our mother, Pearl, Randles's mother, and I stood around his hospital bed while I massaged his feet, and he seemed grateful. We left him to go to dinner and when we came back, he had died. Jerry recoiled, his back against the wall, went a little crazy, and started to scream, "Close his eyes! Close his eyes! Close his eyes!"

My brother Jerry suffered from his AIDS illness more than anyone I knew. He was so bloated, he looked like he was going to give birth to triplets, and when he got news his son, Mark, had died in his sleep at age thirty, he broke out in shingles, which made him writhe in pain.

Jerry and Randles had bought grave sites next to each other in Lodi. Randles was buried first, then Jerry buried his son Mark in *his* grave next to Randles, with instructions to me that Jerry should be cremated, his son's grave opened, and Jerry's ashes placed on top of Mark's casket. I did what he asked. At that final burial, Aaron read the lyrics to "If Ever I Would Leave You" from the musical *Camelot*, Randles and Jerry's favorite song.

Michael Vincent died of cancer. Judd Wirz died of AIDS. I've lost track of Gary Fusfield and Bob Lanci, Michael's lover. My friends Al Husar, Roger Stephens, and Cora Lee aka TWAT, all died of Alzheimer's. During the AIDS crisis, I lost over 50 friends and at least 50 more men I knew socially or sexually. All these deaths of beloved friends and family, as painful as they are for me to remember, cannot compare to the grief I still bear that struck me like a blow to my head, my body, my soul … in 1996.

## Chapter 77
# The End of the Beginning

Being a gay man (or gay woman) in the '60s and '70s wasn't a piece of cake. We lived in fear of the law, of our co-workers and bosses, of our landlords, of homophobic strangers on the street. We especially lived in fear that our families and dearest straight friends would be repulsed and abandon us if they found out whom we were attracted to, whom we loved, whom we had sex with.

On the other hand, we were blessed. Gay bars and baths did standing-room-only business and were brazenly advertised in openly gay papers like the *Sentinel*, the *Berkeley Barb*, *The Slant*, and the *Bay Area Reporter*. Clubs like S.I.R. (Society for Individual Rights) and Mattachine Society demanded respect from the politicians and the police. It was an age of defiance, of finding the joy of being openly gay.

On a more personal level, a common denominator (sex) allowed the lowliest of us to mingle with the loftiest. And we stumbled into encounters only *that* bond can bring. Not that I had sex with them, but being gay put me in contact with Rock Hudson, Danny Kaye, Vincent Price, and Raymond Burr, to name-drop a few movie stars. If I had married Verla and stayed in Brentwood to teach school, I would never have known Harvey Milk, Armistead Maupin, Cleve Jones, or the A-list interior designers of San Francisco like Michael Vincent, Michael Taylor, John Dickinson, or even that snake in the grass, Val Arnold.

I would never have met my dearest friend, Bill Pasek, or been as close to my brother, Jerry.

We went to parties, cocktail parties where your knee might press up against Dave Kopay's knee, and dinner parties where you would leave your job selling lamps at the Emporium to that evening finding yourself at Terrence O'Flaherty's dining room table seated next to Bill Ball, the director of A.C.T. Facing you across the forest of cut-glass goblets sat Agnes Moorehead, who glared contemptuously at Bill Ball's black, broad-rimed hat until he finally removed it.

Luckily, at one of these parties, I met two very handsome, bright men, lovers for 15 years, and both psychologists. Paul and Warner invited me to a dinner party, and at that party I told them about Aaron's strange behavior at school, hoping I might be given some small bit of advice, especially since Warner specialized in child psychology.

"Tell you what, Bill. Bring him over to my office next week, and we'll have a little chat. Okay? No charge on the first one, Guy, so not to worry."

I should have worried. Our little chat turned into four sessions of tests, including neurological ones with wires attached all over Aaron's head, which left Aaron giggling, thinking the whole thing was a big joke. After all, the wires didn't go into his head, so there was no pain, just tapes holding them in place and a lot of attention from the nurses, which he loved. After the tests, Warner spent two more sessions alone with Aaron. Then, he called me into his office to explain what he had found.

"Let's begin with a minor problem, Bill. Aaron's ambidextrous and is confused about his left and right hand. For instance, he throws a ball with his left hand but tries to catch it with his right. With a little encouragement from his teacher, and you, he'll be able to choose the prominent hand in time, and it won't be a problem."

I had never noticed Aaron's being ambidextrous, probably because we never went outside to toss a ball. I felt embarrassed about my own failure to toss and catch a ball like the other boys in school, but now, knowing this about Aaron, I was determined to spend time throwing and catching a ball with him. Both of us could benefit from that.

"We know that Aaron was taken away from his mother right after she gave birth to him and was in intensive care, withdrawing from her drugs for over a

Our miracle worker, Mirabai Baker, Aaron's therapist

week, but we also found neurological damage to one side of his brain, the side that recognizes and computes mathematical problems."

I digested what Warner had just told me for a minute or two, then asked, "Can it be fixed?"

"The damage to his nerves can't be rectified, but there are therapies, both physical and mental, we can use to help him get by."

I blurted out, "My god! I don't know if I can afford it!"

"You love your son, don't you, Bill? You'll find a way to pay for the therapies, but there's something else I have to tell you about Aaron, and that will require long-term therapy. A long, hard road ahead for him."

I know my face gave me away because he came from behind his desk and sat next to me on the couch, patting my hand and looking at me with compassion and I thought a little sorrow.

"In layman's terms, Bill, Aaron is a classic case of what we call 'suffering from the lack of infancy.' You see, it's incredibly important for an infant to be held, stroked. Every nerve under his skin relays messages to the brain about dimensions, length, width, weight. A baby has to be bounced on your knee, lifted into the air. And to trust. Trust the one lifting him. His nerves tell the brain about gravity, about feeling light or feeling heavy. From what I learned from you and him, he lived the first two years of his life isolated from the warmth of human hands."

I found myself gritting my teeth I was so nervous. Warner and I stared at each other, letting his words about Aaron's deprivation take root. Then he continued.

"But even more than that, an infant needs to be held close to his parents' bodies. A healthy baby can feel a parent's love, the beating of the heart, a warm breath, and it nourishes him. If he isn't held and cuddled … you know, talked to, sung to, hugged, it affects him for the rest of his life. Even the tiniest of babies just out of the womb can feel when they aren't loved. They feel abandoned, and that feeling can last."

I was quick to retort, "I hug Aaron all the time, Warner, all the time, and I tell him how much I love him every day. Every single day."

"I'm sure you do, Bill, but I'm talking about his most formative years, the years before you adopted him. You weren't there, and that's the pity. Unfortunately, from what I understand, his foster mother just let him lie in his crib all day. She did only what was needed to feed him and keep him clean. Too bad she didn't give him what he needed the most."

I was perplexed and feeling powerless. "So what can be done, Warner? Can you take him on? Can you take him as a patient?"

"No, I'm not what he needs. He needs a specialist in 'lack of infancy' therapy. To tell the truth, I've heard of only one child psychologist who specializes in this kind of therapy. She's well known and has achieved a great deal of respect in England."

"England!"

"Yeah, she takes children up to ten or eleven years old, and takes them back through infancy, step by step, and I mean every damn step – including nursing!"

"You're kidding me!"

"No, it takes a long time, sometimes years, but this woman has achieved things with her patients that no other therapist has been able to do – anywhere else in the world."

"Jesus, I can't afford to even call her long distance to set up an appointment, much less move to England and pay her a fortune to breastfeed Aaron!"

"Don't be discouraged. Don't feel we've come to a dead end. He's worth it. I'll put the word out. There's gotta be someone in the Bay Area who can help you."

I pulled out my checkbook, reluctantly, I'm afraid, sure Warner's fees for all his time interviewing and testing Aaron was going to bankrupt me. He lifted the pen out of my hand and closed my checkbook.

"Bill, I know it'll be hard for you to understand, but Paul and I have talked about wanting a child of our own for years now, and both of us are thrilled that you've actually done it. It's given us hope that maybe we can do it, too. I feel so privileged to be able to help you. I don't need your money and I don't want your money. You're a gay friend, a gay man who's doing the impossible, and if I can help you, that's making *my* life richer. Your money won't do it."

I was so moved by his generosity and so thankful for all the help my friends and my brother Jerry, had given me to raise Aaron. As Hillary Clinton said, *It takes a village to raise a child*. It *was* taking a village to raise him. Now I had to find one more villager to help me, but I had no idea where to start looking for a female-mother-figure-child-therapist who didn't seem to exist except in jolly olde England!

It was Warner who found her, a superb child psychologist, Mirabi Baker, who lovingly took Aaron as a client when he was nine years old. He could get to her office on Market Street and home again by cable car, and sometimes I went with him. She insisted I "come out" to him because, she said, "The thing that can tear a family apart is a lie. Stop lying to Aaron. Not being upfront and feeling normal about being gay is a lie. It'll comfort him if you're honest. He needs to understand how two adults can be affectionate and loving, but he never sees you that way. It'll help him, not hurt him if he sees you holding a lover's hand. Or kissing occasionally."

And so, with the support of Mirabi, during one session I hesitantly told Aaron I was gay and wanted to marry a man so he could have two fathers. He thought it over for a moment and then said, "Sounds good to me. I need someone on my side."

## Chapter 78

# The Wrecking Ball Phone Call
## August 3, 1996 – Saturday, 6:45 a.m.

When I was eight and the open window in my bedroom brought me a blinding sunrise along with a whiff of freshly cut alfalfa and the steady chugging of a John Deere tractor a mile away, I was thrilled to bound out of bed to embrace a fresh new morning.

Sixty years later on the morning of August 3rd, I tugged at the blanket to cover my head from the morning light sliced by the venetian blinds. I couldn't afford retirement, living on the houseboat, so I sold it and bought another apartment house, #324, the first one on Larkin Street, right in the middle of Civic Center.

Across the street, the heavy equipment that swung the wrecking ball was being fired up with the wrecking crew shouting at each other. The old courthouse was being demolished and a new federal courthouse, a high-rise, would be built right across the street. For weeks, my apartment and all my tenants' apartments were coated with fine dust, and my building shook with every blow of the wrecking ball. If you picked your nose, wet dust would be on your finger. The morning news on TV that had come on automatically at 6:30 wasn't loud enough to muffle the usual, constant street sounds, the hum of motors, a siren, the bleating of a drugged, homeless person.

My cats, a Russian blue named Mercedes, and Cadillac, a yellow and white stray, pinned me down, lying between my spread legs and under my armpit. What the hell! I had nothing much to do on that Saturday, except lie there thinking about the night before in a private sex club on 13th Street that a friend, Derek, told me to check out. A large hot tub squatted under a tree in the backyard of the house, and it was in the tub I'd met and talked to a very attractive, boy-next-door fourth-grade teacher from some god-awful place in Kansas. He was 20 or 30 years younger than I, but I felt a connection, a stirring, and was planning in my head what I would cook for him when we got up the next morning. I was sure he was sending me a message when he told me he was getting out of the tub to leave. I quickly agreed it was time to go and rushed to my locker to get dressed. As I headed for the exit, I heard him call my name, and turned to see him smiling and waving goodbye to me. He was naked, lying in a sling with one bearded man going down on him and another slipping a condom on himself and rubbing lubrication on my new friend's ass. I smiled and waved back, making a beeline for home and to my cats who loved me.

Before Aaron came into my life, my sexual urges drove me to distraction, and I spent hours through the night and into the early hours looking for relief. It couldn't be with just anyone though. I was extremely picky and only the clean-cut, mature man with passion and longing could satisfy me. They were few and far between. So, like a ravenous slut, I cruised bars and baths and streets.

Then a needy little boy showed me that it was love I was looking for all along.

Thinking of the last time I'd seen my son two weeks before made me smile. For the past year, we had barely spoken, and then it was with cold hostility and mistrust. Several of my friends who were recovering alcoholics kept insisting I stop trying to help Aaron every time he ended up in the detox ward of a hospital.

"Let him lie in the gutter the next time he goes down, Bill. Just let him lie there. Helping him get back up on his feet ain't gonna do it, Man. All the king's horses and all the king's men can't put that kid together again, especially you. Yeah, Aaron might die, but *he's* the only one that can save him. He's got to want to live, to *save himself*, and he can do it but only after he hits rock bottom. You've got to hold back, or he'll never quit taking drugs. It's called 'tough love' and you're the one that has got to be tough. Are *you* tough enough to give him the space he needs?"

A couple of months before that August morning, Aaron had called to tell me that he hoped I'd be proud of him. He had admitted himself into rehab in Belmont without my help, and for the first time he was "getting it" and was determined to last 28 days. I went to visit him there and was amazed at the wonderful way he looked and acted. He led me through the facilities and, with a lot of smiles and laughter, introduced me to his new recovering friends and the staff, who lit up when he came into sight.

I'd bought him another keyboard for his 30th birthday in May, hoping that maybe he wouldn't sell this one, like all the others, to buy drugs. And since I didn't allow myself to give it to him – tough love you know – it was still in the trunk of my car. When I showed it to him at the end of our visit, he almost broke down in tears but said he couldn't take it with him then because if he used it … it would be a way of escaping the work he had to finish in rehab.

A week after he got out of the Belmont rehab, I picked him up outside his therapist's office in Palo Alto and took him to lunch at the Olive Garden. He looked very thin, and I insisted he eat something. I drove him to the train station after lunch and gave him the keyboard. He asked me to drive him to San Jose, where he was living in a group home for recovering addicts, but I turned him down because it was getting late in the afternoon and I didn't want to spend the rest of the day fighting commuter traffic … a refusal that I regret to this day. He said he understood, and for the first time in 20 years, leaned over and kissed me on the lips when we said our "goodbyes." The kiss stunned and elated me. My son, my little boy, was back and I drove home feeling really good for the first time in years until a thought came in a quick flash. Aaron always gained weight when he was *off* drugs.

I wiggled out from under the bedding, tossing Mercedes and Cadillac to the floor. It was going to be another hot day, very unusual for San Francisco in the summer, and I wished I could stay naked all day.

Strange, but that's exactly what happened.

I needed to pee or I wouldn't have gotten out of bed. It was cozy cuddling with the cats and the *Today Show* was about to begin. I grabbed my baby blue Princess phone with its 25-foot cord and scurried for the bathroom. I had just shaken off the last few drops when the phone rang. Damn!

(The following conversation was recorded on my answering device).

*Hello.*
*Yeah, I'm sorry to call you so early.*

*Uh huh?*

*It's rather urgent. We're trying to locate a ... Aaron Hunter Jones. We wanna know if your phone number or if your ... anyone of your family is related to this individual.*

*Yeah ... Who are you?*

*This is the – eh – Medical Examiner's Office. We had a deceased by the name of Aaron Hunter Jones. Does, eh, anyone at this number, eh, know him or is related to him?*

(long pause*) I'm his father.*

*You're the father?*

(long pause) *Yes.*

*Is this 1221 Monterey Highway? Number 158?*

*I think that's where he lived ... yes.*

*Hold on for just a minute and let me get another record and I'll have some extra information. Just a moment ...*

*Oh, my god!*

(The recording ended).

The rest of the conversation is a blur. I must have asked him some questions because he told me Aaron was found in a weed-infested garden between a warehouse and an empty, deserted church in San Jose. He held a syringe in his hand. He was taken to the hospital and declared deceased at 7:15 p.m. His belongings would be sent to me, and I could make arrangements to pick up his body.

As he was talking, I was thinking of all the times I had pleaded, cajoled, and bribed him to stop using drugs. It was as if he were still alive and I was berating him, "Get a job, Aaron. Get off the damn drugs, Aaron! I told you. I told you so!"

I hung up the phone, leaving it on the bathroom sink, and started to walk back toward my bed. I grabbed on to something. I don't know what. Something like an asteroid came in a fiery, molten ball toward me. It was a word. DECEASED.

Aaron was dead! Dead! *Deceased!* My knees began to weaken and wobble, and I sank to the floor. I crawled to the side of my bed but couldn't pull myself up to lie in it. So, I stayed there, kneeling, my head pressed against the ever-increasing wet blanket, wet with mucus and tears, repeating over and over, "Oh, my God! Oh, my God!"

I don't recall hearing or seeing the *Today Show* or anything else on the TV that kept droning on and on that long day, but I was all too aware of the room shaking and the tremendous ricocheting boom each time the wrecking ball tore into the concrete walls across the street.

Oh, my God!

## Chapter 79
# I Kiss Aaron Goodnight and Tuck Him In for the Last Time

### The Eulogy

Ramona tells me I stumbled on the altar riser. Blur. I looked out at the blurred faces but didn't recognize anyone. This was my last chance to do something right for my son, but I was terrified I would fuck it up because the lump in my throat had grown to a monstrous size, and I had to constantly wipe my eyes so I could read my notes.

I do remember the feeling of tremendous responsibility, to tell the truth about Aaron so that the blurred faces would know him and love him as I did ... and remember him. I wanted to begin with his name.

\* \* \* \* \*

"Aaron Hunter Jones had two births ... and two deaths. First birth on May 18, 1966 ... screaming pain from the withdrawal of his mother's drugs. Second birth ... on February 13, 1969 ... at City Hall ... was our adoption day. It was full of love, joy, and hope for the future.

"Aaron's first death ... August 2 ... was *alone*, collapsed in a small area between two abandoned buildings in San Jose. His second death is today, August 25 ... at this hour ... in this lovely place. *We* will hold him, and we will be by him, as he slips away from this earth. He will *not* be alone, and he *will* be loved.

"Aaron Hunter Jones was named at a cocktail party given by Uncle Judd. Dennis Redmond made up the rules to choose the name ... It had to look

# AARON HUNTER JONES
May 18, 1966 — August 2, 1996

Sunday August 25, 1996
The Swedenborgian Church of San Francisco

good on a marquee. It had to look good on a marquee, and if you're at a cocktail party ... and he was introduced behind you ... you'd want to turn around and meet him. Aaron Hunter Jones.

"He had the weirdest birth certificate you've ever seen. Since I was the first single male to adopt, they didn't know how to make out his birth certificate. So, at the hospital, it says the father was present, the mother wasn't. And the death certificate says the same thing: Mother Unknown, kind of strange."

I stumbled on for another half hour, wiping my tears away so I could read the extensive list of friends, family, teachers, doctors, nannies, even strangers who helped me raise my son. Then I stopped and took a deep breath.

"So, the answer to the question ... would you do it again, if you had to go through the same thing, all over, again ... everything, with no insight whatsoever?" I had to pause again to get my voice under control. "The answer, of course, is ... *yes*. Aaron gave me so much love! He filled up my whole life."

Like a blind man, I felt my way back to my seat next to Ramona to hold her hand.

Tony Bennett's "For Once in My Life" filled the chapel.

\*     \*     \*     \*     \*

I greeted all the guests in the dreamlike walled-in garden before they went into the reception hall for the catered food and drinks, yet I remember only the hugs I got from a very few. Thankfully, the eulogy had been recorded and the other mourners had signed the guestbook. Otherwise, the whole day would have been lost to me. I do remember two things. A dear friend, Amity Buxton, handed me a single red rose, and another friend sat down at the grand piano in the reception hall and started to play show tunes. Friends crowded around him and after a few glasses of wine, a boisterous chorus was singing their hearts out. And there was laughter. Music, songs, laughter.

Aaron, Pasek, my brother Jerry ... my Group would have loved it!

Especially Aaron.

## Chapter 80
# The Atheist's Heaven

Aaron was only thirty years old when he killed himself accidentally with a syringe of pure heroin. While my son was being cremated in Mill Valley, I sat on a hillside in the back of the mortuary overlooking the crematorium. No smoke rose from the tall round chimney, but the sun shone through the heat waves rising out of it, casting a weird, turbulent light on the dry weeds covering the hill, transforming them into a roiling seascape. I felt myself drifting into that ocean around me. The taste of its saltwater spray ran down my cheeks and into my mouth as I composed his obituary.

The next day the mortician told me I could pick up his ashes, so I drove back to Mill Valley to claim my son. I sat waiting in a small room with nothing but a few straight-backed chairs upholstered in maroon velvet and a brass vase holding paper flowers that rested on a plaster-of-paris Greek column. The one arched window was opaque with rippled, yellowish glass that filled the room with a dismal beige light.

The double doors opened, revealing a slightly plump man in a black suit, holding a square plastic box about the size of a loaf of bread. It matched the maroon chairs, except it was shiny like dried blood.

"So terribly sorry for the loss of your beloved son, Mr. Jones."

He passed the box to me, and I said, "Thank you."

"The invoice will be in the mail tomorrow."

"Thank you."

I sat in my car with the box on the seat next to me for a long, long time, wondering if I was fit to drive back to the city safely. Finally, I turned the key and started the trip back across the Golden Gate, but not until I had put the box on my lap. Aaron used to love to sit on my lap with his tiny hands on the steering wheel. As he grew a little older, I actually let him steer it by himself. It was one of those no-no things that parents do with their kids, even though we know a cop could pull us over. But this was the last time my little boy would be on my lap as I drove us home. It was almost impossible to keep in my lane on the bridge as I blinked away the tears, but we made it home, my son and me.

It's been twenty-five years since he overdosed, and I poured his ashes into a more suitable container, a maple-wood cigar humidor, which dominates the middle shelf of the *Aaron Jones display shelves* in my bedroom. He is surrounded by his sleeping companions, Teddy, Snoopy, and Monkey. On the top shelf are the blue sweater and rompers he arrived in, and the shoes he was wearing, now bronzed and indestructible. On the second shelf is the impressive invitation to our party that Pasek and I designed, celebrating the adoption, along with the baby-shower gifts of silver from Shreve's: two small round pill boxes with 'Son' and 'Daddy' inscribed on their lids, a silver baby comb, a silver baby spoon, and a silver bell. The shelf under his encased ashes and stuffed playmates holds two leather albums displaying photos and mementos of his life I assembled for his memorial at the Swedenborgian Church in Pacific Heights. The bottom shelf is the garage for two of his favorite toys, a wooden truck with his name printed on it I made for him and a model of the blue Volkswagen bus we went camping in.

There's a free-form black fountain under our portrait in my entry hall that has been running for over twenty-five years, and my office walls are covered with photos of Aaron, and some of Aaron and me. He's in my computer as the desktop photo, and framed photos of him in his blue velvet suit are glued to every cabinet door in my kitchen.

I have files and drawers filled with doctors' and teachers' evaluations of my schizophrenic son, who heard "voices;" records of his allergies, rehabs, special ed, private schools, therapists, birthday cards. A cedar chest is filled with his baby clothes, costumes, favorite blanket, plastic cup, spoon, and bowl, and a pile of newspapers and magazines with articles about us.

I opened the chest a few years ago to show a friend Aaron's collection and discovered a large sealed plastic bag that I didn't recognize right away. It held the blue shirt and Levi's he had died in. I burst into sobs, shut the lid quickly, and haven't opened it since.

I think of him every day, and many times in the dark shroud of night I wake myself calling his name. As long as I am alive, I swear he will live in my thoughts and heart.

I tell you all this so you will understand the impact on me of an incident that happened when he was five and had just started kindergarten.

*       *       *       *       *

I was cleaning up the breakfast table and packing his lunch in a paper bag when he came out of his bedroom dressed in his knight costume – silver plastic breast plate, helmet, and sword. "Aaron, for god's sake, you can't go to school dressed like that!"

"Daddy?"

"Take off the costume, Aaron, and make it snappy!"

"Daddy?"

"We don't have all day. Now get going or you'll be late."

"Daddy?"

"What *is* it, Aaron? Get back in there and take off that damn costume!"

"Daddy, something's wrong with Bird. Bird's on the bottom of his cage and won't wake up."

"What!"

We rushed into Aaron's bedroom, and over to Bird's cage. Bird's limp body was sprawled on the bottom of it with a spray of his yellow feathers caught in the bars of the cage and others lying next to his open claws. I lifted him out and gently put him on the table next to the cage.

"Daddy, is he sick?"

"No, Honey. He's dead."

"Dead? I didn't … I didn't mean to hurt him, Daddy. I was … just playing with him."

"Playing? Aaron, what do you mean *playing?*"

"I was playing sword fight with him, and then he fell down and played dead. Is he playing dead, Daddy?"

"Take off your knight's costume, Aaron, and we'll talk about it on the way to school. Don't forget to brush your teeth."

The walk to the school at the bottom of Russian Hill from our apartment at the top of the hill took about 30 minutes, and Aaron questioned me every step of the way. He wasn't sure what *dead* meant, and then he drilled me about what happens to you after you *die*.

Being an atheist, and vowing to always be honest with him, I could hardly paint a picture of us floating around in white-cloud heaven, tossing our halos to each other like Frisbees. I didn't want to frighten him with my true thoughts either, that once you move on to the marble orchard, that's it. Nothing. Nowhere. Zero. Gone.

"Well, Aaron, here's where it gets to be real fun. Every single person in this whole, big world has his or her own idea about what happens after we die. Some people like to think they will be going on a nice trip up through the clouds to be with a bunch of good people just like themselves, but they'd be too boring for me."

"What's your plan, Daddy? Where'll you go after you die?"

"I don't have a real plan, Honey, but if I could make up something that would come true, I think I'd like to die and go to my junior prom again."

"What's a junior prom, Daddy?"

It's a dance in a high school gym at night when the moon is shining and all the young ladies are in beautiful princess formal gowns, smelling of soap and flowers, and all the young men are wearing carnations in the lapels of their new dark blue suits. Romantic music from the electric phonograph is playing Frank Sinatra, Harry James, Jo Stafford, Tommy Dorsey. Everybody's smiling and happy. Everyone's in love and going steady."

"Will I be there, too?"

"Oh, yeah! Of course! And all our family and all our friends will be there, too. And because it's *my* heaven, I can make everyone any age I want. My mother will be forty-two, my brother will be eleven, and all our friends will be thirty again. It'll be the best prom ever, and it'll go on forever. How'd you like that?"

"Can Bird be there too, Daddy?"

"Of course. You can let him out of his cage, and he can fly over us anytime he wants to."

By the time Aaron came home after school, I had stored the cage and swept up the seeds and feathers.

"Where's Bird, Daddy?"

"Wash your hands, Honey. Time for dinner. I wrapped Bird up in newspaper and put him down the garbage chute. Use soap."

Aaron and I went through the same routine we had gone through for the past three years. During dinner, we watched *Sesame Street* and *Mr. Rogers* together, and then he played with his toys until it was time for his bath. After his bath, he got into his jammies and we cuddled on the sofa while I read to him. He loved books. Our favorite pastime was to haunt old bookstores looking for books he would like me to read to him. He had a few favorites, but the one he asked me to read to him, at least once a week, was *The Little Prince* by Antoine De Saint-Exupery, and that is what he asked for that night.

I had just begun the chapter where the Little Prince is cleaning out his two volcanoes and preparing his proud rose to live on his small planet alone when he flew away. Aaron reached up and put his hand over the page I was reading. He looked up at me, and asked in a trembling voice, "Daddy, when I die, will you wrap me up in newspapers and throw me down the garbage chute?"

## Chapter 81
# Come Early!

I walked down the Lombard steps with Aaron every morning to the chain-link fence of the schoolyard for the first two years. Every day, he would hesitate when we arrived, walk partway through the gate, stop, turn those beautiful blue puppy-dog eyes up at me and plead, "Come early!"

When he started the first grade, I thought it was time he walked to school by himself. Each day I would walk with him but kiss him goodbye a few yards farther from the gate. Day by day, the distance between us became longer. It took two weeks before I could wave goodbye to him from the top of Russian Hill. When I was sure he could manage the trip by himself, I kissed him goodbye at our front door. His last words to me each morning were always pleading, "Daddy, come early!"

It bothered me each time we said goodbye. For the first time in my life I, had someone I loved who wanted to be with me more than anyone else. He gave me power over him. He made himself vulnerable to my whims. He was allowing me to hurt him or please him, make him cry, or be happy depending on if I picked him up at five or a few minutes before five ... or a few minutes after five.

It was a power I cherished, but one that frightened me. It gave me a dynamite stick, one that might blow us all to kingdom come if I got careless and misused it.

\* \* \* \* \*

I so wanted to be the perfect son. The perfect teacher. The perfect lover. The perfect friend. But most of all I wanted to be the perfect father for Aaron when all the time I should have been focused on being the perfect me. I wish I had that second chance to be perfect.

If I had only taken the time to do my homework while I was in school. If I had only practiced throwing and catching a ball. If I had only read more books, auditioned for more plays, exercised more, learned to cook, worked harder, stayed in relationships longer. Then maybe I could have been the perfect *whatever*, but I goofed off and let the temptation to take the easy road take over my soul. I cannot shake off the feeling that because I did not perfect myself, Aaron is dead.

Since he died I have lost count of the nights I wake myself in the dead of night with the sound of my own voice calling his name – *Aaron, Aaron!* With his name echoing in my head, my dark bedroom lights up with memories, and the tears start to flow. Wads of tear-soaked Kleenex litter the floor by my bed.

I remember his clean smell as he cuddled on my lap in his Dr. Dentons while I read him fairy tales. I remember how excited he was when I let go of his bicycle and he rode off on his own. I remember the sweet sound of his first word – Daddy. Anguished, I remember him being wheeled into the operating room when he was four, screaming, "I want my Daddy! I want my Daddy!"

I long for something I'll never have – a second chance. I see his blue eyes as I left him at the gate pleading with me "Daddy, come early!"

# Part Three

## After Aaron

## Chapter 82
# Skydiving into Manhood

I was bullied as a freshman in high school by the jocks who played on the basketball, football, and baseball teams. In grammar school, I was always the wimp who was the last one to be chosen to be on a team. Billy couldn't throw a ball or catch a ball or even kick a ball like the other kids. Most of the girls were better at it than I. Even the smallest of balls, a marble, was beyond my thumb and forefinger's ability to move in a straight line to hit another marble. I thought of myself as unworthy to be in the same room with the ones that taunted me.

I hate Mrs. Taylor to this day. She was the custodial teacher in my freshman fourth-period study hall class, a tall, gaunt woman, who kept her squinty eyes on anyone sitting at a desk without an open book in front of them. Judgmental and stern. I hate her because she made absolutely no effort to intervene when four senior jocks came into study hall, strolled over to my desk, and picking me up by my arms and legs, rushed me out into the empty hallway and headed for the boy's bathroom.

My heart was pounding and I was paralyzed with fear when they banged one of the stall doors open and two of them let go of my arms. I was upside down, the blood rushing to my head, when the four of them, two on each leg crowded into the stall, laughing and swearing, swinging my convulsing body over the black oval seat of the smelly toilet. I grabbed the white tank and pushed away with all my might, which made them all the more determined to finish the "royal flush" with me.

I wasn't aware that he had come into the bathroom, but I heard Mr. Callahan, the vice principal, bellow out, "What the hell is going on here?" I was flipped upright. My feet touched the wet concrete floor. The jocks, red-faced, quickly fell in line and followed Mr. Callahan out the door and down to his office.

I just tell you of this nasty incident so you can understand more clearly why at the age of seventy-eight, I decided to literally clear the air once and for all and prove to myself that I was a man among men – brave, fearless, and strong. I decided to take a risk that would free my soul and let me finally walk tall. I signed up to go skydiving.

I don't think my friends took me seriously when I told them what I planned to do because not one of them was willing to accompany me to the airport. In a way I was relieved because what if I got cold feet at the last minute and chickened out? The embarrassment and shame would have been magnified a hundred times if that happened. And so I drove to the Santa Rosa Airport by myself, dreading every mile. The hangar for the skydiving outfit wasn't near the airport terminal but at the end of a long line of Quonset huts that must have been temporary dormitories for flight crews in World War II.

I found the small office busy with others signing their lives away on a 10-page contract that basically said there would be no way in hell that you or your family could sue the sky diving company if anything went wrong. After I watched a 15-minute video about the wonders of falling 120 miles an hour toward earth, attached to another human being who could let you die if the mood moved him, a young man with acne and long hair handed me a "cover your ass" contract to sign. The narrator of the film was a skinny man in his fifties with a mane of white hair that fell down over his shoulders. An aging hippie. Not to be trusted. Did I really want to sign it? No. Did I sign it? Yes.

As much as I wanted it to be over quickly, I endured an agonizing wait for my turn to board the small plane with two or three jumpers ahead of me. I put the jumpsuit on and zipped it up over my khakis and golf shirt and waited with sweaty palms for over an hour, watching the plane take off fully loaded and then land soon after with only the pilot on board. It took off with passengers and landed with none, two more times. My heart was beating faster and faster each time it took off. My turn was approaching too fast.

Jake, my tandem partner, hurried over with last-minute instructions. "On our way up I'll strap us together. You in front, me on your back, so you'll be sitting in front of me on the plane. With me?"

I nodded.

"You'll step out on the struts before me. Capeesh?"

I nodded.

"You'll cross your arms, hands up close to your chest. Put your feet together, lean back, and put your legs between mine. Try to kick my ass that way. With me?"

Before I had a chance to nod again he finished with, "Relax. You'll love it!"

I watched Jake strap on his parachute and double-check all the thick black straps winding around his legs and over his arms. I tried not to look at the bulge in his crotch as he tugged the straps snug, high on his thighs. I had a quick flash of Steve McQueen's tight body, rugged face, and shock of gray and blond hair as I watched Jake twist and turn, buckling himself into a contraption that would bring us back to earth. Not since I was very, very young and felt sexual attraction combined with panicky fear, had I experienced what I felt at that moment. Strapping Steve McQueen on my back had a nice ring to it. But my palms were wet and my mouth was dry.

It was July 12th, my birthday, and I was giving myself a bucket-list gift on this warm summer morning. My thoughts were mostly of dying a tragic death, spinning out of control, splattering my body in somebody's backyard like a fly squashed under a swatter, when I should have been celebrating being alive for another year.

Jake yanked on my chest strap. "Come on!"

We started to walk toward the plane, but the pilot came running to us and yelled something into Jake's ear, which I couldn't hear over the noise of the engine. Jake and I came to an abrupt stop at the hangar door.

For at least 15 minutes, the white and red plane sat on the runway with its propeller rotating just fast enough to become invisible, while two of the crew struggled with the door under the right wing. They walked back toward us, carrying the door between them. I sighed with relief. This must mean I was free! Free to hightail it home without doing the dreaded jump! I almost cried with joy.

That is until one of the men grumbled, "The damn hinge is broke and we can't fix it right now. Wind's bout to come up, so get on board and go without the fuckin' door!" With that, Jake yanked on my strap again, and I felt my legs and feet moving without my permission toward the plane.

I crawled through the opening that once was married to a door, and my heart sank even farther down into my despairing belly. There were only two seats: one for the pilot and one for the photographer. Jake and I put our butts on the metal floor, once painted red to match the red graphic line on the sides of the white body of the plane (or to disguise blood stains), and now worn down by many other butts, belts, and buckles. The glimmer of silver metal peeked through the layer of dust and scratches in the worn splotches of red paint.

Jake sat behind me, resting against the back partition, but I sat uncomfortably cross-legged right smack dab in the middle of the small cabin with nothing to brace my overweight body against. The gunned engine revved up, and the wheels beneath us turned, escalating in speed down the bumpy, potholed runway. I desperately looked for something to hang onto, fearing that I would be jiggled right out the open doorway.

The bumpy ride ended as the wind lifted the wings and we gunned up toward nothing but blue sky. Jake leaned toward me shouting something like, "Garble, garble, takeoff! With me?"

I nodded.

"Did you catch Bush landing on that carrier in a jet? He's my boy!"

I nodded, thinking *that fuckin' moron, Bush, is no hero, you stupid asshole!* I wanted to tell Jake, the jerk, that I willingly got myself arrested at the Federal Building in San Francisco, protesting Bush's shock and awe bombing of Iraq two years before, and I'd do it again gladly. But I bit my tongue and held it in. Way in.

Jake kept yakking about Bush the entire time it took the small, rickety plane to get up to 10,000 feet, and I was not about to challenge him about his fuckin' hero, George Dingleberry Bush. I'm sometimes outspoken and dumb, but not *that* dumb. *He* was the one I was strapped to. *He* would be the one to pull the ripcord. *He* would be the one to bring us to earth again and to a safe landing. I fought my urge to let this guy have it with both barrels, but my mouth was so dry with fear, it felt like I had a box of tissues stuffed into it.

Jake yanked on my straps and yelled, "Get on your knees!"

He pulled me to him, buckling, snapping, pulling on cords, so close that I could feel his garlic-loaded breath on the back of my neck. We edged toward the opening to Hell on our knees. Jake slapped me on my legs.

"Step out on the struts! ... With me?"

The cold, howling wind hit my face, and the photographer, who had crawled out the opening before us, faced us, bracing himself against the two struts that held the right wing to the body of the plane. He was taking photos of me to appear in the papers the next day, lamenting the tragic death of an elderly, misguided fool.

I crossed my hands over my chest just like the undertaker would do as I lay in my casket.

Jake yelled in my ear, "Put your damn feet between my legs and try to kick me in the ass!" I bobbed my head in agreement. *If you only knew how much I'd love to kick you in the ass!*

I looked down and saw hills, roads, and tiny square blocks of houses, slowly moving beneath my tennis shoes. The photographer let go of the struts and stepped off into space. Jake, a moment later, pushed us both off the struts, following the photographer into a blast of air that slapped my face. A blinding sun filled my plastic goggles. For the longest five seconds of my life, I was bombarded with a blast of cold wind. The ear-splitting roar of the plane's engine quickly faded away, but my eyes were unfocused, and my ears were deaf with rushing air.

Jake grabbed my arms, clenched close to my chest, and pulled them out like the cross Jesus suffered and died on. "Relax! Enjoy!" he yelled in my ear. "Fly like a bird!"

It was useless to answer him because I couldn't turn around and get close enough to his ear so he could hear me. My day brightened! I realized that I could yell out anything I damn well wanted to, and *no one* could hear me! Especially Jake!

Suddenly, a swelling feeling of euphoria came over me, and I was scream-ing with delight. I didn't give a shit if I was falling to my death. I was riding the Santa Cruz roller coaster and its tracks were nothing but air. I was ten years old again, howling and loving every second of it. The air whistled by at 120 miles an hour, quickly becoming warmer as we fell closer to the brown hills and freeways. I wanted it to never end. I was alive, arms out like the wings of an eagle, my heart beating so hard my whole body shook with it.

I was close to heaven, and because I felt its closeness, I had to scream out one word. Filled with the wild joy of being alive, I yelled out with all the breath that was in me, the name of the one I knew *could* hear me.

## Bill Jones cites his experience

"AARON!"

He was with me, alive again, clinging to me, falling from heaven back to earth.

Jake pulled the ripcord, and my legs were jerked up over my head with the sudden, explosive deployment of the rectangular chute. The roar of the wind in my ears stopped, and the vast view of the earth loomed on a wide screen below us, gently approaching us with more and more details. What could be more wonderful than the Russian River snaking its way through the rows of grapevines and fir trees? I could see the faces of the crew and the photographer, smiling up at us as we came sweeping down to the sandy field where we landed, not on our butts as I had expected, but on our feet, touching the ground in a walking gait. Imagine that! Strolling at the end of a freefall to earth! The magic of what I had done tingled every vein in my body. My feet were on the sandy ground, but I was walking on air.

I drove back to San Rafael that afternoon, feeling proud, courageous, fearless, full of my manliness. I could face anything after that jump. I was a man among men, and to my friends who saw the photographs of my dive, I was a Superman. I had felt more fear than I had ever felt before, which had dissolved into the courage to face all the devils that had taunted me all my life.

And above all – above the life-changing risk I took – above coming out of my cocoon of unworthiness, like a Tiffany glass butterfly – I had touched my dead son's soul by screaming out his name, high, high above the earth, and as close to heaven – and him as I could get.

**"Aaron!"**

# Acknowledgments and Appreciation

My fabulous writing teacher – Diane Frank
My dear friend who edited the book – Elinor Gale
My eagle-eyed copy editor – Cynthia Hanson
My patient friend who rescued me from the computer age – Brian Johnson
My loyal friend who designed the cover for it – Barry Power
The time-consuming and thoughtful feedback from – Amity Buxton, Ralf Schubert, John Geoghegan, Dennis Elder, Bill Otton, and the other students in Diane's classes.

## The Village that helped me raise Aaron

His nannies: Ronnie, Carol, Akiko, and Helen
His loving kindergarten teacher, Marilyn Diamond; his special ed teachers; his daycare workers; and his doctor, Larry Williams
Our adopted family: Uncle Pasek, Uncles Mike, Bob, Gary, and Dennis, and Dad, Muffer, Grandmother Witchcraft, Aunt Ramona, Aunt Sandi, and especially
   Uncle-Uncle Jerry

## The adoption

Dorothy Murphy, Mary Davidson, and Evander Smith

## The recovery from Aaron's death

My beautiful and caring cousin, Ramona Dittmer

CPSIA information can be obtained
at www.ICGtesting.com
Printed in the USA
JSHW010429281222
35432JS00001B/8